Public Sector Management
in Italy

To all our beloved parents…

Edited by
Massimo Sargiacomo

Public Sector Management in Italy

McGraw-Hill Education

Milano · New York · Bogotà · Lisbon · London
Madrid · Mexico City · Montreal · New Delhi
Santiago · Seoul · Singapore · Sydney · Toronto

This volume has been supported by the research funds assigned to Prof. Massimo Sargiacomo by the University G. d'Annunzio Foundation in 2013.

Publisher: Paolo Roncoroni
Acquisition Editor: Daniele Bonanno, Alessandra Pagani
Proof reading: Sarah Sivieri
Production: Donatella Giuliani
Cover graphic: Feel Italia, Milano
Print: Prontostampa
McGraw-Hill Education (UK), September 2013
ISBN 978-00-771-6099-9

Brief Contents

Contents

Preface

In the last two decades major reforms have been addressed to the broad Italian Public Sector, requiring the introduction of New Public Management-inspired ideas and tools, thus calling for further research in this field. The convergence of EU Countries towards the Euro deadline of December 31, 2013 has also accelerated the managerial transformation process, as well as the consequent deployment in the Public Sector of techniques and practices widely adopted in the private sector. This refereed volume has been written and designed to provide a cross-areas examination of a selection of the main present Italian Public Sector issues and challenges.

In Chapter 1 Del Vecchio and Lecci seek to introduce researchers, students and professionals into the characteristics of stakeholder and governance structures in public organizations. After a literature review they describe how corporate governance mechanisms work in public entities vis-à-vis private firms. They also discuss the respective implications of interests and political systems on public organizations, and later provide conclusions and suggest future research directions on corporate governance in public organizations.

In Chapter 2 Preite and De Matteis analyse cutback management of the Italian bureaucratic apparatus. After a brief overview on the International and Italian economic scenario, they portray the financial constraints raised by the European Union Stability Programme on the Italian public spending. Accordingly they highlight the characteristics of the financial management of the State, which required a thorough examination of the main sources of financial waste, and the deployment of a Spending Review process, through a cutback management approach.

In Chapter 3 Maggi and Morelli focus on planning and control systems of Italian Regions. After a description of Italian Regional Governments, they illustrate the changes occurred in the process of strategic planning and programming in Italian Regions in the aftermath of the major reforms. By so doing they show a reference model which works both for the Strategic Planning process in the Regions, as well as for the respective Programming and Control of management. An empirical analysis of the programming, planning and control systems in use in several Italian Regions concludes their analysis.

In Chapter 4 Ziruolo provides a portrayal of the intersection of accounting and management practices in Italian Local Governments. After a necessary contextualization, which depicts the main Local Governments Reforms which triggered the shift to prior paradigms and techniques, the author explains the changes from cash into accrual accounting, and related relevant accounting and reporting documents and methodologies. The introduction of the Executive Management Plan as a new management tool is later discussed. In the conclusions the 2015 accounting harmonisation scenario is presented, as well as possible future research trends.

In Chapter 5 Gitto and Della Porta present an analysis of the the impact of Management Control on Italian Provinces. The authors firstly highlight the main characteristics of the Italian Provinces socio-economic scenario and organization, thus providing the main contextualization features of these peculiar Italian Local Governments. Then, they illustrate how New Public Management ideas has made Public Sector more output oriented, thus giving the abbrivium to Provinces to introduce new performance management logics and techniques. With these premises, the authors elucidate the implementation of management control systems in the Province of Ancona, located in the Marche Region.

In Chapter 6 Della Porta and Gitto explain how Public Transport sector has not escaped the major impetus provided by Italian reforms oriented towards the continuous search for spending better. After a synthetic recapitulation of the reform path, they illustrate how local transport services have been for a long time so difficult to improve, thus illuminating an extreme resistance to the deployment of efficiency mechanisms and tools, which hampered the reforms'implementation process. In light of past issues, the recent measures imposed by central government are illustrated, thus highlighting how they are supposed to push forward the public transports never ending improvement process.

In Chapter 7 D'Andreamatteo, Ianni and Sargiacomo unveil how lean thinking practices may be used to enhance performance improvement of healthcare organizations. After a brief portrayal of the main challenges affecting the Italian National Healthcare System (INHS), and the consequent emerging need to boost performance improvement, they highlight the principal benefits and approaches of lean healthcare practices. Three Italian case-studies are subsequently presented, thus offering empirical evidences which demonstrate the main features of early lean implementations in the INHS where, at the moment, Lean has not yet been chosen explicitly as means of public reform.

In Chapter 8 Ianni, D'Andreamatteo and Sargiacomo aim to illustrate the impact of the future introduction of standard costing on healthcare management and services delivery in the light of the latest federalist reform in Italy (Legislative Decree 68/2011). They initially discuss how in order to better address the issues raised by funding and healthcare delivery, and concurrently guarantee more efficiency and effectiveness within the INHS, the per capita and retrospective expenditure criteria will be replaced by the future introduction of standard costing criterion already deployed in other countries. The chapter finally unveils and discusses the managerial implications and impact on healthcare management and delivery both at a macro and at a micro level.

In Chapter 9 Della Porta, Sargiacomo and Venditti investigate how performance measurement has recently tried to make Italian Universities more financially sustainable. A critical analysis of the main reform waves affecting the Italian scenario across the last three decade is initially presented, thus illustrating – through the help of different empirical evidences – how the University system has failed to manage financial autonomy and accountability there allocated by the State. The consequent rather clear financial distress status of different public universities triggered the last 2010 reform. Indeed, the co-authors argue that Law 240/2010 has been a true restoration of central power and control through an MBO type performance management system, which seeks to achieve a more financially sustainable university system.

In Chapter 10 Lucianetti and Franco-Santos examines the relationships between diagnostic and interactive role of Human Resource Performance Management (HRPM) – and their connections with social capital, sense of community and the individual well-being inside the Italian University system. Admittedly, the recent introduction of new performance evaluation system in the academia has indicated that scholars are increasingly experiencing a sense of losing their academic freedom and autonomy. The co-authors conclusively present and discuss the results of data collected from a broad sample of academics – belonging to 17 different academic research field – and administrative employees working in 77 Italian Universities.

Pescara, 10 September 2013

Prof. Massimo Sargiacomo

Authors

Antonio D'Andreamatteo is Senior Lecturer in Accounting and Public Management at the Open University Leonardo da Vinci

Mario Del Vecchio is Associate Professor in Public Management at the University of Florence

Armando Della Porta is Senior Lecturer in Accounting and Public Management at the Department of Management and Business Administration of University G. d'Annunzio

Fabio De Matteis is PhD in Management at the University of Salento

Monica Franco-Santos, is Senior Research Fellow in Performance Measurement and Management at the School of Management of Cranfield University

Antonio Gitto is Senior Lecturer in Accounting and Public Management at the Department of Management and Business Administration of University G. d'Annunzio

Luca Ianni is Senior Lecturer in Accounting and Public Management at the Open University Leonardo da Vinci

Francesca Lecci is PhD in Public Sector Management at Bocconi University

Lorenzo Lucianetti is Senior Lecturer in Management Accounting at the Department of Management and Business Administration of University G. d'Annunzio

Davide Maggi is Associate Professor in Management Theory, Accounting and Public Management at the University of Eastern Piedmont

Chiara Morelli is Assistant Professor of Business Organization and Human Resources Management at the University of Eastern Piedmont

Daniela Preite is Senior Lecturer in Public Management and Policy at the University of Salento

Massimo Sargiacomo is Professor of Accounting and Public Management at the Department of Management and Business Administration of University G. d'Annunzio

Michela Venditti is Professor of Accounting and Public Management at the Department of Management and Business Administration of University G. d'Annunzio

Andrea Ziruolo is Professor of Accounting and Public Management at the Department of Management and Business Administration of University G. d'Annunzio

1

Stakeholder and Governance structures in public organizations[1]

Understanding the logic behind the definition of stakeholder and governance structures has always been a central issue in the Italian research stream of Management. Within this theoretical framework, the chapter assumes that the stakeholder and governance structure relates to the organizations structure and composition, as well as its various management and project teams. In the chapter we present an in-depth analysis of stakeholder groups and contributions expected and organizational structures and mechanisms that allow coordinating activities. As far as public organizations are concerned, the likelihood of public organizations being perceived as effective increases when they manage to align the, possibly very diverse, expectations of stakeholder groups with respect to good governance. How can public-sector regimes, agencies, programs, and activities be organized and managed to achieve public purposes? This question, of fundamental importance in the fields of politics, policy implementation, public administration, and public management, motivates the systematic study of stakeholder and governance structure. The reminder of the chapter is structured as follows. Paragraph 1.1 reviews the literature on stakeholder and governance structure. Paragraph 1.2 describes corporate governance frameworks within private firms. Paragraph 1.3 presents stakeholder and governance structures in public organizations, while paragraph 1.4 discusses interests, political system and public organizations. Finally, paragraph 1.5 provides conclusions and suggests future research directions on corporate governance in public organizations.

Learning objectives

After reading this chapter you should be able to:

- Understand the characteristics of stakeholder and governance structure in private firms;
- Understand the characteristics of stakeholder and governance structure in public organizations;
- Discuss the implications of interests and political system on public organizations;
- Recognize major trends on stakeholder and governance structure in public organizations.

---

[1] Mario Del Vecchio (corresponding author) wrote paragraphs 1.1, 1.4 and 1.5; Francesca Lecci wrote paragraphs 1.2 and 1.3.

1.1   Stakeholder and governance structures

1.1.1   The Italian approach to management theory

Understanding the logic behind the definition of stakeholder and governance structures has always been a central issue in the Italian research stream of 'Economia Aziendale'. In particular, there has been a long debate about the theoretical construct of "institution" (Masini, 1979; North, 1990; Airoldi et al, 1994; Borgonovi et al, 2009). According to North (1990), the word "institution" may have two different meanings:

- "institutions are the rules of the game in a society or, more formally, are the humanly devised constraints that shape human interaction. In consequence they structure incentives in human exchange, whether political, social or economic" (p.3);
- institutions may be intended as "organizations" which "include political bodies (political parties, the Senate, a city council, a regulatory agency), economic bodies (firms, trade unions, family farms, cooperatives), social bodies (churches, clubs, athletic associations), and educational bodies (schools, universities, vocational training centres). They are groups of individuals bound by some common purpose to achieve objectives" (p.5).

In the Italian approach to management theory and in this chapter, we assume a definition of "institutions" as systems of people, powers and goods which are well coordinated to pursue a common goal. Such definition of institutions enables to (Borgonovi 1993a; 1993b):

- build theories about economic events without neglecting the complex twine of interests of multiple actors that live any social institution;
- make a distinction among the interests of the networks that the actors build to satisfy their personal and multiple needs and the other dimensions that can still be relevant for their regular operation (for instance, the economic dimension of the institution that are not mainly driven by such aim);
- unify the economic events according to an ultimate goal to be achieved by an integrated and everlasting system, called "organization";[2]
- identify the context with its conditions, restrictions, formal and substantial rules that shape the decision making process, and the main interactions between actors and groups of actors involved in the institution itself.

Both the Italian and the Central European approaches to management theory highlight the role of individuals and institutions when studying economic events. Masini (1979) considers the work of individuals as a fundamental pillar of institutions. In that respect, management theory covers all activities belonging to the following three categories: (i) the production of private goods and services; (ii) the production of public goods and

---

[2] According to the italian approach to management theory, "organization" identifies a specific set of activities performed by an institution, affecting the organizational structure, the operating mechanisms and personnel (Anessi Pessina, 2002).

services; (iii) the consumption of such private and public services. Moreover, the ultimate goal of economic activities is to satisfy people needs. To that extent, we can assume that consumption processes are the end, whereas production is the mean of such end. Finally, Italian approach (Rossi, 1921) to management theory suggests that economic activities tend to be performed within institutions, rather than on individual basis.

Thus, management theory is the discipline that focuses on the "economic dimension of all classes of institutions, characterized by relevant production or consumption activities" (Airoldi et al., 1994: p. 28). Therefore, institutions are (i) durable entities, (ii) composed of individuals and resources (tangible and intangible), (iii) operating under a stable set of norms, rules and structures, (iv) performing a set of integrated activities, (v) with the ultimate goal of satisfying human needs. Italian approach to management theory (Zappa, 1957; Onida, 1965; Amaduzzi, 1992; Giannessi 1979) recognizes the existence of four main classes of institutions: (i) firms, focusing on production; (ii) families, focusing on consumption; (iii) public organizations, performing both production and consumption and (iv) other institutions, mainly including non profit organizations.

Although the four classes are different in terms of norms, rules and structures, they share a number of general features. They are (Masini 1979: p. 10-11):

- unitary entities across space and over time;
- systematic, that is with an immediate objective (production or consumption) and an ultimate goal (satisfy human needs);
- relatively autonomous, even if mutually interdependent with the environments in which they operate;
- durable, since they're expected to operate indefinitely;
- dynamic, since they need to change according to their environments in order to survive;
- organized according to a defined set of norms, rules and structures;
- composed of an economic dimension and several non-economic dimensions.

More specifically, according to Viganò (2000), characteristics of being unitary, systematic (with an immediate objective and an ultimate goal) and durable represent a common endowment of Italian approach to management theory (Ferrero 1968: p. 13), since many relevant Italian researchers have highlighted such peculiar characteristics (Zappa 1957: p. 10; Onida 1965: p. 4; Amaduzzi 1992: p. 18-19; Giannessi 1979).

Within this theoretical framework, we assume that the stakeholder and governance structure relates to the organizations structure and composition, as well as its various management and project teams. It is aimed at defining the organizations stakeholders and stakeholder groups, their relative importance; the contributions expected by each group and the structures, rules and procedures for determining and balancing each group contributions and rewards. Governance includes the formal lines of authority and accountability as well as the systems which are in place to ensure that representatives of the various functions and organizational units meet to co-ordinate their activities both vertically and horizontally. In the next pages we will present and in-depth analysis of: (i) stakeholder groups and contributions expected and (ii) organizational structures and mechanisms that allow coordinating activities.

1.1.2 Stakeholder and governance structure

Institutions'stakeholder and governance structures are crucial in defining the ultimate institutions'goals. Freeman (1984) defined the concept of "stakeholder" to include any individual or group who can affect the organization's performance or who is affected by the achievement of the organization's objectives. Within the Italian (and, partly, European) approach to management theory, there are two different streams of literature within the scientific debate. The two streams differ in terms of composition of the two main stakeholder groups, which are (Anessi Pessina, 2002: p. 33):

- primary stakeholders, the satisfaction of whose expectations is the institution's ultimate goal. This group includes stakeholders without whose participation the organization cannot survive, like shareholders, employees, customers, suppliers, government and communities;
- other stakeholders, the satisfaction of whose expectations is a constraint on the institution's autonomy and its ability to pursue its own goals. This group includes those who influence or affect, or are influenced or affected by, the organization, but they are not engaged in transactions with the organization itself and are not essential for its survival.

The first stream (Onida, 1965: p. 21; Ardemani, 1993: p. 23; Ferrero, 1968: p. 52-53; Frooman, 1999) considers primary stakeholder, usually internal stakeholders, those that engage in economic transactions with the business and are characterized by three attributes, namely power, legitimacy and urgency. It would be more proper, in this case, to define such a category as "real stakeholders" or "stakeowners", since they include genuine stakeholders with a legitimate stake. Stakeowners own and deserve a stake in the firm. Following Clarkson (1994: p. 5), are primary stakeholders those who "bear some form of risk as a result of having invested some form of capital, human or financial, something of value, in a firm". These stakeholders are those without whose participation the corporation cannot survive (Clarkson, 1995). The second stream considers primary stakeholder any person or organization that has a legitimate interest in a project or entity. In discussing the decision-making process for institutions – including large business corporations, government agencies, and non-profit organizations – the concept has been broadened to include everyone with an interest (or "stake") in what the entity does and achieves. This includes not only its employees and customers, but even members of a community where its offices or factory may affect the local economy or environment. Clarkson (1995: 106) argues that "primary stakeholder groups typically are comprised of shareholders and investors, employees, customers, and suppliers, together with what is defined as the public stakeholders group: the governments and communities that provide infrastructures and markets, whose laws and regulations must be obeyed, and to whom taxes and other obligations may be due". While not all community residents are employees, suppliers, customers or investors, they do provide various forms of important infrastructure for the organization and, in turn, are impacted directly by tax revenues and physical environment. The survival and continuing sustainability of institutions depends upon their ability to fulfil their economic and social purposes, which are to create and distribute wealth or value sufficient to ensure that each primary stakeholders group continues as part of the institutions'stakeholders system. Thus, an institution can be viewed as a set of interdependent relationships among primary stakeholders (Chakravarthy, 1986; Donaldson and Preston, 1995; Evan and Freeman, 1988; Greenley and Foxall, 1996; Harrison and St. John, 1994; Hill and Jones, 1992; Jones, 1995; Kotter and Heskett, 1992).

Such an enlargement of primary stakeholders group need to be carefully managed. In fact, Hansmann (1996) argues that there is, in such a view, a problem related to the decision-making process. The more groups of stakeholders there are, the more complicated it will be to make a decision, especially considering that stakeholders often have different goals. In that respect, it may be useful to integrate three different approaches to stakeholder theory, in order to better define the composition and the characteristics of primary stakeholders group.

- The ontological perspective of stakeholder and governance structure disserts about the fundamental nature and purpose of the organization. In that respect, the latter is essentially an "organizational entity through which many different individuals and groups attempt to achieve their ends"(Boatright, 2003: p. 391). So, "the very purpose of the organization [...] is to serve as a vehicle for coordinating stakeholder interests"(Evan and Freeman, 1988: p. 314). This stands in contrast to the shareholder-centred view of the organization as an economic entity that marshals resources for the purpose of making a profit for its owners. This perspective may also be defined as "normative" (in contrast with a "descriptive" approach).
- The deontic approach to stakeholder theory determines the legitimate interests and rights of various stakeholders (presumably going above and beyond their legal rights), and uses these as a way of determining corporate and managerial duties (Zan, 1990).
- The governance approach is about how certain stakeholders groups should exercise oversight and control over management (e. g. which groups, in addition to shareholders, should be represented on the board and how the board should function).

As far as public organizations are concerned (Coda, 1988; Ansoff, 1984), several researchers find that the likelihood of such organizations being perceived as effective increases when they manage to align the, possibly very diverse, expectations of stakeholder groups with respect to good governance (Abzug & Galaskiewicz, 2001; Balser & McClusky, 2005; Herman & Renz, 2008; Hsieh et al., 2010; Kilby, 2004; Ospina, Diaz, & O' Sullivan, 2002; Studer & von Schnurbein, 2012). How can public-sector regimes, agencies, programs, and activities be organized and managed to achieve public purposes? This question, of fundamental importance in the fields of politics, policy implementation, public administration, and public management, motivates the systematic study of stakeholder and governance structure. Two distinct or paradigmatic approaches to public management may be identified within this logic of governance. First, public managers may optimize outcomes within a given system of formal authority. This essentially short-run view of public management emphasizes the quotidian, repetitive aspects of managerial roles and features the psychology, tactics, and political intercourse aspects of management (descriptive approach). A second approach views public managers as proactive participants in coalition politics, as representatives of elected executives, as representatives of agency constituencies, or as goal-seeking actors in their own right. This longer-run view broadens the subject of public management to the wider domain of governance and administrative control of bureaucracy, and it broadens the content of management to include the design of governance arrangements (normative approach). This normative approach to stakeholder and governance structure has been increasingly confirmed by facts (Del Vecchio, 2001: p. 25). By now, in fact, the positive correlation between the social performance of any institution and its financial and competitive results are not questionable (Coda, 1988: p. 218-243).

Before discussing organizational structure and operational mechanisms, we will sum up the key issues presented so far. Institutions are characterized by several interests and actors, without whose participation the institutions themselves may not be able to survive and whose expectations are goals or constraints on the institutions'autonomy and their ability to pursue their own goals. The survival and continuing sustainability of institutions depends upon their ability to fulfil their economic and social purposes, which are to create and distribute wealth or value sufficient to ensure that each stakeholders group continues as part of the institutions'stakeholder system. In that respect, some expectations must be intended as institutions'goals, while some others as constraints on their autonomy. The distinction between the two kinds of expectations, not always immediate in practice, should derive from the ultimate goals of institutions'themselves.

1.1.3 Organizational structure and operational mechanisms

An important component of institutions'stakeholder and governance structure refers to the set of structures, rules and procedures for determining and balancing each stakeholder group's contribution, and rewards. These components may be classified into two main groups, referring to:

- environmental and inter-institutional relationships;
- internal organizational structure, rules and procedures.

The first group refers to the set of environmental conditions and institutional relationship with other entities. Those relationships have an economic and several non economic components. The economic component of the environment includes such elements as the industry to which the institutions belongs, the industries with which it interacts, the markets in which it performs the input-acquisition and output-delivery processes, the government's economic policies. The non economic components refer to social, political, cultural, legal, technological and geographical events or conditions. Institutional relationships with other entities include, but are not limited to, competition and market exchanges. For example, firms establish institutional relations with other legal entities in order to perform joint ventures, cartels, franchising agreements and so on. For public organizations, institutional relationship may occur at different levels:

- all public entities of a given country operate under an overall constitutional framework;
- all public entities are related with one another in terms of overlapped jurisdictions; shared competencies; provided funds and appointed governing bodies;

- public institutions may establish, just like firms, economic entities composed of separate legal entities;
- public entities operate within complex networks of public organizations, private firms and non-profit institutions in order to provide public services.

The second group of components refers to intra-organizational structures, rules and procedures. In private firms these include issues regarding "the composition, appointment systems, prerogatives, duties and mutual relationship of the general shareholder meeting, the board of directors, the key executives, and the board of auditors" (Anessi Pessina, 2002: p. 35). As far as public institutions are concerned, it is useful to distinguish between:

- organization design and structure. It is an important control device, since it can encourage certain types of contact and relationships. It works through divisional or functional specialization and reduce the variability of behaviour. The focus on specialization has had a direct impact on the new operating models and organizational structures that are emerging in the public sector. Increasingly clear functions are evident in public sector. More specifically, they refer to: (i) regulatory functions and oversight; (ii) service delivery and (iii) policy development. These three areas can be viewed as the core elements of almost any public sector organization, each requiring a different operating model, with peculiar implications on organizational structure and design. The Italian public organizations have experimented significant changes in their organizational design and structure, mainly because of the transition from the bureaucratic model to the managerial one. It implied, in most cases, the adoption of a divisional structure (or a mixed structure with a major divisional component) and the creation of wider-scope, more autonomous organizational units in charge of entire areas of need (Del Vecchio, 2000);
- the use of policies and procedures is the bureaucratic approach to specifying the processes and behaviour within an organisation. Policies are statements of intentions and actions that are meant to guide how a government, a department, a service or an individual works or behaves. Written policies usually consist of a set of principles, a purpose or aims/objectives or outcomes and strategies. Policies and procedures include such approaches as standard operating procedures and practices (Macintosh and Daft, 1987) and rules and policies (Simons, 1987).

1.2   Corporate governance within firms

During the 1990s, corporate governance became a hot issue in all of the advanced economies. We have defined governance as the determination of the broad uses to which organizational resources will be deployed and the resolution of conflicts among the myriad participants in organizations. In a 1997 review of corporate governance research, Shleifer and Vishny (1997) noted that "the subject of corporate governance is of enormous practical importance" (p. 737). Corporate governance refers to the system by which corporations are directed and controlled. The governance structure specifies the distribution of rights and responsibilities among different participants in the corporation (such as the board of directors, managers, shareholders, creditors, auditors, regulators, and other stakeholders) and defines the rules and procedures for making and disclosuring decisions and their impacts to various stakeholders (Hodges, Wright e Keasey, 1996: p. 7). Another well-known definition is the one provided by the Cadbury Committee (1992: p. 14) according to which "corporate governance is the system by which companies are directed and controlled. Boards of directors are responsible for the governance of their companies. The shareholders'role in governance is to appoint the directors and the auditors and to satisfy themselves that an appropriate governance structure is in place. The responsibilities of the board include setting the company's strategic aims, providing the leadership to put them into effect, supervising the management of the business and reporting to shareholders on their stewardship. The board's actions are subject to laws, regulations and the shareholders in general meeting".

The overwhelmingly dominant theoretical perspective applied in corporate governance studies is agency theory (Dalton, Daily, EllStrand, & Johnson, 1998; Shleifer & Vishny, 1997). Jensen and Meckling (1976) proposed agency theory as an explanation of how firms could exist, given the assumption that managers are self-interested, and a context in which those managers do not bear the full wealth effects of their decisions This was the first satisfactory explanation of the corporate governance since Berle and Means (1932) pointed out some of the key problems inherent in the separation of ownership and control. The concept of "effective governance" evolved from the above relationship between the agency theories determined participants of an organization, and was deemed to be achieved when governance mechanisms and processes were developed and implemented to an extent when interests between the principal and agent were fully aligned (Forestieri, 1998; Brennan and Solomon, 2008; Davis, 2005; Parkinson, 1993). The agency-oriented concept of "effective governance" essentially defined the extent of the governance paradigm of an institution and was generally described as being constrained to only refer to or address the regulatory and administrative framework that defined the board's monitoring and control functions in meeting its accountability requirements towards shareholders (Cutting and Kouzmin, 2001).

While agency theory dominates corporate governance research (Dalton et al., 2003), parts of the governance literature stem from a wider range of theoretical perspectives. Clarke (2005) suggested that under an agency-shareholder centric approach, the economic relations were limited to a series of contracts between the agent and shareholder. Consequently, the approach was suggested to have failed to take into account the increased accountabilities to shareholders and other constituents of the organization resulting from these wider environmental influencing forces. Roberts (2001) also in defining the problem of corporate governance referred to such wider interdependencies in an organization and suggested that a combination of its corresponding accountability processes together with agency theory oriented accountability processes constituted effective processes for corporate accountability.

Once we recognized the potential misalignment between the principal and agent interests, the question is how to avoid and eventually manage such a misalignment. Even in this case there are two possible approaches: the first one refers to external control and market mechanisms, while the second one refers to internal control and accountability. External, market-based control mechanisms and internal, organizationally based mechanisms of corporate control can be both employed to help align the diverse interests of managers and shareholders.

External corporate governance mechanisms encompass the controls external stakeholders exercise over the organization (*market for corporate control*). The theory of the market for corporate control was suggested by Manne (1965) and then refined in a series of articles by Jensen and Meckling (1976), Fama (1980), and Fama and Jensen (1983a, 1983b). According to this theory, as top managers engage in self-interested behaviour, their company's performance is likely to increasingly diverge from its maximum potential. This underperformance is reflected in the value of the company's stock. Under such circumstances, other management teams are likely to offer themselves to the shareholders as alternatives to the incumbent management. The "market for corporate control", then, is the competition among these management teams for the rights to manage corporate resources. Other examples of market for corporate control mechanisms include: debt covenants; demand for and assessment of performance information (especially financial statements); government regulations; managerial labour market; media pressure and takeovers (Capasso, 1996: p. 17-19).

Internal control mechanisms are designed to bring the interests of managers and shareholders into congruence. As required by law, the board of directors in a publicly held company is charged with the responsibility of developing and implementing these mechanisms. With the creation of a board, a division of labour emerges in the management and control of organizational decision making. The managers initiate and implement their decisions, while the board members ratify them and, in general, monitor the conduct of the firm's top managers (Fama and Jensen, 1983a, 1983b; Airoldi et al., 1998: p. 180). The board of directors has many broad classes of internal control options available to it. It can either alter the incentives of its managerial team or dismiss them. Other internal mechanisms include board structure variables such as duality and the proportion of non-executive directors, debt financing and executive director shareholdings. Finally, other internal control procedures are policies implemented by an entity's board of directors, audit committee, management, and other personnel to provide reasonable assurance of the entity achieving its objectives related to reliable financial reporting, operating efficiency, and compliance with laws and regulations.

From a management theory perspective, the corporate governance requires the concrete implementation within organizations of principles defined by the Cadbury Report (1992) and the Sarbanes-Oxley Act (2002) in terms of:

- rights and treatment of shareholders. In that respect, organizations should respect the rights of shareholders and make them able to exercise those rights. To those extents it can be useful to openly and effectively communicating relevant information and encouraging shareholders to participate in general meetings;
- interests of other stakeholders. Organizations must recognize legal, contractual, social, and market driven obligations to other stakeholders, including employees, investors, creditors, suppliers, local communities, customers, and policy makers;
- role and responsibilities of the board. The board is in charge of reviewing and challenging management performance. It also needs adequate size and appropriate levels of independence and commitment;

- integrity and ethical behaviour. Corporate officers and board members are required to have integrity and organizations should develop a code of conduct for their directors and executives that promotes ethical and responsible decision-making;
- accountability and transparency. Organizations should clarify and make publicly known the roles and responsibilities of board and management to provide stakeholders with a level of accountability. Disclosure of material matters concerning the organization should be timely and balanced to ensure that all investors have access to clear, factual information.

Summing up, as far as firms are concerned, corporate governance is a relevant issue from a management theory perspective. Its characteristics, however, are not still easy to be defined, because of two different groups of reasons.

Firstly, a multi-theoretic approach to corporate governance is essential for recognizing the many mechanisms and structures that might reasonably enhance organizational functioning. Our intent is not to provide a comprehensive list of the many theoretical perspectives (from the applicability of class hegemony theory to the legalistic perspective in the corporate governance field) appearing in the corporate governance literature, but to highlight that this unavoidable and desirable multi-theoretic approach to corporate governance requires to be read according to a systematic view, in order to produce a unitary framework. Secondly, there is still not an orthodox use of theoretical paradigms by management theory researchers: this leads to the definition of wide propositions that aren't able to support the practitioners perspective.

As far as future research trends on corporate governance are concerned, the theoretical perspectives we have identified — and those we have not mentioned — suggest that researchers face a considerable challenge in determining those settings that best fit the assumptions in a given theory.

1.3 Stakeholder and governance structures in public organizations

As mentioned in § 1.1, the definition of the governance structure of any institution requires a clear identification of the main groups of its primary stakeholders. This is particularly critical in public organizations, since the heterogeneity of primary stakeholders has major implications in terms of:

- structures, rules and procedures that allow the different stakeholders to take part to the decision-making process;
- number, types and mutual relationship of public organizations.

In that respect, presenting two strictly related, relevant issues, such as the governance structure and its pervasiveness in public institutions, may be considered a useful starting point,.

As already mentioned, the term governance is widely used in public and private sectors, in characterizing global and local arrangements, and in reference to formal and informal norms and understanding. Because the term has a strong intuitive appeal, precise definitions are seldom thought to be necessary by those who use it. As a result, when researchers identify governance as important to achieving policy or organizational objectives, it may be unclear whether the reference is to organizational structures, administrative processes, managerial judgment, systems of incentives and rules, administrative philosophies, or combinations of these elements. Despite ambiguity of definitions, governance generally refers to the means for achieving direction, control, and coordination of wholly or partially autonomous individuals or organizations on behalf of interests to which they jointly contribute. According to the prevailing theories, public organizations are supposed to operate in the "general interest" of their communities (Borgonovi, 2000: p. 4). More specifically, they should specify the general interest, identify and implement a set of actions to pursue such an interest and collect the financial resources needed to implement these actions (Anessi Pessina, 2000: p. 99). As society grows more diverse, the identifications of the public interests and the related actions become increasingly difficult. Governance structures reflect these priorities: thus non economic issues usually take precedence whereas economic issues are important, but not dominant. At best, public organizations show a sort of "benign neglect" (Del Vecchio, 2001: p. 35) toward economic dimensions and they explicitly sacrifice the economic component to better serve government's non economic goals. Thus, for example, most governments are characterized by systems of check and balances and by formalized decision-making procedures, which certainly do not increase their efficiency or flexibility, but are intended to protect various rights and interests.

As far as the governance structure pervasiveness is concerned, such pervasiveness is partly linked to the governance structure itself. The presence of formalized decision-making procedures is a crucial feature of public institutions governance structure. To some extent, the reliance on formalized procedure is common to all private and public bureaucracies. The pillar of bureaucratic model refers to the possibility to break down the organization through a systematic division of labour: it implies that (i) for each position there's a set of tasks to be assigned; (ii) for each task, it's possible to define a set of rules and procedures; (iii) the compliance to rules and procedures is the only condition to reach the task. In that respect, bureaucratic model require the use of rules, policies, hierarchy of authority, written documentation, reward systems and other formal mechanisms to influence employee's behaviour.[3]

Thus, what private firms view as a mean to an end, in public organizations often becomes an end in itself, or has a significant impact on the institution's ultimate goals.

Partly, this condition derives and is stressed by the small degree of autonomy that characterizes public organizations. Largely this is caused by the fact that public interests are never entrusted to a single, all inclusive public institutions, but rather to a public sector, in which operate a number of independent entities (§ 1.1.3), that: (i) operate under an overall constitutional framework; (ii) are related with one another in terms of

---

[3] Bureaucratic model stimulates at least three types of responses: (i) rigid bureaucratic behaviour occurs when bureaucratic systems prompt employees to stay out of trouble by following the rules rather than doing the right thing; (ii) tactical behaviour leads to ineffective behaviour, because employees try to beat the system; (iii) resistance to control occurs because control systems uncover mistakes, threaten job security and status, decrease autonomy and may be seen as an invasion of privacy.

overlapped jurisdictions; shared competencies; provided funds and appointed governing bodies; (iii) may include, such as any other economic entities, separate legal entities.

Thus the necessity to provide coordination between public organizations arises. There are several tools that may ensure such coordination. The main relevant one refers to the vertical coordination within the overall public sector, especially with reference to the territorial government bodies. A territorial government (Anessi Pessina, 2000: p.117) may be defined as "a general purpose government, composed of all the people residing in its territory. It usually has a legislature elected by the relevant population and executive". The presence of several levels of governments implies that a given territory and its population will simultaneously fall within the jurisdiction of different public organizations. This overlapping jurisdiction may be managed by:

- the allocation of competencies among level of governments. It refers to what and whose needs each public organization is supposed to satisfy, which activities are necessary to be performed to this end and, if it's possible, how such activities should be performed. The implications of such an allocation of competencies are the overall mission of any public institution. However, this mission is not defined by the institution itself, but rather by the country institutional arrangements. This is obviously a major difference between private firms and public entities and it derives from different expectations of the organizations'primary stakeholders. In practical terms, the distribution of competencies requires that one or more lists of competencies are assigned to each level of governments. The clearer the definition of responsibilities is, the more efficient and effective the coordination among tiers of government becomes;
- allocation of taxation authority. The overall structure of the public sector requires an alignment between the fiscal resources available and the competencies held. In theory, it's possible that competencies can be devolved to lower ties of government even without a corresponding fiscal power. This, however, may create perverse incentives since, at a lower level public organizations may be induced to overspend their appropriations, thus requiring the upper level to provide with supplementary funds. The principles that must be accomplished in order to have a good allocation of resources, according to the World Bank, refer to: autonomy (sub-national governments should have complete independence and flexibility in setting priorities); revenue adequacy to discharge designated responsibilities; equity and predictability; efficiency (the resource allocation should be neutral with respect to public organization choices of resource allocation to different sectors or different types of activity); simplicity (the allocation should be based on objective factors); incentive (the allocation should provide for sound fiscal management and discourage inefficient practices);
- introduction of general rules and mechanisms to ensure coordination and homogeneity through the public sector, especially with reference to health care, education and employment. In that respect, higher level or governments are required to define laws and guidelines in order to limit the discretion of lower tiers of government and ensure homogeneity in behaviour, decision-making process and needs satisfied.

Public sector, indeed, is not only characterized by several levels of government, but also by the presence, in each level, of many different organizations. This requires the provisions of horizontal coordination. Horizontal coordination initiatives may take place across levels of government, across boundaries between units of a single department or agency or among multiple departments or agencies, or across public, private and voluntary sectors. In that respect, horizontal practice may be defined by the concept of coordinated government, emphasizing the need for departments to work together and not to produce either redundancy or gaps in services.

In conclusions, as far as stakeholders and governance structure is concerned, public organizations are characterized by heterogeneous stakeholders and conflicting expectations, a limited importance of economic issues and a pervasiveness of governance structure within both organization's internal features and its relations with the environment. Internally governance structure covers a number of issues that have not governance relevance in private firms (establishment of new departments, personnel management systems, decision-making procedures, etc). Externally public organizations operate under an overall constitutional framework; they are related with one another in terms of overlapped jurisdictions, shared competencies, provided funds and appointed governing bodies; they may include, such as any other economic entities, separate legal entities. For all those reasons, it's necessary to activate vertical and horizontal coordination mechanisms.

1.4 Interests, political system and public organizations

A major implication of stakeholders heterogeneity is the role of political representation and its impact on public organizations. As already mentioned, public organizations are characterized by a number of economic and non economic goals: those goals derive from the principle that public organizations operate in the general interests of their communities.

Since the general interests are often wide, public organizations perform a wide range of activities, characterized by a relevant diversification and horizontal extension. According to Borgonovi's taxonomy (2000: p. 15) such activities my belong to five groups: (i) protection of fundamental rights, public order and safety, regulation; (ii) provision of collective good and services; (iii) provision of technically private goods and services; (iv) financial transfer to firms, families, non-profit organizations and individuals; (v) socio-economic planning. For any of these activities it's necessary to define the groups of recipients, which, in turn, can be defined according to different criteria (age, income, occupation, etc). In all these choices the role of politics is central.

Firstly, it's important to recognize that politician play a number of roles at a variety of levels: leadership of their polity; policy-making for society; strategy-making for organizations; partnership building with other organizations and other stakeholder; watchdog over the decision made in their polity; lobbyist in relation to the decisions made in other polities and representation of their constituents. All these roles assume different configuration at different levels (global, national, local, etc.), however the contribution to policy-making is often intended as the most relevant. The question of the political influence on decisions raises one of the most relevant issue in the organizational literature on decision-making. In that respect, political researchers have always highlighted that the political system of a nation and its traditions, institutions and values heavily influence the actions and functioning of public organizations.

Secondly, separating politics and administration has long been a feature of public administrative systems, so as to attempt to maintain distance between politicians and administrators roles. However, modern empirical research has established that public administration is also involved in politics. In reality the public administration has considerable possibilities to exert political influence, regardless of which part of the public decision making process we examine, and to be influenced by politics. This realization raises several topical issues:

- the governing politicians must develop an administrative apparatus that creates the best possible conditions for ensuring that their policies are actually put into effect (governance and steering problem);
- the assertion that the public administration is involved in politics means that there are democratic issues to be faced. In fact, even though according to democracy theory power must be coupled with responsibility, yet the assertion that the public administration exerts political power raises issues of how the administration can be held accountable (accountability problem);
- from a citizen's perspective it's necessary to define how the role of public administrators can be justified in a democracy as legitimate and which type of institutions are required to guarantee that the public administration does not abuse its powers.

These interpretations are here discussed in order to highlight the difference between private firms and public institutions. Firms are characterized by a top-down delegation process, according to which shareholders appoint board members, who, in their turns, select top managers based on their ability and willingness to pursue firms'ultimate goals. The assumptions are: market is able to punish any possible firm's inefficiency or ineffectiveness; shareholders have the ability and the power to avoid inefficiency and ineffectiveness and other stakeholders are accountable about firm's performance and have abilities to prevent undesirable outcomes. In public organizations, on the contrary, the relationship between politicians and managers have been characterized by the well-known public-administration paradigm (Wilson, 1887), which calls for the separation of politics and administration. The normative approach highlights that we observe some separation but not a complete separation between public administration and politics. According to Goodnow (2008), while, "the function of politics [...] consists in the expression of the will of the state" (p. 23), "the function of executing the will of the state has been called administration" (p. 72). The relation of politics to administration is one of subordination. Goodnow (2003) argues that while politics can never be completely apart from administration, "government requires that it is the executing authority (administration) which shall be subordinate to the expressing authority (politics)" (p. 24). Political parties are central to public institutions'architecture and efficient administration. The reason is that the role of powerful yet responsible political parties is a necessary means of expressing and executing the will of the state. Having powerful political parties ensures that the will of the people is the will of the legislature, and thus through the aforementioned subordinate relationship, results in the effective administration of the people's will.

The politics-administration dichotomy has had a strange history in public administration. It expands and contracts, rises and falls, but never to go away (Svara & Overeem, 2006: p. 121). At the heart of the public administration there is the relationship between administrators, on one hand, and politicians and the public, on the other hand. The nature of such relationship and the proper role of political leaders and administrators in the administrative and political process have been the subject of considerable debate. About the importance of the politics and administration, Waldo (1987) wrote: "nothing is more central in thinking about public administration than the nature and interrelations of politics and administration. Nor are the nature and interrelations of politics and administration matters only for academic theorizing. What is more important in the day-today, year-to-year, decade-to-decade operation of government than the ways in which politics and administration are conceptualized, rationalized, and related one to the other".

Thus, the politics'nature, characteristics and concrete behaviours are crucial for the understanding and functioning of public organizations. In the following pages we discuss about:

- the relation between governance structures and politics;
- spoils and merit system;
- political goals and deviations from the public interests;
- impact on the consensus enjoined by public institutions.

As far as the relation between governance structures and politics in concerned, we observe that, in public organizations, governance structures are mostly based on political representation. In fact, according to the doctrine of popular sovereignty, the ultimate political authority resides not in the government or in any other political officials, but rather in the people that is the government's constituents. This is translated into a set of rules of political rights and responsibilities, thus defining the governance structure. Political system and governance structure are mutually interdependent: on one hand the governance structure may be intended as the arena in which the general interests are mediated and interpreted by the political system; on the other hand, the political system influence the governance structure according to its needs, by shaping rules and principles. The interactions between political system and governance structure constitute the environment in which public organizations operate. Such an environment may influence the functioning of public administrations in terms of power distributions, allocation of competencies and degree of financial autonomy, etc. This is particularly relevant if we consider that such an environment derive from stakeholders'expectations, which are largely non-economic and often vague and conflicting, so that politician must be good interpreters and mediators of expectations rather than good managers (Anessi Pessina, 2000). Thus the interactions between political system and governance structure not always generate higher level of efficiency and effectiveness in public sector. Moreover, public administrations activities are significantly affected by political cycles (Borgonovi, 2000). This partly affects the characteristic of unitary of public institutions over the time. In order to better understand political cycle influence, let's consider the variations generated by elections approach on the public organizations activities. We observe postponing of unpopular decisions (such as a higher level of taxation) and introducing new policies, able to bring additional votes (public investments, for example). Obviously, this impact is particularly critical for unstable political system, where elections are frequent and politician have to face short representation horizon. Greater stability should (Del Vecchio, 2001):

- extend public organizations decision making time horizons;
- give continuity to their policies, where continuity is often a prerequisite for effectiveness;
- reduce their need to rely on "announcement effects", intended as the process whereby the presentation of plans and commitments is perceived by public opinion as if such plans and commitments had already been implemented, thus inflating expectations;
- reduce the waste of resources that stems from the lack of long-term planning processes.

As far as spoils and merit system are concerned, the first one implies that politicians can, after winning an election, give government jobs to their voters as a reward for working toward victory, and as an incentive to keep working for the party; whereas the second one requires that offices are awarded on the basis of some measure of merit, independent of political activity. The spoils system involves political activity by public employees in support of their party and the employees'removal from office if their party loses the election. A change in party control of government necessarily brings new officials to high positions carrying political responsibility, but the spoils system extends personnel turnover down to routine or subordinate governmental positions. Arguments in favour of the spoils system defend it as a means of maintaining an active party organization by offering loyal workers occupational rewards. It also guarantees the ruling party loyal and cooperative employees. On the other hand, the spoils system too often resulted in appointments that were based strictly on the needs of the politics, without regard for the appointee's qualifications or ability to do the job. However, even the merit system may produce undesirable effects, since it makes responsibilities on final outcome unclear and overloads politicians with minor decisions, which negatively affect both the quality and timeliness of decision-making process.

As far as political goals and deviations from the general interests are concerned, it's necessary to highlight the role of interest groups, which are associations of individuals who have common goals and who work together to achieve their goals by attempting to influence government policy. These groups are also sometimes referred to as voluntary association or pressure groups. Although interest groups may articulate and aggregate the diverse interests found in society in the scope of the political arena, they are not synonymous with political parties. This is because they seek only to influence government in their member's favour. Peters (1991: 203-241), classified influences (mediated by politics) pursued by formal and informal interests groups on public administrations as follows:

- institutionalized interest groups are characterized by well structured and enduring organization, stable membership, clear objectives, and exclusive knowledge of the appropriate sectors of government and their clients. They begin for purposes other than political activity and only engage in such activity in order to defend their own interests in the government's policy decisions. They are a part of government, departments or agencies, but they are politically neutral;

- non-associational interest groups are in essence the complete opposite of associational interest groups. They lack any formal organization whatsoever, instead, they are composed of individuals who share some common, defining characteristic such as class, ethnicity, race, religion, culture, or gender. They seldom act as coherent political groups, but they are often treated by others as if they did. Despite their lack of political organization, the members of these groups tend to be seen as representatives of the group;
- associational interest groups are often the political branch of a group that already exists for other reasons such as professional associations. Thus, they regard political activity as only one of their primary activities. These groups are characterized by their ongoing, formal organization which is a product of their efforts to influence public policy and articulate the interests of their members over the long term;
- anomic interest groups are generally the result of turmoil and excitement. Consequently, their actions are often violent. They are characterized by their lack of formal organization, absence of obvious leaders, as well as their temporary and loose coordination of efforts. They are short lived, spontaneous aggregations of people who share a common concern over a particular issue.

As far as impact on the consensus enjoined by public organizations is concerned, again it's necessary to highlight that consensus is crucial for public institutions, since it allows public organizations to raise funds (through taxes, tariffs and loans) and provide public services. If public organizations have more funds, they can operate more effectively, thus improving the quantity and quality of the services they provide, and, again, generating more consensus. What happens within political arena can affect such virtuous circle by two mechanisms (Del Vecchio, 2001; Anessi Pessina, 2002):

- the community's judgments on politicians and public institutions tend to overlap to such an extent that if politicians'approval ratings fall, the same will happen to the consensus towards public institutions, regardless of their actual performance;
- politicians may build their political platforms around the myth to downsize the public sector, thus designing public organizations unable to satisfy all complex needs coming from different stakeholders, or may use public organizations'dysfunctions to justify the inability of political systems to be effective and efficient.

In conclusions, it's now clearer that governance structures in public organizations must balance three different and often conflicting logics: constitutional, political and managerial (Borgonovi, 2000: p. 50-51), described as follows:

- the constitutional logic is based on the leading principle of legality and has the final purpose of establishing a set of individual rights and ensuring that such rights are not violated by other individuals and institutions, included public ones. The result is a system of rules and constraints that public administrations must comply with and ensure;
- the constitutional logic is based on the leading principle of consensus, which, in turns, depends on politicians'ability to fulfil voters'expectations. Since interests and

expectations are often vague, politicians are expected to interpret them and reach an adequate compromise;

- the managerial logic is based on the leading principle of financial viability, which derives from public organizations'ability to purse efficiency and effectiveness, thus balancing between expanding needs and scarce resources.

Even if the three logics are often in conflict, is not possible to choose one instead of another. It's crucial to maintain equilibrium among them: when the constitutional logic dominates there is a bureaucratic excess; when the political logic dominate there are risks of favouritisms and corruptions, when the managerial logic dominate there is place for undemocratic technocracy.

1.5   Corporate governance in public organizations

For at least the last 15 years governance has been a prominent subject in public administration. Governance, defined by Lynn et al. (2001: p. 7) as the "regimes, laws, rules, judicial decisions, and administrative practices that constrain, prescribe, and enable the provision of publicly supported goals and services", holds strong interest for public administration researchers.

The Report of the Committee on the Financial Aspects of Corporate Governance (the Cadbury report) defined corporate governance as "the system by which organizations are directed and controlled". It identified the three fundamental principles of corporate governance as: (i) openness; (ii) integrity; (iii) accountability. These principles are relevant to public sector entities as they are to private sector entities. They apply equally to all public sector entities, irrespective of whether governing bodies are elected or appointed, and whether or not they comprise a group of people or an individual. In the context of the public sector, the definitions of these principles need to be adapted to reflect the key characteristics of public sector entities, which distinguish them from the private sector. In particular, public sector entities have to satisfy a more complex range of political, economic and social objectives, which subject them to a different set of external constraints and influences; and are subject to forms of accountability to their various stakeholders which are different than those that a company in the private sector owes to its shareholders. In that respect, the IFAC Public Sector Committee (2001) argues that in public organizations:

- openness is required to ensure that stakeholders can have confidence in the decision-making processes and actions of public sector entities, in the management of their activities, and in the individuals within them;
- integrity comprises both straightforward dealing and completeness. It is based upon honesty and objectivity, and high standards of propriety and probity in the stewardship of public funds and resources, and management of an entity's affairs;
- accountability is the process whereby public sector entities, and the individuals within them, are responsible for their decisions and actions, including their stewardship of public funds and all aspects of performance, and submit themselves to appropriate external scrutiny.

Thus, there is an increasing recognition that the corporate governance in public organization is more about finding ways to ensure that decisions are made effectively in a 'governed' rather than 'managed' sense (Barrett, 1997). There is a difference between these two concepts. The role of management is primarily concerned with running the business operations efficiently and effectively within the boundaries of the organisation under which it operates. By contrast, the governance role is concerned with giving overall direction, overseeing and controlling the executive actions of management and satisfying legitimate expectations (Tricker, 1984). Therefore, "if management is about running business, governance is about seeing that it is run properly"(Tricker, 1984: 7) It is aimed at defining the organizations stakeholders and their relative importance; the contributions expected by each group and the structures, rules and procedures for determining and balancing each group contributions and rewards. Tricker (1994) argues that there are two aspects of corporate governance: conformance and performance. Conformance, he argues, "consists of two elements, firstly monitoring and supervising executive performance, and secondly maintaining accountability to all those with the legitimate right to expect that feedback" (Tricker, 1994: p. 150). Performance, on the other hand, consists of strategy formulation and policymaking, and is thus the contribution of those who govern the organisation to its performance (Tricker, 1994). While it is the conformance aspect of corporate governance that is emphasised in the private sector, in the public sector it is argued that the performance dimension is at least as important as the conformance dimension (Hodges et al., 1996). Thus, we describe governance in the public sector as basically concerned with structures and processes for decision-making and with the controls and behaviour that support effective accountability for performance outcomes. Corporate governance includes the formal lines of authority and accountability as well as the systems which are in place to ensure that representatives of the various functions and organizational units meet to coordinate their activities both vertically and horizontally.

In recent years, many developed and developing countries have started a deep reevaluation of the role of public organizations in their societies. In that respect, a redefinition of the political-administrative relationship has evolved, designed to ensure greater accountability and a greater devolution of power to managers. The focus of governance in the private sector is on the board of directors. In the public sector context, boards are sometimes difficult to identify and define, as they operate in different statutory and managerial frameworks. In particular, public sector entities have to satisfy complex range objectives (political, economic and social) under a set of several external constraints (Figure 1.1). That way, for example, the UK Public Accounts Committee noted in their Report on the Proper Conduct of Public Business (2009) that it's "[…] a framework […] (which) must include effective systems of control and accountability, and above all responsible attitudes on the part of those handling public money. It is important that the drive to provide improved services at reduced costs should be sustained and that this drive should not be stifled by unnecessary bureaucracy. At such time it is even more essential to maintain honesty in the spending of public money and to ensure that traditional public sector values are not neglected in the effort to maximize economy and efficiency".

If we assume the validity of corporate governance framework in order to design effective public organization according to the traditional paradigm of public institutions, we need to critically discuss the role of external and internal control mechanisms.

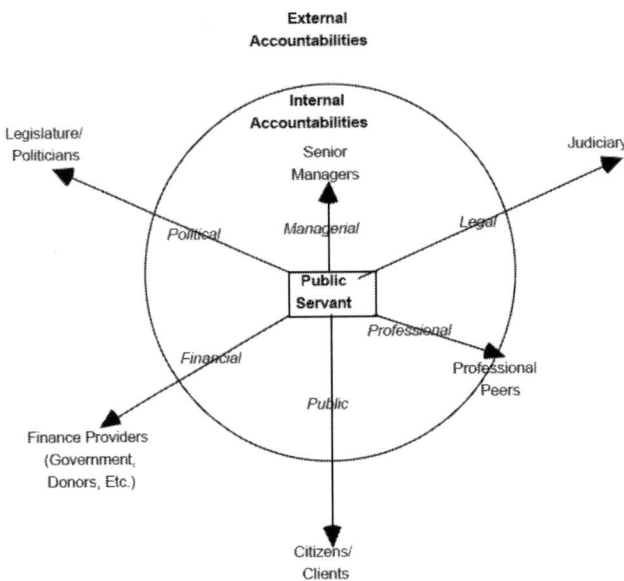

Figure 1.1 Example of overall accountability process in the public sector (Heeks, 1998).

External corporate governance mechanisms should encompass the controls external stakeholders (mainly citizens) exercise over the organization. In the traditional approach, as top managers or politics deviate from the general interest, the public organizations'performance is likely to increasingly diverge from its maximum potential. This underperformance is recognized by citizens, which may use an exit strategy — according to Hirschman (1970) model — during elections. Publishing on a timely basis an annual report (including financial statements), presenting an objective, balanced and understandable account and assessment of the entity's activities can make more effective external mechanisms.

As far as internal control is concerned the need is for designing clear roles and responsibilities of top management, and in particular the relative roles and responsibilities of non-executive members and executive management of each public organization. In the traditional approach, one way of achieving such a balance is for the politicians to include a balance of executive and nonexecutive members (including independent non-executives), so that no individual or small group of individuals can dominate the politicians'decision-making. Moreover a good governance should requires clear definitions of responsibility and a clear understanding of relationships between the organization's stakeholders and those entrusted to manage resources. It needs to be based on an acceptance by all involved in top management that the highest standards of integrity are expected of them, and it needs to be clearly visible in all their actions.

In this approach, accountability appears to be crucial, but, as well explained by Day and Klein (1987: p. 51), "the view of accountability, seen as flowing from the fact of election, springs from traditional democratic theory uncontaminated by consideration about the complexities of large modern organisations or about the problems of large, uninterested electorates. It is a view which takes the linkages in the system of accountability for granted, since it assumes that councillors [politicians] are automatically answerable to their voters and unquestionably in control of the organisation for which they are accountable. As we have seen, the debate and developments of the past two decades reflect precisely the realisation that neither of these two assumptions stands up".

In the next pages we present the debate and theoretical developments which have been characterizing the last two decades, by recognizing that the traditional approach failed in catching all the complex objectives pursued by public sector in a continuously changing environment and generated inefficiency, inefficacy, delays and dysfunctions. The more general claim of the managerial model in the public sector is to transform the traditional public administrations into a new set of organizations, characterized by:

- a separation of strategic policy from operational management;
- a concern with results rather than process and procedure;
- an orientation to the needs of citizens rather than the interests of bureaucrats;
- a new entrepreneurial management culture.

New public management presents a complex set of ideas that have evolved and developed different themes (Hood, 1995). The version most clearly embraced by the governments across the Western world rests on a critique of monopolistic forms of service provision and an argument for a wider range of service providers and a more market-oriented approach to management. Public service organizations, so the argument has it, tend to be dominated by producer interests (the bureaucrats and the various ranks of other employees). According to Ferlie et al. (1996: p. 10-16) at least four new public management models can be discerned and, while each of them represent an innovation of the traditional public organization models, they are all different.

The earliest model to emerge can be defined as "the efficiency drive". It represents an attempt to make public organizations more business-like, led by crude notion of efficiency. Core themes include:

- an increased attention to financial control and a strong concern with value for money and efficiency gains;
- a stronger general managerial spine, even of hierarchical nature; a command-and-control mode of working and clear target setting and performance monitoring;
- an extension of audit; an insistence of more transparent methods for reviewing the performance and more standard settings and benchmarking;
- new forms of corporate governance; marginalization of elected representatives and trade-unionists and a more entrepreneurial management.

The second model can be defined as "downsizing and decentralization" and involves reducing workforce numbers, decentralization of financial budgets and contracting-out. It also involves a more concerted focus on the introduction of quasi-markets and distinctions between purchaser and provider organizations. According to this model, which gained raising importance in the 90s, flexibility and unbundling vertically integrated organizations are crucial issues in order to support a new course of actions in public institutions. This model emphasizes quasi-market, management by contract, a small strategic core and a large operational periphery, delayering and downsizing, split of private and public funding, management by influence and networks, a service by flexibility and variety.

The third model, "in search of excellence", represents a focus on changing the organizational culture of the public sector. On the one hand, a 'top-down'approach views a public sector organization's culture as malleable and capable of being altered by a charismatic leader espousing a new vision. An alternative 'bottom-up'approach emphasizes introducing concepts from the organizational development literature such as the "learning organization".

The fourth model, "public service orientation", seeks to bring together a range of public and private sector management approaches. It involves to "reinventing" the public sector by extolling managers to be more entrepreneurial, results-oriented and mission-driven. This model also emphasizes the provision of quality public services and total quality management initiatives. The focus is believed to be on citizens rather than customers, and proponents of the model are critical of the introduction of market-based solutions into the public sector. Returning power to elected rather than appointed local councils is advocated as is an awareness of the distinctiveness of public sector tasks and values.

NPM principles share precise trends in public administrations change processes. These trends are observable in Italy, too. In fact, in the last two decades Italian public administrations have been characterized by a gradual break-down of the classical and mostly theoretical accountability chain. In fact, we can identify the following major trends:

- the introduction of direct popular election of the head of the executive, which is designed to make the executive more accountable to the population;
- the introduction of public competition and internal or quasi-market mechanisms;
- territorial governments managers have achieved greater autonomy, since their fiduciary relationship with politicians;
- the increased importance of economic issues;
- the introduction of performance-related and position-related pay systems.

In this new setting, a crucial issue is how to define proper corporate governance mechanisms. Obviously, the answer to that question cannot be searched within the traditional (bureaucratic) framework of public administrations.

The principal goal of public organizations change processes is to empower public employees, create autonomous and effective public managers and make government a more attractive employer. But effective government will only work by reducing the power of the civil service and empowering their nominal political masters. Both freedoms and accountability are desirable for effective public management. Public sectors that fail to provide sufficient managerial freedoms will foster unresponsive, bureaucratic behaviour of the sort that created an appetite for the NPM proposals. On the other hand public sectors that fail to hold their managers accountable, risk loss of control by democratically elected representatives to unelected public entrepreneurs who choose how they spend the public's money.

Reforming public management impels governments to assess and modify existing organisational structures. The assessment might lead to the establishment of new entities, a redefinition of organisational boundaries and responsibilities or the elimination of some units. The major trend consists in breaking up functionally integrated, multi-purpose departments into a number of service delivery entities, each with a clearly defined mission, operating independence and performance targets. One of the main reasons for such a change is that large departments, which are structured as holding companies for loosely related activities tend to be top-heavy, slow-moving and inefficient entities that have high operating costs. On the other hand, in functionally integrated departments, service providers "capture" policy-makers, feeding them advice that blunts innovation and weakens accountability. As far as this form of organisation is concerned, risk has been voiced that departments may have been weakened to the extent that they cannot carry out essential co-ordinating functions.

Finally public organizations face a two steps challenge of balancing freedom and control—within each organization and in relationships between officials and elected representatives. The issue of democratic control over management action is central to the political process because public agencies have awesome powers of compulsion. They can tax, regulate, inspect, arrest and can reward through subsidies, purchases or protection (Wilson, 1887; Mussari, 1994). Control systems are defined as the "formal, information-based routines and procedures managers use to maintain or alter patterns in organizational activities" (Simons, 1995). New control systems have to provide the link between political strategy and administrative delivery. These new control systems descend from the work of Frederick Taylor (1911), which emphasizes the quest for efficiency through identifying the best possible ways of working; include forms of political pressure focusing on achieving economy in public spending and stimulate a citizens and political movement that emphasizes openness of information as a form of control which will ensure fairness in the implementation of public services.

Summing up, we can comment with Shick (1999) that, even if the traditional, centralized bureaucracy has been replaced by a system that seeks to hold public sector managers accountable for delivering good performances, "one area of concern is the link between 'letting'and 'making'managers manage. It is much easier to fulfil the first part of the bargain than the second. It is much easier to remove control than to enforce accountability. In fact, accountability frameworks — the specification of targets, reporting on results, and audit of performance — still are relatively undeveloped" (Shick, 1999: 12-13).

Summary

Understanding the logic behind the definition of stakeholder and governance structures has always been a central issue in the Italian research stream of Management. Within this theoretical framework, the chapter assumes that the stakeholder and governance structure relates to the organizations'structure and composition, as well as its various management and project teams.

In the chapter we presented an in-depth analysis of stakeholders group and contributions expected and organizational structures and mechanisms that allow coordinating activities. As far as public organizations are concerned, major trends described require a new corporate governance framework, which must include effective systems of control and accountability, and above all responsible attitudes on the part of those handling public money. It is important that the drive to provide improved services at reduced costs should be sustained and that this drive should not be stifled by unnecessary bureaucracy. At such time it is even more essential to maintain honesty in the spending of public money and to ensure that traditional public sector values are not neglected in the effort to maximize economy and efficiency.

References

ABZUG R., GALASKIEWICZ J. (2001), "Nonprofit Boards: Crucibles of Expertise or Symbols of Local Identities?", *Nonprofit and Voluntary Sector Quarterly*, Vol 30: 51-73.

AIROLDI G., BRUNETTI G., CODA V. (1994), *Economia Aziendale*, Il Mulino, Bologna.

AIROLDI G., GNAN L., MONTEMERLO D. (1998), "Strutture proprietarie, complessità gestionale e sistemi di governance nelle piccole e medie imprese", in AIROLDI G., FORESTIERI G. (EDS), *Corporate governance: analisi e prospettive del caso italiano*, Etas Libri, Milano.

AMADUZZI A. (1992), *L'azienda nel suo sistema e nei suoi princìpi*, UTET, Torino.

ANESSI PESSINA E. (2000), *La contabilità delle aziende pubbliche*, Giuffrè, Milano.

ANESSI PESSINA E. (2002), *Principles of Public Management*, Egea, Milano.

ANSOFF H. I. (1984), "Le strategie sociali per l'impresa", in PASTORE R., PIANTONI G. (EDS), *Strategia sociale dell'impresa*, Etas Libri, Milano.

ARDEMANI E. (1993), *L'impresa: economia, controllo, bilancio, gestione straordinaria, 4a ed.*, Giuffrè editore, Milano.

BALSER D., McCLUSKY J. (2005), "Managing stakeholder relationships and nonprofit organization effectiveness", *Nonprofit Management and Leadership*, Vol 15 (3): 295-315.

BOATRIGHT J. R. (2003), "The Ethics of Arbitration in the Securities Industry", *Business and Society Review*, Vol 99 (1): 19-24.

BORGONOVI E. (1993a), "La rilevanza del concetto di istituto in Economia aziendale", in CATTANEO M., CODA V., GALASSI G., PELLICELLI G., PROVASOLI A., SUPERTI FURGA F. (EDS), *Scritti in onore di Carlo Masini, Vol. 1*, Egea, Milano.

BORGONOVI, E. (1993b), "Non cercare nelle leggi ciò che in esse non si trova", *Mecosan*, 6: 2-6.

BORGONOVI E., FATTORE G., LONGO F. (2009), *Management delle istituzioni pubbliche*, Egea, Milano.

BORGONOVI E. (2000), *Principi e sistemi aziendali per le amministrazioni pubbliche*, EGEA, Milano.

BRENNAN N. M., SOLOMON J. (2008), "Corporate governance, accountability and mechanisms of accountability: an overview", *Accounting, Auditing & Accountability Journal*, Vol. 7: 885 – 906.

CADBURY COMMITTEE (1992), *Report of the Committee on the Financial Aspects of Corporate Governance*, Professional Publishing, London.

CAPASSO A. (1996), *Assetti proprietari e governo di impresa: "corporate governance" e assetti proprietari*, CEDAM, Padova.

CHAKRAVARTHY B. S. (1986), "Measuring strategic performance", *Strategic Management Journal*, 7: 437-458.

CLARKE T. (2005), "Accounting for Enron: shareholder value and stakeholder interests", *Corporate Governance*, Vol. 13 (5): 598-612.

CLARKSON MBE. (1994), "A stakeholder framework for analyzing and evaluating corporate social performance", *Academy of Management Review*, Vol. 20: 92-117.

CODA V. (1988), *L'orientamento strategico dell'impresa*, Utet, Torino.

CUTTING B., KOUZMIN A. (2001), "Formulating a metaphysics of governance: Explaining the dynamics of governance using the new JEWAL synthesis framework", *Journal of Management Development*, Vol. 20 (6): 526 – 564.

DALTON D. R., DAILY C. M., CERTO S. T., ROENGPITYA R. (2003), "Meta-analyses of financial performance and equity: Fusion or confusion?", *Academy of Management Journal*, Vol. 46: 13-26.

DALTON D. R., DAILY C. M., ELLSTRAND A. E., JOHNSON J. L. (1998), "Meta-analytic reviews of board composition, leadership structure, and financial performance", *Strategic Management Journal*, Vol. 24: 269-290.

DAVIS G. F. (2005), "New directions in corporate governance", *Annual Review of Sociology*, Vol. 31 (1): 143-62.

DAY P., KLEIN R. (1987), *Accountabilities: Five Public Services*, Tavistock, London.

DEL VECCHIO M. (2001), *Dirigere e governare le amministrazioni pubbliche. Economicità, controllo e valutazione dei risultati*. Egea, Milano.

DONALDSON T., PRESTON L. E. (1995), "The Stakeholder Theory of the Corporation: Concepts, Evidence, and Implications", *Academy of Management Review*, Vol. 20 (1): 65-91.

EVAN W. M., FREEMAN R. E. (1988), "A Stakeholder Theory of the Modern Corporation: Kantian Capitalism", in BEAUCHAMP T. L., BOWIE N. E. (EDS.), *Ethical Theory and Business, 3rd edition*, Englewood Cliffs.

FAMA E. (1980), "Agency problems and the theory of the firm", *Journal of Political Economy*, Vol. 88: 288-307.

FAMA E., JENSEN M. (1983a), "Separation of ownership and control", *Journal of Law and Economics*, Vol. 26: 301-325.

FAMA E., JENSEN M. (1983b), "Agency problems and residual claims,", *Journal of Law and Economics*, Vol. 26: 327-349.

FERLIE E., PETTIGREW A., ASHBURNER L., FITZGERALD L. (1996), *The New Public Management in action*, Oxford University Press, Oxford.

FERRERO G. (1968), *Istituzioni di economia d'azienda*, Giuffrè, Milano.

FORESTIERI G. (1998), "La corporate governance negli schemi interpretativi della letteratura", AIROLDI G., FORESTIERI G. (EDS), *Corporate governance: analisi e prospettive del caso italiano*, Etas Libri, Milano.

FROOMAN J. (1999), "Stakeholder influence strategies", *Academy of Management Review*, Vol. 24 (2): 191-205.

GIANNESSI E. (1979), *Appunti di economia aziendale con particolare riferimento alle aziende agricole*, Pacini Editore, Pisa.

GOODNOW F. J. (2003), *Politics and Administration: A Study in Government*, Transaction Publishers, New Brunswick, NJ.

GREENLEY G., FOXALL G. (1996), "Multiple stakeholder orientation in UK companies and the implications for company performance", *Journal of Management Studies*, Vol. 34: 259-284.

HANSMANN H. (1996), *The Ownership of Enterprise*, Harvard University Press, Cambridge.

HARRISON J., ST. JOHN C. (1994), *Strategic Management of Organizations and Stakeholders*, West Publishing, St Paul.

HEEKS R. (1998), "Information systems and public sector accountability", *Information Systems for Public Sector Management Working Paper 1*, IDPM, Manchester.

HERMAN R. D., RENZ D. O. (2008), "Advancing nonprofit organizational research and theory: Nine theses", *Nonprofit Management and Leadership*, Vol. 18 (4): 399-415.

HILL C. W. L., JONES T. M. (1992), "Stakeholder–agency theory", *Journal of Management Studies*, Vol. 29: 131-54.

HIRSCHMAN A. O. (1970), *Exit, Voice and Loyalty*, Harvard University Press, Cambridge (MA).

HODGES R., WRIGHT M., KEASEY K. (1996), "Corporate governance in the public services: concept and issues", *Public Money & Management*, VOL. 16 (2), 7-13.

HOOD C. (1995), *The Art of the State. Culture, Rhetoric, and Public Management*, Clarendon, Oxford.

HSIEH L. H. Y., RODRIGUES S. B., TSAI F. S. (2010), "The Governance of Knowledge Heterogeneity by Multinational Corporations", *European Group for Organizational Studies Colloquium*, Lisbon, Portugal, June 28 – July 3, 2010.

IFAC (INTERNATIONAL FEDERATION OF ACCOUNTANTS) PUBLIC SECTOR COMMITTEE (2001), "Governance in the Public Sector: A Governing Body Perspective", *Study 13*, August 2001, http://www.ifac.org/sites/default/files/publications/files/study-13-Governance-in-th.pd.

JENSE M., MECKLING W. (1976), "Theory of the Firm: Managerial Behavior, Agency Cost and Ownership Structure", *The Journal of Financial Economics*, n. 3.

JONES R. (1995), "Accounts of Government of UK", in MONTESINOS V., VELA J. M.. (EDS), *International research in public sector accounting, reporting and auditing*, Istituto Valenciano de Investigaciones Economicas, Valencia.

KILBY P. (2004), "Is Empowerment Possible under a New Public Management Environment? some lessons from India", *International Public Management Journal*, Vol. 7 (2): 207-225.

KOTTER J., HESKETT J. (1992), *Corporate Culture and Performance*, Free Press: New York.

LYNN L. E, HEINRICH C. J., HILL C. J. (2001), "Studying Governance and Public Management: Challenges and Prospects", *Journal of Public Administration Research and Theory*, Vol. 10 (2): 233-261.

MANNE H. G. (1965), "Mergers and the Market for Corporate Control", *Journal of Political Economy*, Vol. 73 (2): 110-120.

MASINI C. (1979), *Lavoro e risparmio, 2a ed.*, UTET, Torino.

MUSSARI R. (1994), *Il management delle aziende pubbliche. Profili teorici*, CEDAM, Padova.

NORTH D. C. (1990), *Institutions, institutional change and economic performance*, Cambridge University Press, Cambridge.

ONIDA P. (1965), *Economia d'azienda*, UTET, Torino.

OSPINA S., DIAZ W., O'SULLIVAN J. (2002), "Negotiating Accountability: Managerial Lessons from Identity-Based Nonprofit Organizations", *Nonprofit and Voluntary Sector Quarterly*, Vol. 31 (1): 5-31.

PARKINSON J. (1993), *Corporate power and responsibility, issues in the theory of company law*, Oxford University Press, Oxford.

ROBERTS J. (2001), "Trust and control in Anglo-American systems of corporate governance: the individualizing and socializing effects of processes of accountability", *Human Relations*, Vol. 54 (12): 1547-72.

ROSSI G. (1921), *Trattato di ragioneria scientifica*, Reggio Emilia.

SARBANES-OXLEY ACT (2002), *Congress of the United States of America Sarbanes-Oxley legislation*, http://www.soxlaw.com/.

Shick, A. (1999), Opportunity, strategy, and tactics *in reforming public management*, OECD/PUMA, Paris.

SHLEIFER A., VISHNY R. W. (1997), "A survey of corporate governance", *Journal of Finance*, Vol. 52: 737-783.

SIMONS R. (1995), *Levers of Control*, Harvard Business School Press, Boston.

STUDER G. VON SCHNURBEIN S. (2012), "Literature Review on Volunteer Coordination", *VOLUNTAS: International Journal of Voluntary and Nonprofit Organizations*, Vol. 23 (1): 236-256.

SVARA J. H., OVEREEM P. (2006), "Complexity in Political-Administrative Relations and the Limits of the Dichotomy Concept/in Defense of the Dichotomy: A Response to JAMES H. SVARA", *Administrative Theory and Praxis*, Vol. 28: 121-148.

TAYLOR F. W. (1911), *The Principles of Scientific Management*, Harper & Brothers, London.

UK PUBLIC ACCOUNTS COMMITTEE (2009), "Report on the Proper Conduct of Public Business", *Report 39*, March 2009, http://www.publications.parliament.uk.

VIGANÒ E. (2000), "Il concetto generale di azienda", in VIGANÒ E. (ED), *Azienda: contributi per un rinnovato concetto generale*, CEDAM, Padova.

WALDO, D. (1948), *The administrative state: a study of the political theory of public administration*, Ronald, New York.

WILSON W. (1887), "The Study of Administration", *Political Science Quarterly*, Reprinted in 1997 in *Classics of Public Administration*, 2d ed. Shafritz J., Hyde A., Dorsey Press, Chicago.

ZAN L. (1990), *L'economia dell'impresa cooperativa*, UTET, Torino.

ZAPPA G. (1957), *Le produzioni nell'economia delle imprese*, Giuffrè, Milano.

BARRETT P. (1997), "Corporate Governance: P–S Style", *Australian Accountant*, August: 30-31.

TRICKER R. I. (1984), *Corporate Governance: Practices, Procedures and Powers in British Companies and Their Boards of Directors*, Gower Publishing Company, Vermont.

TRICKER R. I. (1994), *International Corporate Governance: Text, Readings and Cases*, Prentice Hall, New York.

HODGES R., WRIGHT M., KEASEY K. (1996), "Corporate Governance in the Public Services: Concepts and Issues", *Public Money and Management*, April-June: 7-13.

2

Cutback Management of the Italian bureaucratic apparatus[1]

The crisis is affecting the international economic environment with serious repercussions also on the Italian Public Sector, highlighting the need to rationalize public spending.

From this situation, after a short overview on the international and Italian recent economic scenario, arise the objectives of this chapter: describing the financial constraints on the Italian public spending due to the Stability Programme defined by the European Union, identifying the financial waste sources related to the Italian bureaucratic apparatus, focusing on the cutback management approach adopted at a national level through the Italian Spending Review process.

The study of these aspects leads to some discussion about the criticisms that come from the coexistence of the necessary managerial approach in the Public Sector (i. e. introduction of efficiency and effectiveness) and the constraints imposed by the Stability Programme.

Learning objectives

After reading this chapter you should be able to:

- International crisis and Italian public debt;
- Stability program and financial management of the State;
- Italian Public Sector and financial waste;
- Cutback management in Italy: the spending review process.

[1] This chapter was prepared jointly by the two authors. However, it is possible to assign paragraphs 2.3 and 2.4 to Daniela Preite (corresponding author), paragraphs 2.1 and 2.2 to Fabio De Matteis.

2.1   International crisis: what impact on the Italian Public Sector resources

The international economic crisis began in 2007 in the United States of America having a financial origin. In 2008, the crisis began to spread outside of the U. S. borders and reach, especially from 2009, the rest of the world and, in particular, Western countries. Between 2010 and 2011 the crisis hit the sovereign debt, greatly affecting the public finances of many countries and hitting the euro zone states especially. Some of these states escaped the default thanks to substantial funding from the International Monetary Fund and the European Union.

Also, during 2012, the international macroeconomic scenario continued to denote a generalized crisis above all in the European Union. In fact, the general situation of uncertainty and tension relating to the sovereign debt that still characterize the euro zone countries today is producing a prolonged delay in the pursuit of greater stability and in achieving better economic performance (Ministero dell'Economia e delle Finanze, 2012a). The economic downturn has led to a 0,6% decrease in Gross Domestic Product (GDP) and an increase of 11,4% in the unemployment rate, aspects which were also affected by the weakness of domestic demand in the countries that implemented policies of fiscal adjustment. In the last quarter of 2012, this situation also affected Germany, which is considered the most resilient country in dealing with the euro zone crisis.

On the other hand, the United States of America saw an improvement in economy with a GDP which increased by 2,2% and an unemployment rate which dropped to 8,1% in 2012. In addition, some extraordinary measurers accompanied by an accommodating monetary policy of the Federal Reserve, led to an improvement in both the real estate market and in equities.

In Japan, there was an increase in GDP of 2%, but over time economic growth has been slowing down and, therefore, the government has adopted a plan that aims to lead the country through the deflationary situation which has characterized it for more than a decade.

The growing trend remains for the developing countries and their perspective for 2013 is positive.

The deterioration that characterized the final months of 2012 has led to a downward revision of the estimates of the global economy. Albeit in a generalized situation of contraction, in 2013 the U. S. GDP is expected to grow by 1,9%, in Japan it should be around 1%, while in the euro area the GDP is expected to decline by 0,3% with an increase in the unemployment rate to 12,2%. (Ministero dell'Economia e delle Finanze, 2013a).

The international scenario shows that Europe is currently an area particularly hit by the crisis.

Countries with the highest incidence of public debt to GDP (referred to 2011) are Ireland (106,4%), Portugal (108,1%), Italy (120,7%) and Greece (170,6%), compared to a European average of 82,5%.

In addition, from a recent focus on primary expenditure, i. e. expenditure net of interest expense, it is evident that, in Europe, the main areas of absorption of financial resources are represented by Social Security, Health and Education. It is noted that, in this economic downturn, the voice of Economic Affairs has taken on greater importance as a result of the interventions of many governments supporting the national economy and, in particular, the banking system (Ministero dell'Economia e delle Finanze, 2013b).

With specific reference to the Italian economy, the recession that began in 2011 extended through 2012, leading to a reduction in GDP of 2,4% and to a very weak performance of the economy in the last quarter.

Especially in the last months of 2012, a considerable decrease in the spread between the yields on Italian and German government bonds occurred, but it has not yet resulted in a positive impact on the national credit system. This involves, among other things:

- a cost of loans to business higher than most European countries;
- a very conservative attitude on the part of banks to grant loans to companies (as a result of bad debts on loans).

The difficulties in accessing credit, combined with the impact of fiscal policies had a negative impact on domestic demand, investment, and consequently on industrial production that decreased significantly. The disposable income of households decreased in the first three quarters of 2012, by 4,1% compared to the same period in 2011, leading to a fall in consumption. The reduction of imports and the stability of exportation led to an improvement in the current balance of payments.

This situation took its toll on the labor market in which there was an increase in unemployment.

In Italian public finances, in 2012, the total revenue increased compared to the previous year. This increase derived from growth in current revenue due, essentially, to the higher tax revenue:

- both indirect, due to the revenue from municipality tax and the increased excise duties on mineral oils;
- and direct, as a result of exacerbation of the Personal Income Tax (and of its additional regional tax) and tax on other income.

Total expenditure increased compared to the previous year in an amount almost coincident with current expenditure, essentially arising from interest.

While the dynamics of revenue and expenses led to a decrease in the net borrowing of public administration.

The Italian public debt is equivalent to the nominal value of all consolidated liabilities of all the public administration: the national ones, the local governments and the social security institutions. At the end of 2012 about 82% of the Italian public debt was made up of government bonds. During the year, the management of the public debt was particularly complex given the context of profound instability in the financial markets and a negative economic cycle. Despite such a difficult market situation, the Treasury was able to allocate the debt, as seen in the following table, growing both in absolute values and in terms of the ratio of government debt to GDP (Table 2.1).

Table 2.1   Italian public debt trend

Year	Public Debt	GDP
2009	1.769.254	1.519.695
2010	1.851.252	1.551.886
2011	1.907.392	1.578.497
2012	1.988.658	1.565.916

Source: *http://www.dt.tesoro.it/it/debito_pubblico/_link_rapidi/debito_pubblico.html.*

Important legislative measures were adopted in 2012 to try to deal with this very difficult period. The main ones (converted into Law no. 135 of 2012) were aimed at:

1. the comprehensive revision of public spending through the implementation of structural savings and selective cuts to expenditure;
2. the enhancement and sale of public assets by using investment funds in order to decrease the stock of public debt.

The situation of great difficulty has continued into the early months of 2013. Starting from the second half of the year, an improvement of the economic situation is expected thanks to the recent law (Legislative Decree 35/2013) relating to the payment of trade debts of the Public Administration (Ministero dell'Economia e delle Finanze, 2013a).

The above brief description shows how the crisis – affecting the international economic environment with serious repercussions in the Italian context – leads to some considerations on the possible paths that can be followed to face this serious situation. From a strict financial point of view and specifically considering Italian public administration, the need to rationalize public spending is evident. This topic has been debated in international literature for more than thirty years (Levine, 1978; Bozeman, 2010).

Since the early insights on this issue, its importance has been emphasized making the following points essential (Levine, 1979):

- the development of tools and techniques to support the process of cutback;
- management which can be of support to public organizations both to implement cuts in public spending, and to evaluate the performance of public administrations;
- the search for credibility and consensus in the early stages of deep spending review, through processes of allocation of spending reductions that allow for effective and equitable cuts;
- the study of the ethical dimension of the cuts in public spending, trying to consider the ethical responsibility of a public organization implementing such cuts;
- the analysis of the impact of the cuts on the expectations of the community.

Equally important is the approach to the policies of downsizing public spending which, if addressed in the short term and in a reductionist way, can cause organizational tensions and difficulty in achieving goals. Therefore, the need for a holistic perspective and long term approach (Pandey, 2010).

The difficult economic situation, together with the contributions of the literature on cutback management, denote the relevance and importance of an in depth analysis of the spending review policy planned and currently underway in the Italian context.

The international crisis and the increase in public debt previously outlined, have led the EU member countries to the creation of constraints to respect the balance of public finances.

The measures under the European Regulation strongly influence the choices of public finance and lead states to carry out their budgetary policies in relation to European constraints. Indeed, through the Stability Programme, Member States pledge to pursue the objectives contained in the document and to make appropriate policy choices that impact the government budget.

This has led some academics in management (Pezzani, 2008; Pattaro et. al., 2009) to question the real impact of applying this mechanism. It has been questioned whether the application of such stringent rules brings public administration to immobility, by increasing the complexity and creating obstacles to development. Therefore, over the years it has increased the need to provide a key to understanding the political and administrative phenomena which allows for the observation of the actual dynamics of the country, by adopting specific effective solutions.

The impact of public finance decisions at the central level is also reflected in the coordination of regional and local finance, through the introduction of the Internal Stability Pact (Guarini, 2008), generating different effects on the national territory. If on one hand, the Stability Pact provides for the resetting of the ratio between deficit and GDP, in any case no more than 3%, on the other hand, the ratio between GDP and debt should not exceed 60%. Italy, in order to respect the Stability Pact, has set the objective of maintaining a constant level of the primary surplus (excluding interest charges) equal to 5% per annum.

In order to understand the phenomenon, it may be helpful to consider the effects of these actions on the Italian plan, which have led to the emission of the Internal Stability Pact.

As shown by some studies that analyze the application of the Internal Stability Pact in some European countries (Pattaro et al., 2009), the approaches implemented to introduce the constraints can be summarized as follows:

- legally binding (Morris et al., 2006) which is based on the introduction of guidelines and requirements of the law. This approach differs from the reputation based model focused on the weight of prestige among administrations;
- cooperative approach (Ambrosanio et. al, 2006), where targets for the headline balance and expenditure growth are set for different levels of government, in Belgium, while a domestic stability pact is in place, in Germany; fiscal rule, in Italy, in domestic stability pact sets ceilings on expenditure and the deficit of sub-national Governments and, in Spain, all levels of government face a balanced budget constraint.

In Italy, the Internal Stability Pact was regulated by Law 448/1998 and introduced in 1999. The aim was to involve regions and local governments to converge on the objectives of public finances through (Liguori et al., 2009):

- the progressive reduction of the use of deficit to cover expenses;

- the reduction of the ratio between the amount of debt of each entity and the national GDP.

Failure to meet the defined objectives led, over the years, to a series of penalties ranging from the reduction of transfers, to the hiring freeze and to limiting the possibility of borrowing.

Subsequently, the Internal Stability Pact has been changed limiting the scope more and more, placing limits on current expenditure, imposing obligations on competence and also on cash accounting, varying the scope (initially including municipalities with a population more than 3,000 inhabitants and later increasing the threshold to municipalities with a population greater than 5,000 inhabitants), and identifying a reward for virtuous institutions, to the detriment of the non-virtuous. An important change was the transition from the logic of "financial balances" (implemented from 1999 to 2004) to "spending caps" (applied from 2005 to 2006) and a subsequent return to the logic of "financial balances" (from 2007).

At present, the Domestic Stability Pact, updated with Law 228/2012, provides for a range of measures for the observance by regional and local governments for the period 2013-2015 (Ministero dell'Economia e delle Finanze, 2013c, p.7 et seq.).

Since 2013, compliance with the Stability Pact has been expanded. The application covers both provinces and municipalities with a population greater than 5.000 inhabitants and municipalities with populations between 1.001 and 5.000 inhabitants. So, even small municipalities are subject to the strict rules laid down by the Domestic Stability Pact.

As the document points out, a significant change in the rules governing the Internal Stability Pact of 2013 is represented by the update of the reference base for the calculation of the objective. This base is represented by the average of the current cash obligations recorded in 2007-2009 instead of 2006-2008. This update includes an assessment of the virtuosity of the public administration: in fact, the institutions which reduced the current cash obligations in 2009 were given a smaller objective than those who did not respect the Pact. In this sense, the rule confirms the allocation mechanism, based on the criteria of virtuosity defined by four elements:

- compliance with the Internal Stability Pact;
- the presence of financial autonomy;
- a balance between current revenue and current expenditure;
- the relationship between collection and assessment of current revenue.

In order to comply with the Internal Stability Pact, public administrations are provided with four alternative methods for calculating targets to rebalance public finances (Ministero dell'Economia e delle Finanze, 2013c):

1. target balance as a percentage of average expenditure;
2. target balance net of the reduction in transfers;
3. target balance as reward on the basis of "virtuosity" linked to participation and testing of new accounting standards;
4. target balance restated (Solidarity Pacts).

Table 2.2 Target balance as a percentage of average expenditure

	2013	2014-2015
Provinces	18,8%	18,8%
Municipalities with a population greater than 5,000 inhabitants	14,8%	14,8%
Municipalities with a population between 1,001 and 5,000 inhabitants	12%	14,8%

Source: Ministero dell'Economia e delle Finanze– Dipartimento della Ragioneria Generale dello Stato (2013c).

The first target balance, as a percentage of average expenditure, requires institutions subject to the Internal Stability Pact to apply a percentage (provided in Table 2.2) to the average of the cash obligations of their current expenditure recorded in 2007-2009. The percentages shown represent the participation in the balance of public finances by local authorities, in order to respect the Stability Programme, presented to the European Union by the Italian government.

The second value, the target balance net of the reduction in transfers, is calculated starting from the procedure provided for the determination of the first target balance. This value should be reduced by state transfers to the local authorities, following the existing rules.

The third value is the target balance intended as a reward. It is assessed on the basis of "virtuosity" and participation and experimentation of new accounting standards. This application comes from an annual breakdown of local authorities into virtuous and non-virtuous entities, based on the parameters identified by the Stability Act 2013.

For local authorities in the virtuous class, a target balance, expressed in terms of mixed competence (equal to zero), is attributed for the year 2013. The greater financial freedom granted to the virtuous institutions is offset by the more stringent commitment imposed on the non-virtuous. The placement in the bands of virtuosity is done through the adoption of a decree. If this decree is not approved, the contribution of each institution to the containment of public finance balances is determined by identifying the objective of each institution on the basis of the average current expenditure sustained in 2007-2009, as described for the determination of previous balances.

The determination of the fourth and final goal only applies to those entities not involved in the rules laid down by the Solidarity Pact between local authorities (Vertical and Horizontal Regional Pact and National Horizontal Pact). It provides for the coordination of public finance targets, by Regions, which may intervene on the rules of local finance, through vertical (regions, provinces, municipalities) or horizontal offsets (Guarini et al., 2012) (between provinces and between municipalities). Therefore, the balance target to be considered for 2013 will be that resulting from the sum of the target balance calculated on the basis of previous balances and the variation of the objective determined by the Solidarity Pact.

Compliance with the restrictions imposed by the Stability Programme has led to the adoption of the Internal Stability Pact which, despite continuous improvements, still provides stringent rules for the Italian public administration.

2.2 Financial waste in the Italian bureaucratic apparatus

The effects of the international crisis on the situation that characterizes the Italian public sector and the constraints on public finances required by the Stability Programme discussed in previous sections, lead to a deepening of what are the main sources of financial waste within the Italian public administration.

Preliminarily, it is opportune to briefly expose some aspects that define the essential features which characterize Italian public spending (Giarda, 2012):

1. Levels and the structure of public spending. Italian public spending is characterized by a very high level, greater than the international average. In addition, its structure has profound anomalies not found in other countries. In particular, the expenditure for the provision of public services and for the support of people and businesses who find themselves in a difficult economic situation, is less than the average for OECD countries. On the other hand, spending for interest and pensions is much greater than this average. Interest expenditure derives from the large amount of public debt; pension expenditure involves a particularly significant portion of the population. This situation results in a public system bound by two elements (interest expenditure and pensions) which place particularly heavy constraints on management flexibility that needs adaptation to external changes from the economy.

2. Cost of public production. The costs incurred for public services have increased more than proportionally compared to those of the private sector. The Italian Public Sector has not proved to be particularly used to innovation in the provision process, and this has led to the need to increase the financial resources required from the community through fiscal pressure. This situation also occurs in other countries, but its incidence is particularly relevant in the Italian context. Therefore, a special focus on the innovation process is necessary. The process would require investments and organizational changes that are difficult due to the current difficult situation in public finance. Digitalization is feasible and less expensive, but requires greater commitment in the training of administrative staff.

3. Management control. The costs incurred for the provision of public services, in addition to the factors mentioned in the previous paragraph, also stem from the lack of management skills in terms of work organization and purchasing processes necessary for the provision of the same services. There is much criticism about the low efficiency of the purchasing procedures in public administration which, if innovated, could lead to savings and more uniform prices throughout the country. The same applies to contributions to households, businesses and institutions: these transfers represent significant expenditures for which an increase in efficiency would lead to less waste and greater redistributive equity. What is missing is a detailed analysis which could define a macro-economic profile of the inefficiencies

and their impact on public spending. Informed choices for the rationalization of expenditures could be derived from this analysis.

After this brief reference to some typical features of Italian public spending, follows an analysis of the areas in which inefficiencies are generated, leading to financial waste.

In fact, in order to: evaluate the different possible alternatives to achieve the reduction of inefficiencies and eliminating waste; understand the feasibility and extent of these alternatives; implement the most suitable interventions for the rationalization of public spending, it is important to identify the sources of waste and inefficiency in the provision of services and in public funding (Giarda, 2012). Three main areas represent the most important sources of waste and inefficiency:

1. Production inefficiency. This is waste arising from the production or the organization of public services and activities. Some typical examples of this category of inefficiencies occur if:
   - the factors of production used in the process of production/provision are greater than those actually needed;
   - financial benefits are given to individuals who are not really in need;
   - implemented processes are more costly than the alternative procedures which could replace them.
2. Management inefficiency. A first situation of management inefficiency comes from the lack of correlation between the financial resources deployed and the resulting benefits. In other words, resources are used for a specific purpose of public utility while, even if only part of the same resources were used for another purpose, this would generate results which would be more beneficial to the community. In Italy, where there is a lack of comparative analysis between the benefits generated and those expected, decisions on public spending produce many different consequences for the community. Consequently, there are margins for rationalization where financial resources could be used for activities generating greater benefits for the population. Another case of management inefficiency – strongly connected to the previous one – occurs when the collective benefits generated by a specific public action are marginal or non-existent..
3. Macroeconomic inefficiency. In this case, public expenditure is used for activities whose benefits do not compensate for the financial effort required to implement them. In particular, the funding of this type of public spending, whether it takes place through taxation or through debt, has a negative impact on economic growth which is not offset by the benefits generated by public intervention.

In the three above-mentioned macro areas of inefficiency, it is possible to identify some types of waste typically found in Italian public administration.

The provision of public services is wasteful when:

- input is greater than actually required;
- input is purchased at a cost higher than the market value or higher than the actual value;
- incorrect production processes involve excessive use of financial resources;
- obsolete provision processes are more expensive than the more innovative ones;

- production processes are carried out using incompatible factors (i. e., using non-specialized staff for innovative technological tools).

In the field of redistributive policies, a typical type of waste comes from the incorrect identification of subjects deserving public support. In this case, the selection procedures are inefficient and imply the provision of subsidies to non-deserving subjects (with a consequent waste of resources).

As for public investment, the main types of waste are attributable to the following:

- delays in public intervention which lead to incomplete projects or projects which take decidedly longer than planned;
- realization of projects of excessive size compared to the real possibility of exploitation, or use of materials that are too valuable and, therefore, excessively expensive;
- implementation of programs not preceded by a cost-benefit analysis or for which this analysis has not had positive results (this is often the case of infrastructure);
- definition of spending measures that do not conform or adapt belatedly to changes in the demand expressed by the community (traditionally in public administration there is a tendency to maintain over time facilities and activities which are no longer relevant from the point of view of community satisfaction);
- the launch of spending programs with anti-cyclical goals implemented with expenditure of a permanent nature. In other words, in times of economic vitality a tax increase is used to finance a permanent expenditure (interpreting the acceleration of the economy as lasting).

The identification of sources of inefficiency and types of waste should be analyzed in conjunction with the portion of public expenditure on which medium term rationalization measures can be programmed (modifiable spending). In other words, it is necessary to identify the items composing the total public expenditure that can be reviewed. The following matrix summarizes these items and their related amounts: the rows provide the modifiable voices of public spending, while the columns view the levels of government responsible for such items.

The effects of the international crisis on the situation that characterizes the Italian public sector and the constraints on public finances required by the Stability Programme seen in previous sections, lead to a deepening of what are the main sources of financial waste within the Italian public administration.

At the outset, it is appropriate to briefly expose some aspects that define the essential features that characterize the Italian public spending (Giarda, 2012). ***Levels and the structure of public spending.*** Italian public spending is characterized by a very high level and magnitude higher than the international average. In addition, its structure has profound abnormalities not found in other countries. In particular, the expenditure for the provision of public services and support to people and businesses who find themselves in a difficult situation economy, are smaller than the average for OECD countries. On the other hand, spending on interest expense and on pensions are much higher than this average. Interest payments derived by the extent of public debt, the pension expenditure relates to a particularly significant portion of the population. This situation results in a public system stiffened by two elements (interest expenditure and spending on pensions) which place particularly heavy constraints to management flexibility that requires adaptation to the demands from the economy. *Cost of public production.* The costs incurred for the delivery of public services have increased more than proportionally than those in the private sector. The Italian government has proved not particularly accustomed to innovations in the delivery process, and this has led to the need for increasing financial resources required to the community through the tax burden. This situation also occurs in other countries, but its incidence is particularly relevant in the Italian context. It is necessary, therefore, a special focus on innovation process that would require investments and organizational changes that the current situation in which there is a public finance makes it difficult to accomplish. It is feasible the way of digitization, less expensive, but requires major interventions in the training of administrative staff. *Management control.* The costs incurred for the delivery of public services, in addition to the factors mentioned in the previous paragraph, also stem from the lack of management skills in terms of work organization and processes necessary for the provision of purchase of goods. There are many criticisms about the low efficiency of the purchasing procedures in public administration that if innovated, could lead to savings in more uniform purchase prices throughout the country. The same applies to transfers in relation to households, businesses and institutions: it is significant expenditure for which the efficiency gains would lead to less waste and greater redistributive equity. What is missing is a detailed analysis that allows to give evidence to the macro-economic inefficiencies and their impact on the public spending. From this analysis derive informed choices in relation to rationalizing expenditure (Table 2.3).

Of the more than 295 billion euro of modifiable expenditure, the highest percentage is found in Healthcare (33,1%), although when considering the total expense of the State, "Other national administrations" and "Social security institutions" (all considerable national governments) it reaches 37,4%. Municipalities (15%) together with Provinces and Regions reach 24,3%.

Considering the time needed for analysis, for approval of legislation necessary to regulate the spending review process, and for the implementation of the cuts themselves, the intervention on modifiable expenditures requires at least medium-term horizons.

From the above, it is clear that, in the short term, the amount of modifiable spending is much lower than that outlined in the previous matrix.

These observations show that there are opportunities for public spending review and that, to avoid linear cuts (without considering merits), it is necessary to intervene rapidly, given the urgency imposed by the critical national and international economic situation, to start the process of analysis of the modifiable expenditure and the formulation and approval of the necessary rules for the rationalization.

2.3   Cutback Management in Italy: Spending Review process

The cutback management for government is how to achieve cuts in public expenditure and personnel at minimum cost to political objectives (Dunsire, 1989). According to Wynne G. (1983), cutback management "is an acutely practical issue among urban decision makers in most countries, caught as they are between declining resources (reflected in lower budgets) and continuing or even rising demands for public services".

Table 2.3 Medium term modifiable public expenditure

	State	Other National administrations	E.P.	Regions	Province	Municipality	Health	University	Tot.
Gross wages	61,8	2,6	2,2	4,5	1,9	12,8	28,3	7,8	122,1
Intermediate consumption	21,3	3,9	2,9	5,5	3,1	25,3	69,0	4,7	135,6
Subsidies on production	2,9	0,1	0,0	6,3	1,6	2,6	0,0	0,7	14,2
Contribution to Social institutions	2,0	0,0	1,0	0,7	0,1	0,7	0,0	0,1	4,8
Current contributions to families	1,9	0,0	1,2	0,5	0,3	1,0	0,1	1,5	6,5
Current contributions to businesses	0,1	0,3	0,1	0,4	0,0	0,3	0,0	0,2	1,3
Capital grants to businesses	5,2	0,4	0,0	1,6	0,2	0,9	0,0	0,3	8,6
Capital grants to families	0,6	0,0	0,0	0,6	0,0	0,6	0,0	0,1	1,9
Tot. Modifiable expenditure	95,9	7,2	7,4	20,2	7,3	44,2	97,6	15,4	295,1
% Modifiable expenditure	32,5%	2,4%	2,5%	6,8%	2,5%	15,0%	33,1%	5,2%	100,0%

Source: Giarda (2012).

This process can be analyzed through three kinds of problems (Dunsire, 1989):

- macro-problems, related to questions such as to whether face the imbalance by cutting expenditure or raising revenue; whether to cut uniformly or selectively, etc.;
- meso-problems, related to organization issues (at the level of department or agency) concerning some questions as whether and how to close down units; how to keep morale up, etc.;
- micro-problems regarding single workers or small work-groups. This kind of problem is professional (promotion prospects and career choice; same standards with less resources) and also social (effects on family and social stresses).

In Italy the cutback Management is realized through the so called Spending Review process and it is here analyzed through the related macro problems.

The Spending Review process started in Italy is part of a framework of public administration reforms which have been underway for some time, pushing towards the applicability of the managerial model, based on the principles of efficiency, effectiveness and economy (Anselmi, 1995; Meneguzzo, 2001; Pollitt et al., 2002).

The debate often arises from the contrast between the institutional and managerial approaches. In the first case, the process of public administration reform is intended as a "change in the general structure of the public system" (Borgonovi, 2006) and is based on a general adaptation of the rules of the system. This attitude is based on the belief that the set of rules, both existing and new, is sufficient to ensure a balanced performance of the public work, from the economic, organizational and managerial points of view. Based on this assumption or legal-institutional logic, public organizations are considered as a unitary and uniform body operating with a homogeneous legal approach, regardless of the specific operative, cultural, local, managerial, organizational and economic "identity". The change occurs through a transformation of the functions, formal responsibilities and administrative processes. In the second case, the rule becomes only a tool to facilitate a process of evolution based on autonomy, and the change is represented by an adjustment of managerial models, oriented to the improvement of achieving institutional goals (Valotti, 2005). In the managerial logic, the public institute, understood as a set of people who are organized according to certain rules to achieve "common good", reaches its goals (social, ethical, economic, political, etc.) through the public economic organization, which is considered the economic order of this institute, that is, the set of economic events unified under their own laws (Masini, 1979). Therefore, the public institute, which is both unitary and autonomous, has the purpose to protect and meet public needs.

The coincidence between the two conceptual schemes creates confusion in terms of deployment of operating systems that allow public administrations to overcome the weaknesses of mechanistic and bureaucratic order, that affect them.

On an institutional level, of the Spending Review process began with the approval of Law Decree 201/2011, the so-called "Save Italy Law", through which both the number of institutions, and public managers'salaries were reduced, followed by diversified changes on public spending.

The first phase began with Decree n.52/2012 converted into Law n.94/2012, the so-called "Spending Review 1". Subsequently, the government issued Decree n.95/2012, converted into Law 135/2012, the so-called "Spending Review 2". The reform process is still ongoing, continuing through the enactment of the Law of Stability 2013.

The content of the Spending Review process is mainly based on four aspects:

- the organs;
- the deadlines;
- the guidelines;
- the other public entities.

1. **Organs.**   With the enactment of the Spending Review 1, appropriate bodies have been identified to carry out the process. Firstly, a separate body called "Inter-ministerial Committee for the review of public expenditure" was formed. It was in charge of coordinating the government's actions and policies of the spending review. In addition, the rule considers the possibility of appointing a special Commissioner for the rationalization of expenditure for the purchase of goods and services. The Commissioner also supervises and monitors the activities related to purchases and he has the right to request any information from the public administration, in order carry out his role. If the Commissioner finds rules that can be suppressed to facilitate the spending review, he reports them to the Council of Ministers.

2. **Deadlines.**   Spending review interventions can be divided into short term ones and those that require longer periods. For short-term interventions, estimated around 80 billion euro (Giarda, 2012), the procedure of the so-called "linear cuts" was used following the model of bureaucratic control based on the verification of the acts and procedures (Pezzani et al., 2003). With this approach, the focus is on financial flows acquired and used by the public authorities, on the basis of a perspective on their regulation aimed at achieving the economic policy goals (Borgonovi, 2006). Linear cuts exercise a significant influence not only in the transfer of funds from the State to peripheral administrations, but also in the formulation of rules relating to the budgets of Regions and Local Authorities, on which the Spending Review process has an impact. In contrast, medium-term structural interventions, totaling about 295 billion euro (Giarda, 2012) require reorganization within the public sector. This means reviewing the management model of public administration and the way services are offered.

3. **Guidelines.**   The guidelines of the Spending Review process are contained in a Directive of the Prime Minister (Presidenza del Consiglio dei Ministri, 2012), on which the action of expenditure should be concentrated. It can be summarized as follows:

4. better management of expenditure, to be carried out with the review of spending programs (including purchases) and transfers, and downsizing of the existing managerial structure; together with a rationalization of activities and services offered throughout the territory and abroad;

5. better management of instrumental organizations, through reduction or elimination of the instrumental organizations and participated entities;

6. better property management, through a reduction in rental expenditure and an optimization of the use of public buildings including consolidations of offices;

7. better management of compensation, through an extension to the in-house companies of the constraints concerning consultancy and reduction of expenses for conferences and representation.

8. **Other public entities.** The Spending Review process involved all public administrations (local and national). Regarding local government, on the one hand, standard costs and needs were identified and, on the other, transfers were reduced and the Internal Stability Pact was exacerbated, as seen above. Spending Review 2 implies a reordering for the provinces, saving between 5 and 7% of the total current expenditure. As the following Table shows, during the period 2001-2011, the primary expenditure of local government appears to be quite stable (around 33%). Specifically, the reduction in spending mainly concerns the Regions (from 5,5% to 4,8%) and the municipalities (from 9,6% to 8,5%). The expense of the provinces, however, has increased slightly (from 1,5 to 1,6%).

On a national level, in a first phase (Giarda, 2012) expenditure was revised for: the Ministry of Internal Affairs (wages and peripheral structures), the Ministry of Education, University and Research (central and territorial administration), the Ministry of Justice (reduction of offices), the Ministry of Infrastructure and Transport (streamlining and reorganization) and the Institute for Social Security (unification of other social security bodies) (Table 2.4).

Looking at the total expenditure, the above Table highlights an overall reduction in central government (from 27,5 to 24,5%) and a corresponding increase in the weight of social security institutions (from 38,9 to 42,4%). While, considering only the expense of the State, it shows a significant reduction (from 24,3 to 22,4%), which was recorded during the course of the last five years.

Analyzing the budget of the State, Table 2.5 shows a gradual improvement in the main financial balances (Ministero dell'Economia e delle Finanze – Dipartimento della Ragioneria Generale dello Stato, 2012b):

- public savings ("tax revenue" + "extra-tax revenue" – "current expenditure") after a peak of 1,5 billion raises to 46.1 billion;
- the net balance to finance (final income – final expenditure) reaches a negative peak in 2008 (-37 billion), then starts to grow, becoming positive in 2011 (900 million euro). In last year there is a significant increase in final revenue, which rises from 505,3 to 521,7 billion, and a net reduction of final expenditure, from 526,9 to 520,8 billion).

In order to assess the impact of the Spending Review, it is necessary to examine the maneuvers enacted in the delicate process of reform. In 2011, the impact of financial maneuvers generated a reduction in expenditure of 6.9 billion, that jumped to −33,5 billion in 2012.

Specifically, analyzing the impact of the Spending Review 1 a reduction in spending of 2,8 billion occurred already in 2012. This impact should generate an expected reduction of 5,2 billion in 2013 and 8,3 billion in 2014 (Table 2.6).

Table 2.4   Primary expenditure consolidated by general government subsector. Various years. Percentage of GDP, share over total expenditure and index numbers 2001 = 100 (on nominal values)

Subsector and division	2001			2005			2010			2011		
	% GDP	% share	index number 2001 = 100	% GDP	% share	index number 2001 = 100	% GDP	% share	index number 2001 = 100	% GDP	% share	index number 2001 = 100
Central administrations	11,5	27,5	100,0	11,6	26,5	115,8	11,7	25,2	126,9	11,2	24,5	123,0
– of which State	10,1	24,3	100,0	10,7	24,4	121,0	10,8	23,1	131,9	10,2	22,4	127,6
Local administations	14,0	33,6	100,0	15,2	34,7	124,2	15,6	33,4	138,0	15,1	33,1	135,7
– of which Regions	2,3	5,5	100,0	2,4	5,6	122,4	2,3	4,9	124,2	2,2	4,8	120,6
– of which Provinces	0,6	1,5	100,0	0,8	1,8	137,3	0,7	1,6	144,1	0,7	1,6	139,9
– of which Municipalities	4,0	9,6	100,0	4,1	9,4	117,3	4,0	8,7	125,1	3,9	8,5	122,5
– of which local healthcare authorities	6,0	14,4	100,0	6,7	15,3	127,8	7,3	15,6	150,3	7,1	15,5	149,3
Social security authorities	16,2	38,9	100,0	16,9	38,7	119,8	19,3	41,4	147,7	19,3	42,4	150,6
Public Administrations	**41,6**	**100,0**	**100,0**	**43,7**	**100,0**	**120,2**	**46,6**	**100,0**	**138,7**	**45,6**	**100,0**	**138,0**

Source: Ministero dell'Economia e delle Finanze – Dipartimento della Ragioneria Generale dello Stato (2012b).

Table 2.5 Final statement of accounts – State Budget: assessed revenue and commitment expenditure. Years 2003-2011. Million Euros

	2003	2004	2005	2006	2007	2008	2009	2010	2011
Tax revenue	367.408	380.062	377.854	429.363	444.168	446.165	439.017	441.614	452.731
Extra-tax revenue	34.150	35.715	44.105	48.759	49.382	49.400	66.150	61.791	65.698
Sale and amortisation of assets and collection of debts	17.949	10.992	10.075	1.921	6.121	2.182	2.630	1.921	3.313
FINAL INCOME	**419.507**	**426.769**	**432.034**	**480.043**	**499.671**	**497.746**	**507.796**	**505.325**	**521.742**
Current expenses	391.593	400.651	420.449	428.139	437.189	472.685	481.578	474.662	472.320
of which interests	71.304	60.964	70.671	70.800	68.202	79.867	73.239	69.523	73.748
Capital expenses	60.035	47.364	46.794	38.954	53.157	63.052	58.913	52.282	48.502
FINAL EXPENDITURE	**451.629**	**447.925**	**467.243**	**467.094**	**490.346**	**535.737**	**540.492**	**526.944**	**520.822**
Differential results									
Public savings	9.964	15.217	1.509	49.983	56.361	22.880	23.588	28.742	46.109
Net balance to finance	–32.122	–21.155	–35.210	12.949	9.325	–37.990	–32.695	–21.619	921

Source: Ministero dell'Economia e delle Finanze – Dipartimento della Ragioneria Generale dello Stato (2012b).

Table 2.6 Main legislative interventions on the expenses of the state budget since 2008. (million)

	2008	2009	2010	2011	2012	2013	2014
DL 112/2008	1.163,3	-9.557,5	-9.354,2	-17.841,3	-15.430,9	-13.140,6	-10.850,3
DL 185/2008	0,0	3.043,4	847,4	762,6	775,1	787,7	800,2
LF 2009	0,0	-919,1	-329,1	4.750,8	-1.805,0	-1.811,6	-1.818,2
DL 5/2009	0,0	1.088,1	-19,5	-200,0	-166,0	-132,0	-98,0
LF 2010	0,0	0,0	9.275,6	8.396,6	5.509,1	727,7	533,0
DL 78/2010	0,0	0,0	1.123,4	-8.273,1	-13.485,4	-14.405,7	-14.027,4
LS 2011	0,0	0,0	10,4	4.241,1	3.661,2	10.089,7	1.088,7
DL 98/2011 e DL 138/2011	0,0	0,0	0,0	1.106,3	-6.322,6	-11.253,0	-14.715,3
LS 2012	0,0	0,0	0,0	67,6	1.062,4	1.440,1	7.620,1
DL 201/2011	0,0	0,0	0,0	0,0	-4.515,6	-3.834,8	-4.872,9
DL 95/2012	0,0	0,0	0,0	0,0	-2.871,5	-5.284,2	-8.324,2
TOTALE	1.163,3	-6.345,1	1.554,0	-6.989,4	-33.589,2	-36.816,9	-44.664,2

Source: Ministero dell'Economia e delle Finanze – Dipartimento della Ragioneria Generale dello Stato (2012b).

2.4 Discussion and conclusion

The theme of the reduction in government expenditure has been debated for several years, not only in terms of international literature (CH Levine, 1978; Dunsire, 1989; B. Bozeman, 2010), but also in terms of Italian doctrine (Anselmi, 1995; Pezzani et. al., 2003; Borgonovi, 2006; Valotti, 2005) that leads to a managerial approach to public entities.

This clarification is intended to shed light on the mistaken belief that the acceptance of the managerial model for public institutions implies, therefore, that they are exclusively companies operating for profit. In truth, the acceptance of the managerial model does not change the specific purposes of public institutions which are expressed through the attainment of common good and public interest, using tools of an economic nature.

The fulfillment of the "common good" can be pursued by making use of economic instruments typical of the management approach in order to organize economic activity which, in turn, is accomplished through the acquisition of input necessary to enable the provision of public services.

So, the "immediate economic goals" of the public sector organizations are (Masini, 1979):

- the satisfaction of public needs through the production and consumption of goods and/or services (as opposed to companies in the public sector where the production and/or consumption of goods is the end and not the means);
- the remuneration of workers (government organs and administrative bodies);
- redistribution of wealth and eventual remuneration to suppliers of monetary means.

The acceptance of this conceptual model involves the application of managerial principles and criteria, methods and tools (Airoldi et. al, 1989), aimed at achieving a balance between scarce resources and needs to be met, and between supply and demand of public services. Among the various principles, autonomy is particularly important to the purposes of this paper. Autonomy is defined as the ability of the public institute to govern the economic processes in order to achieve the institutional goals without supporting interventions by other public institutions. Autonomy can be either organizational or financial. The former is inherent to definition of service, personnel management, identification of organizational schemes and external control systems; the latter is related to the ability to acquire financial resources and to implement input purchase processes (Zangrandi, 1994).

The application of the managerial approach to public bodies allows for a cultural perspective which pushes towards the search for the criteria of:

- efficiency, understood as the relationship between quantity and quality of resources used and services provided;
- effectiveness, understood as the coherency between the "intermediate result" (internal), and "final result" (external);
- economy, defined as the durable ability to meet the needs of public interest, based on a flow of wealth that is "economically viable and socially acceptable" (Borgonovi, 2006).

Moreover, for a long time it has been stated that economy "does not aim to achieve a 'contingent result', but instead, a 'lasting result' and its improvement, as often as possible" (Giannessi, 1961).

The use of the managerial approach to public bodies should not replace the legal and institutional approach, but should integrate with it, because their goals are different.

The cut-back management theme fits into this debate contextualized in the Italian public administration, that is affected by the urgencies of the international crisis and the growth of public debt.

Therefore, if on the one hand, the introduction of efficiency and effectiveness in the public administration is needed, on the other hand, the public sector must deal with the constraints imposed by the Stability Programme, which affect the local government, through the Internal Stability Pact.

Analyzing the data emerging from this work, some aspects can be observed.

1. Public debt. Italy is one of the European countries which has a higher incidence of public debt (120,7), after Greece (170,6), compared to a European average of 82,5%. This figure comes from an uncontrollable growth in spending. In fact, total spending increased compared to the previous year almost coincidentally with the current expenditures, among which interest increased notably. The increase in public debt leads to a natural consequence of actions to be carried out from an administrative point of view on two fronts: revenue and expenditure. On the revenue side, the increase in fiscal pressure and the fight against tax evasion have been implemented. On the expenditure side, the Spending Review process has been put into effect.

2. Stability Programme. The rise of sovereign public debts has led to the need to create a package of constraints to enforce on the European Union member states. As shown by the data (European Commission, 2012, p.16), Italy has managed to improve data in Budget Balance, Balance Structural and Structural Primary Balance, even rising above the EA27 countries'average. This leads Italy (Ministero dell'Economia e delle Finanze, 2013a, p.10) to make a prediction of growth already in 2014, equal to 1.3% up to 1,5% in 2015. The respect of the Stability Programme has been made possible by the enactment of the Domestic Stability Pact, based on fiscal rule (Ambrosanio et al., 2006). At this point, the impact of these constraints must be considered. One criticism about the application of rigid rules concerns the difficulty of realizing unified management and focusing on results, which should, instead, characterize public administration oriented to a managerial approach (Borgonovi, 2005; Pezzani, 2009). In fact, trying to respect the Pact under these conditions leads to scarce transparency in the financial statements.

3. The lack of clarity in the definition of areas of responsibility, i. e. between national and local administrations, makes it difficult to identify and may encourage unethical behavior.

4. Spending Review. In Italy, the Spending Review process has started after a series of fruitless efforts related to the cutback management. In the past, there has been a series of actions aimed at reducing the public spending, through a hiring freeze for civil servants, the increased use of performance management systems, or operations of institutional restructuring in the health sector (Cuccurullo et al., 2005). These operations, however, have not yielded the desired results. For example, if the blockage of turnover, on the one hand, led to a reduction in public spending, on the other hand they generated rather high "organizational costs", often compounded by the absence of real reorganizations, symptom of bad man-

agement (Cuccurullo, 2012). The lack of a structured system of cutback management is essentially due to two factors: a) the absence of a strong political will, b) the "crisis" factor.

Of different capacity appears, instead, the process of Spending Review that is booted, which attempts to give light to a system of cutback management. In fact, this process starts in a context radically changed and more complex: the urgency of the financial crisis and the extent of the Italian public debt led the political class to the rethinking of the failed attempts to cutback management. Hence the need to give a concrete answer to the citizens, through a series of bills that appear more consistent than the sporadic answers of the past. The Spending Review process, in some respects, may also adopt a strategic approach (Mintzberg et al., 1998), if the adopted instruments support the decision-making processes in the context of strategic management and if they lead to the carrying out projects for the improvement of the performance (Clark, 1997). As Behn has emphasized (Behn, 1980) the development of a strategic plan for an organization requires not only the examination of alternatives, but also the examination of the purposes for which these alternatives might be used. In order to see a strategic matrix, it is necessary to analyze the path of Spendig Review. Compared to past interventions, the Spending Review process is supported by methods and tools, it is prolonged in time, it considers different variables (not just the linear cut) and it appears more organic (Nag et al., 2007), compared to past interventions. In fact, in the guidelines of the Spending Review activities, it is possible to identify strategic actions (March, 2006) related to problem solving (e. g., review of spending program) or to decision-making (e. g. reduction or elimination of instrumental organizations).

The Italian Spending Review process follows a dual mode: "linear cuts" and reorganization of services, where there is a strategic approach.

Linear cuts are characterized by a prevalence of the legal-administrative approach resulting from subjecting the public administrations to a "bureaucratic" control. This approach does not allow for the proper appraisal of the results and the conditions necessary to achieve economy. Therefore, this prevents the implementation of control over the economic performance which, examining the valuesraised by the exchange operations, allows for assessments that are useful for management decisions.

In the reorganization of services, instead, where the review of management models is foreseen, there is a real opportunity to rethink the organization of public administration, introducing the management approach, based on a functional model of efficiency and effectiveness.

At this level it is possible to apply the strategic approach. The organizational rethinking of the bureaucratic apparatus can lead to the achievement of public policy objectives established by each Ministry that acts and decides how to fill in autonomy its own strategic space (Del Vecchio, 1995). In order to operationalize the Spending Review process, to fully achieve the strategic purpose, it is necessary, however, to encourage discussion among actors operating at different organizational levels (Grant, 2003; Chelsey et al., 1999). In fact, the Italian Ministries are complex structures, from a strategic and organizational point of view, and they may seem "distant" to local governments. In this sense, a rationalization action of activities and services across the country without a comparison with the local authorities is unthinkable. Instead, the approach of Spending Review addressed to local authorities appears different.

In local government, the process of Spending Review identifies standard costs and requirements. This approach does not follow the managerial model, and it cannot be considered as a part of a strategic planning. It relocates the public administration to a legal-institutional level.

In conclusion, cut-back management (based on the assumptions of debt reduction, the observation of the constraints imposed by the Pact, and the Spending review), follows a legal-institutional approach that can be considered acceptable only in a state of emergency and for a limited time.

In order to achieve the efficiency, effectiveness and economy of public administration with a managerial and strategic approach, it is necessary to review the management model in the medium term and to identify strategic policies aimed at improving the provision of public services.

Therefore, the quality of a good administration stems from balancing the different requirements intended to ensure other equilibria, besides that of the "managerial system", which are critical for the proper implementation of activities (Borgonovi, 2006).

Public authorities should, in fact, operate in order to achieve "a balance between the formal powers of the various internal organs and the relationships of rights and duties with external legal entities", according to the principles and criteria typical of the "institutional system". Also, "balanced development between values, expectations and interests of various social groups" should be ensured, according to the rules of the "political system".

Therefore, public authorities must be prepared to guarantee a contemporary balance between the managerial, the institutional and political systems, thereby favoring the Italian process of new public management which has been developing over the last twenty years.

Summary

The difficult economic situation, together with the contributions of the literature on cutback management, denote the relevance and importance of an in depth analysis of the spending review policy planned and currently underway in the Italian context.

Compliance with the restrictions imposed by the European Stability Programme has led to the adoption of the Internal Stability Pact which, despite continuous improvements, still provides stringent rules for the Italian public administration.

This implies an analysis on the sources of inefficiency in the Italian Public Sector and on the modifiable public expenditure. This analysis aims to establish "where" useless expenditure is generated and "how much" of the expenditure amount can be reduced. Considering the time needed for analysis, for approval of the legislation necessary to regulate the spending review process, and for the implementation of the financial cuts, the intervention on modifiable expenditures requires at least medium-term horizons. So, there are opportunities for public spending review and, in order to avoid linear cuts (without considering merits), it is necessary to intervene rapidly, given the urgency imposed by the critical national and international economic situation, to start the process of analysis of the modifiable expenditure and the formulation and approval of the necessary rules for the rationalization.

Cut-back management applied to Italian public apparatus at a national level, needs the integration of managerial and institutional approach. Especially the former can create some difficulties facing the constraints imposed by the Stability Programme.

References

AIROLDI G., BRUNETTI G., CODA V. (1989), *Lezioni di economia aziendale*, Il Mulino, Milano.

AMBROSANIO M. F., BORDIGNON M. (2006), "Internal Stability Pacts: The European Experience", European Economic Governance Monitor, Papers.

ANSELMI L. (1995), *Il processo di trasformazione della pubblica amministrazione: il percorso aziendale*, Giappichelli, Torino.

BEHN R. D. (1980), *Leadership for cut-back management: the use of corporate strategy*, "Public Administration Review", Vol. 40, n. 6, November-December: 613-620.

BORGONOVI E. (2005), *Principi e sistemi aziendali per le amministrazioni pubbliche*, V edizione, Egea, Milano.

BOZEMAN B. (2010), *Hard Lessons from Hard Times: Reconsidering and Reorienting the "Managing Decline" Literature*, "Public Administration Review", July/August:.557-563.

CHESLEY J. E WENGER M. (1999), *Transforming an Organization: Using Models to Foster a Strategic Conversation*, "California Management Review", 41 (3): 54-73.

CLARK D. N. (1997), *Strategic management tool usage: a comparative study*, "Strategic Change", 6 (7): 417-427.

CUCCURULLO C., (2012), *Propositi, proprietà e legittimazione degli strumenti impiegati dai Piani di rientro*, in CANTÙ E. (a cura di), *L'aziendalizzazione della sanità in Italia. Rapporto OASI 2012*.

CUCCURULLO C., MENEGUZZO M. (2005), *Dai piani strategici ai piani per la salute: tendenze in atto nella pianificazione strategica delle Aziende sanitarie italiane*, Roma, Rapporto Ceis.

DEL VECCHIO M. (1995), *Strategia e pianificazione strategica nelle aziende sanitarie pubbliche, un'introduzione*, in "Mecosan", 4 (14): 20-32.

DUNSIRE A, HOOD C. C. (1989), *Cutback Management in Public Bureaucracies*, Cambridge, Cambridge University Press.

EUROPEAN COMMISSION (2012), *Report on Public Finance in EMU*, European Economy, n.4.

GIANNESSI E. (1961), *Interpretazione del concetto di azienda pubblica*, in AA. VV., *Saggi in memoria di Gino Zappa*, Giuffrè, Milano.

GIARDA P. (2012), *Elementi per una revisione della spesa pubblica*, Ministro per i Rapporti con il Parlamento e il programma di governo, 8 maggio, Roma.

GRANT R. M. (2003), *Strategic Planning in a Turbulent Environment: Evidence from the Oil Majors*, "Strategic Management Journal", 24 (6): 491-517.

GUARINI E. (2008), *Il patto di stabilità interno: confronto fra equilibri di bilancio e dinamiche reali*, in PEZZANI F. (a cura di), *Il patto di lucidità. Come avvicinare istituzioni e paese reale*, Università Bocconi Editore, Milano.

GUARINI E. (2009), *Un modello di riferimento per la revisione del patto di stabilità interno*, in AMATUCCI F., VECCHI V. (a cura di), *Le scelte di finanziamento degli enti locali*, Egea, Milano.

GUARINI E., PATTARO A. F. (2012). *Il patto di stabilità territoriale. Uno strumento efficace di governo della finanza pubblica?*, Intervento presentato al Convegno Nazionale della Società Italiana dei Docenti di Ragioneria e di Economia Aziendale (SIDREA), "Innovare per crescere: quali proposte per il governo e l'amministrazione delle aziende?", Università di Modena e Reggio Emilia, Modena, 27-28 Novembre, 2012.

LEVIN, C. H. (1978), *Organizational Decline and Cutback Management*, "Public Administration Review", July/August: 316-325.

LEVINE C. H. (1979), *More on Cutback Management: Hard Questions for Hard Times*, "Public Administration Review", March/April: 179-183.

LIGUORI M., PATTARO A. F., SICILIA M. F. (2009), *Gli effetti dell'applicazione del patto di stabilità interno sulle scelte di indebitamento e di investimento degli enti locali*, in AMATUCCI F., VECCHI V. (a cura di), *Le scelte di finanziamento degli enti locali*, Egea, Milano.

MARCH J. G. (2006), *Rationality, foolishness, and adaptive intelligence*, "Strategic Management Journal", 27 (3): 201-214.

MASINI C. (1979), *Lavoro e risparmio*, 2a Ed., Utet, Torino.

MENEGUZZO M. (2001), *Managerialità, innovazione e governance*, Aracne, Roma.

MINISTERO DELL'ECONOMIA E DELLE FINANZE (2013a), *Documento di Economia e Finanza 2013*, Roma.

MINISTERO DELL'ECONOMIA E DELLE FINANZE – DIPARTIMENTO DELLA RAGIONERIA GENERALE DELLO STATO (2013b), *La spesa pubblica in Europa: anni 2000-2011*, Roma.

MINISTERO DELL'ECONOMIA E DELLE FINANZE – DIPARTIMENTO DELLA RAGIONERIA GENERALE DELLO STATO (2013c), *Circolare concernente il patto di stabilità interno per il triennio 2013-2015*, n.5.

MINISTERO DELL'ECONOMIA E DELLE FINANZE (2012a), *Update of the 2012 Economic and Financial Document*, Roma.

MINISTERO DELL'ECONOMIA E DELLE FINANZE – DIPARTIMENTO DELLA RAGIONERIA GENERALE DELLO STATO (2012b), *Lo Stato e le Amministrazioni pubbliche*, Roma.

MINTZBERG H., AHLSTRAND B. E LAMPEL. J. (1998), *Strategy Safari: A Guided Tour Through the Wilds of Strategic Management*, New York, The Free Press.

MORRIS R., ONGENA H., SCHUKNECHT L. (2006), *The reform and implementation of the Stability and Growth Pact, European Central Bank*, Occasional Paper Series, n. 47.

NAG R., DONALD C., HAMBRICK D. C. E CHEN M. (2007), *What is Strategic Management, Really? Inductive Derivation of a Consensus Definition of the Field*, "Strategic Management Journal", 28 (9): 935-955.

PANDEY S. K. (2010), *Cutback Management and the Paradox of Publicness*, "Public Administration Review", July/August: 564-571.

PATTARO A. F. (2011), *Il patto di stabilità interno e l'orientamento della gestione al breve periodo. Alcune osservazioni in ottica aziendale sugli effetti tra i comuni italiani*, "Rivista Italiana di Economia Aziendale", 1-2: 58-69.

PATTARO A. F., CAPERCHIONE E., SANCINO A. (2009), *Un confronto internazionale: come altri Paesi europei hanno declinato il Patto di stabilità interno*, in AMATUCCI F., VECCHI V. (a cura di), *Le scelte di finanziamento degli enti locali*, Egea, Milano.

PEZZANI F. (2008), *Il patto di lucidità. Come avvicinare istituzioni e paese reale*, Università Bocconi Editore, Milano.

PEZZANI F. (2009), *Prefazione*, in AMATUCCI F., VECCHI V. (a cura di), *Le scelte di finanziamento degli enti locali*, Egea, Milano.

PEZZANI F., GARLATTI A. (2003), *I sistemi di programmazione e controllo negli enti locali*, Etas, Milano.

POLLITT C., BOUCKAERT G. (2002), *La riforma del management pubblico*, Università Bocconi Editore, Milano.

PRESIDENZA DEL CONSIGLIO DEI MINISTRI (2012), Direttiva del 03 maggio, Roma.

VALOTTI G. (2005), *Management pubblico. Temi per il cambiamento*, Egea, Milano.

WYNNE G. C. (1983), *Cutback Management: A Trinational Perspective*, Council for International Urban Liaison, Washington, D. C.

ZANGRANDI A. (1994), *Autonomia ed economicità nelle aziende pubbliche*, Giuffrè Milano.

3
Planning and Control Systems of Italian Regions[1]

This chapter aims to assess the changes in the processes of strategic planning and programming and the role of public managers in Italian regions. It hopes to identify possible alternatives for governance and suggests a reference model, although this can only be applied in the individual regions further to the implementation of appropriate corrective actions in order to bring it in line with the specific situation.

Learning objectives

After reading this chapter you should be able to:

- the processes of strategic planning and programming
- the changes in the processes of strategic planning and programming in Italian regions
- the role of public managers in Italian regions
- an empirical analysis of the programming, planning and control systems in use in several Italian regions

3.1 Introduction

Since the mid-Nineties, a new paradigm called public governance (PG) has been emerging in public administration as an alternative to New Public Management (NPM), which was considered too close to the world of business and insufficiently

---

[1] Davide Maggi (corresponding author) wrote paragraphs 3.1, 3.2, 3.3 and conclusions. Chiara Morelli wrote paragraph 3.4

critical, too mechanistic and incapable of highlighting the specific nature of decision-making and management in public administration.[2, 3]

The need for a new paradigm for public administration, centred on the development of governance ability, can be traced back to ongoing trends, such as internationalisation, the need to protect the environment, the development of technology and the culture of individuality. To respond to these trends, innovative methods of governance and coordination of socio-economic systems must be implemented, based on interaction between government and society, between public and private sectors, and on the materialisation of a new relationship between decisive action managed at the political-administrative level and forms of self-organisation at the social level.

In Italy, Regional Governments are confronting the issue of governance more than any other form of public administration: at micro level, they are redefining their organisational structures with regard to their role.

A network of public administration and agencies, revolving around the central Regional hub, is becoming increasingly consolidated and consists of municipal and provincial administration, new agencies and bodies linked to forms of inter-institutional cooperation such as Mountain Communities, Metropolitan Cities and associations of municipalities, Local Health Authorities and hospitals, regional agencies protecting the right to education and social housing, the many regional and local public agencies and companies operating in a variety of fields and, since 1994, regional agencies for the protection of the environment and human health.

At macro level, the Regions aim to initiate, consolidate and support processes for growth and local development by implementing Regional Development Plans[4] and ROP (Regional Operational Programmes) in Objective 1 regions.

Socioeconomic planning tools are linked to tools for urban planning and land management (territorial coordination plans) and sectoral action plans, such as regional healthcare plans and/or social and healthcare plans, social services plans and regional transport plans.

---

[2] NPM and PG have received considerable academic attention over the last few decades, referred to as "the two grand narratives of public management reform" (Fattore et. al, 2012; Andresani and Ferlie, 2006)".

[3] If NPM aims to increase efficiency and effectiveness in order to reduce costs and to improve performance, PG suggests rebuilding the relationship with society and increasing public participation (Trotta et al., 2011). Both NPM and PG require more than minor changes of existing services or processes. Instead, they demand the introduction of fundamentally new ways of doing things with sweeping changes in the organizational, social and cultural arrangements of public sector organizations. Therefore, abandoning the "rational approach" and considering the administration as an operational system (Friedberg, 1996) the literature highlights a challenge in the merger between the prescriptions of the reforms and the effective practices of organizations (Caiden, 1991; Weick et al, 2005).

[4] The Regional Development Plan is intended as a programming guideline document closely linked with the Government Programme as it is an implementation tool for priority interventions during its period of office. It is, therefore, a tool that is aimed at the medium to long term, divided into strategic programmes that take up the contents of the Government Programme and supplement it with greater explanation of the political priorities.

The consolidation of the process for institutional decentralisation and regional federalism, endorsed by the reform of Article V, requires Italian Regions to have an ever increasing capacity for governance, nevertheless there is an obvious risk of a significant lack of standard[5] conduct between the various Regions, as seen in their different speeds of decision-making and operating processes, scant exploitation of the room for manoeuvre and limited institutional performance.

3.2 Italian Regional Governments: description and developments

It is not possible to design and implement the processes required for planning, programming and controlling management practices in the abstract sense, i.e. without a prior assessment of the nature of the agency where they will be employed, the operations it carries out and the information needed by the bodies handling its finances (Brusa, Zamprogna, 2000). For this reason, this section provides a brief illustration of the institutional functions of Regional Governments.

Public agencies can be divided into two basic categories: territorial agencies and derived agencies. In Italy, the former include the State, the Regional Governments, the Provincial Governments and the Municipalities. There are numerous derived agencies that are very different to one another, however they always depend on one of the upper levels, which represents its higher-level agency and, in a certain sense, owns them. The former generally hold office whereas the latter are more focused on services. The former tend to be more stable over time in institutional terms; the latter have a higher level of institutional dynamism.

Regional governments belong to the category of economic institutions as they have the service delivering agency in-house. They acquire resources and production inputs from the environment, combining them and delivering the output of their economic operations to the community.

The Regional Governments were established by the Italian Constitution of 1947 but actually only came to light in 1972 when the first decrees were issued to transfer responsibilities from Central Government, with additional duties provided for in law 616/77. The Regional Governments have political autonomy and are able to express their political orientation (within the general orientation of the State) and can determine the scope of their actions. Regional Governments can only perform their duties within their own territory and impact on the population residing there. Furthermore,

---

[5] Law 76/2000 regarding "fundamental principles and regulations for coordination for the budgeting and accounting of Regional Governments" leaves them an ample degree of freedom to choose systems for planning, scheduling and control. This leads to a greatly differing scenario, within which it is difficult to extrapolate a system that can adapt to all regional situations. However, it is useful as a reference model, while bearing in mind that it may be applied in the various regions only after appropriate corrective action has been put in place to ensure it is suitable for the situation in question.

a Regional Government is linked to its territory and population by virtue of the mechanism of electoral representation.

The Regional Governments have legislative initiative; they may submit laws to Central Government, petition for public referendums and take part in electing the President of the Republic. Regional Governments may also set their own taxes in the areas where they have financial autonomy. Regional Governments carry out their duties based on four basic principles:

- the Right to Education: each Region has to promote the cultural growth of its population, from all points of view and making use of every possible means;
- the Right to Health: each Region has the duty of safeguarding the health and well-being of its population through the establishment of laws, regulations and instruments employed in the area;
- the Right to Work: Region must aim to promote employment for all by coordinating economic activities, cooperation and association of self-employed workers. Regions must also aim to help young and disabled people enter the job market;
- improving the local territory: eliminating any economic imbalance, promoting harmonious development of the territory.

The Regions are composed of several bodies: the Regional Council and the Executive. The Regional Council is the decision-making body for the region. It handles any legislative duties related to matters carried out by the Regional Government. The Council appoints a President to convene council meetings, chair discussions, draw up the agenda, represent the Region and coordinate the activities of the various permanent committees.

The Executive is the executive body for the region. The Executive is elected by the Council. It is formed of councillors who have specific powers. The Executive implements regional laws and decisions made by the Council. The President of the Executive is elected by the Executive and represents the region. He or she promulgates regional laws and regulations, directs administrative operations and coordinates the work of the councillors.

The recent decentralisation process (Laws 59/97, 112/98 and 1/99) defined the beginning of what is probably an irreversible process by establishing that the primary duty of the State lies only in matters of general interest (such as foreign affairs, defence, protection of cultural heritage, public order, justice, scientific research and social security), limited by an inclusive list and consequently allocating all other duties to local authorities. It also provided for the extensive use of the principle of subsidiarity, whose vertical dimension drives the Regional Governments to establish levels of decentralisation within their own organisation in favour of Municipal and Provincial Authorities and second level agencies. The process requires the introduction of fiscal federalism in favour of the Regions with a predefined path to increase its intensity, and increases the power of consultation of Regional and local authorities with the State, generating flow from State to Regions as regards central functions and for representation with the European Union.

Therefore, Regional Governments are able to draw up their own local systems independently, as they have a considerable degree of freedom as regards the infra-regional distribution of their functions, their macro-structural configuration and management of the system in accordance with the provisions of Article 4 of Law 59/97.

The main weaknesses of Regional Governments include the absolute predominance of a bureaucratic and administrative model and the resulting lack of business type logic and tools, especially those needed by a "parent agency"; their still rigidly sectoral and functional organisations resulting in a difficulty to reconcile the general and individual logic needed for effective communication with decentralised agencies; their lack of the culture and operational set up of a parent agency and lack of general and strategic coordination between agencies; their mainly specialist professional know-how resulting from their legal and administrative background and lack of general skills.

3.3   Theoretical framework: the development of strategic planning

Several schools of thought can be identified in literature. The first is known as the strategic design school and was introduced in the Seventies by Andrews (1971). This theory sees strategy as the pursuit for coherence between the sources of strength and weakness within the organisation in question and the threats/opportunities originating outside it.

A second important school, led by Ansoff (1968) and developed in parallel with the strategic design school, is known as formal planning. It shares numerous points of contact with the former, but differs significantly in that it upholds the centrality of formal and rational processes, divided into separate and distinct phases, supported by techniques and methods, and focusing on objectives, budgets, programmes and operational plans.

These two schools of thought were brought together by the positioning strategy, better known as the competitive strategy and the business strategy.

Competitive strategy, developed by Porter (1982), has witnessed the emergence of concepts such as strategic areas of operation, strategic groups and chain of value.

The business strategy focuses on intuition, on the positive impact created by changes and business turnarounds, and on creative ability, establishing a link with authors such as Schumpeter.

The formal, rational and managerial schools contrast with informal and relational schools on strategy, including strategy as power, the outcome of a negotiation process within the agency. Strategy as power goes beyond the boundaries of the agency and enables negotiation processes with other organisations in the form of partnerships, joint ventures, alliances and networks. Strategy as a social process is also included in this school, whereby the cultural factor in the agencies and public administration takes on more importance. Normann (1977) and Rhenman (1973) were the first to suggest the possibility of cross-fertilisation between managerial practices and logic, including strategic planning, between the public and private spheres, in particular with regard to the management of services.

The approach whereby strategy is a cognitive mental process is linked to the informal schools. Here, a central role is given to the reconstruction of the cognitive maps of the different actors and parties involved in the strategic process, the processing and communication of information, and the management of knowledge. The mental cognitive approach, conceptualised and developed by March and Simon (1958), has subsequently progressed towards subjective logic, in which strategy itself is the result of a creative process of interpretation. Strategy as learning represents a trend that is growing in importance and was developed and added to in following years by Quinn's work (1980) on logical incrementalism and the work of Mintzberg, Ahlstrand and Lampel (1998). Strategies are the outcome of internal learning processes; they apply across the entire organisation and are manifested as emerging phenomena and signals.

Finally, another two important schools should be mentioned: the environmental school, which focuses on how an individual organisation moves within the environment or rather its context of reference, and the school on strategic configurations. In the former, there is a significant relationship with the logic of strategic management, especially with the contingency theory and above all with institutional theories. In the public sector, the environmental school, which applies to all public management and public governance logic, is represented by the strategies implemented by certain public organisations, typically local governments and agencies operating in the field of healthcare and social services, in order to respond to environmental changes. According to the school of strategic configurations, agencies and public administration are considered to be groups of segments of internal decision-makers and actors, with their own characteristics and expectations, affected by processes of change and transformation.

The adoption of New Public Management (NPM) logic by public administration and the resulting autonomy given to public managers makes it vital to have a strategic plan capable of controlling that objectives are met and that the necessary results-oriented approach is in place.

Therefore, formal planning approaches have a high degree of consistency with NPM logic, as they are marked by a strong link between long-term choices, systems for budgeting and operational planning, and control systems. These schools of thought are weakly linked to competitive strategy and business strategy.

The form of strategy introduced by the model of public governance is profoundly different. Compared to NPM, it refers to the operating logic in the individual public administration; it pays more attention to the recovery of the ability to govern systems and networks of economic and social subjects and to the development of the role of control. Environmental strategy becomes central, especially strategy as a learning process based on comparing the ideas, expectations and interests of the internal and external stakeholders.

3.3.1 Strategic Planning in the Regions: a reference model

The strategic planning process can be defined as the set of methodologies, processes and tools supporting the development of policies and strategic plans and their conversion into the budget as applicable, and the implementation of corrective measures in line with the guidelines available.

Based on this definition, the strategic planning process can be divided up into the following stages:

- formulation of medium-long term objectives;
- assessment of action plans with selection of the various strategic alternatives;
- preliminary strategic control;
- implementation of the strategy;
- concurrent strategic control;

- reviews to the plan, if necessary;
- post action strategic control.

Although the definition of medium-long term objectives is normally delegated to the political body, however, there is a clear opportunity to establish dialogue with upper level managers, since the latter implement the steps needed to execute the chosen plans of action and accordingly have the necessary skills to assess the financial viability and technical feasibility of the objectives. The dialogue between the management and the political body may be direct or mediated by supporting organisations, such as Evaluation Units.[6] Furthermore, this stage often sees the involvement of other parties involved in the community, administered in various capacities. With regard to this, it should be noted that the process of defining objectives does not focus exclusively on financial questions, especially in the case of public agencies, because they do not operate for profit, and so the process is strongly influenced by the needs of the various stakeholders (Intrieri, 1980). As a result, not only is it desirable to establish dialogue between the political body and the managers, but negotiation should also be initiated between a variety of social powers, including:

- representatives of political parties;
- trade unions;
- representatives of consumers;
- professional associations;
- other pressure groups.

The outcome of this comparison and negotiation, in terms of defining objectives, must be actually achievable, i.e. fulfilling the needs of the various stakeholders must be balanced with the conditions of efficiency, effectiveness and economy (Zappa, 1951) in order to achieve sustainable and feasible action plans. As regards the feasibility of the projects, it is notable how this is determined by relevant factors within the agency that affect its operations, such as the availability of technical and human resources over and above financial resources, the running of its bureaucratic organisation and its relationships with the external environment, especially the synergies that can be achieved by working with other public and possibly private agencies. The evaluation of the technical feasibility and the financial viability of the projects are part of the preliminary strategic control phase, according to the provisions in Article 6 of Italian Law 286 issued on 30th July 1999. Accordingly, evaluation and strategic control "consists of the prior and subsequent analysis of the correspondence and/or any deviation between the assigned missions and the regulations, the chosen operating objectives,

---

[6] The evaluation unit, which entered the Italian legal system with Law 29/93, was originally an organisation primarily for control, given the job of assessing the degree of achievement of objectives, the efficient use of resources, impartiality and the performance of the administration. However, today, in addition to its original role, the evaluation unit acts as an agent for change, whose added value is found mainly in its ability to introduce new management methods requiring radical changes in the culture adopted by region.

the operating decisions taken and the human, financial and material resources assigned, in addition to the identification of any impeding factors". This refers in particular to a process put in place by the political body, usually supported in technical terms by specific departments (such as the planning and control department) or bodies, such as the aforementioned Evaluation Unit, in order to employ suitable methodologies to assess the strategy and adequate tools and analysis models. This phase also includes the opinions of sector or service managers as well as those of the general level managers in order to assess whether the quality and quantity of the human and material resources at their disposal are adequate for implementing the projects. In particular, we should point out that any changes to the organisation or to the facilities available can only be achieved in the medium-long term and so they must be part of strategic planning.

Besides identifying the strategic objectives to be assigned to the different organisational units, the lines of action must be defined in order to pursue them and achieve the fulfillment of a plan covering several years (usually three or five years). In particular, the region's portfolio strategy must be identified, defining which areas of activity will continue to operate, any new areas it will enter and any that should be abandoned (Coda, 1989), as well as deciding which activities will be handled directly and which will be delegated to other public or private agencies. The implementation of these lines of action will be subject to verification during the concurrent control stage with the aim of routinely checking the degree of implementation of the strategic objectives and constantly monitoring the dynamics of the internal variables and environmental factors, since sudden changes in the reference context may demand adjustments even at the strategic planning level. The phases analysed are iterative, since managers can ask for the objectives to be reviewed during the implementation of the strategies should they consider them to be out of date and so no longer concretely pursuable, initiating a new planning process (Brusa, Zamprogna, 2000).

At the end of the pre-assigned period allocated to the plan, post action control is needed to check the conformity of the results and the objectives, and represents the final stage in the strategic planning process. This is an unequivocal requisite in Article 6 of Italian Law 286 of 30 July 1999, which stipulates "based on the exercising of the policy powers of the competent bodies, the phase of assessment and strategic control aims to check the actual implementation of the decisions contained in the directives and other policy documents". The starting point for this monitoring system are the general and specific objectives that are set out in the Regional Development Plan, often expressed in terms of expected results, in the form of indicators, and compared with other results indicators at the end of the set period of time representing the impact and effects of the governance on the regional community, primarily for the purposes of assessment. Given the vastness of the context analysed, the organisation of an adequate system of monitoring will require:

- all those responsible for the planning actions to be involved in the setup and management of the system;
- links with sectoral information systems.

Given the complexity involved in managing a system with a similar configuration, the control and evaluation operations normally carried out by the political body have to be supported by other bodies and offices for any technical issues (such as the department for strategic control). Art.6 of Italian Law 286 of 30th July 1999 states: "the offices and persons responsible for evaluation and strategic control report the results of their analysis to the political bodies in confidence. As a rule, they also support the political body during the appraisal of the managers reporting directly to the body itself as regards the achievement of the objectives they were assigned by it."

3.3.2   Programming and control of management: a reference model

The system used to plan and control management can be defined as: "the set of methodologies, processes and tools supporting the management for the definition and achievement of managerial objectives, for the allocation and use of resources and for carrying out corrective measures in line with the management tools available at the different levels of responsibility".[7]

The interpretation of this definition reveals that, as programming focuses on the definition of the managerial objectives, it has a short-term timeframe and is expressed by the drafting of two key documents:

- the Financial Planning Document, which provides an overview of the activities that the Region intends to execute within one year, designed for pursuing its strategic objectives;
- the Budget, drawn up in order to allocate resources according to the plans and programmes outlined in the Regional Development Plan and the Financial Planning Document.

More specifically, the process of management planning and control can be divided into the following phases:

- preparation of the Financial Planning Document, including the definition of annual targets to be achieved during the financial year;
- preparation of the annual Budget, including the definition of the map of centres of responsibility;
- preliminary control with the aim of verifying the financial viability and the technical feasibility of the programme;
- concurrent control carried out during the year with the aim of revealing any differences between the objectives and actual results, and reviewing programmes should any significant differences be found;
- post action control.

With regard to the first phase, the main purpose pursued when the Financial Planning Document is prepared is to turn the government guidelines into objectives that must be assigned to the administration's organisation, thereby giving the political body the possibility to influence how the Administration operates and assess the results

---

[7] Various Authors. Permanent Conference of Internal Control Services of the Regions and Autonomous Provinces.

achieved by the individual structures in order to create a integrated system consisting of programming and evaluation processes.

Normally the document, adopted by the Executive and submitted to the Council, is prepared after careful preliminary analysis of the current situation, i.e. the general situation of the community and the economy in the region; however, the bulk of the work is based on the description of the regional objectives and policies for each sector achieved via the breakdown into macro areas (for example: individuals and families, the local area, the environment and infrastructures, internationalisation and development of the economy, the institutional organisation and governance).[8] Subsequently, the intended impact of these lines of action on public finances should be described, presenting a forecast of the income and outlay making use of the cooperation and involvement of supporting structures (such as the Management of Financial Resources) in order to provide general information that will be examined in greater detail during the preparation of the annual budget.

The preparation of the latter document aims to assign resources to the various centres of responsibility based on their allocated plans and programmes, thus going beyond the traditional methods used for allocating resources based on the incremental approach, closely linked to how much funding was allocated the previous financial year. In this way, it is possible to assess the actual level of efficiency, effectiveness and economy achieved by the various centres by comparing objectives and actual results. This development has certainly had an impact on the relationships between managers and political bodies: the incremental approach, marked by greater rigidity and consistency in the allocation of resources, reduces the level of conflict between them. Vice versa, an approach closely linked to the definition of objectives implies flexibility in the preparation of budgets and, therefore, room for conflict during the allocation of resources. During this phase, therefore, it is important how the centres of responsibility are defined because the following needs must be safeguarded:

- establishing optimum conditions to subsequently exercise management control;
- preventing possible conflict between the different units involved in the pursuit of the goals.

The centres of responsibility can be created in one of two ways: by identifying a single level of responsibility – the general management – or by identifying a double level of responsibility, the general management and the management of the unit or service.

With regard to this, we should consider that the second comma of Article 3 in Italian Law 29/1993 states: "the managers are responsible for the adoption of administrative acts and measures, including all acts that create a commitment between the administration and third parties, as well as for the financial, technical and administrative management by means of autonomous powers as regards spending, organising human resources, equipment and control. They are solely responsible for administration, management and the associated results". This Article gives department and service managers, as well as general managers, the authority to handle management and spending as needed in order to achieve their assigned objectives, giving them full and sole responsibility for the final results. Thus, it is considered preferable to create the

---

[8] Macro areas taken from the 2006 Financial Planning Document of the Region of Veneto.

map of the centres of responsibility by identifying two levels of responsibility, general management and department or service management, since this type of structure configuration makes more information available for assessing second level managers who have been given more extensive management authority.

Finally, the map of the centres of responsibility should be designed bearing in mind the need to control the management. Art. 4 of Italian Law 286 of 30th July 1999 states: "for the purposes of controlling the management, each public administration defines:

- the unit or units responsible for the design and handling of the management controls;
- the organisational units at whose level the effectiveness, efficiency and cost of the administration's operations will be measured;
- the procedures for defining the management objectives and the persons responsible;
- the set of products and aims for the administration, with reference to the entire administration or single organisational units;
- the methods for identifying and allocating costs among the organisational units and for identifying the objectives for which the costs were incurred;
- specific indicators to measure effectiveness, efficiency and economy".

The budget is a key document in management control as it is a tool for preliminary, concurrent and post action control. For preliminary control, the budget enables the financial viability and the technical feasibility of the annual programmes to be assessed: in particular, by dividing the year into infra-annual periods (one month, two months, quarters) it becomes possible to control whether the resources of the agency are sufficient to meet its financial needs for each period. Similarly, identifying different centres of responsibility enables each organisational unit's capacity to reach its chosen programmes to be tested from a technical and analytical viewpoint.

These divisions are also helpful during the process of concurrent control, namely the routine measuring of any differences between objectives and results, in order to take appropriate corrective action promptly and achieve a process that is iterative and not merely consequential.

Finally, the budget also provides the necessary information for post action control, i.e. when the degree of achievement of the annual objectives by the various centres of responsibility is assessed in accordance with art. 5 of Italian Law 286 of 30th September 1999, which states: "public administration assess the performance of their managers and conduct in relation to the development of the professional, human and organisational resources they have been assigned (organisational skills), in line with the provisions established by national collective employment agreements and also based on the results of their management control".

3.3.3 The actors involved in planning, programming and control processes: the relationship between political bodies and administrative bodies

In addition to the study of the processes of planning, programming and control in the regions, we should consider the actors involved in the decision-making process and the relationship between political bodies (referring primarily to the Regional Executive) and the administrative body (or managers), who are traditionally assigned different tasks such as:

- the political body is mainly given the role of representing and mediating interests and carries out duties associated with policy and control with regard to those issues involved in administration;
- the administrative body has the task of turning the general aims of the Region into objectives that will be pursued by choosing appropriate monetary combinations, exercising management powers and guiding and controlling the staff.

The relationships that can be formed between the above-mentioned bodies and the degree of cooperation that can occur between them depend on a variable set of factors: in each Region, the separation between the identification of the two bodies can be preserved or collaboration can be promoted to a lesser or greater extent as a result of the methods chosen to allocate tasks, thus affecting the model of corporate-governance. In this regard, it is worth considering two models of corporate-governance that are directly opposed to one other:

- the traditional, hierarchical-bureaucratic model;
- the decentralised model.

The former features a clear separation of the duties allocated to the political body and to the managers, as the latter act as mere executors of the decisions taken by the politicians, and so their authority is mainly in terms of compliance with procedures and not on the tangible pursuit of the objectives based on conditions of efficiency, effectiveness and economy. This model, which has gradually generated inefficiencies and a lack of a results-oriented approach, should already have been replaced with the implementation of a decentralised system, featuring a high degree of cooperation between politicians and managers: in particular, the political body defines the strategies and guidelines with the help of the managers and the latter, who have a certain amount of organisational and managerial autonomy, manage and use resources to turn objectives into tangible results. Therefore, there is a growing need for interdependence between the different roles, requiring first and foremost a rethinking of the process for formulating the agency's strategies and of the planning and control process in order to achieve greater manager participation in the Region's policy-making and to promote the introduction of results-based mechanisms of control and accountability. The actions that may prove useful in this sense may include:

- creating ad hoc bodies with an assorted political-managerial formation to support the planning and programming processes by means of comparison as well to intervene during the allocation of resources;
- involving existing bodies with the aim of promoting dialogue between the political body and management.

Regarding the latter, we should note the role played by the Evaluation Unit in many regions. This Unit, introduced into the Italian legal system by Law 29 on 3rd February

1993, traditionally has had "the task of verifying the achievement of objectives, the correct and cost effective management of public resources, the impartiality and efficiency of the administration, by means of comparative assessment of costs and performance" operating primarily from a position of autonomy and responding solely to the political leadership. What's more, the general approach of Law 29 of 3rd February 1993 already guaranteed that individual agencies had an element of autonomy for the design and configuration of the Evaluation unit, for example by providing for the possibility to issue a special regulation concerning the functions, powers and set-up of the unit. For this reason, different scenarios may be encountered in the actual administration, in particular:

- the evaluation unit is used exclusively for certification purposes, i.e. the formal verification of compliance with procedures;
- the evaluation unit acts as an internal consultant for the Region, as its operations are seen to be useful for promoting the introduction of new management methods and for facilitating the renewal of culture and dominant values;
- the region adopts an intermediate solution with respect to the extremes described above, which may vary depending on the scope of the roles assigned to the evaluation unit.

Clearly, when the evaluation unit also has the role of internal consultant, it must take part in planning and programming too, offering technical-methodological support during the definition of strategic plans and annual programmes as well as for the execution of the preliminary investigation that is essential for the appraisal of the managers. In this way, the unit is not merely a tool for the accomplishment of the political manifesto but acts as an intermediary in relationships established between the political body and the management.

To put it briefly, there is a need to maintain a proper dialectic between the political body and the management, based on a collaborative relationship and not one of subordination in order to:

- allow them to offer their opinions and skills to contribute to the defining of plans and programmes that are to guide the agency's operations;
- promote accountability among the management[9]

In this sense, the system of planning and control has a central role in the relationships between politics and management as well as demanding the involvement of both parties in order to work properly (Rebora, 1999); it is clear that if adequate systems of planning and control are in place within the region, this not only represents an essential tool for the policy and control of strategic actions and operations, but it also

---

[9] Undoubtedly, the budget is a tool that promotes the assigning of responsibility to the management as it is also used to allocate the resources that the singles managers will have to manage. Thus, it is important to make full use of the expertise of the political body and the managers during its preparation.

represents an opportunity to reconcile the roles and responsibilities of politicians with the autonomy of the managers. This result can be achieved when certain essential conditions are guaranteed:

- plans and programmes expressed by the political body are in line with the programmes and management objectives guiding the actions of the managers so that a homogeneous area is created within which each body can exercise its role;
- using forms of management by objectives encourages accountability among those involved in the management of the agency and does not translate into a system where the formal observance of procedures prevails.

Despite the validity of the information provided above, it seems excessive to assume that systems of planning, programming and control are the only fertile ground for combining the functions assigned to the political body with the autonomy given to the managers, because there remains the risk of overloading the systems themselves with even more work than the traditionally assigned tasks. It is unconceivable that the only space for interaction between politics and management is during the negotiation phases when strategic plans, annual programmes and the strategic and management control are defined, and that it marks the confines safeguarding the autonomy of both bodies. It is also restrictive to think that the implementation of plans and programmes defined during the strategic planning and the annual planning should coincide with the achievement of all the results the Region wants to achieve. For this reason, it is inadequate to assess the management by measuring numbers or by comparing the agreed actions with the achieved actions. This is because changes in key context variables during the implementation of plans and programmes may persuade managers to alter choices already made as these are no longer consistent with the reference context. As a result, the achieving results may differ to some extent to what was planned but they are no less valid. Iterative planning and scheduling processes must be implemented, i.e. that can be altered during execution, in order to successfully define objectives that can actually be pursued.

3.4 Empirical research: An analysis of the programming, planning and control systems in use in several Italian regions

The above analysis has helped to outline a theoretical model consisting of systems and processes for programming, planning and controlling that may be adapted to fit various regional contexts.

Empirical research conducted in different Italian regions has revealed how the systems actually implemented do not always comply with the model proposed. This is understandable if we consider that each Region has its own economy and social context: the starting point for programming.

In particular, the planning, programming and control processes were analysed in conjunction with the associated supporting documents, focusing on the relationships created between the Regional Executive and the directors/managers during these phases in the following regions:

- Veneto;
- Piedmont;
- Emilia Romagna;
- Tuscany;
- Marche;
- Basilicata.

The main intention was to reveal any differences between the actual practices implemented by the Regions and the theoretical model proposed.

3.4.1   Veneto

The planning, programming, budgeting and control processes are very complex and impact on the entire organisation of the Regional government. However, as regards the instruments used, we should mention:

- the Regional Development Plan (RDP), the Implementation and Spending Plan (ISP) and the Financial Planning Document (FPD) at the planning and programming level;
- the budget document at budgeting level;
- the Budget Report and the Management Analysis Report at control level.

It is not possible to identify a specific set of reference methods applied in its entirety according to traditional developments in methodology (such as Zero Based Budgeting, Performance-Based Budgeting System, Activity Based Budgeting) for the preparation of these documents. Nevertheless, we can say that the Region has adopted planning and programming logic based on the definition of objectives using a method of resource allocation, referring to the functional needs and objectives identified in the timeframe in question. The main purpose of this approach is to overcome a method of allocating resources based on allocations in previous years, i.e. incremental logic which is thought to lack rationality since it is unsuitable for controlling the consistency of the relationship between the allocated resources and the programmes to be implemented. Moreover, in recent years, the region has supported the notion of linking the budget with financial programming by creating a link between the financial planning data, the budget and the cycle of the balance sheet, with the aim of creating a complete information system capable of guiding governing bodies and achieving informed decisions relating to the allocation of resources and facilitating controls carried out by the political body.

Looking at each of the documents mentioned in greater detail, we should first consider the Regional Development Plan, i.e. an instrument for knowledge and long-term strategy definition developed by the Executive using the method of consultation with the various public and private parties. The Region made use of IT systems to create a "Forum on Competitivity", i.e. a form of active consultation available to the various legitimate stakeholders in Veneto for participation in the definition of political and administrative decisions.

Moving on from the analysis of the planning phases to the programming phases, we should consider a document that represents a policy document for the following year's governance for the Region, agencies, companies and regional bodies, i.e. the Financial Planning Document (Article 5 of Regional Law 35/2001). It is an instrument of knowledge providing an overview of the activities that the Region intends to carry out within the year, translating Government policies into objectives assigned to the Administration, thus enabling the connection with the system used to assess the results achieved by the individual organisations. Specifically, this document enables regional organisations to provide a detailed yet focused picture of its operations, thus acknowledging the value of the work carried out by the Regional Administration.

The Financial Planning Document also has a close association with the Regional Development Plan, for the purpose of ensuring the aims of its operations comply with the strategic plan, and subsequently with the sector plans[10] and the Implementation and Spending Plans.[11] The Financial Planning Document in particular, includes an element of assessment, featuring an analysis of the results of the sector plans and the Implementation and Spending Plans, and any proposed reviews. As for the preparation of the Regional Development Plan, the Financial Planning Document also requires the cooperation of various parties: the Regional Executive, regional structures and the economic and social partners, as well as the intensive exchange of information between the managers and councillors involved, in order to produce a document shared by the various stakeholders.

These documents are the outcome of the planning and programming phases and influence the formulation of the Budget for the financial year, a budget document that shows how resources are allocated to the responsibility centres.

3.4.2   Emilia-Romagna

The planning and programming system in use in the Region of Emilia Romagna is based primarily on the preparation of the following basic documents:[12]

- a Regional Territorial Plan;
- a Financial Planning Document.

The Regional territorial plan (RTP) is a planning tool used by the region to outline its development strategy and define its strategic motives for pursuing the development of its social and environmental resources and enhancing the quality and efficiency of

---

[10] The Sector Plan defines the specific goals and administrative and regulatory aspects for the production of services or work by both public and private entities, also when jointly financed and under public-private management.

[11] ISP (Implementation and Spending Plans) are medium-term operating instruments that define the priorities for use of the available resources, allocating them among homogeneous action groups.

[12] Aspects relating to sectoral programming are not covered in this study.

the regional system. The term "territorial" is used in a broad sense: this is not simply a document concerning urban planning, it is a strategic plan prepared according to European and national strategies in order to define its medium to long term objectives. However, these conclusions are based on an interpretation of the various applicable regional laws, as there is still no approved Regional Territorial Plan but simply some preliminary documents. This shortcoming brought to light the need for a tool that is predominantly for the purpose of communication: as a result, the Financial Planning Document has been in use in the region since 2000. This has predominantly two goals, the first is distinctly for communication purposes and the second is political. The Financial Planning Document is a knowledge and relational tool addressing the whole community, which is useful for explaining the objectives and strategies of the region and for summing up the political options of the majority, especially the President. Thus, this document offers an explanation of the President's programme and as a result it has a five-year timeframe to coincide with the entire legislature, even if it is updated annually by the Statistics and Strategic Control Department. For the same reason, the central section of the document consists of the strategic priorities, i.e. the policies of the region linked directly to President's mandate and very closely associated with the general situation of public finances and the economy in general.

Given the vastness of the context analysed and the lack of references taken from an approved strategic planning document, the region's entire organisation has to be involved in preparing the Financial Planning Document. In actual fact, this necessity is actually only partially fulfilled, as the document is drawn up by the Regional Executive and incorporated by the Legislature in the session examining the budget. It is analysed and updated with the support of the General Management, which mainly intervenes on areas involving regional policy. In particular, each General Manager offers his input for his specific area, with regard to projects and actions supporting the achievement of the legislative objectives, also indicating the expected results and the financial resources that are expected to be used. The relationship between the political bodies and the management are in part direct and partly mediated by the Statistics and Strategic Control Department, a special Executive body for handling data collection for the reconstruction of the general reference context, preparing drafts for discussion and drawing up the final version of the document. It is also involved in the annual updating of the document and in post action strategic control, collecting and processing the information needed to measure the degree of implementation of the necessary actions to achieve the expected results, the level of use of the available resources and the degree of achievement of priority strategic objectives. These activities fall under the strategic controls carried out by the Regional Executive on the basis of data and information provided by the Statistics and Strategic Control Department, whose results are then reported and discussed by the Legislature. This is actually a control of the outcome or results achieved in terms of user satisfaction and of the impact of policies at community level (for example, assessing whether the actions undertaken have helped reduce the level of unemployment and consequently lower the distress of the families living in Emilia Romagna).

These considerations regarding the planning stages of the overall activities undertaken by the Regional government show how a decentralised system of corporate governance is implemented within the region, marked by intense, direct or mediated relationship flows between politicians and managers. In particular, the political body defines the strategies and guidelines supported by the managers; the latter enjoy a certain degree of organisational and managerial autonomy to manage and make use of resources in order to translate the objectives into tangible results. Furthermore, general and department managers are also allowed to decide the programmes within their specific areas, provided they remain in line with the general objectives set out in the Financial Planning Document. Consequently, management and department programmes are prepared every year and are subject to self-monitoring: each management assesses the results achieved at the end of the reference period, and subsequently reports them to the political body so it, in turn, can assess the managers, the administrative staff and officers. Thus, a flow of information is also produced at department level, originating from the managers and used by the political body for assessment purposes.

3.4.3   Basilicata

The planning and control systems in use in the region of Basilicata are aimed at pursuing balanced socio-economic and territorial development by means of discussion and cooperation with the stakeholders in the area and in line with the plans and programmes defined at national and community level. In order to achieve this, the Region ensures that representatives of the local agencies and communities and representatives of economic and social organisations are involved in the planning and programming process. The programming method is governed by Regional Law n. 30 issued on June 24th 1997, based on the Regional Development Plan (RDP), the Region's main policy document, containing guidelines that are checked once a year and specified further during the approval of the Annual Financial Planning Document (AFPD). The following documents also fall under the regional planning instruments and are closely linked to the Regional Development Plan and the Annual Financial Planning Document:

- the regional territorial reference plan and the associated provincial territorial co-ordination plans;
- the catchment plans resulting from Law n. 183 issued on May 18th 1989 and Regional Law n. 43 issued on September 2nd, 1996;
- sectoral plans and special projects undertaken at regional level;
- provincial programmes with a duration of several years and socio-economic development plans for Mountain Communities and the Parks Management authorities;
- negotiated planning documents;
- programmes co-funded by the EU;
- plans of activities of Regional agencies.

The planning and programming methods adopted by the region and the instruments considered, make it possible to go beyond the traditional incremental approach used for the allocation of resources. In particular it follows a logic whose starting point is the definition of the objectives, while considering a financial constraint, i.e. the total amount of resources available, in order to guarantee the feasibility of the plans and programmes. The resources are, therefore, allocated considering the relevance of the objectives in political terms, overlooking how they were allocated previously. This conclusion is also the outcome of the analysis of the documents forming the core of the planning and programming system, i.e. the Regional Development Plan and the Annual Financial Planning Document: the central part of these consists of an analysis of the objectives that may be pursued during the relative timeframe and the instruments that may be used in operations in order to achieve them. The Regional Development Plan, in particular, is a governing document, and all other general and sectoral planning documents are based on this; its acts like a summary, as it considers all sectors and the total amount of financial resources that are available for use.

The Regional Executive has the task of preparing the outline of the Regional Development Plan for the five year period in question, providing the information indicated. The drafting of the document is done in conjunction with the Promotion Office (a body run by the Office of the President of the Executive) and the Evaluation Unit, which falls outside the region and has an advisory capacity. In this way, the Evaluation Unit provides technical-methodological support during the definition of the strategic plans and the annual programmes as well as during the essential preliminary stage for the appraisal of the managers.

The Unit is not simply a tool used to carry out political intentions, but acts as an intermediary in the relationships that are established between the political body and the management. We should consider that the preparation of the Regional Development Plan requires an exchange of information and opinions between the Regional Executive and the managers through direct discussion or in meetings and debates on politically relevant points in order to identify the most effective tools to achieve the strategic objectives. In this way, the relationship between the political bodies and the managers does not only take the form of a transfer of orders, but becomes a collaborative relationship that demonstrates that there is a largely decentralised system of governance in place in the region, whereby the political bodies define the plans and programmes with the help of the managers and the latter manage these resources with the ultimate goal of turning objectives into tangible results.

The implementation of the Regional Development Plan is verified annually during the preparation of the Annual Financial Planning Document. The latter is a planning and control tool used by the region to determine its operational objectives and to remodel its strategic objectives, producing an iterative process. Changes in the region's external and internal variables may, in fact, demand modifications to its strategies in order to bring them in line with the current situation.

By drafting the Annual Financial Planning Document, the region clarifies and updates its governance priorities with the aim of creating the conditions for greater and balanced development in the area. Basically, this document contains three main guidelines. First, the analysis of the status of implementation of the Regional Development Plan considered both as a whole and in its sectoral and regional subdivisions, in addition to the repositioning and the annual updating of the strategic objectives in the Regional Development Plan. Secondly, the definition of annual objectives and specific objectives to be assigned to the individual general managers, according to their specific fields. Third, the document carries out a detailed analysis of the resources available for the implementation of the various projects. In order to do this, it considers the situation and the expected development of the regional financial flows and the Region's financial management policies and defines the framework for the financial resources in the budget that can be assigned to the various plans and programmes.

The Regional Executive is in charge of preparing the Annual Financial Planning Document; it then adopts it after discussion with local institutions, specially convened in a plenary session. The Programming Office and the Evaluation Unit provide technical support for the drafting of the document. Furthermore, both the Annual Financial Planning Document and the Regional Development Plan involve discussion with the general managers: relationships between the political body and the managers may be direct or be mediated by the Evaluation Unit. This Unit, in fact, provides support and evaluation not only for the definition of operating objectives but also to verify the degree of achievement of the strategic objectives contained in the Regional Development Plan during the preparation of the Annual Financial Planning Document. Should it be seen that the long-term objectives do not comply with the current situation and as a result are no longer feasible, the Evaluation Unit has the duty to offer advice for the purpose of reviewing the plans.

The Regional Development Plan and the Annual Financial Planning Document are preliminary documents for the preparation of annual and multiple-year budgets. The Region's budgets make it possible to allocate financial resources based on the objectives set out in the above documents. This creates a sort of sequentiality, as the preliminary definition of the objectives (in the Regional Development Plan and the Annual Financial Planning Document) is needed to achieve the rational and analytical distribution of resources. When resources are allocated to offices, which have to have appropriate tools to reach their objectives, it is also important to be aware of the costs incurred in previous years for the implementation of the same tools. This approach does not imply the total adoption of the incremental approach, as the allocation of resources is not achieved by simply adjusting the allocations of previous years. Reference is only made to past spending in order to verify the economic feasibility of the various solutions to ensure a certain degree of consistency between the financial resources allocated to each organisational unit and the programmes that each must implement.

3.4.4   Marche

The planning and control system in the region of the Marche is governed by Regional Law n. 31 issued on December 11th 2001. It consists of a set of tools and processes designed to develop strategic plans and operational programmes that necessarily have to be turned into annual and multiple-year budgets. As far as the overall planning is concerned, since there is no Regional Development Plan, the framework for the sectoral Plans and Programmes and for the preparation of the annual and multiple-year budgets is provided by the RFPD (Regional Financial Planning Document) alongside the instruments for community programming (Regional Strategy Document and Regional Operational Programmes for 2007-2013) and territorial programming (Territorial Strategy Document).

The Financial Planning Document in particular, is a document with two main functions: firstly it acts as an instrument bringing together the budget programming and the other regional planning instruments, as the strategies described in the Financial Planning Document are turned into the annual and multiple-year budgets in financial terms. In turn, the spending constraints, resulting from the implementation of the budget and financial policy, affect the definition of the objectives. Secondly, the Regional Financial Planning Document outlines the contents of the strategies that can be concretely pursued in the medium to long term, i.e. the reference period in the multiple-year budget.

Therefore, the document is not limited to describing the manoeuvres of the government impacting on the preparation of the annual budget, as it also sets down the guidelines for the strategic development in the region and the activities assigned to each regional structure. As a result, it is a fundamental planning and programming document capable of filling the gap caused by the lack of a regional development plan. According to established practice, this document is drafted by the "Programming, Budget and Community Policies" Department, based primarily on instructions received from top managers, who offer input with regard to their specific fields in agreement with the associated Councillor. Together with the Regional Financial Planning Document, the Regional Strategy Document (RSD) and the Territorial Strategy Document (TSD) are key elements for regional programming. These three tools provide the main references for defining integrated policies for regional operations. The Regional Strategy Document is used to identify the specific aims that the Region intends to pursue by making use of European funding.

The Territorial Strategy Document, on the other hand, is used to promote social cohesion and the competitive system by integrating the territorial vision with the financial vision of the Regional Strategy Document. In this way, integration is achieved between the regional and local community, as these documents are not only intended for regional bodies (Regional Council, Executive, Councillors, regional organising bodies), but also for local authorities and financial and social organisations.

The plans and programmes described in the Regional Financial Planning Document must be turned into the multiple-year budget in financial terms, a document drafted for a three year period, representing the overall resources that the region plans to acquire and use in the period in question and that must be attached to the annual budget. In this way, a link is preserved between the objectives deriving from the joint efforts of the Executive and the managers and the resources that are allocated to the individual production departments. When plans and programmes are altered, it becomes necessary to review the criteria used for allocating equipment and human and financial resources. This system configuration has a high degree of flexibility and can lead to conflict between the managers in charge of the various departments, who are well known to prefer a certain degree of stability in budgeted resources available for carrying out operations. The solution adopted by the region consists of offering managers the possibility to pro-actively take part in the programming phase, offering their input in agreement with the Councillor in question. This avoids giving the political bodies too much discretion for decisions regarding the allocation of resources and reduces the risk of internal conflict.

3.4.5 Tuscany

Tuscany's regional planning is based on well-identified guiding principles, including sustainability, consistency between strategic objectives and the programmes to implement them, subsidiarity and adequacy during the allocation of resources and assignment of responsibilities, institutional cohesion, consultation between the institutional representatives and the stakeholders. The methodology used enables the systematic linking of the allocation of financial, technical and human resources to the various projects for implementation, gradually pursuing Zero Based Budget programming logic. The aim is to redefine budgets on an annual basis and avoiding using the previous year's level of expenditure as a benchmark.

The Regional Development Plan (RDP) is the basic policy document for regional programming that defines its policy options in a medium-term timeframe which are consistent with government programme and represent guidelines for the region's programming and intervention strategies, resulting in the general objectives and policies that should be implemented in order to achieve them. It is a document adopted by the Executive and submitted to the Regional Council but whose preparation requires the contribution of several stakeholders from within the regional structure, the general managers, as well as external parties, i.e. the members of the consultation committee.

The general managers are involved in the process for drafting the Regional Development Plan in collaboration with the Regional Executive (thecoordination planning and control department, in particular) and above all with the benefit of the support of the Technical Programming Committee, the advisory body to the President of the Executive and the Regional Executive itself which unavoidably expresses its opinion on the proposed laws, regulations, general programming documents, sectoral policy programmes and the organisation documents handled by the Regional Executive. The members of the consultation committee are, on the other hand, parties from outside the regional organisation, in particular local authorities and social and business parties, who are involved in defining the most important decisions on social and financial policies and for the implementation of regional action policies by way of comparison.

By adopting the method of consultation and cooperation between political bodies and managers, the region of Tuscany intends to acknowledge the positive contribution that proposals, discussion and debate can make to governance. For this reason, the behaviour of the various regional agencies must bear the mark of transparency, readiness to inform and compare, and the ability to encapsulate different positions. This approach is also manifest during the drafting process of the Financial Planning Document (FPD), providing the guidelines for the region's programming and financial governance for the coming year, strongly linked to the Regional Development Plan. The two documents are linked, as the Financial Planning Document contains explicit operating references for the individual years of implementation of the Regional Development Plan. This is also possible thanks to the decidedly planning-related content of the latter document, whose division into Integrated Regional Projects links it to short-term planning activities and sectoral programmes. For example, the specific actions relating to the individual integrated regional projects contained in the Regional Development Plan are normally indicated in the Financial Planning Document, accompanied by the envisaged financial situation for the year in question, making a balanced distribution of resources among the various production units based on their assigned projects.

The defined plans and programmes are subject to monitoring and evaluation by the Regional Executive which presents documents annually to the Regional Council attesting the degree of achievement. In particular, a process of integrated assessment is implemented in the region during the drafting of the plans and programmes, showing the internal and external coherence with respect to individual programming instruments and evaluating the expected effects in environmental, territorial, economic and social terms. In this way, it also provides an analysis of the feasibility of the plan, both from technical and financial points of view, requiring a review of the process for drafting the plan or programme, showing the logical and functional sequence of the drafting stages, the time required to implement the various phases, the estimated resources for its implementation and distinguishing between those available and those that must still be activated.

A system of concurrent and post action monitoring and evaluation runs alongside the preliminary evaluation system in order to measure the consistency between end results and objectives and expected results, enabling any unexpected problems to be revealed and the necessary corrective action to be put in place or, should this not be possible, to identify more effective solutions that should be considered in future programming phases. A special technical unit, the Single Regional Evaluation and Verification Unit (SRAVU) has been set up in the region to support the Regional Executive for its duties relating to the evaluation, monitoring and verification of regional programming and public investments, as well as for coordinating integrated evaluation processes. The SRAVU also works in conjunction with the general managers, thus helping to create a bond between them and the Regional Executive: this is logical, because it considers and evaluates the requests and opinions of the various managers even if it is subject to the directives of the Executive, and reports them to the political body.

3.4.6 Piedmont

The region of Piedmont has adopted a planning and control system that focuses primarily on a number of generic documents. Firstly, the regional Financial Planning Document, which complies with the guidelines contained in the Legislative Programme, determines the objectives, action plans and programmes and defines the financial relations on an annual basis, with forecasts covering a period of no less than three years.

Again, on a general level, it uses planning documents for its strategy and operating strategy with regard to community resources, i.e. the Preliminary Strategy Document (PSD), the Regional Strategy Document (RSD), the Regional Territorial Plan, the Operating Strategy Planning Document (OSPD), Regional Operating Plans (ROP) and the Rural Development Plan (RDP). These tend to be general instruments and are produced over and above sectoral programming documents, such as the Regional Healthcare Plan, the Transport Plan and the Regional Territorial Plans (RTP) etc. Finally, it also makes use of negotiated programming, based on Interinstitutional Programme Agreements, Framework Programme Agreements, Territorial Pacts, Programme Contracts and Area Contracts, tending, therefore, to move towards increasingly integrated forms of programming. In the region, the RFPD is the administrative policy document that sets down the guidelines for the preparation of annual and multiple year budgets and represents the link between the general and sectoral programmes.

This document takes the form of a report and is a preliminary assessment of the national budgetary policies, the overall economic trends and the current status and trends of Piedmont's economy. It then offers guidance with regard to the necessary criteria and parameters for the preparation of the annual and multiple-year budgets.

Moreover, although it considers a period spanning several years (three years), it is updated once a year and so produces an iterative process capable of maintaining on-going consistency between the programmes and the internal and external conditions in the region. As the RFPD is a generic instrument, it is approved by the Council and drawn up by the Regional Executive, in particular by its operational departments (the Department for Planning and Statistics, the Department of Budget and Finance and other regional departments) in conjunction with the stakeholders and general managers. An interchange of information is created with the latter in particular via systematic and mutual consultation. This creates a direct relationship between the political body and the management that does not require mediation by other parties and encourages the organisation of a planning and programming system capable of also including sectoral demands. In particular, the single strategic plan is subsequently broken down to identify strategic initiatives relating to individual sectors via the drafting of an additional document: the Operational Programme. In this instrument, the policies contained in the strategic planning documents are translated into actual facts intending to obtain resources and use production factors. Those in charge of centres of administrative responsibility may, in fact, only commit to spending within the limits of their budgets as allocated in the operational programme and for the purposes of achieving the objectives set out in the programme. The latter document also provides the basis for the execution of the phases of strategic control by the special Department for Management Control and the Assessment unit, a body that operates within the Regional Department of Statistics and Programming – Regional Planning Sector.

In the region, the concept of assessment can have different meanings, including preliminary assessment, especially with regard to documents for strategic planning and operating strategy relating to community resources. This form of control is clear during the construction of the plans, as it helps to clarify their general and specific objectives and to verify the consistency of the proposed action strategy with the stated purposes and with the current situation in the region and in the sectors affected. This type of analysis is carried out by independent experts who are not directly involved in the creation or management of the action. Furthermore, the region has developed a monitoring system (or concurrent control), namely the systematic reading of the progress of the individual projects.

This confirms the very widespread tendency to collect data relating to the funded projects predominantly for the purposes of reporting and control. Finally, the region has a system of post action control designed to assess the effects of policies, i.e. to control the ability of the actions already undertaken by the region to produce an impact on a particular area of collective interest (such as employment, pollution, domestic production, exports and imports). Despite its name, the evaluation unit, therefore, does not carry out any assessment directly but provides the necessary support to assessment bodies or political bodies and the general management for specific areas.

The possibility to interface with both bodies (the political body and the managements) gives the evaluation unit an important role for the promotion of dialogue and collaboration, and so also contributing to maintaining a decentralised system of corporate governance in addition to the use of results-based control and accountability mechanisms.

Summary

The regions have taken different directions based on the type, functions, organisation and the information content of their planning and programming documents (Table 3.1). In the regions of Tuscany and Piedmont, for example, the strategic options of legislature, indicated in what is called the Regional Strategic Plan (RDP), include an analytical specification in sectoral plans (such as the healthcare plan, the plan of public works, the plan for tourism), which constitute an important reference point for the management of their operations by the responsibility centres and for drafting the annual preliminary and multiple year budgets.

The regions of Basilicata, Emilia Romagna, Marche, Tuscany and Veneto have divided this document into Files summing up their sectoral policies and part of their FPD.

Like the RDP and also with regard to the FPD, the Regional governments have come to different decisions based on function, object and information content. In Basilicata, for example, this document was specifically given the task of integrating all the programming subsystems, as well as acting as the instrument used to divide the strategic plan into annual programmes, review strategic objectives, analyse the current implementation of the RDP and allocate targets and programmes to individual general managers.

In Piedmont, however, the content of the FPD contains little analytical information. The accompanying note reads "the function of the FPD is not to neatly illustrate the activities and spending of the Regional Administration based on its functions and powers, but to provide an assessment of the current status and future trend of regional spending and of the social situation, the overall picture of public finances, its objectives and the functions to be implemented, the areas of structural intervention that the Region intends to implement and where it will converge its programmes, projects and sectoral policies".

The introduction of strategic planning, as has been noted in the analysis of the regional cases, led to the decline of programming, or at least of the assumptions and models that inspired programming policies in the Seventies, which resulted in the ritualistic production of regional programming documents.

Steps were taken in Italy in the early Nineties to update the regional models of regional planning as a result of the experience gained in territorial and regional planning (such as the strategic plans in major European and American cities). From the situation in Tuscany to that in certain regions in southern Italy (e. g. Basilicata), conditions became ripe for a rethinking of the programming logic, triggering the development of negotiated programming models and the associated instruments (territorial pacts, programme agreements, area contracts).

The New Public Management (NPM) paradigm encouraged the adoption of strategic planning systems, represented by the logic of strategic design and formal planning. As regards the descriptive models of the process for formulating public policies, the same paradigm was developed to a greater extent in public administration systems adopting rational models or with a limited degree of rationality, which then evolved towards the managerial paradigm.

The spread of rational, long-term planning systems followed by strategic planning and management systems was facilitated by the implementation of an extensive process whereby management systems from the private sector were transferred across to the public sector. As with other public administration systems at international level, NPM logic in Italy did not focus on strategic planning but indirectly encouraged the spread of formal/rational logic and models.

Table 3.1 Comparison between Regions.

Region/ Analysis	Veneto	Emilia–Romagna	Basilicata
Tools	Regional Development Plan (RDP); Implementation and Spending Plan (ISP); Financial Planning Document (FPD); Budget document; Budget Report and the Management Analysis Report.	Regional Territorial Plan; Financial Planning Document.	Regional Development Plan (RDP); Annual Financial Planning Document (AFPD); Regional Development Plan.
Methodology	Based on the definition of objectives using a method of resource allocation.	Explains the objectives and strategies of the region; Control of the outcome.	Follows logic whose starting point is the definition of objectives, while considering a financial constraint.
Actors	Cooperation of various parties: the Regional Executive, regional structures and the economic and social partners, as well as the intensive exchange of information between the managers and councillors involved, in order to produce a document shared by the various stakeholders.	The region's entire organisation has to be involved; The relationship between the political bodies and the management are in part direct and partly mediated by the Statistics and Strategic Control Department.	Regional Executive, Promotion Office and the Evaluation Unit; Relationships between the political body and the managers may be direct or be mediated by the Evaluation Unit.

In regions where the regional programming laws changed the previous regulations (Law 335 issued on May 19th 1976), by introducing budget planning and programming systems using the model of PPBS logic (Planning Programming Budgeting systems), regional development plans and financial planning documents were also reformulated based on the logic of strategic programming.

With the onset of public governance, the distinctive contents and approach of public management, and thus the strategic approach taken by public administration, were developed and brought the following to the centre of attention: the relevance of interaction with the actors at various levels in the political and social context, the governance and coordination of complex networks in the social system; the external orientation, especially with regard to the economic and social climate.

Marche	Tuscany	Piedmont
Regional Financial Planning Document; Regional Strategy Document; Regional Operational Programmes for 2007-2013; Territorial Strategy Document.	Regional Development Plan; Financial Planning Document.	Regional Financial Planning Document and Preliminary Strategy Documen;, Regional Strategy Document and Regional Territorial Plan; Operating Strategy Planning Document; Regional Operating Plans and Rural Development Plan.
Strategies described in the Financial Planning Document affect the definition of the objectives.	Zero Based Budget programming logic. The aim is to redefine budgets on an annual basis, avoiding using the previous year's level of expenditure as a benchmark.	Determines the objectives, action plans and programmes and defines the financial relations on an annual basis.
Documents are drafted by the "Programming, Budget and Community policies"; The solution adopted by the region consists of offering managers the possibility to pro-actively take part in the programming phase, offering their input in agreement with the Councillor in question.	Documents adopted by the Executive and submitted to the Regional Council; Contribution of several stakeholders from within the regional structure, the general managers, as well as external parties, i.e. the members of the consultation committee; By adopting the method of consultation.	Documents approved by the Council and drawn up by the Regional Executive, in particular by its operational departments in conjunction with the stakeholders and general managers; Direct relationship between the political body and the management that does not require mediation by other parties.

It is interesting to note how the opening up of the outlook achieved via the transition from NPM to Public Governance puts the focus back on a number of previously neglected areas, such as public policies, the delivery of public services and public participation and involvement, alongside the attention placed on the internal management.

In the regions analysed, an interesting debate emerged between the political body and the management by way of a collaborative relationship aiming to contribute to the defining of plans and programmes to guide the activities of the regional government.

The plans and programmes expressed by the political body are consistent with the programmes and management objectives that guide the activities of the management; the use of forms of managing-by-objectives promotes accountability for those involved in managing the regional government.

It was also interesting to examine the role played by the Evaluation Unit, which in some cases acts as an internal consultant for the Region, as its operations are seen to be useful for promoting the introduction of new management methods and for facilitating the renewal of culture and dominant values.

References

AA. VV. (2000), *Programmazione Bilancio Controlli. Il caso della Regione Lombardia*, I. R. E. F., Lattanzio & Associati, Milano.

AA. VV. (2003), *L'accountability delle amministrazioni pubbliche*, Egea, Milano.

AIROLDI G., BRUNETTI G., CODA V. (1994), *Lezioni di Economia Aziendale*, Il Mulino, Bologna.

ANDRESANI G. AND FERLIE E. (2006) *Studying governance within the British public sector and without*, "Public Management Review", n. 8: 415-431.

ANDREWS K. R. (1971), *The Concept of Corporate Strategy*, Irwin, Homewood, IL.

ANSOFF H. I (1969), *Business Strategy*, Harmondsworth, Penguin.

ANTONY R. N., YOUNG D. W. (1988), *Controllo di gestione per gli enti locali e le organizzazioni non profit*, Mc Graw-Hill, Milano.

ANTONY R. N., YOUNG D. W. (1988), *Management Control in Nonprofit Organizations*, 7th ed., Mc Graw-Hill/Irwin, New York, NY.

BORGONOVI, E. (1996), *Principi e sistemi aziendali per le amministrazioni pubbliche*, EGEA, Milano.

BRUSA L., ZAMPROGNA L. (2000), *Il controllo di gestione nelle regioni: alcune riflessioni sui più recenti orientamenti*, "Azienda Pubblica", n. 1.

BRYSON J. M. (1988), *Strategic Planning for Public and Nonprofit Organizations*, Jossey-Bass, San Francisco.

CAIDEN G. E. (1991), *Administrative Reform comes of Age*, De Gruyter, Berlin-New York.

CODA V. (1989), *L'orientamento strategico dell'impresa*, UTET, Torino.

COOPER R., KAPLAN R. S. (1988), *How Cost Accounting Distorts Product Cost*, "Management Accounting", 69, 10.

D'ALESSIO L. (1999), *Intervento sul tempo. Il Controllo Interno della PA*, Atti del Seminario di Studi del 21 ottobre, Università degli Studi di Roma Tre, Roma.

FATTORE G., DUBOIS H. F. W. AND LAPENTA A. (2012), *Measuring New Public Management and Governance in Political Debate*, "Public Administration Review", 72 (2): 218-227.

FRIEDBERG E. (1996), *Power and Rules: The Organizational Dynamics of Collective Action*, London, Avebury.

GARLATTI A., PEZZANI F. (2000), *I sistemi di programmazione e controllo negli enti locali. Progettazione, sviluppo e impiego*, Etas, Milano.

GUARINI E. (2003), *Un modello di riferimento per la progettazione dei meccanismi di accountability delle aziende pubbliche*, AA. VV., *L'accountability delle amministrazioni pubbliche*, Egea, Milano.

HOODGE L. AND MARKS G. (1996), *Europe with Regions: Channels of Regional Representation in the European Union*, "The Journal of Federalism", 2 (1).

HUGHES O. E. (1998), *Public Management and Administration*, Macmillan Press, London.

INTRIERI A. (1980), *Il sistema di impresa e le indagini quantitative per la formulazione di giudizi di convenienza economica*, Tipolito Zona, Messina.

JONES R., PENDLEBURY M. (1992), *Public Sector Accounting*, Pitman Publishing London.

LARSSON T., NOMDEN K., PETITEVILLE F. (1999), *The Intermediate Level of Government in European States,* European Institute of Public Administration, Maastricht.

LATTANZIO E. (2000), *Il ridisegno dei modelli di governance come strumento per il cambiamento delle regioni,* I. R. E. F. E LATTANZIO E ASSOCIATI (a cura di), *Programmazione, bilancio e controlli. Il caso della regione Lombardia,* I. R. E. F. e Lattanzio e Associati, Lattanzio & Associati, Milano.

LATTANZIO E. (2000), *La nuova struttura del bilancio per unità previsionali di base, Programmazione Bilancio Controlli. Il caso della Regione Lombardia,* I. R. E. F., Lattanzio & Associati, Milano.

LEACH S., STEWART J., WALSH K., (1994), *The Changing Organisation and Management of Local Government,* Macmillan Press, London.

LE GALÉS P., LEQUENSE C. (1998), *Regions of Europe,* Routledge, London.

MARCH J. S., SIMON H. A. (1958), *Organizations,* Wiley, New York.

MARCON G. (1978), *Bilancio, Programmazione e razionalità delle decisioni pubbliche,* Franco Angeli, Milano.

MENEGUZZO M., ORIZIO R. (1998), *Il Programma Regionale di Sviluppo: il caso della Lombardia,* Azienda Pubblica, n. 5.

MINTZBERG H., (1993), *Power in and around Organizations,* Prentice-Hall, Englewood Cliffs.

MINTZBERG H., AHLSTRAND B., LAMPEL J., (1998), *Strategy Safari: a Guided Tour through the Wilds of Strategic Management,* Free Press, New York.

NORMANN R. (1977), *Management for Growth,* Wiley, New York.

OSBORNE D., GAEBLER T. (1992), *Reinventing Government: How the Entrepreneurial Spirit is Transforming The Public Sector,* Addison-Wesley.

PEZZANI F. (2003), *L'accountability delle amministrazioni pubbliche,* F. PEZZANI (a cura di), *L'accountability delle amministrazioni pubbliche,* Egea, Milano.

PORTER M. E., (1982), *La strategia competitiva, analisi per le decisioni,* Compositori, Bologna.

QUAGLIANI A., ROBOTTI L. (2002), *Il controllo strategico nelle regioni,* Franco Angeli, Milano.

QUINN J. B. (1980), *Strategies for Change: Logical Incrementalism,* Irwin, Homewood.

REBORA G. (1999), *Un decennio di riforme: nuovi modelli organizzativi e processi di cambiamento delle amministrazioni pubbliche,* Guerini, Milano.

RHENMANN E. (1973), *Organization Theory for Long-Range Planning,* Wiley, London.

STIGLER G. J. (1957), *The Tenable Range of Functions of Local Government,* Joint Economic Committee, Subcommittee on Fiscal Policy, US Congress, Federal Expenditure Policy for Economic Growth and Stability, Government Printing Office, Washington.

TROTTA M., SCAROZZA D., HINNA A, GNAN L. (2011), *Can Information Systems Facilitate the Integration of New Public Management and Public Governance? Evidence from an Italian Public Organization,* "Information Policy", 16: 23-34.

VERMIGLIO F. (1982), *Considerazioni sulla economicità e sull'efficienza del sistema aziendale,* Grapho editor, Messina.

WEICK K. E., SUTCLIFFE K. M: AND OBSTFELD (2004), *Organizing and the Process of Sensemaking,* "Organization Science", 16 (4): 1.

ZAPPA G. (1951), *Le produzioni nell'economia delle imprese,* Giuffrè, Milano.

4

Accounting and Management Practices in Italian Local Governments[1]

In the last quarter of a century, besides the new accounting tools, the regulation has also aimed at introducing some management enhancement with explicit reference to management models taken from the operating experience of the companies, in an attempt to influence the culture and behaviours of the players. This project, however, has substantially failed because it has never been supported all the way and it has been, in fact, disturbed by continuous legislative measures consequence of the various emergencies experienced by the country. This led to a modus operandi in which the accounting system has never educated the players on its use within the decision making processes as hoped for by the legislator. All this, however, instead of adjusting the correct application of the system and its tools to the problems encountered, caused the system to be questioned again, in the manners that will be described below, and led to the adoption of a more complex accounting system that, given the current shortage of human and financial resources in the local public administrations, is not going to succeed, in the opinion of the author, where the previous project failed, but will hold back the elusive managerial behaviours encountered in the last few years. The reminder of the chapter is structured as follows. Paragraph 4.1 introduces the general framework presenting the contents that will be analyzed. Paragraph 4.2 describes the reform of the accounting system in Italian local governments introduced in 1995, which led to a paradigm shift with respect to the previous situation, thus laying the basis for the passage to accrual accounting as explained in paragraph 4.3. Paragraph 4.4 presents the reporting and the relevant accounting documents, while accounting methodologies are presented in paragraph 4.5. Paragraph 4.6 describes the impact of EMP as a new management tool besides the accounting tool. Paragraph 4.7 deals with the future scenario that the new accounting harmonisation will introduce from 2015. Finally, paragraph 4.8 presents the conclusions and future trends in research on accounting and management practices in the Italian local Governments.

---

[1] By Andrea Ziruolo.

Learning objectives

After reading this chapter you should be able to:

- understand the evolution of the accounting system of Italian local governments;
- implement the introduction of a new harmonised accounting system;
- choose the accounting method to support the accrual accounting system;
- set the budgetary system within the wider context of the evolution of Italian local Governments.

4.1   Introduction

The reformism of the budget structure of public administrations has, in the last thirty years, gone through at least three significant seasons, all focused on the realisation of some native forms of "Planning Programming Budgeting System" (Canaletti, Morgese, 1998).

The aforementioned process is linked to the transformation of the environment in which the public administrations operate. In fact, as time goes by, the purposes of the companies, the institutional structures and the economic combinations change, and when the evolution reaches the point of inconsistency, a review of the accounting theories and systems is required, so that the latter may maintain their functions and facilitate the effectiveness of the company (Di Maggio, Powel, 1991; Meyer, Rowan, 1991, 1997; Caperchione, 2000). Following the law No. 42/2009 on fiscal federalism, which creates the basis for an accounting system harmonised at every level of government (Ricci, 2009), now we are living the start of the fourth stage of the PPBS, which, given the rules subsequently introduced, points towards a greater autonomy of the territorial entities only in its title, whereas, as a matter of fact, involves an increasingly stricter centralisation of the control levers on public finance, as a consequence of the effects of the international economic crisis of 2009.

This work addresses the accounting system of the Italian local governments[2] and the evolution thereof. The latter will be limited to the two most recent events, which

---

[2] The Republic of Italy (art. 114 of the Italian Constitution) is comprised of municipalities, provinces, metropolitan cities, region and state. The local governments (provinces, municipalities, metropolitan cities, mountain and island communities, i. e. associations of municipalities in mountain areas and islands, unions and associations of municipalities), are public entities the bodies of which (council, committee and managers) exercise their respective duties within the limits of the territorial context to which they belong (that is why they are also known, together with the regions, as territorial entities). As opposite to the local governments, there are the national governments that have bodies the competence of which is extended to the entire national territory, or which, although they are intended to operate within a limited territorial context, nonetheless pursue public interests of a national reach. The context of the local governments includes the territorial entities, for which the territory of the district does not represent only the limit of the jurisdiction of their bodies but also a constituent element of such government, the bodies of which are representative of the resident population. It is through these entities that the self-government of the community resident in the district is realised, according to different levels of autonomy that reaches the maximum level in the federal sys-

coincided, and will coincide, with the introduction (Legislative Decree No. 77/1995) and abandonment of the current accounting system (second part of the consolidated text on local governments – TUEL – Legislative Decree No. 267/2000, in which the Legislative Decree No 77 converged in its entirety) towards the harmonised one.

4.2 The 1995 Reform in Italian Local Governments: from cash accounting to accrual accounting

4.2.1 The current accounting system between accounting and management

The current financial and accounting legislation of the local governments was introduced with the legislative decree No. 77 dated 25 February 1995, and it represented the overcoming of the predominance of the legal aspects on the budgetary information so as to give room, at last, to the decision making purposes that must be supported by such information (Farneti, 1995; Ziruolo, 1996). Just like any other public administrations, the local governments have specific operating features related to the institutional objectives assigned, that determine the structure and content of the forecast budget (FB) and of the annual account (AA).

The principles and criteria underling the accounting discipline of the local public administrations lie in the law and accounting principles (Pcel) prepared by the Observatory; given that such accounting principles refer only to the general principles, in case of legislative deficiencies (Borghi, 1996: Ziruolo, 1999), it is possible to resort to the professional accounting principles and to the provisions of the Civil Code where applicable (nowadays, this principle may also be found in the regulation, under art. 3 of the Legislative Decree No. 118/2011).

Focusing on the regulations currently in force, the financial and accounting system of the local governments is based on the second part of the TUEL, which fully implements the provisions of the Legislative Decree No. 77/1995. In fact, with such Decree the government has not introduced any new accounting provision, but implemented, virtually to the fullest extent, the content of the previous system, simplifying the legislative jungle existing at the time, all of this in line with the then prevailing

---

tems. Consequently, the concept of local government is wider than that of local territorial government, although the first term is commonly used as a synonym of the second. Moreover, the State itself may be considered as a territorial government, although not local, and, specifically, the wider territorial government, since it includes the territory amongst its constituent elements. Local governments are autonomous governments provided with own by-laws, powers and functions according to the principles set forth in the Constitution and, being public entities, they may be provided with administrative (autarchy) and regulatory (autonomy) jurisdiction. Therefore, the allocation of functions (art. 118 of the Constitution) to the local governments realises the so called autarchic decentralisation, as opposed to the bureaucratic decentralisation where, on the contrary, the functions are assigned to peripheral bodies of State departments (or of a wider local government).

doctrine of the New Public Financial Management (Guhtrie, et al, 1999), but with the effects that we can imagine (Pollit, Bouckaert, 2000).

With the Legislative Decree No. 77/1995, the legislator intended to deeply affect the local administration system, of which it redefined the entire accounting legislation which replaced the old one introduced with the Presidential Decree No. 421/1979. The grey areas and the deficiencies evidenced on this subject by the previous legislation, and which allowed the emergence of anomalies, were thus cancelled. With the new regulation, and specifically in the part related to the executive management plan (EMP), the legislator intended to adjust the directional model of the territorial public entities to the increasingly pressing needs for a response based on contents and no longer on form, coming from the community after the end of the first Republic, changing the bureaucratic activity (Borgonovi, 1989) of the "management by tasks" into the management activity of the "management by targets" (Farneti, 1995).

The accounting IT system of the local governments, just as that of any other public administration, may be identified and commented on with reference to the three phases of the administrative activities:

- forecasting;
- management;
- reporting.

Therefore, operating documents and conducts correspond to each one of such phases, which are clearly defined by administrative-accounting regulations and accounting principles.

The legislator, driven by the reasons listed above, tried to facilitate the realisation of an information-accounting system capable of satisfying the information on the nature of the items of expenditure (reclassification by nature), as well as their destination (reclassification by destination) instrumental for the management accounting (Ziruolo, 2000).

Therefore, going back to the phases of the financial management of territorial administrations, it should be noted that the forecasting, regulated by the TUEL under articles from 162 to 174 and in the Pcel No. 1, satisfies the need of the technical structure to be authorised by the decision-making body to act according to the descriptions and content of the planning documents.

The authorisation documents of the local governments are the annual forecast budget (AFB), the multi-year forecast budget (MFB) and the EMP; the first two are related to the strategic-administrative policy and the latter to the administrative-management policy. Both documents must be consistent (consistency principle) with the policy guidelines (PG) related to the activities and projects to be realised during the period (program for the mandate period, or PMP) presented to the board by the mayor or by the president of the province, subject to the opinion of the committee, within the deadline set by the statute and formalised in the general development plan (GDP). A recent research identified an average consistency level of less than 30% between the PGs and the budgetary documents (Deidda, Gagliardo, 2013).

The management activities, regulated by the articles of the TUEL from 175 to 185 and in the Pcel No, 2, refer to the aggregate of the transactions that affect the accounting after having been authorised by a resolution of the council on the AFB and by a resolution of the committee on the EMP. The administrative activities must comply with the provisions of the financial and accounting system that governs the performance of the other activities necessary to achieve revenues and cover the expenses. The phases to be followed are: assessment, collection and payment for revenues, and commitment, liquidation, order and payment for expenditures. Moreover, during the management period it is possible to overcome the rigidity of the financial provisions of the budget by using specific accounting tools, the so called flexibility tools, designed to preserve the cost effective management from the strict authorisation and monitoring requirements on public expenditures, adjusting them to management needs.

With the reporting, governed by articles from 227 to 233 of the TUEL and in the Pcel No. 3, the legislator requests that the administrative activities carried out in the financial year of reference be evidenced, with reference to the financial and cash results (balance sheet account, BSA), to the economic result (statement of operations, SO) and to the financial position (statement of assets, SA) of the local government.

Finally the Pcel No. 4 regulates the preparation of the consolidated budget (Grossi, 2001; Pozzoli, 2006). With this principle, the Observatory anticipated the reform brought by the Legislative Decree No. 118/2011 that, pursuant to the joint provisions of the recently introduced art.147-quater of the TUEL (Decree Law No. 174/2012) provides for the mandatory nature thereof in entities with more than 15,000 inhabitants. In any case, the vision of a local government more complex than that recognised in the accounting practices, was already included in articles 2 and 72 of the Legislative Decree No. 77/1995.

4.2.2   The annual forecast budget

The Pcel No. 1 for the local governments, known as "planning and forecasting in the budgetary system" and approved in its first release on 3 July 2003, and subsequently reviewed with the document approved on 12 March 2008, under point 1 clarifies that the provisions of the regulations governing forecasting and programming are essential for the proper preparation of the economic-financial activities of the local governments. The same principle, under point 2, continues specifying that the subject of forecasting and programming is currently based on the discipline referred to in Chapter III of the Legislative Decree No. 170 dated 12 April 2006, in the second part of the TUEL, in the relevant regulation (Presidential Decree No. 194 dated 31 January 1996) and in the implementation rules of the internal stability pact of the local governments.

The Pcel No. 1, however, does not include the further requirements for the programming, introduced after its approval, such as the integration with the performance cycle referred to in article 4 of the Legislative Decree No. 150/2009.

The discipline of the AFB is contained in Title II, of the TUEL, dedicated to the "programming and budgets". This Decree, under Chapter I, concerning the "programming", identifies the following budgetary accounting documents to be prepared not later than on 31 December of the financial year prior to that to which they refer:

- the AFB (article 165);
- the forecasting and programmatic report (FPR, article 170);
- the MFB (article 171);

- other annexes (article 172);
- the EMP (article 169).

Whereas chapter II, governing the "competences as regards to the budgets", regulates the procedures for the approval of the AFB and the annexes thereto.

The programming activity is the process of analysing and assessing, in compliance with the economic-financial compatibilities, the possible evolution of the administration of the local government, which ends with the formalisation of the policy and management decisions that provide the content of future plans and programs. Therefore, it must be truly and accurately represented in the programming and forecasting models of the budgetary system and it represents the "contract" assumed by the political governing body of the local government vis-a-vis the citizens and the other users of such budgetary system. The reliability, adequacy and consistency of the budgets reflect the reliability and credibility of the Administration. The users of the budgetary system must be provided with the information necessary to assess the political commitments assumed and the consequent decisions, their burden and, with the reporting, the level of their maintenance.

Before going into the merits of the AFB, it is necessary to point out the intentions, besides the authorisation of the expenditures, of the accounting legislator in defining the entire regulatory schedule. To this regard, the framework (point 4) specifies that in the formalisation of the forecasting and programming process within the budgetary system, three key elements, typical of the financial and accounting legislation, must be taken into account:

- the multi-year validity of the system;
- the fact that the impact of the documents is not only of an accounting nature;
- the necessary consistency and interdependence of the different segments of the budgetary system (reference here is made to the aforementioned restrictions and partial and interim balances).

Contrary to what happened with the previous system (Presidential Decree No. 421/1979), only a political-administrative role has been assigned to the AFB, whereas the management-related role, competence of the committee, has been assigned to the EMP. In fact, prior to 1995, the excessive level of details of the AFB induced the political side to interfere with the management. Therefore, with the introduction of Law No. 142/1990 (art. 55) the independence of the technical competences from those of a political nature was established, principle (the separation of the competences) which was subsequently confirmed by art. 3 of the Legislative Decree No. 29/1993, now art. 2 of the Legislative Decree No. 165/2001. In order to obtain this shift, the level of details of the information contained in the budget has been reduced in the new accounting legislation, given that the management purposes had been transferred to the EMP.

This information, reclassified as detailed below, allows a competitive benchmarking (comparability principle) between uniform local governments by demographic class and geographic position, in order to trigger, amongst the different governments, that competitive process aimed at enhancing their actions, compared with what was done by the other administrations (Farneti, 1995; Sargiacomo, 2000; Ziruolo, 2000, 2001, 2002; Farneti, Padovani, 2003) and at benefiting from the relevant incentives provided for by law.

In the accounting regulations, the AFB seems to have a central role in the entire information system, since it is with reference to the AFB that the other accounting and programming documents are regulated. The MFB and the FPR, in fact, seem to have a secondary role compared to that of the AFB, only because they are defined as "annexes" by the regulation. This is due to Law No. 142/1990, to which the wording of the current financial and accounting system is subject.

Nowadays, the AFB no longer has this central role, which has been effectively replaced, both in the form and in the substance, with the assignment of the authorisation power also to the MFB, in which the annual information represents only the part related to the programming of the first of the financial years envisaged. Additionally, since the information based only on the amounts included in the tables and schedules of the budget is somehow reductive, with the FPR the legislator has intended to exceed again the contents of the AFB. In fact, in describing the forecasting activities divided by programs and, possibly, by projects, it offers a further element of knowledge that the AFB cannot provide.

The authorisation to act directly, on the contrary, belongs only to the EMP, which is mandatory for the municipalities with more than 15,000 inhabitants and in the provinces, whereas is optional in the other local governments. In the latter, given their small size, the authorisation to manage is the competence of the AFB and of the MFB.

The programming documents, therefore, prospectively express what the administration intends to do in the period subject matter of the authorisation, evidencing the resources available and their destination. Just like any other programming activity, however, the preparation of the budget must be part of the wider scope of the strategic planning, expression of the program for the mandate period.

4.2.3 The principles of the budget

The guiding principles of the budget of the local governments are set forth in article 162 of the TUEL. However, since the TUEL sets forth the general clauses and the principles for the preparation of the budget indiscriminately, here we provide a first list thereof dividing them by general principles and preparation principles. So, the general principles are:

- correctness;
- reliability;
- publicity.

Whereas, the principles for the preparation of the budget are:

- unity;
- annual frequency;
- universality;
- integrity;
- financial balance.

The principles listed above, also referred to as assumptions in point 35 of the framework, are of a general nature and are thus related to the entire budget – forecasting

(Pcel No. 1), management (Pcel No. 2) and reporting (Pcel No. 3) systems and not just to the forecast budget.

Besides the principles listed above, the Observatory has added other principles introduced, in point 56 of the framework, by the definition of accounting principles as those "principles, including the criteria, procedures and methods of application, that establish the identification of the facts to be recorded, the procedures to account for the events, the assessment criteria and those for the presentation of the values in the budget system, for the purposes of the performance of the programming and auditing processes". Thereafter, under point 57, the Observatory divides the accounting principles in general accounting principles or assumptions and applied accounting principles, and identifies the content thereof in the following point 58: "the assumptions of the budget represent the basis and general rules which must be complied with by the accounting principles applied to the individual items of the budget system".

The main assumptions are:

- understandability (clarity);
- significance and relevance;
- reliable information;
- consistency;
- reliability and consistency;
- reasonable flexibility;
- neutrality (impartiality);
- prudence;
- comparability;
- cash basis;
- accruals basis;
- compliance of the overall process for the formation of the budget system with the appropriate accounting principles;
- verifiability of the information.

As regards to the principles described above, the administrative-accounting experiences made and the doctrinal debate observed evidenced only a partial success in the Italian PA (Ziruolo, 1998), since the legal status still prevails over the economic substance. The existence of some regulatory deficiencies magnifies, in the literature, the lack of shared views between the many experts, with the consequence that, in addition to the criteria set forth in article 162 of the legislative Decree No. 267/2000, other criteria are available, other than those listed in the framework (Bellesia, 1996; Borghi, 1996, D'Aries, D'Atri, Mazzara, 1998; Anessi Pessina, 2000; Ziruolo, 2000).

4.2.4   Structure of the annual forecast budget

Consistently with the principles described in the preceding paragraph, the pattern of the AFB, introduced with the Presidential Decree No. 194 dated 31 January 1996, though maintaining the same structure, changes its contents depending on the type of local government to which it refers, given that the needs to represent the various local self-governments are different since the regulations provided them with different institutional functions. In fact, the Presidential Decree referred to above identifies four categories of local governments, according to which it is possible to characterise the contents of the budget (provinces, municipalities and associations of municipalities, mountain communities and metropolitan cities).

The AFB is, but this is true, as discussed below, also for the multi-year forecast budget (MFB) and for the balance sheet account (BSA, document of the report prepared on cash basis), structured in separate and opposite sections, that only in the summary sections (included at the end of the AFB) are shown in the same page since it is a synthetic representation. In the text of the AFB, instead, in light of the extent of the information present for revenues and expenses, the two sections are presented one after the other.

In the first of the two sections, related to the revenues, pursuant to article 165, second paragraph, of the TUEL, the (vertical) structure is ordered in titles, categories and resources, with regard to, respectively, the source, the type and the specific identification of the subject matter of the revenues. The section related to the expenses, on the other hand, pursuant to the fifth paragraph of the aforementioned article 165, is vertically structured in titles, functions, services and interventions, according, respectively, to the main economic aggregates, functions of the governments, the individual offices that operate a set of activities and the economic nature of the productive factors within the scope of each service, for a total of 1002 items for the expenditures of the municipalities (Anessi Pessina, 2000; Ziruolo, 2000).

The AFB model, prepared in the form with separate and side-by-side sections, for the expenditures-related part presents a reclassification by nature, as regards to the titles and interventions, and by destination, as regards to the functions and services. This dual information content satisfies a dual fact-finding need, allowing, on one side, the disclosure of the operations events and, on the other, their representation for management purposes, showing the resources absorbed for performing the different services. This purpose, however, needs to be supported by an accrual-based accounting system, essential cornerstone of the current as well as of the future accounting legislation now being tested.

4.2.5   The forecasting and programmatic report and the multi-year forecast budget

The FPR and the MFB comprise the annexes to the AFB (article 151 of the Legislative Decree No. 267/2000).

The models of the FPR, the contents of which are regulated by article 170 of the TUEL, were introduced with the Presidential Decree No. 326/1998 (Mazzara, 1998). In the programming process, the FPR plays a major role, since it represents the link between the AFB and the administrative and political principles that will be followed in the period under review. Additionally, the FPR must evidence the compliance with the principle of consistency, since it describes the management activities of the local government, which must be consistent with the strategic guidelines for the period set forth in the GDP.

The period to which the FPR must refer is that of the MFB, which, in turn, is equal to that of the budget of the relevant region (not less than three years), since, at least in formal terms, the legislator had assumed a programming system consistent as between the local governments that resulted from the planning of the higher ranking governments.

The MFB (Pcel No. 1, points 35-41), on the contrary, is the instrument that translates in financial terms the programs and projects described in the FPR, ensuring consistency and cash-based reconciliation between the multi-year forecasts of the sectors (public works and personnel) that, pursuant to the law, are addressed by other programmatic documents.

Just as for the AFB, of which it has the same structure except for the period of time, the MFB is prepared on a cash basis and its expenditure forecasts have a multi-year authorisation nature. Current expenditures, on the other hand, are divided in consolidated and development expenditure, evidencing a more analytical information compared to that of the AFB.

4.3   The passage from cash basis to accrual basis: the reporting

The modernisation process of public accounting in Italy, which is at an intermediate stage compared to the countries more evolved in accounting terms (Pine, Torres, 2003; Benito, Brusca, 2011), has been inspired and driven by the wider international process led by the IPSASs (Giovannelli, 2009; Cristiaens et al., 2011). As mentioned above, the accrual accounting method in Italy has been subject to an in-depth debate. Specifically, the reference made by the Observatory to the preface to international public sector accounting standards and the drafting of the first version of the Pcel No. 3, have been interpreted by the majority as being the end of the cash-based accounting in favour of accrual accounting. This led to a passionate debate between three parties: those who still believed that the cash basis had to prevail, especially as regards to its authorisation function (Grandis, 2006); those who believed that it should have been abandoned in favour of the accrual basis, so as to obtain more significant documents within the decision making process, assigning the authorisation function of the programmatic documents to solutions that would affect the entire accounting system only to a minimum extent (Anessi Pessina et al., 2006; Pozzoli, 2006); and those who had always been in favour of documents prepared according to accrual accounting, including programmatic documents, but without disregarding the cash-based documents, not only for their authorisation function and the culture of the players, but also for the financial requirements to be met, with the internal stability pact above all (Ziruolo, 2006). The current legislation is aligned to this latter position, as will be the legislation that will shortly come into force (Legislative Decree No. 118/2011).

Neither of the three opinions mentioned above denies the importance of the accrual basis information but, rather, its pre-eminence over the cash basis information. In fact the accrual basis information:

- allows a greater transparency since, according to the approach of the New Public Management, by adopting instruments popular amongst the enterprises its reading would be easier (Farneti, 2003; Pozzoli, 2006);
- allows for the harmonisation of the accounting systems (Borgonovi, 2000; Pozzoli, 2005; Anessi Pessina et al., 2008);

- makes it possible to prepare the consolidated budget of the group of companies that has the local government as its holding (Grossi, 2002; Ziruolo, 2002).

As from 17 May 1995, date in which the Legislative Decree No. 77/1995 enters into force, art.74 introduces more clearly the accrual basis principle in the accounting regulations of the local governments. Previously, the aforementioned principle was included in art. 55 of the Law No. 142/1990, paragraph 6. It established that the operating results should be recognised through the accrual accounting and evidenced in the annual account (AA) that includes the BSA and the SA. The fact that the preparation of the SO has not been provided for, however, prevented the application of such assumption. In fact, almost in every territorial authority this requirement has been interpreted simply as a fulfilment necessary to prepare inventories previously unknown to virtually all local governments, without subsequently updating them, however, after their first draft (Ziruolo, 1997). Even today, many local governments still do not have the inventory.[3]

Article 74 referred to above, now art. 232 of the TUEL, establishes that the "accrual accounting system is a free system", since the legislator himself has designed a method (art. 71, paragraph 9 of the Legislative Decree No. 77/1995) that would allow for the preparation of the SO and the SA even without a general ledger accounting. This option has been designed in order to facilitate the implementation of the accrual accounting in an environment that was not professionally and culturally prepared to adopt it (Ezzamel et al., 2008), by leaving the possibility to keep, at the same time, the double entries if so desired (Ziruolo, 2000). And it is indeed the granting of this option that led to the increased adoption of the bureaucratic culture compared to the management culture; in fact, only a very limited number of local governments in Italy have adopted a general ledger system[4] contrary to what happened in other countries with an advanced economy (Pina, Torres, 2003; Jones, Pendlebury, 2004; Alvino, 2005; Caperchione, 2005; Pozzoli, 2005; Luciannelli, 2009; Benito, Brusca, 2011).

4.4 Reporting

Through the reporting, the local governments evidence the cash basis and accrual basis results related to the calendar year in question. Given that the regulation governs only the accounting statements, the Observatory (Pcel No. 3) strongly demands also the preparation of a descriptive final document to supplement the accounting data, which must recognise to the administered community the right to know, participate and monitor the public finance. Consequently, the reporting must provide a structured representation of the operations carried out by the local government. Therefore, the "general purposes" of the communication related to the operations must provide useful information to high-

---

[3] A survey conducted by interviewing the managers of the financial departments evidences that of a casual national panel of 400 governments with less than 15,000 inhabitants, 14% does not have the inventory yet, whereas 63% has an inventory which is not up to date.
[4] The survey referred to in this note evidences that only 4% of the responding municipalities adopted the general ledger.

light the liabilities of the local government in managing the resources available and to take decisions. For this purpose, it must contain information (Pcel No. 3, page 7):

- regarding the sources, allocation and use of the financial assets and on how the local government funded the relevant activities, fulfilled its commitments and satisfied the relevant financial and cash needs;
- for the understanding of the performance of the local government in terms of costs of the services, efficiency and effectiveness.

Under point 8, the Pcel No. 3 confirms that the communication must also provide the users with information:

- specifying whether the resources have been obtained and used in compliance with the forecast budget prepared according to the provisions in force on the subject;
- reporting whether the resources have been obtained and used in compliance with the provisions of law and with the contractual requirements, including the financial limits established by the competent legislative authorities.

Under a political-administrative profile, the reporting makes it possible to exercise the control that the council of the local government has over the committee as executive body, in the exercise of the guiding and political-administrative control rights assigned by the regulation to the deliberative body.

Under the technical-accounting profile, on the contrary, the reporting must allow the verification of both the authorisation-financial phase included in the budget system, and the economic and property-financial situation of the local government and any changes of such situation also with reference to the economic performance planned by the local government. Additionally, it is not sufficient to achieve an overall cash basis balance to express a full judgement on the current and expected performance of the local government; therefore, the accrual basis balance in time is a key objective of the government, that is to be continuously verified and analysed with the review and approval of the annual account. To this regard, the report must allow for the real verification of the level of achievement of the objectives attained and of the realisation of the programs in accordance with the economic and financial balances, the measurement of which might not be always reflected by accounting data.

Therefore, the local government must give evidence, through the accompanying report, also of the socially relevant results generated. There are many local governments that also use other and more important tools of social reporting such as: sustainability report (Hinna, 2004), the sustainability report for the mandate period (Farneti, Pozzoli, 2006), the gender budget statement and the environmental budget, for the purpose of demonstrating the accountability profile (Farneti, 2004) achieved (Pcel No. 3).

4.4.1   The reporting of the local governments

The AA, pursuant to article 227 of the TUEL, is the document through which the administrative action is finally reported. It is comprised of:

- BSA (article 228);
- SO (article 229);
- SA (article 230).

Through these tools, evidence must be given of the operational results achieved, in financial, economic and property terms. Furthermore, although it is not requested in the first paragraph of the aforementioned article 227, there is an additional fourth document, provided for in the financial and accounting legislation as well as amongst the models (model No. 18) introduced with the Presidential Decree No. 194/1996, which contains the methodology provided by the legislator for the reconciliation of the financial results related to the financial year ended, in economic and capital terms. This is the reconciliation statement (RS, article 229, ninth paragraph).

The function of the AA is to provide a final statement of the results of operations in financial, economic and property terms, which the committee submits to the decision of the council. The resolution on the AA must be passed by the council not later than on 30 April of the financial year immediately after that of reference. Failure by the council to approve the AA, just as for the failure to approve the AFB, determines the dissolution of the City council.

The annual account, if limited only to the documents listed above, satisfies only the provisions of law, whereas if, at the discretion of the local government, it also refers to the details provided for in the EMP, it would allow an in-depth analysis more useful for management purposes (Farneti, Ziruolo, 1998; Ziruolo, 2000).

This information, moreover, is available within every government, given that, if the AFB is the summary of the forecasts of the EMP, the BSA cannot be other than the aggregation of the results obtained through the accounting management of the EMP.

The accounting principle No. 3, points 36-37, encourages the local governments to adopt a general ledger system, since this would facilitate the drafting of a true and correct reporting, as regards to the SO and the SA. The accrual basis accounting has only external information purposes, and as such it does not replace the cash-based accounting nor the analytical accounting. However, by introducing the knowledge of the consumptions for the period, it also represents the basis for the correct programming of the subsequent financial years (Ziruolo, 2001).

4.5   The accounting methodologies

Since the legislator recognised to the local governments the right to decide the methods for keeping the accrual accounting, four different approaches have been identified.

Within the context of the accounting system of the capital and of the results of operations (Amaduzzi, 1978), the bookkeeping method to be adopted is restricted to the double-entry method. Consequently, the link between cash-based accounting and accrual accounting has in the logic of the double entry method, its lowest common denominator of the possible accounting application approaches, which are:

- the metodo minimale (minimum level) system;
- the single system;
- the integrated system resulting from cash-based accounting;
- the integrated system resulting from accrual accounting;

The minimum level system is the system required to satisfy only the legal requirements, preparing only the SO and the SA through the adjustment and integration of the values of the BSA by means of the RS. In this system, the operating procedures are manual, i. e. not automated by the IT system, but registered individually by the operator.

The single system, simultaneously measures the financial and the economic aspects of the events of the external operations. However, it refers to a realisation method of the accrual accounting that is accepted only by part of the literature, whereas it has no operating validation.

The integrated system resulting from cash-based accounting, on the contrary, gets from the latter the database on which adjustments and additions may be made to determine the economic results of operations for the financial year.

According to this bookkeeping method, there are two accounting methods, whereas there is only one accounting measurement instrument (Figure 4.1).

Finally, the integrated system resulting from accrual accounting recognises the administrative events in the cash-based accounting, in the accrual accounting and in the analytical accounting. Consequently, in this system the cash-based accounting is perceived only in its authorisation function.

Also this system originally focuses on the cash-based events, therefore only after their recognition there may be the links with the accrual, capital and analytical accounting.

For the purpose of integrating the subsystems referred to above, (Bellesia, 1996) it is necessary to create a chart of accounts on which all possible links may be realised between the cash-based, accrual, capital and analytical subsystems, so that the entering of the data of each individual transaction, according to the double entry method (recording of the cash-accrual aspect), may automatically generate the relevant en-

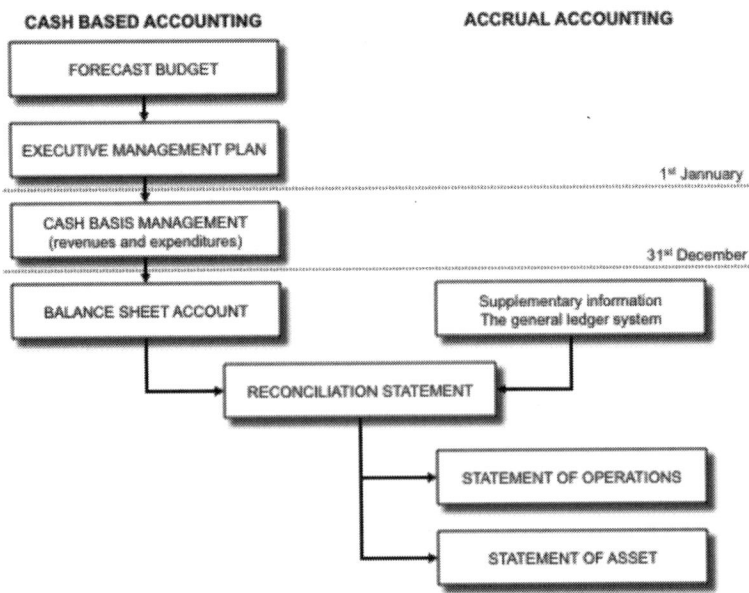

Figure 4.1 The integrated system resulting from cash-based accounting.

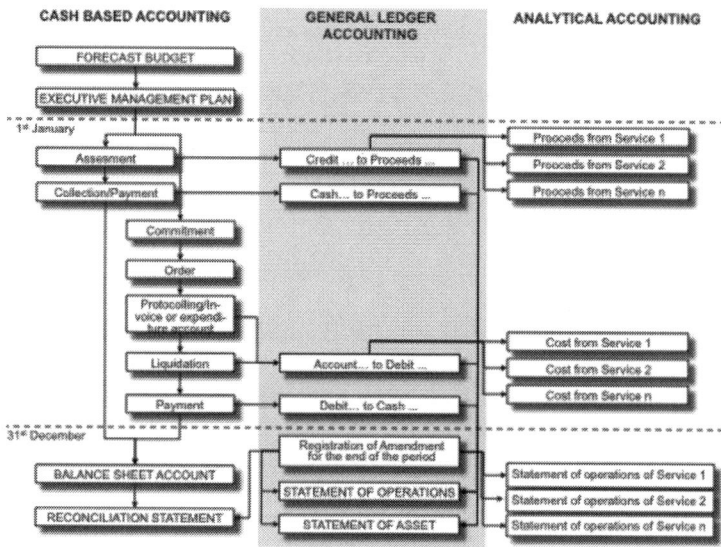

Figure 4.2   The integrated system resulting from accrual accounting.

tries, according to the single entry method, in the accrual accounting and in the analytical accounting (Figure 4.2).

4.6   The impact of EMP as a new management tool

4.6.1   A portrayal of EMP

The EMP is the document with which the accounting legislator intended to realise the segregation between political and management guidelines. In fact, it is through its content that the committee, in compliance with the guidelines set forth in the AFB and in the FPR, authorises its managers, or senior staff in those governments with no managers, to realise the operating targets that, together with the financial resources necessary for the attainment thereof, are formalised in the EMP itself. Additionally, the legislator has recently repositioned the EMP at the centre of the performance management cycle referred to in article No. 10 of the Legislative Decree No. 150/2009; in fact, through art. 3 of the Law Decree No. 174/201, it introduced a new paragraph, 3-bis, in which, besides expressly referring to the FPR as the document of reference for the creation of the EMP, the legislator highlights the fact that the detailed plan of the targets (DPT, article 197, paragraph 2 of the TUEL) and the performance plan (PP, article 10 of the Legislative Decree No. 150/2009) are organically unified in the EMP, consistently with the guidelines on the performance referred to in the resolution No. 121/2010 of CiVIT (the ministerial committee in charge of the coordination of and supervision on the performance of the PA).

The EMP, unlike the AFB and the other accounting statements required by law, has no model provided by the legislator, but only the preparation principles contained in article 169 of the TUEL and in the Pcel No. 1, points 56-67. Additionally, its preparation by 31 December of each year is mandatory for all local governments, except for the municipalities with a population of less than 15,000 inhabitants and the mountain communities for which the EMP is an optional document, except where its preparation is required in the accounting regulation also for these governments.

4.6.2   The intersection of accounting, management and organization in Local Governments

In accounting terms, the EMP is a cash-based budget that expresses the impact of the forecast budget on the organisation of the local government, through the breakdown of the resources in chapters, for the revenue side and, for the expenditures side, of the services in cost centres, and of the investments in chapters. The structure of the services and interventions should be construed so as to satisfy the requirement resulting from the need to provide the planned targets with a real operating content. Therefore, there shall be no predefined rules; the above mentioned structure must be instrumental to the exercise of the mandate, allowing the transfer of the responsibilities from the political body to the management body.

Consequently, through the EMP of each unit, it will be possible to know, through the further analysis, the responsibility centres (inappropriately named by the legislator "cost centres") in charge of the activities included in the budgetary services specified in the official statements, and the revenues and expenditures, recognised in the chapters, that will be obtained and incurred in each cost centre. To this regard, it should be noted that, within the scope of the allocation of the financial provision, this must also include the management of the residual assets and liabilities for the period and the three year perspective of the FPR and of the MFB, consistently with the authorisation nature of the latter.

Therefore, it is evident that the EMP provides a more analytical information compared to that of the AFB, which has only the role of political document, whereas the EMP has the function of a guideline on the operations, thus strengthening the principle of the segregation of the competences as referred to above. Furthermore, given that the organisation of each territorial administration is different from the others, the breakdown of the content of the budget in cost centres allows the connection between the organisational chart of the local government and that defined by the reclassification by destination of the AFB pursuant to the Presidential Decree No. 194/1996, provided that every cost centre must refer to only one budget service.

Having established the preparation principle through which the cost centre must be realised, there are other criteria, in literature, to be taken into account. In brief, it is possible to identify cost centres to:

- link budget services and responsibility centres;
- identify second level responsibility centres;
- break down services comprised of elements of different nature under the technical-productive profile or, in any case, to identify their aggregates of uniform transactions that result in one single product;
- ensure a more appropriate and binding authorisation of the expenditures;

- connect the responsibility centres and the "assessorati" (departments);
- find a basic unit of recognition with which responsibility centres, programs and projects may be connected (Farneti, Ziruolo, 1998; Anessi, Pessina, 1998; Ziruolo, 2000).

The line followed in this work, has in the cost centre the responsibility centre that, according to the meaning assigned thereto in the executive control practice, is defined as the functional context under a manager, who is in charge, in a formal manner, of the resources necessary to attain the predefined targets (Anthony, Young, 1992). To this regard, in fact, it is necessary to highlight that the definition of "cost centre" is inappropriate since, given the financial nature of the document, it should have been an "expense centre", even though expense centre in the literature is defined as a specific management responsibility (Brusa, 1995; Ziruolo, 2000).

The EMP, however, is mainly an accounting document through which the relevant managers of the expenditure process are authorised to operate; consequently, the accounting entries will be included in the related accounts, expressing the details of the general accounting framework. In too many cases, however, an EMP was registered that was still being used only as an accounting document and not as a performance management document.

4.6 Local government traditional practices before 1995

The accounting legislation of the local governments prior to 1995 was represented by the Presidential Decree No. 421/1979 and was applied with regard to models used in the legal framework of the Public Accounts and in rules that, sometimes, were still the expression of "royal decrees" issued at the beginning of 1900 and in an environment in which "politics" was included in every single phase of the administrative life of the country. As a matter of fact, it was in charge of managing as well as controlling the accounts, with a clear conflict of interests.

Particularly critical elements that characterised the previous accounting legislation, which the current legislation intends to overcome, may be identified in the expenditure phase named "commitment" and in the structure of the expenditures side of the budget. As regards to the commitment, the reasons behind its subsequent structure may be traced back to before 1979.

At the beginning, the commitments were divided into provisional and final (Carpino, 1987), pursuant to art. 327 of the municipal and provincial law No. 383/1934, which has now been repealed.

After the provincial and municipal law of 1934, the commitment discipline was represented by art. 20 of the Presidential Decree No. 421/1979, which has now been repealed. Such Presidential Decree established that commitments on the competent funds allocated were to be considered as the amounts due by law (legislative commitments), under a contract (contractual commitments), following a ruling (judicial commitments) or for some other reasons (administrative commitments), provided that the relevant resolution was passed prior to the end of the financial year.

Part of the doctrine (Brancasi, Ancillotti, 1986) criticised the fact that the commitment resulted directly from the legal obligation, since the commitment itself was at the basis of the assumption of the legal obligation, and not the other way round. Additionally, the further requirement of the prior passing of the relevant resolution within the financial year did not clarify what was its relation with the obligation incurred. As a consequence, the commitment was made simultaneous to the approval of the expenditure resolution and thus preceded, especially in the contractual procedures, the implementation of the obligations.

The discussion in doctrine on the contents and nature of the commitment remained, at the time, confined within the scope of the public accounts. Zaccaria (1967) brought the commitment within the scope of the administration activity of the local government, and qualified as such also the legislative and contractual commitments since they had, in any case, to be prepared at an administrative level.

With the aforementioned art. 20, second paragraph, within the local governments the notion of commitment meant a completely different discipline from that resulting from the third paragraph of art. 20 of the law No.468/1978 as regards to the notion of commitment within the State; for provinces and municipalities any reference to the obligation legally implemented had been omitted (Lupò Avigliano, 1986).

On this element, a weakness was found in this regulation which was adjusted by the Presidential Decree No. 421/1979. Therefore, unlike in the past, when it was simply a requirement on the budget appropriations, with the Legislative Decree No. 77/1995 it becomes, with specific exceptions of law, a legally implemented obligation. A corrective action that practice proved to be still insufficient to improve the truthfulness of cash-based accounting, often subdues to the elusive needs of the failure to comply with the aforementioned legal financial restrictions, and in fact the Legislative Decree No. 118/2011 provides for the enhancing thereof as from 2015, with the methods commented below.

As regards to the structure, on the contrary, the approach referred to in the Presidential Decree No. 421/1979 has been used by the local governments until the end of the financial year.

With the accounting regulation currently in force, even though the macro-classification of the budget remains formally unchanged, the allocation of the expenses was carried out in compliance with stricter principles, closer to the management needs of a modern local government.

The classification by titles provided for in the Presidential Decree No. 194/1996 mirrors that of the Presidential Decree No. 421/1979, except for Title IV of the revenue side and Title I of the expenditure side, where the items "amortisations" and "notional rents" are not included. A more in-depth comparison of the financial statements under the two regulations, however, evidences substantial differences.

With reference to the revenues, the scheme from the Presidential Decree No. 194/1996 is characterised by the absence of the columns related to the residuals and to the cash-based figures.

The part related to the expenditure, in the Legislative Decree No. 77, under article 7, paragraph 5, is ordered in titles, functions, services and interventions. Here, the titles represent the main economic aggregates of the expenditure side (current expenses, capital expenditures, expenses related to the repayment of loans and expenses related to services for outside entities) whereas the functions contain the groups of assets which are uniform as regards to the model adopted by the legislator, of which the services represent the individual offices in charge of the management thereof. Finally, the interventions represent the factors available to the service, which are deeply different from the previous basic unit, the chapter, used to describe the subject matter of the expenditure. This latter aspect has a great impact, besides the information contents of the document, also on the volume of the document itself, by reducing it, also following other changes, to approximately one fifth of the previous budget. The structure of the budget is similar to that of the revenue side.

The simplification of the cash-based accounting, as commented above for the revenues, led also to the elimination of the column related to the cash-based figures and to the residuals, since it does not diminish its information scope, but, on the contrary, it made the preparation and reading thereof more immediate. This choice, (Farneti, 1993, 1995, 1997) was also the consequence of the way in which the local administrations carried out the programming of the cash flows. The cash flows were determined, in bureaucratic terms, simply by the sum of the current forecasts and the residuals, and not as a consequence of the analysis of the flows that would have occurred in the following financial year. Moreover, the column related to the residuals, given that the institution, now abrogated, of the administrative peremption was still in force, did not contain all of the liabilities generated in the previous financial years, and those that were in fact included did not specify a legally implemented obligation, since the commitment phase of the expenditures only formalised a bond on the budget appropriations.

4.7 Toward a new accounting and management architecture: future scenarios

4.7.1 The completed regulatory path

For the purpose of providing the different governance bodies of the European Union and of the member countries with an information system to decide and, therefore, manage (Simon, 1977), the harmonisation of the public accounting systems originates from the inadequacy of the mechanism of the governance and of the accounting information of the different public local, national and European administrations. Every public administration, in fact, now has its own recognition principles and methods available, with the consequent heterogeneity of the representation procedures also amongst governments of the same segment.

The harmonisation system in question was implemented also for the purposes of the statistical monitoring of public expenditures.

Accounting harmonisation means the process for the homogenisation of the accounting methods and systems of the different Public Administrations, aimed at obtaining homogeneous and uniform information, so as to represent a "single accounting language".

The homogenisation of the heterogeneity of information pursues, more in general, the following purposes:

a. to allow accounting comparisons:
b. to allow accounting consolidations;

c. to allow a new and more effective dialogue;
d. to allow the tracing of useful information:
    1. for a better governance of the individual PA by its political-technical bodies;
    2. to increase effectiveness of both guidelines and controls on European policies by the competent institutions, and the satisfaction of the targets and public finance requirements by the PAs of the different countries (all of it for the purpose of limiting the deficits through the curbing of expenditures) (Deidda Gagliardo, 2013).

The harmonisation of the public accounting systems of the different governance levels differs from the standardisation of the national accounting systems with reference to the European System of Accounts (SEC 95). The first level, of an information-management nature is related to the purposes c) -d) 1; the second level, with an information-statistical character, is related to the purposes d) 2; they both pursue a) -b) purposes, and on these they must be reconciled.

The two levels referred to above, moreover, follow a double regulatory path for the accounting harmonisation:

- that with an information-statistical character, which is based on the Community laws;
- that with an information-management character, is based on the national laws;

The regulatory path based on Community laws and having an information-statistical character was introduced with the Community regulation No.2223/1996, related to the "European system of national and regional accounts in the Community". In fact, the establishment of the SEC 95 had the purpose of defining a common national accounting pattern, fed by every public administration, capable of allowing diagonal accounting comparisons between the different European member states.

The regulatory path based on national laws and having an information-management character, on the other hand, was first introduced with the Legislative Decree No. 170/2006, known as "Recognition of the key principles as regards to the harmonisation of the public accounts, pursuant to article 1 of the Law No. 131, dated 5 June 2003"; this regulation defined the scope of application of the harmonisation of the budgets and of the accounting systems in the regions and local governments, as compared with the budget of the State, and carried out a preliminary and not binding verification of the principles already existing in the accounting regulations related to regions and local governments

The regulatory path based on national laws and having an information-management character, received a new and more decisive impulse with Law No. 42/2009. This rule defined the accounting principles underlying the regional and local harmonisation in order to facilitate the preparation of the territorial budgets according to pre-set criteria horizontally uniform, as well as vertically consistent with the State criteria. Afterwards, Law No. 196/2009, known as "Law on public accounting and finance", laid the basis for the definition, through subsequent decree laws, of common reclassification and consolidation patterns, of deadlines for the filing and approval of the budgets according to the planning, management and reporting needs of the public accounts, and of accounting rules needed to standardise the accounting actions.

To this regard, the Ragioneria Generale dello Stato (General Accountancy Office)[5] identifies two different lines of action: a decentralisation of political and administrative functions towards the peripheral areas, and a first coordination of certain key central State functions vis-a-vis the European Union.[6]

As a consequence, the regulatory path based on the national laws and having an information-management character is divided into a twofold implementation track:

- central implementation track – Law No.196/2009 contains the delegation to the government for the adoption of successive legislative decrees for the implementation of the accounting harmonisation of the other public administrations, except for regions and local governments;
- territorial implementation track – Law No.42/2009 contains the delegation to the government for the adoption of successive legislative decrees for the implementation of the accounting harmonisation of regions and local governments.

The Legislative Decree No. 118, dated 23 June 2011, containing "Provisions for the harmonisation of the accounting systems and balance sheet formats of the regions, local governments and their bodies, pursuant to articles 1 and 2 of the Law No. 42 dated 5 May 2009", defines the framework and the essential principles of accounting harmonisation delegating the definition of the application details to the implementation decrees; moreover, article 36, paragraph 2 of the Legislative Decree No. 118, provides that the test procedures referred to in article No. 36, paragraph 1 of such decree be defined.

The first implementation decree, comprised of the d.p.c.m. (decree of the Prime Minister) dated 28 December 2011, approved in the Official Gazette dated 31 December 2011 and titled "Test of the discipline regarding the accounting systems and balance sheet formats of the regions, local governments and their entities and bodies, referred to in art. 36 of the Legislative Decree No. 118 dated 23 June 2011", is integrated into the track towards the accounting harmonisation of regions and local governments designed by the Legislative Decree No. 118.

4.7.2 The future accounting system

The general contents of the accounting harmonisation are outlined in art. 2 of the Legislative Decree No. 118. According to this Legislative Decree, the accounting system, cornerstone of the harmonisation, is comprised mainly of the cash-based accounting sub-system together, for fact-finding purposes, with the accrual accounting system named "general accrual" system. The unitary recognition of the operational

---

[5] Hearing of the Ragioniere Generale dello Stato (Italian Chief Government Accountant), on 1 April 2009 at the Fifth Permanent Commission of the Senate on the reform of the Public accounts.

[6] This is evidenced by the fact that art. 1 of Law No. 196/2009 provides that the PAs must concur in pursuing the objectives of public finance, defined, in the national context, consistently with those of the European Union, based on the principles of harmonisation of public budgets.

events between the two sub-systems must aim at the homogeneity of the general accounting system of each territorial administration and of each body instrumental for the latter.

In the d.p.c.m. referred to above, just as in the Legislative Decree No. 118/2011, it is specified that the unitary recognition of the operational events between the two sub-systems must aim at a "common integrated accounting system" comprised of the general accrual accounting sub-system that should allow the comparability thereof.

Annex 1 to the Legislative Decree No. 118/2011 identifies the general principles, referred to in art. 3, which must inspire the accounting actions of the regions and local governments. Moreover, compared with it, art. 7 of the d.p.c.m. in question identifies, amongst other principles, the general accounting principle of the "enhanced" obligation basis. Unlike the current accounting legislation, the obligation basis principle is "enhanced" in order to eliminate all alterations to which the accounting of the local governments is subject today, for the elusive purposes mentioned in the introduction.

According to the new principle, all legally implemented obligations, active and passive, that give rise to assessments of revenues and expenditure commitments for the local government, must be recorded in the accounting entries when the obligation is implemented, charged to the financial year in which the obligation expires. Expiry of the obligation means the moment in which such obligation becomes due and payable. Therefore, unlike what happens today, the assessment is to be charged to the financial year in which the active obligation expires and the credit becomes due and payable; similarly, the commitments must be charged to the financial year in which the passive obligations expires.

In order to reconcile the financial cover of the expenditure to be incurred with the new contents of the commitment, annex 2 clarifies that the commitment order must specify the entire amount of the expenditure to incur (financial cover), whereas it must be charged to the financial years in which the individual passive obligations are due and payable.

Essentially, the moment of the accounting of revenues and expenditures is a step forward towards the end of the relevant financial path, or to that of the cash movements (receipts and payments). Furthermore, by significantly reducing the formation of any current uncollected assessments and unpaid commitments, the results of the cash-based accounting will be similar to those of the accrual accounting.

The creation of the single language, within the regulatory system, passes through the integrated charter of accounts, outlined by art. 4 of the Legislative Decree No. 118/2011 and subsequently reviewed and detailed by art. 8 and by the annexes 5) and 6) of the d.p.c.m. 28/12/2011. The charter of accounts is structured in a modular form so as to allow reclassifications useful for information-management purposes, the information required for information-statistical purposes, and the consolidation of the public accounts of the different public administrations. Additionally, through the list of the divisions of the basic units of the cash-based accounts and of the accrual based accounts, the integration is realised between cash-based accounting and the accrual accounting.

The charter of accounts currently in force is not unchangeable, but may be subject to improvements resulting from the outcome of the tests being carried out.

The unitary and integrated recognition of the operational events under the cash-based and accrual-based profiles, results from the financial movements. Even though there is not a unique relation between the different phases of the path of cash-based recognition of revenues and expenditures, and the path for the accrual-based recognition of the revenues/proceeds and costs/charges, unlike the current legislation, the legislator considered it appropriate to set, with reference to the case of revenues and expenditures, the different management phases to which the cash-based principle is to be connected. Additionally, as regards to the unitary recognition of the operational events under the cash-based profile as well as under the general accrual-based perspective, either the double entry method or the single entry method may be used.

4.7.3   The future harmonised budget

The features of the harmonised forecast budgets are defined by articles 9-18 of the Legislative Decree No. 118/2011. Within the scope of the aforementioned guidelines, art. 9 and annex 7 of the d.p.c.m. regulate the harmonised forecast budgets based, substantially, on the following nine criteria:

1. overall forecast architecture;
2. nature of the budget;
3. role;
4. character;
5. time frame;
6. timetable of approvals;
7. configuration of the budget meant as a set of features of content;
8. structure and form;[7]
9. flexibility mechanisms.

The *architecture* of the harmonised forecast budgets, as specified in art. 9 of the d.p.c.m. dated 28/12/2011, is structured as follows:

- cash-based forecast budget:
  - annual financial forecast budget, obligation-basis and cash-based (annex 7)[8], of an authorising nature and complete with the general summary of the expenditures by missions, the general summary framework and the differential results;
  - multi-year financial forecast budget, obligation-basis only, (annex 7), of an authorising nature and complete with the general summary of the expenditures by missions, with the general summary framework and with the differential results;
- annexes to the financial forecast budget:

---

[7] Configuration of the budget means the set of features of content, structure and form. Content is considered as every element necessary to define the information framework; the structure is linked to the information-related organisation of the contents; form means the conditions, also of a graphical nature, to facilitate the reading of the document.
[8] The AFB and the MFB of the regions may be comprised of the MFB only, which should include, for the first year, the cash forecasts.

- the preliminary note for the regions and the programmatic report for the local governments, that comply with the new structure of the budget as referred to in paragraph 1;
- statement of multi-year budget revenues divided by titles, types and categories, with the separate disclosure of non recurring revenues (annex No. 7-a);
- statement of the multi-year budget expenditures divided by missions, programs and macro-aggregates for each one of the years considered in the multi-year budget (annex No. 7-b);
- explanatory statement of the administrative result assumed (annex No. 7-c);
- the list of the programs divided by investment expenditures funded through indebtedness and with the resources available;
- the report of the Audit Committee, except for those regions that have no Audit Committee;
- the list of the obligation-based and cash-based annual forecasts according to the structure of the charter of accounts (annex No. 7-d);
- composition by missions and programs of the multi-year restricted fund of the reference financial year n of the budget (annex No. 7-e);
- composition of the provision for bad debts (annex No. 7-f).

The re-introduction of the cash forecasts evidences the need to verify the existence of the cash balances starting from the programming phase.

The revenues section of the single balance sheet format presents, pursuant to art. 15 of the Legislative Decree No. 118/2011, the following structure:

- titles: based on the source of the revenues;
- types: based on the nature of the revenues, within the Title;
- categories: based on the subject matter of the revenues, within the Type;
- chapters: based on the specific subject matter within the Category;
- articles: based on the specific subject matter within the Chapter.

The type identifies the basic vote units for the purposes of the approval of the AFB by the Council.

The chapters and the articles represent the basic units for the purposes of the management programming referred to in the EMP and/or in the DPT.

The categories define the management forecast budget that is not provided for in the current balance sheet forms. The actual management program is comprised of the EMP/DPT in both cases.

As regards to the structure of the forecast budget, it may be useful to compare the provisions of the old form with those of the new one, with specific reference to the level of the revenue side Titles (Table 4.1).

It is clear that the main new features are represented by Title V (Revenues from the reduction of financial assets) and Title VII (Advances from treasurer/cashier). Furthermore, the legislator did not achieve a precise correspondence with the structure of the current charter of accounts: with reference to the first two Titles of the revenues side, the types coincide with the III level of the charter of accounts; as regards to all other titles, on the other hand, the Types are equivalent to the II level of the charter of accounts (whereas the categories correspond to the III level).

Table 4.1 The structure of the budget titles for the revenue side

Old budget (Presidential Decree No. 194/1996 and Legislative Decree 267/2000)	New budget (Legislative Decree 118/2011 and d.p.c.m. 28/12/2011)
Title I: Tax revenues	Title I: Current revenues of a tax, contribution and equalisation nature
Title II: Revenues resulting from contributions and current transfers from the State, the region and other public governments, also with reference to the exercise of the functions delegated by the region	Title II: Current transfers
Title III: Non tax-related revenues	Title III: Non tax-related revenues
Title IV: Revenues resulting from disposals, transfers of capital and collection of credits	Title IV: Capital revenues
	Title V: Revenue from the reduction of financial assets
Title V: Revenues from borrowing	Title VI: Borrowing
	Title VII: Advances from a treasurer institution/cashier
Title VI: Revenues on behalf of third parties	Title IX: Revenues on behalf of third parties and clearing entries

Having clarified the content and structure of the AFB, the presentation form thereof is outlined below.

For each entry, the following will be specified:

- with reference to the financial year being closed (N):
  - the uncollected assessments and unpaid commitments assumed;
  - the final forecasts;
- with reference to the financial year subject matter of the forecast (N + 1):
  - the accrual-based forecasts;
  - the cash-based forecasts.

The forecasts (only of an accrual nature) related to the financial years N + 2 and N + 3, shall also be included in the MFB. In such MFB, the non-recurrent revenues within each category shall be identified.

The single balance sheet form, under the expenditure section, provides that the contents must be organised according to the following structure (art. 12 of the Legislative Decree No. 118/2011):

- missions (art. 13 of the Legislative Decree No. 118/2011): they represent the main functions and strategic targets pursued by the territorial governments, using the financial, human and instrumental resources allocated to them;

- programs: within each Mission, they represent the homogeneous aggregates of activities aimed at pursuing the targets defined in the context of the missions. The realisation of each program is assigned to one single centre of responsibility (art. 14, Legislative Decree No. 118/2011). The programs, that represent also the link with the SEC 95, through the COFOG classification, are structured in lower accounting levels, such as:
  - macro-aggregates: according to the accrual-based nature of the expenses within each Program; the Macro-aggregates are grouped in Titles, based on the source of the expenditures;
  - chapters: based on the specific subject matter of the expenditure, within each Macro-aggregate;
  - articles: based on the specific subject matter of the expenditure, within each Chapter.

The program represents the basic vote units for the purposes of the approval of the AFB by the Council.

The chapters and the articles represent the basic units for the purposes of the management programming referred to in the EMP and/or in the DPT.

The political or decision making forecast budget goes up to the interventions in the old balance sheet forms, and to the programs in the harmonised forms.

The management forecast budget was not envisaged in the old financial statements, whereas, in the harmonised statements, is represented by the macro-aggregates.

The actual management program is comprised of the EMP/DPT in both cases (Table 4.2).

In the structure of the expenditure side of the management forecast budget, which may be compared with the current AFB, the main new features are represented by

Table 4.2 The structure of the expenditure side budget

Structure of the expenditures			
Old budget (Presidential Decree No. 194/1996 and Legislative Decree No. 267/2000)		**New budget (Legislative Decree No. 118/2011 and d.p.c.m. dated 28/12/2011)**	
	Forecast budget: approval by the Council	Missions	Political forecast budget: Council
		(EU vote) programs	
Titles			General forecast budget: Committee
Functions			
Services			
(EU vote) interventions		Macro-aggregates (grouped by Title)	
Chapters	EMP and/or DPT: approval by the Committee	Chapters	EMP and/or DPT: approval by the Committee
Articles		Articles	

Table 4.3   The structure of the revenue and expenditure titles

New budget (Legislative Decree 118/2011 and d.p.c.m. 28/12/2011)	
Revenues	Expenditures
Title I: Current revenues of a tax, contribution and equalisation nature	Title I: Current expenditures
Title II: Current transfers	
Title III: Non tax-related revenues	
Title IV: Capital revenues	Title II: Capital expenditures
Title V: Revenue from the reduction of financial assets	Title III: Expenditures for the increase in financial assets
Title VI: Borrowing	Title IV: Loans repayment
Title VII: Advances from a treasurer institution/cashier	Title V: Closure of advances from cashier or treasurer
Title IX: Revenues on behalf of third parties and clearing entries	Title VII: Expenditures on behalf of third parties and clearing entries

Title III (Expenditures due to the increase of financial assets) and Title V (Closure of advances from cashier/treasurer institution). Tithe II of the old form, within the context of the harmonised budget, has been divided into Titles II and III.

The harmonised budget presents the following form (Table 4.3).

The new features contained in the d.p.c.m. that have the greater impact on the system of the preventive recognition, include, but are not limited to: the restricted multi-year fund (fondo pluriennale vincolato) and the provisions for bad debts (fondo svalutazione crediti). If the first is the real new element, consequence of the introduction of the enhanced obligation basis principle, the second is a new implementation of the current institution which is already supported by regulations that make it mandatory (Ricci, 1998; Ziruolo, 2000, 2013).

For the purposes of this work, the reporting does not present any particularly interesting elements other than those already discussed with reference to the programming. The only exception, for accountability purposes, is the Legislative Decree No. 118 that, under art. 11, requires the preparation of a simplified reporting for the citizens, to be disclosed through the relevant institutional website. Additionally, as a supplement of the reports, the same article provides for the realisation of a system of simple result indicators which can be measured, and which are referred to budget programs, delegating its general discipline to Title IV, articles 17-18 of the d.p.c.m. dated 28/12/2011.[9]

---

[9] The specific discipline of the indicators system has been delegated to the dpcm dated 18/09/2012, for the PAs referred to in art. 1, paragraph 2, of the law No. 196 dated 31 December 2009, except for the regions, the local governments, their entities and instrumental bodies and the entities of the National Health Service, regulated by the Legislative Decree No. 118/2011

4.8   Conclusions

The evolution framework outlined evidences the alternation of the accounting systems of the local governments from 1979 to date. Such systems have never been fully implemented and, probably, they will never be, due to the administrative culture of the players involved, even more than due to their professionalism.

In Italy, the simultaneous lack of political structures capable of preparing their own leaders to the management of public affairs, has meant that, in the second Republic, the majority of the decision making persons arrived at government positions without an adequate preparation. Moreover, the spending review, to which, in the last decade, the territorial public administration has been subject, since it was carried out with linear cuts to the public expenditure and not through paths for the streamlining of the activities performed, particularly as regards to the personnel, generated a slow emptying of the professional profiles of the territorial public organisations, preventing the generation renewal.[10] This condition, together with the aforementioned inadequacy of the politicians, led to a destructive mix of the results which may be clearly seen today.

Consequently, with less financial and human resources compared with the previous years, with a collective sentiment of disaffection towards the PAs, within the context of reorganisation of the entire public system, further considering that more than 75% of the local governments has less than 5,000 inhabitants and that the cuts referred to above have a greater impact on such governments compared to the other municipalities, in the opinion of the author the harmonisation will not achieve the desired changes because new needs will probably come to light, driven by an emergency of which all the conditions can already be seen, that will cause the relevance of the new accounting legislation to be overshadowed.

The principle of the enhanced cash basis will certainly prevail so that the national accounts, too often altered by the numerous local needs to satisfy the internal stability pact and to maintain the level of the services delivered, could regain credibility. And it is just as certain that the general accrual accounting will be introduced and that the consolidated budget will be prepared. This will avoid the need to shift on the affiliate bodies the debt of their parent governments and the relevant patronage systems, but what should have made the so called turning point possible has not been correctly introduced. In fact, the desired planning for the definition of the missions and of the programs referred to in the Legislative Decree No. 118/20121, with the usual exceptions, shall have to wait.

Having identified the vulnus of the system in the culture of the players, in the opinion of the author, the local governments have already available the solutions to overcome the problems faced today, i. e. the auditors and performance assessment

---

and by the dpcm dated 28/12/2011. Therefore, the dpcm dated 18/09/2011 does not apply to regions and local governments, but it is believed that, appropriately, its contents might provide the guidelines, on an optional basis, for the preparation of the indicators system.

[10] The Dipartimento della Funzione pubblica (Department of public administration) reports that the average age of the employees of local governments is over 50 years.

bodies. The aforementioned competences, however, should at least be relieved from the many tasks related to the administrative regularity by which they are now being strangled. This would make it possible to assert the business principles of consistency, reliability and correctness of the programming documents of the respective governments, by not considering them as simple declarations of principles, and to relaunch the role of the territorial governments as engine for the local development.

Summary

The chapter has led the evolution path of the accounting legislation of local governments from the entry into force of the Presidential Decree No. 421/1979 to date, when we are creating the conditions for the introduction, starting from 2015, of the next legislation.

After having introduced the environmental challenges in which the territorial public administrations operate, for the purposes of this work the main problems have been highlighted, such as the reliability of the cash-based recognitions and of the procedure for the commitment of the expenses, as well as the quality of the accounting information.

On this latter aspect, particular attention was paid to the EMP, as the main operational tool provided for in the regulation in favour of the public management and as a connection point between the current accounting system of the local governments and the next one. Finally, with reference to the shift to an accrual system, even if not as exclusive as provided for by the regulation, the principles and methodology have been provided which are necessary for the completion of this shift in compliance with the law and the decision making processes.

References

ALVINO F. (2005), *Il sistema contabile delle pubbliche amministrazioni: l'esperienza francese*, in FARNETI G., POZZOLI S., *Principi e sistemi contabili negli enti locali. Il panorama internazionale, le prospettive in Italia*, Franco Angeli, Milano.

AMADUZZI A. (1978), *L'azienda nel suo sistema e nell'ordine delle sue rilevazioni*, UTET, Torino.

ANESSI PESSINA E. (1998), *Il piano esecutivo di gestione: un'analisi critica della letteratura*, "Azienda Pubblica", n. 5.

ANESSI PESSINA E. (2000), *La contabilità delle aziende pubbliche. Contabilità finanziaria e contabilità generale negli enti locali*, EGEA, Milano.

ANESSI PESSINA A., BORGONOVI E., CANTÙ E., SICILIA M., STECCOLINI I. (2008), *Alcune proposte per una riforma dell'ordinamento contabile degli enti locali*, "Azienda Pubblica", n. 1.

ANESSI PESSINA A., STECCOLINI I. (2007), *Contabilità finanziaria ed economico-patrimoniale: una convivenza forzata?*, "Azienda Pubblica", n. 2.

ANTONY, R. N. (2000), *The Fatal Defect in the Federal Accounting System*, "Public Budgeting and Finance", Vol. 20 No. 4: 1-10.

ANTHONY R. N., YOUNG D. W. (1984), *Management Control in Nonprofit Organizations*, Irwin.

BELLESIA M. (1996), *Manuale di contabilità per gli enti locali*, Editrice CEL.

BENITO, B. L., BRUSCA, I. (2004), *International Classification of Local Government Accounting System*, "Journal of Comparative Policy Analysis", Vol. 6 No. 1: 57-80.

BENITO, B. L., BRUSCA, I., MONTESINOS, V. (2007), *The Harmonization of Government Financial Information Systems: the Role of the IPSASs*, "International Review of Administrative Sciences", n. 73: 294-317.

BERGMAN A. (2008), *Public Sector Financial Management*, FT Prentice Hall.

BISIO L., MASTROGIUSEPPE P. (1996), *Il piano esecutivo di gestione*, Il Sole 24 Ore, Milano.

BOCCALETTI V. (2001), *Osservazioni sulla contabilità finanziaria e sul concetto di impegno*, Finanza locale, n. 9: 1181.

BONETTI S. (2010), *L'applicazione degli IPSAS agli enti locali nell'ambito del New Public Management Approach: alcune riflessioni*, "Azienda Pubblica", n. 2.

BORGHI A. (1996), *Il conto del patrimonio*, "Azienditalia", n. 6.

BORGONOVI E. (1988), *I concetti di controllo burocratico e controllo manageriale nella pubblica amministrazione*, "Azienda Pubblica", n. 1.

BORGONOVI E. (1996), *Princìpi e sistemi per le amministrazioni pubbliche*, EGEA, Milano.

BRANCASI A., ANCILLOTTI A. (1986), *L'ordinamento finanziario e contabile degli enti locali*, Maggioli, Rimini, p. 163.

BROADBENT, J., LAUGHLIN R. (1998), *Resisting the New Public Management: Absorption and Absorbing Groups in Schools and GP Practices in the U. K.*, "Accounting, Auditing and Accountability Journal", Vol. 11 No. 4: 403-435.

BROADBENT, J., DIETRICH, M., LAUGHLIN, R. (1996), *The Development of Principal-Agent, Contracting and Accountability Relationships in the Public Sector: Conceptual and Cultural Problems*, "Critical Perspectives on Accounting", Vol. 7 No. 3: 259-284.

BRUSA L. (1995), *Contabilità dei costi. Contabilità per centri di costo e Activity Based Costing*, Giuffrè, Milano.

BULIIVANT J. R. N. (1994), *Benchmarking for Continuous Improvement in the Public Sector*, Longman.

CANALETTI F., MORGESE W. (1998), *Nuove strutture contabili e controllo di gestione: i bilanci ammi– nistrativi nazionali e territoriali*, in BIANCHI M. (a cura di), *La Pubblica Amministrazione di fronte all'Europa. Tre culture dello Stato a confronto*, Società Editrice "Il Ponte Vecchio", Cesena.

CAPERCHIONE E. (2005), *Sistema contabile e prospettive di riforma in Germania*, in FARNETI G., POZZOLI S. (a cura di), *Principi e sistemi contabili negli enti locali. Il panorama internazionale, le prospettive in Italia*, Franco Angeli, Milano.

CAPERCHIONE E. (2000), *I sistemi informativo-contabili nella Pubblica Amministrazione. Profili com– parati e criteri per la progettazione*, EGEA, Milano.

CAPERCHIONE E., STECCOLINI I. (2000), *L'impatto dell'introduzione della contabilità economico-patrimoniale negli enti locali della Francia e del Belgio*, Egea, Milano.

CARLIN, T., GUTHRIE, J. (2003), *Accrual Output Based Budgeting Systems in Australia: the Rhetoric–Reality Gap*, "Public Management Review", Vol. 5 No. 2: 145-162.

CARLIN, T. M. (2006), *Victoria's Accrual Output Based Budgeting System—Delivering as Promised? Some Empirical Evidence*, "Financial Accountability and Management", Vol. 22 No. 1: 1-19.

CARPINO R. (1987), *Manuale del bilancio di previsione dei comuni*, Maggioli, Rimini, p. 41.

CHAN, J. (2003), *Government Accounting: an Assessment of Theory, Purposes and Standards*, "Public Money and Management", Vol. 23, No. 1: 13-20.

CHOW, D., HUMPHREY, C., MOLL, J. (2007), *Developing Whole of Government Accounting in the UK: Grand Claims, Practical Complexities and a Suggested Future Research Agenda*, "Financial Accountability and Management", Vol. 23 No. 1: 27-54,.

CHRISTENSEN, T., LAEGRAID, P. (2007), *Transcending New Public Management. The Transformation of Public Sector Reforms,* Ashgate Publishing Company, Furnham.

CHRISTIAENS, J., REYNIERS, B., ROLLÈ, C. (2010), *Impact of IPSAS in Reforming Governmental Financial Information Systems: a Comparative Study,* "International Review of Administrative Sciences", Vol. 76 No. 3: 537-554.

D'ARIES C., D'ATRI A., MAZZARA L. (1998), *Il sistema informativo contabile. Dalla programmazione alla rendicontazione dei risultati,* IPSOA, Milano.

DEIDDA GAGLIARDO E. (2002), *La creazione del valore nell'ente locale. Il nuovo modello di governo economico,* Giuffrè, Milano.

DEIDDA GAGLIARDO E. (2007), *Il sistema multidimensionale di programmazione a supporto della governance locale,* Giuffrè, Milano.

DEIDDA GAGLIARDO E. (2013), *L'armonizzazione del sistema contabile degli enti locali,* in ZIRUOLO A. (a cura di), *Contabilità e bilancio degli enti locali,* Maggioli, Rimini.

DEIDDA GAGLIARDO E., BIGONI M. (2012), *Il Piano della Performance nei Comuni medi. La proposta di un nuovo modello per superare l'inadeguatezza delle prime applicazioni,* "Rivista RIREA", maggio-giugno.

DI MAGGIO P. J., POWELL W. (1991), *The New Istitutionalism in Organisational Analysis,* The University of Chicago Press.

DI MAGGIO P. J., POWELL W. (1983), *The Iron Cage Revisited: Institutional Isomorphism and Collective Rationality in Organizational Fields,* "American Sociological Review".

EZZAMEL, M., WILLMOTT, H., WORTHINGTON, F. (2008), *Manufacturing Shareholder Value: The Role of Accounting in Organizational Transformation,* "Accounting, Organizations and Society".

EZZAMEL, M., HYNDMAN, N., JOHNSEN, A., LAPSLEY I., PALLOT J. (2007), *Experiencing Institutionalization: the Development of New Budgets in the U. K. Devolved Bodies,* "Accounting, Auditing and Accountability Journal", Vol. 20 No. 1: 11-40.

FARNETI F. (2004), *Il progressivo affermarsi del principio di accountability negli enti locali. Le implicazioni di tipo manageriale,* Franco Angeli, Milano.

FARNETI G. (1993), *Il bilancio dell'ente locale,* Giappichelli, Torino.

FARNETI G. (1995), *Introduzione all'economia dell'azienda pubblica,* Giappichelli, Torino.

FARNETI G. (1996), *Gestione e contabilità dell'ente locale,* Maggioli, Rimini.

FARNETI G. (1997), *Il bilancio dell'ente locale,* seconda edizione, Giappichelli, Torino.

FARNETI G. (1999), *Verso una nuova definizione di "azienda", con quali conseguenze sull'economia aziendale: prime riflessioni,* "Rirea", n. 7-8.

FARNETI G., MAZZARA L., SAVIOLI G. (1996), *Il sistema degli indicatori negli enti locali,* Giappichelli, Torino.

FARNETI G., PADOVANI E. (2003), IL *check up dell'ente locale,* Il Sole 24 Ore, Milano.

FARNETI G., POZZOLI S. (a cura di) (2005), *Principi e sistemi contabili negli enti locali,* Franco Angeli, Milano.

FARNETI G., POZZOLI S. (a cura di) (2005), *Bilancio sociale di mandato,* IPSOA, Milano.

FARNETI G., ZIRUOLO A. (1998), *Il piano esecutivo di gestione. Principi, metodologie e casi,* IPSOA, Milano.

GRANDIS F. G. (2006), *Le ambiguità nelle riforme dei sistemi contabili,* Rirea, Roma.

GROSSI G. (2001), *Il gruppo comunale e le sue dinamiche economico-gestionali,* CEDAM, Padova.

GUTHRIE, J., HUMPHREY, C. (1996), *Public Sector Financial Management Developments in Australia and Britain: Trends and Contradictions,* "Research in Governmental and Nonprofit Accounting", Vol. 9: 283-302.

GUTHRIE J. ET AL. (2005), *International Public Financial Management Reform: Progress, Contradiction and Challenges*, Information Age Publishing Inc.

GUTHRIE J., OLSON O., HUMPHREY C. (1999), *Debating Developments in New Public Financial Management: the Limits of Global Theorizing and Some New Ways Forward*, "Financial Accountability & Management", Vol 15, n. 3-4, August/November.

HINNA L. (2004), *Il bilancio sociale nelle amministrazioni pubbliche*, Franco Angeli, Milano.

IFAC – CONSIGLIO NAZIONALE DEI DOTTORI COMMERCIALISTI (2003), *Princìpi contabili internazionali nel settore pubblico*, EGEA, Milano.

HOOD C. (1985), *The New Public Management in the 1980s: Variation on a Theme*, "Accounting Organizations and Society", vol. 20.

IJIRI Y. (1986), *A Framework for Triple-Entry Book-keeping*, "The Accounting Review", ottobre, n. 4.

JONES, L. (2007), *The Function of Management Accounting*, "Polytechnical Studies Review", Vol IV, n. 7.

JONES, L., GUTHRIE, J., STEANE P. (2001), *Learning from International Public Management Reform*, Elsevier Science, Oxford.

KETTL, D. F. (2005), *The Global Public Management Revolution*, 2nd. Ed., Brookings Institution, Washington.

LAPSLEY, I. (1999), *Accounting and the New Public Management: Instruments of Substantive Efficiency or Rationalizing Modernity?*, "Financial Accountability and Management", Vol. 15 No. 3/4: 201-207.

LUPÒ AVIGLIANO M. V. (1998), *La riforma del bilancio dello Stato*, CEDAM, Padova.

LUCIANELLI G. (2009), *Accrual Accounting and International Public Sector Accounting Standards (IPSASs) in Universities*, "Rirea", n. 7-8.

MASTRAGOSTINO F. (2004), *Impegni di spesa, l'evoluzione dell'ordinamento contabile dell'ente locale*, Noccioli editore, Firenze, n. 6.

MAZZARA L. (1998), *Obiettivi e programmazione finanziaria: gli strumenti di previsione. La relazione previsionale e programmatica*, "Azienditalia", I Corsi, n. 3.

MEYER H. D., ROWAN B. (2006), *The New Institutionalism in Education*, Albany, NY: SUNY Press..

MEYER H. D., ROWAN B. (1991), *Institutionalized Organizations: Formal Structure as Myth and Ceremony* in POWELL W., DI MAGGIO P. (EDS), *The New Institutionalism in Organizational Analysis*, Chicago, Illinois: University of Chicago Press.

MEYER H. D., ROWAN B. (1977), *Institutionalized Organizations: Formal Structure as Myth and Ceremony*, "American Journal of Sociology".

MEYER J. W., ROWAN B. (2000), *Le organizzazioni istituzionalizzate. La struttura formale come mito e cerionia*, in POWEL W., DI MAGGIO P. J. (a cura di), *il neoistituzionalismo nell'analisi organizzativa*, Edizioni Comunità, Torino.

MICALLEF, F., PIERSON, G. (1997), *Financial Reporting of Cultural, Heritage, Scientific and Community Collections*, "Australian Accounting Review", Vol. 7 No. 1: 31-37.

MOONITZ, M. (1942), *The Entity Approach to Consolidated Statements*, "The Accounting Review", Vol. 17 No. 3: 236-242.

MOONITZ, M. (1951), *The Entity Theory of Consolidated Statements*, The Foundation Press Inc., Brooklyn.

MONTEDURO F., NARDO MT., NARDO L., PADOVANI E. (2011), *Misurazione, gestione e valutazione della performance negli enti locali*, Lezione 1, Riforma Brunetta: le logiche, le parole chiave e il ruolo degli OIV, "Azienditalia", I Corsi, n. 1.

MOORE M. H. (1995), *Creating Public Value*, President and Fellows of Harvard College.

NASI, G., STECCOLINI, I. (2008), *Implementation of Accounting Reforms: an Empirical Investigation into Italian Local Governments*, "Public Management Review", Rev. 10 No. 2: 175-196.

OLSON, O., HUMPHREY, C., GUTHRIE, J. (1998), *International Experiences With "New" Public Financial Management (NPFM) reforms: new world? Small world? Better world?*, in OLSON, O., HUMPHREY, C., GUTHRIE, J. (Eds.), *Global Warning: Debating International Developments in New Public Financial Management*, Capelen Akademisk Forlag As.

OSBORNE, D., GAEBLER, T. (1992), *Re-inventing Government*, Addison Weley, Reading, MA.

OSSERVATORIO SULLA FINANZA E LA CONTABILITÀ DEGLI ENTI LOCALI (2004), *I principi contabili per gli enti locali*, Roma, marzo.

OSSERVATORIO SULLA FINANZA E LA CONTABILITÀ DEGLI ENTI LOCALI (2006), *I principi contabili per gli enti locali*, Roma, 18 ottobre.

PAOLONE G., D'AMICO L. (2001), *L'economia aziendale nei suoi principi parametrici e modelli applicativi*, Giappichelli, Torino.

PAOLONE G., D'AMICO L. (a cura di) (2002), *La ragioneria nei suoi principi applicativi e modelli contabili*, Giappichelli, Torino.

PILCHER, R. (2005), *Financial Reporting and Local Government Reform – a (Mis) Match?*, "Qualitative Research in Accounting & Management", Vol. 2 No. 2: 171-192.

PILCHER, R., DEAN, G. (2009), *Implementing IFRS in Local Government: Value Adding or Additional Pain?*, "Qualitative Research in Accounting & Management", Vol. 6 No. 3: 180-196.

PINA V., TORRES L. (2003), *Reshaping Public Sector Accounting: An International Comparative View*, "Canadian Journal of Administrative Sciences/Revue Canadienne des Sciences de l'Administration", Vol. 20, No. 4, December.

POLLITT, C., BOUCKAERT, G. (2000), *Public Management Reform: A Comparative Analysis*, Oxford University Press, Oxford.

POZZOLI S. (a cura di) (2010), *Guida al bilancio consolidato degli enti locali*, Il Sole 24 Ore, Milano.

POZZOLI S. (2010), *La riforma del sistema dei controlli negli enti locali*, "Azienditalia", n. 8.

POZZOLI S. (2005), *Autonomia e sistemi contabili negli enti locali*, in FARNETI G., POZZOLI S., *Principi e sistemi contabili negli enti locali. Il panorama internazionale e le prospettive in Italia*, Franco angeli, Milano.

RICCI P. (1998), *Il controllo interno negli enti locali e il piano esecutivo di gestione: alcune riflessioni metodologiche*, "La Finanza Locale", n. 12.

RICCI P. (1999), *Il fondo svalutazione crediti nell'ordinamento contabile e finanziario degli enti locali: alcuni aspetti contabili*, "La Finanza Locale", n. 7/8.

RICCI P. (2000), *L'inesigibilità dei crediti e il vincolo di destinazione del fondo svalutazione crediti negli enti locali*, "La Finanza Locale", n. 2.

RICCI P. (2005), *principi contabili per gli enti locali e Principi IPSAS: un confronto impossibile*, "La Finanza Locale", n. 9.

RICCI P., DE LUCA A. (2009), *Una nuova riforma dei sistemi contabili e dei documenti di bilancio delle amministrazioni pubbliche*, "RIREA", n. 1-2, gennaio e febbraio.

RYAN, C., GUTHRIE, J., DAY, R. (2007), *Politics of Financial Reporting and the Consequences for the Public Sector*, "Abacus", Vol. 43 No. 4: 474-487.

SARGIACOMO M. (2000), *Il benchmarking nell'azienda comune. Profilo economico-aziendale, approccio metodologico, sistema di rating delle condizioni di successo e spunti di riflessione dalle ricerche*, Giappichelli, Torino.

SCIULLI, N. (2004), *The Use of Management Accounting Information to Support Contracting Out Decision Making in the Public Sector*, "Qualitative Research in Accounting & Management", Vol. 1 No. 2: 43-67.

SIBONI B. (2007), La *rendicontazione sociale negli enti locali. Analisi dello stato dell'arte*, FrancoAngeli, Milano.

SIMON H. A. (1967), *Il comportamento amministrativo*, Il Mulino, Bologna.

TER BOGT, H. J., VAN HELDEN, G. J. (2000), *Accounting Change in Dutch Government: Exploring the Gap Between Expectations and Realizations*, "Management Accounting Research", Vol. 11 No. 2: 263-279.

WALKER, R. G. (1978), *Consolidated Statements: A History and Analysis*, Arno Press, New York, NY.

ZACCARIA F. (1967), *Corso di contabilità di Stato*, Casa Editrice stamperia Nazionale, Roma, p. 436.

ZIRUOLO A. (1998), *Rendiconto di gestione: strumenti e metodi. La misurazione della situazione patrimoniale*, "Azienditalia", I Corsi, n. 3.

ZIRUOLO A. (2000), *Il supporto informativo-contabile degli enti locali nel processo di programmazione e controllo*, Giappichelli, Torino.

ZIRUOLO A. (2001), *Veridicità e correttezza dei documenti contabili degli enti locali*, "Azienditalia", n. 1.

ZIRUOLO A. (2001), *L'evoluzione del sistema dei controlli interni: profili giuridici ed economico-aziendali*, "La Finanza Locale", n. 11.

ZIRUOLO A. (2002), *Il principio della contabilità e dei bilanci delle amministrazioni pubbliche*, in PAOLONE G., D'AMICO L. (a cura di), *La ragioneria nei suoi principi applicativi e modelli contabili*, Giappichelli, Torino.

ZIRUOLO A. (2003), *Le rilevazioni contabili nelle aziende pubbliche non lucrative*, Libreria dell'Università, Pescara.

ZIRUOLO A. (2006), *Il sistema di bilancio degli enti locali*, Edizioni Simone, Napoli.

ZIRUOLO A. (2008), *L'ICT a supporto dei processi decisionali del management pubblico e di comunicazione*, in *Gruppo di Studio e Attenzione AIDEA, Innovazione e accountability nella Pubblica Amministrazione. I drivers del cambiamento*, Rirea, Roma.

ZIRUOLO A. (2008), *Dal piano strategico al piano degli obiettivi degli enti locali attraverso la balanced scorecard*, "La Finanza Locale", n. 3.

ZIRUOLO A. (2012), *L'organo di revisione: controllo sugli organismi partecipati*, in MULAZZANI M. (a cura di), *La revisione degli enti locali*, Maggioli, Rimini.

ZIRUOLO A. (a cura di) (2013), *Contabilità e bilancio degli enti locali*, Maggioli, Rimini.

5

The impact of management control on Italian Provinces[1]

The chapter aims at investigating the effects of the adoption of management control systems by Italian provinces, after the fiscal federalist reform and the "Stability Pact" to which they were subjected. This has required a strong cultural change towards a more results-oriented culture. In comparison to other countries which have already learned pros and cons of NPM based reforms to improve their public services performance, this occasion represents a cultural revolution for Italian local governments which never seriously applied performance management logics and techniques to improve their public services performance. In light of these premises, our case study describes the efforts of the province of Ancona to comply with this new efficiency-oriented logics. In broad terms, this study aims at showing how a new output-oriented culture, following the reform, has become to replace a previously "too much" outcome-oriented one.

Our case shows that the main consequence of the reform has been a change towards more tangible and measurable results: the financial ones. In fact, we observe general improvements in the financial and economic situation of the province. Moreover, the introduction of the management control systems has generated and is generating a first positive effect of internal rationalization of structures, activities, management responsibilities and resource allocation processes. Some deterioration of the social outcomes signals that is difficult to find a balance between output and outcome without using the debt lever and without a strong cut of the current expenses.

Learning objectives

After reading this chapter you should be able to:

• Understand how external pressures force public organizations to change their culture;

---

[1] The chapter is the result of a joint effort and formulation. However, Antonio Gitto (corresponding author), wrote sections 5.1, 5.4 and 5.6; Armando Della Porta, wrote sections 5.2, 5.3 and 5.5. The authors thank Mr. Lorenzo Torbidoni, Head of Budget and Management Control of the Province of Ancona, and Mr. Pasquale Bitonto, Secretary General of the Province of Ancona.

- Understand the impacts of management control tools on the performances of Italian provinces;
- Discuss the implications of the adoption of a new NPM based culture on the outputs and outcomes of Italian Provinces.

5.1   Introduction

Compared to other countries', the Italian Public sector reforms of 80s and 90s have not substantially affected the way public services were managed (Anselmi, 2005; Borgonovi, 2004; Farneti, 2004) and so they have not improved their performance. To boost the improvement process a fiscal federalist reform was approved in Italy and a Stability Pact was established in the European zone.

The role of Local authorities has become much more important following the reform of Title V of the Italian Constitution, which brings Italy closer to the organizational model of a Federal State (Bibbee, 2007; Mulazzani, 2006; Oates, 2008).

These federalists reforms increased the functions attributed to Local authorities (Municipalities and Provinces) forcing them to reduce the financial dependence from central government. How this new federalist model will function in the next future? There is a broad agreement in the sense that fundamental services should be entirely covered by the State, whereas the remaining services should be partially leveled through fiscal equalization (Osservatorio, 2006). How much the central state will pay for these fundamental services? It will pay the due, not more nor less. So, the main point of the reform is a new simple rule: the funds that will be transferred in the next future to local governments will be quantified by central government not using the historical spending criterion but the more efficiency-enhanced one of standard costing. What matters now is that the local service provider is an efficient one. So, an efficiency-enhanced criterion to quantify the right price to pay to local governments provider is that of standard costing (Weingast, 2009). Therefore it is of utmost urgency to quantify standard costs, to define homogenous measures to be interpreted as significant benchmark for strategic cost reduction initiatives that will be carried out by local governments (Anthony et al., 2008; Ter-Minassian, 1997; Guthrie, 1998).

In light of these premises our case study describes the efforts of the province of Ancona to comply with this new efficiency-oriented logics. The first efforts started in 2007 with the adoption of a new management control system. Some first results were noticed in 2009 when the Financial Statement of the Province of Ancona showed for the first time, not a clear identification of standard costs, but the quantification of the costs of the main services provided on the territory by drawing information from an integrated accounting system that included financial accounting, management accounting, economic-patrimonial accounting, and income and inventory accounting. Usually local government institutions don't know how much is the cost of the services they provide and consequently they don't show it in formal documents. Such knowledge has been useful because these costs have been compared to the indicators identified for each single service, thus creating a system that begun to allow internal and external benchmarking activities with the aim to reduce efficiency performance gaps (Camp, 1989; Camp, 1994; Leibfried, Mc Nair, 1992; Watson, 1993; De Toro, 1995;

Frost, Pringle, 1993; Kouzmin et al., 1999; Helden, Tillema, 2005; Rondo-Brovetto, Saliterer, 2007; Sargiacomo, 2000; Triantafillou, 2007; Sargiacomo, 2005) and, more important, to promote a change towards a more results-oriented culture.

In more general terms, standard costs as elements that bring out efficiency, represent useful indicators for the comparison and evaluation of public action. They reward and stimulate more efficient local government managerial practices. But equally important is the ability of local governments to diversify and to obtain more revenues by enhancing territorial attractiveness and not only to cut costs (Carnegie, West, 2005: 905-928).

This study, therefore, has sought to draw a reliable overview of revenues and expenditures of Provinces, and to assess their role, their operating efficiency as well as their ability to find a relevant part of the revenues necessary for the provision of services in their own territories (Robinson, 1998: 21-37).

Since an empirical research needs to have "study objects" (Fattore, 2005: 85), Italian Provinces were used as units and the "case study" methodology was used for the specific objectives of the present work (Eisenhardt, 1989; Eisenhardt e Graebner, 2007). This methodology is considered suitable for the study of a new phenomenon in a real context (Yin, 2008). Moreover, such methodology allows to elaborate new theories or to enhance the ones already existing.

This work presents the case study of the Province of Ancona.

The research is based on different sources, which can be broadly divided into:

- bibliographic, historiographical, and, in general, textual research (see Bibliography);
- empirical research through the analysis of accounting records, reports, questionnaires and, when necessary, interviews.[2]

In Italian literature there are no studies regarding the processes of adoption of Management control systems by the Provinces. Moreover, there are no empirical data of single administrations, which could show the effects of the use of such tools. Therefore, the present work is theoretically based on the analysis of literature relating to private sector management, on literature relating to public sector, and on the first–hand opinions of managers and public operators (Orelli, Visani, 2004: 587-606; Orelli, Visani, 2005: 381-400; Gori, Fissi, 2010: 369-387; Del Bene, Marasca, 2009: 285-310).

Such methodological choice is internationally practiced when dealing with studies on the impact of public reforms (Humphrey, Miller, Scapens, 1993; Schick, 1996; Pollitt, Bouckaert, 2004; Andrews, Moynihan, 2002).

Therefore, the study of the case of the Province of Ancona, by focusing on the development of a broad performance management system, cannot be used to make general statements but, rather, should be regarded as a specific empirical exploration of what is debated at the theoretical level (Yin, 2003).

The work is structured in the following way. In the next section we present a brief history of the Italian Provinces. Then we show at an aggregate level which were the

---

[2] The oral interview, subsequently transcribed, was made to Mr. Lorenzo Torbidoni, Head of Budget and Management Control of the Province of Ancona, and to Mr. Pasquale Bitonto, Secretary General of the Province of Ancona, in February/April 2013.

financial effects of the federalist reform that, following the Stability Pact, prohibited Local governments to increase their debts. In section 5.3 we describe New public Management main logics and tools (management control is a central one) that are the theoretical drivers of the this Public Sector reform. In Section 5.4 we analyze the case of the Province of Ancona. In section 5.5 we discuss the case and finally in section 5.6 we present some concluding remarks.

In particular, the paper is interested in understanding the effects derived from the adoption of Management control system (Anderson, Young, 1999; Caccia, Steccolini, 2006).

The study focuses on the reforms in Local authorities and within this show how management control systems and practices are shaped and reshaped (Markus, Pfeffer, 1983; Soin, Seal, Cullen, 2002). Thus, the main aims of the paper are to examine the role of Management control system in a specific context and how this was shaped as a result of its adoption (Burns, Vaivio, 2001; Burns, Scapens, 2000; Coad, Cullen, 2006).

5.2   The Italian Provinces Socio-Economic Scenario And Organization

5.2.1   A brief History of Italian Provinces

According to the Italian Constitution, a Province is a local territorial authority, whose territorial extension is inferior to that of a Region and includes the territory of different Municipalities (see Part II, Title V, articles 114).

Law No. 142/1990, in reforming Local authorities defined a Province as "the intermediate local authority between the Region and the Municipality", that "provides for the interests of provincial community, and promotes its development".

While in 2012 Italian central government discussed how to abolish Provinces, in 1859 (Law No. 3702/1859), the then central government, to legitimate the French Provincial system of Savoy, provided that the level of reference for Central political power was the Provincial level. So the Province became "a large association of Municipalities aimed at ensuring the protection of their rights, and at managing their common moral and material interests".

Provinces are the result of complex political and historical events, and have been affected by the territorial and administrative modifications[3] of the national territory (transformations, acquisitions, abolitions and new institutions): starting from the initial 58 Provinces at the time of Unification of Italy, today there are 110 autonomies[4] that constitute the articulated mosaic of Italian identities, all of which are intertwined with the history of Italian institutions.

---

[3] Historical data are based on UPI (2008) and UPI (2011).

[4] Because of continuous changes in the Institutional structures, abolishment of Provinces, and modifications of national borders, data do not always coincide with the observations made in the text.

Until today, every reform – either constitutional or ordinary, implemented or merely planned – has questioned the existence of Provinces, but they have never been actually abolished: as acknowledged by history, any attempt to abolish Provinces has been and is problematic, given the territorial and social-economic complexity of Italy. The reform of Part II, Title V of the Italian Constitution, amending the original text of 1948, divides the Italian Republic into different constituent parts and explicitly envisages the existence of Provinces. Looking at other European countries – such as Germany, France and Spain – it is common to find a third level of government. Indeed, from the Unification of Italy, the number of Provinces has steadily increased and has almost doubled: this has brought to a situation with intermediate authorities that are not homogenous as regards population and territorial extension.

In 1861, the Kingdom of Italy was divided into 58 Provincial administrations, and did not include the territories of Veneto, the part of the Province of Mantova on the left of Oglio river, Friuli Venezia Giulia, Trentino Alto-Adige, and Lazio – except for the administrative districts of Rieti (part of the Province of Perugia), Citta Ducale (part of the Province of L'Aquila), and Gaeta and Sora (part of the Province of Terra di Lavoro). In 2011, however, in Italy there were 110 Provinces.

Under the institutional point of view, 107 Provinces form the Union of Italian Provinces and are classified as such; three Provinces (namely Aosta, Trento, and Bolzano) are part of the Conference of Regions and are classified as Special Regions or Autonomous Provinces.

5.2.2 The functions of the Italian provinces

We have already seen that the law expressly recognizes them an active role in the co-ordination of local development, as a local authority intermediate between the City and Region, in the representation of the communities and in the promotion of their development.

The provincial space (wider than municipality) has emerged historically and was considered as the ideal one for optimal coordination between public and private entities (regions, local authorities, national governments, business associations, trade unions, etc.) and for new public service reforms (see for example L. 151/1981 on local public transport that considered the provincial area as the ideal space for an integrated local transport service network).

The province, (L.267/2000), carries out the administrative functions in the following areas:

- soil conservation, protection and enhancement of the environment and disaster preparedness;
- protection and enhancement of water and energy resources;
- promotion of cultural heritage;
- roads and transport;
- protection of flora and fauna, parks and nature reserves;
- hunting and fishing in inland waters;
- organization of waste management at the provincial level, bearing, discipline and control of discharges of water and air emissions and noise;

- health services, public hygiene and prophylaxis, awarded by the national and regional legislation;
- tasks related to secondary education degree and artistic and vocational training, including school construction, attributed by national and regional legislation.

The province, in collaboration with municipalities and on the basis of its proposed programs, promotes and coordinates activities and creates works of great interest both in the provincial economic, production, trade and tourism, both in the social, cultural and sports. The organizational forms of these activities is prescribed by public services laws.

5.2.3 The financial data of the Italian Provinces

In this section we present, at an aggregate level, the main components and the dynamics of the Italian provinces revenues and expenses in the years 2009-2010-2011. Such data clearly show how relevant was the impact of the Fiscal Federalism and of the Stability Pact in reducing their deficit (Table 5.1).

Table 5.1 presents the current revenues of Provinces in the light of Fiscal Federalism: in the analyzed period there was a shift in the current revenues composition: a decline in State transfers and an increase in autonomous provincial taxes (for example, the automotive sector: insurance and Itp, the Provincial vehicle registration tax) and also a decline in non-tax revenues. The net result was negative in the 2009/10 period (-2,59%) but positive in the 2010/11 period (+ 2,99%). Less central transfers, more local taxes.

Table 5.2 shows how provinces reacted to a decline in state transfers: they managed local taxes (+ 10,69% in the 2010/2011 period compared to the + 0,90% in the 2009/2010 period) as we can see in more detail in Table 5.3.

From Table 5.3 we see that Italian provinces increased, mainly, insurance car taxes (+ 18,80%) and provincial vehicle registration taxes (+ 7,74%). They lost the additional tax on municipal solid waste (-10,09%).

The decline of resources was not only registered in the current revenues but also in the capital revenues as we can see in Table 5.4.

We can observe a decline in the revenues deriving from assets disposal (-10,18%) and loans (-30,95% in the 2009/2010 period). Less loans derive from strict European rules (The Stability Pact) that do not allow local governments to increase their debts.

Table 5.1 (values expressed in €/000.000)

	2009	**2010**	**2011**	**Variation % 2009/2010**	**Variation % 2010/2011**
Tax Revenues	4.652	4.694	5.196	0,90	10,69
Subsidies and tranfers from the State	4.390	4123	3.938	−6,08	−4,49
Non-Tax Revenues	702	675	642	−3,85	−4,89
Current revenues	**9.744**	**9.492**	**9.776**	**−2,59**	**2,99**

Source: Supreme Audit Institution on data SIOPE.

Table 5.2 Revenues (values expressed in €/000.000)

	2009	2010	2011	Variation % 2009/2010	Variation % 2010/2011
Taxes	4.556	4.593	5.041	0,59	9,75
Other taxes	16	26	85	62,50	226,92
Special-Tax and Other Own revenues	70	75	70	7,14	−6,67
Total	**4.652**	**4.694**	**5.196**	**0,90**	**10,69**

Source: Supreme Audit Institution on data SIOPE.

Table 5.3 Main taxes (values expressed in €/000.000)

	2009	2010	2011	Variation % 2009/2010	Variation % 2010/2011
Provincial vehicle registration tax	1.134	1.111	1.197	−2,03	**7,74**
Tax on R. C. car insurance	1.929	1.984	2.357	2,85	**18,80**
Tax addition on energetic consumption	838	828	858	−1,19	3,62
Provincial tax addition on Municipal solid waste	335	337	303	0,60	−10,09
Provincial tax environmental	239	254	259	6,28	1,97

Source: Supreme Audit Institution on data SIOPE.

Table 5.4 Capital revenues (values expressed in €/000.000)

	2009	2010	2011	Variation % 2009/2010	Variation % 2010/2011
Disposal of assets, transfers of capital and collection of receivables	1.526	1.523	1.368	−0,20	**−10,18**
Taking out loans	840	580	585	**−30,95**	0,86
Total capital revenues	**2.366**	**2.103**	**1.953**	**−11,12**	**−7,13**

Source: Supreme Audit Institution on data SIOPE.

In Table 5.5 we can assess the dynamic of province current expenditures that show a tiny decline of −1,35% in the 2010/11 period. The main component of the province expenses are 1) purchase of services; 2) personnel; 3) transfers and 4) interest expenses (Table 5.6).

Table 5.5 Current expenditures (values expressed in €/000.000)

	2009	2010	2011	Variation % 2009/2010	Variation % 2010/2011
Personnel	2.331	2.281	2.219	–2,15	–2,72
Purchase of goods	134	112	109	–16,42	–2,68
Purchase of services	3.150	3.624	3.624	3,25	0,00
Rent third party assets	219	214	222	–2,28	3,74
Transfers	1.723	1.557	1.512	–8,47	–4,12
Interest expenses	464	431	434	–7,11	0,70
Taxes	186	185	179	–0,54	–3,24
Other current expenditure	111	140	149	26,13	6,43
Total current expenditure	**8.678**	**8.564**	**8.448**	**–1,31**	**–1,35**

Source: Supreme Audit Institution on data SIOPE.

Table 5.6 Capital expenditures (values expressed in €/000.000)

	2009	2010	2011	Variation % 2009/2010	Variation % 2010/2011
Purchasing real estate	2.323	1.197	1.832	–14,03	–8,26
Expropriation	23	13	18	–43,48	38,46
Purchase of goods	17	13	7	–25,53	–46,15
Rent third party assets	0	0	0	0,00	0.00
Acquisition of movable property	128	93	66	–27,34	–29,03
Professional assignments	39	29	22	–25,64	–24,14
Transfers	525	438	429	–16,57	–2,05
Shareholdings	37	50	22	35,14	–56,00
Contributions of capital	34	8	3	–76,47	–62,50
Total	**3.126**	**2.641**	**2.399**	**–15,52**	**–9,16**

Source: Supreme Audit Institution on data SIOPE

A more marked decline is observed in the capital expenditures. In the 2009/2010 period we have a – 15,52% while in the 2010/2011 period a – 9,16%.

The whole picture represented in Table 5.7 shows that Italian provinces are in structural deficit in the period under examination: –1,869 millions of euro deficit in 2009; – 1,311 millions euro in 2010; – 990 millions of euros in 2011. The good news

Table 5.7 Total expenditure and revenues (values expressed in €/000.000)

	2009	2010	2011	Variation % 2009/2010	Variation % 2009/2010
Current expenditures	8.678	8.564	8.448	−1,31	−1,35
Capital expenditures	3.553	2.937	2.634	−17,34	−10,32
Special-Tax and Other Own revenues	669	659	710	−1,49	7,74
Expenses from services for third parties	1,079	1.030	927	−4,54	−10,00
Total Expenses	**13.979**	**13.190**	**12.719**	**−5,64**	**−3,57**
Total Capital revenues	**2.366**	**2.103**	**1.953**	**−11,12**	**−7,13**
Total Current revenues	**9.744**	**9.492**	**9.776**	**−2,59**	**2,99**
Difference	**−1.869**	**−1.311**	**−990**	**−42,56%**	**−32,42%**

Source: Supreme Audit Institution on data SIOPE.

is that the deficit is declining at a significant rate – 42,56% in 2009/2010 and – 32,42% in 2010/2011. From the expenses side, the main contribution derives from the reduction of capital expenditure. From the revenues side, the main reduction is in the capital revenues (less loans). At the moment, Italian provinces are still not able to provide the same quantity and quality of public services without using the debt lever. So we generally observe a decline in public services providing, or better a necessary resizing in some or all the functions they provide following The Stability Pact. The real challenge, therefore, is to continue to provide essentials public services in an efficient and responsible manner by reducing current expenditures without increasing the debts. To achieve this goal, it is important to adopt a new performance management culture that helps reduce current expenditures and wastes.

5.3 New Public Management: making the Public Sector more output-oriented

New Public Management (Aucoin, 1990; Hood, 1991, 1995; Gruening, 2001, Le Grand, 2003), as we know, is a theoretical framework comprising concepts and instruments deriving mainly from management and economics disciplines whose principal aim is to improve public service performance (Boyne, 2003) by transforming the public sector from an input-oriented to an output-oriented one. The adoption of a New Public Management-type culture requires the implementation of systems capable of connecting actions to results, rather than to formal administrative rules (De Bruijn, 2002; Holzer, Yang, 2004; Hood, 1991; Pollitt, Bouckaert, 2004). To achieve this goal a fundamental shift is required in the mechanisms used to steer and manage public sector organizations. From trust-based logics, typical of the Public Administration culture, we need to adopt performance management and market-based logics (Le Grand, 2003).

In general terms, the adoption of performance management logic in the public sector has improved efficiency and reduced costs, has contributed, not without problems (Bozeman, 2007; Radin, 2006, Hood, 2011), in changing public sector organizations from input to output-oriented ones. In the next sub-section we explore in more depth the performance management logic.

5.3.1 Performance management in the public sector: logics and techniques

Performance measurement and management in the public sector, as we know, is complicated by the peculiarities that characterize its institutional context. It is a difficult task to define and measure the ultimate public value created (outcome) because a lot of internal and external variables influence the final result (Boyne, 2003b) i.e. the impact on citizens, on the environment, etc. On the contrary, relatively more easy is the measurement of financial outputs, that are intermediate results (Noordegraaf, Abma, 2003; Lonti, Gregory, 2007).

As a consequence if it is difficult to define and measure public value, it is also difficult to assess whether public service performance improvement has occurred or not. We cannot use simple hypothesis (Boyne, 2003b; Brignall, Modell, 2000; Ballantine et al., 1998; Brignall, 1997; Broadbent, Guthrie, 1992; Covaleski, Dirsmith, Samuel, 1996; Henri, 2006), such that better strategies and better management (Boyne, 2004), are the real drivers of the public service improvement instead of more resources or a new regulation or a better citizen behavior, because different external and territorial contexts require different definition of what public value is and, therefore, require different regulatory regimes, different managerial cultures and competences as well as different volumes of resources, i.e. a different mix of improvement levers.

But in crisis times, such as the one we are living, as we know, is crucial to achieve financial autonomy and, so, to focus the attention on financial outputs as a condition for survival (Anselmi,2005; Borgonovi, 2004). To face the declining state resource transfers, therefore, it is important to reduce the resource consumption of local government organizations to match revenues and expenses (Covaleski, Dirsmith, 1983). The most important thing is to recognize that current revenues are the real limiting factor, the constraint, and that capital revenues (especially debts) can't be increased, as happened in the past, because new strict and not negotiable rules have been requested by the European Union and subsequently accepted by the Italian government (Corte dei Conti, 2012). So, in order to provide fundamental public services, local governments managers must control and possibly reduce their current expenses and, possibly, increase their local taxes in a more creative and social responsible way. Their task is to find a better balance between reduced state transfers, local tax revenues and current and capital expenses to best provide their fundamental services (Longo, Cristofoli, 2007; Farneti, 2004).

In more general terms a strong cultural change is required to adopt the tools and the techniques necessary to implement such result-oriented logics. Researchers have investigated the adoption of these techniques in the context of New Public Management (Longo, Cristofoli, 2007). These studies have been conducted in different countries (Preston et al., 1992; Lapsley, Pallot, 2000; Lowe, 2000; Broadbent et al., 2001; Modell, 2001; Caccia, Steccolini, 2006).

The elements collected are not new per se: in fact, they recall proposals already put forward in private and profit-oriented contexts (Della Porta, 2003). In fact, in the local government setting, performance management was implemented through a number of "well known" accounting techniques generally labeled as "New Public Financial Management" (NPFM) (Olson et al., 1998).

Such techniques can be classified as follows:

1. changes in the Financial accounting system, through the introduction of economic-patrimonial systems (Romzek, Dubnick, 1987; Brignall, Modell, 2000);
2. implementation of managing systems that are strongly market-oriented (Henri, 2006; Jacobs, 1998; Noordegraaf, Abma, 2003; Simons, 1990);
3. introduction of performance measurement systems (Farneti, Mazzara, Savioli, 1996);
4. introduction of program evaluation methods (De Bruijn, 2002; Kloot, Martin, 2000);
5. development of budgets (Jacobs, 1995; Jacobs 1998; Marginson, 1999; Subramaniam, Mia, 2003; Fernandez-Revuelta Perez, Robson, 1999; Covaleski, Dirsmith, 1983; Covaleski, Dirsmith, 1986; Czarniawska-Joerges, Jacobsson, 1989) capable of integrating operating and financial management within a structure of responsibilities and expected results;
6. radical changes in internal and external audit and control systems, as well as the introduction of elements to evaluate public policies (Scapens, Roberts, 1993).

Such techniques can be quite easily applied to outputs (especially financials), but not to outcomes (Otley, 1999; Modell, 2001). So they must be used in a responsible way to prevent an outcome deterioration (Pallott, 2003; Lonti, Gregory, 2007). From a more organizational point of view, to effectively implement performance management logics, it is fundamental that the local government organization ensures maximum transparency and information comparability (benchmarking), as regards the results of the evaluation and the elements on which it is based. Nevertheless, there are some criticalities, especially in countries like Italy. Italian public administration, in fact, has always been process-oriented and legal-rule compliant, rather than output and results-oriented (Borgonovi, 2004; Halachmi, 1982; Halachmi, 1992; Thompson, 2006: 496; Wholey, 1983: 5). In the next section we'll examine the case of the Province of Ancona.

5.4 The Case of the Province of Ancona

This province is situated in Marche, where the city of Ancona is also the capital of the region. Overlooking the Adriatic Sea to the east, bordered to the north-west by the province of Pesaro and Urbino, to the south by the province of Macerata, on the west by Umbria (province of Perugia).

Area: 1.940.16 km²
Population: 481.028 (1-1-2011)
Density: 247.93 inhab./Km²
Municipalities: 49

5.4.1 The functions of the Province of Ancona

Before analyzing the performance information relating to its activities, processes and services we present the organizational structure of the Province of Ancona. It is organized in three departments, within which exist sectors and specific areas of expertise. The coordination between the Departments is entrusted to the General Secretary. It appears the following:

GENERAL-SECRETARY Staff Area General Secretary
DEPARTMENT I – INSTITUTIONAL BUSINESS, ORGANIZATION AND HUMAN RESOURCES
SECTOR GENERAL AND INSTITUTIONAL AFFAIRS General Affairs Area Area Provincial Police, Flora and Fauna Area Informatics and Telematics
SECTOR HUMAN RESOURCES, ORGANIZATION, CONTRACTS AND ADVOCACY Area Human Resources and Organisation Area Procurement and Contracts Area Advocacy
DEPARTMENT II – GOVERNANCE AND FINANCE PROJECTS Departmental Area Activities Construction Area Area Planning and Works
FINANCIAL SECTORCOMPANIES AND POLICY ISSUES Area Budget Revenue Area Management Expenditure Area Community Projects
TREASURER'S EQUITY SECURITIES INDUSTRY AND REPORTING Area Treasurer, Heritage securities and school services Area Monitoring and inspection services
EDUCATION SECTOR JOB TRAINING Work Area Area Vocational Education and Training Area Accounting and Monitoring Area Ciof Ancona Area Ciof Senigallia Area Ciof Jesi Area Ciof Fabriano
CULTURE INDUSTRY, TOURISM AND SOCIAL Area Culture and Tourism Area of Social
DEPARTMENT III-GOVERNMENT DEPARTMENT OF LAND Departmental Area Activities Area Procedures permits and environmental assessments Area Civil Protection and hydrogeological Area SIT PTC

> SECTOR PROTECTION AND ENHANCEMENT OF THE ENVIRONMENT
> Area Ecology
> Area-planning and economic development
> Area Coordination external units
> Administrative Area, concessions and authorizations

As we can see, the whole province organization is composed of three departments:

1. Institutional Affairs, Organization and Human Resources;
2. Governance Projects and Finance;
3. Government of the Territory.

Each department is headed by a Director. Each of it, in turn, is organized into sectors, within which the various areas of expertise are included. The current staff amount approximately to 750 units.

5.4.2 The analysis of the financial and economic situation of the Province of Ancona

To analyze the financial and economic situation of the Province of Ancona we'll use the official information deriving from the economic and financial statements referred to the period 2008/2011.

Table 5.8 shows the evolution of the annual financial result of the Province of Ancona. From a positive result of + 4.607 in the 2008 we observe a global negative result of –4.426 in the 2011.

As we can see this negative global financial margin came, mainly:

- from the reduction of capital revenues (from 19.940 in 2008 to 4.598 in 2011).

The difference between current revenues and current expenditures is positive and growing during the period.

Table 5.8 Annual financial result: trends (values expressed in €/000)

	2008	2009	2010	2011
Current revenues	101.811	101.633	101.783	96.435
Current expenditures	97.832	95.878	94.765	88.203
Current balance	+ 3.979	+ 5.755	+ 7.018	+ 8.232
Capital revenues	19.940	13.676	13.258	**4.598**
Capital expenditures	19.312	24.134	23.703	17.256
Capital balance	+ 628	–10.458	–10.445	–12.658
Difference between total revenues and total expenditures (Province of Ancona annual financial result)	+ 4.607	–4.703	–3.427	**–4.426**

The trend of the current financial result is therefore, positive while the trend of the whole annual financial results is negative, due to the strong reduction of the debts following the respect of the Stability Pact.

Table 5.9 shows that, in face of the negative trend of the annual financial result, the Province of Ancona was able to achieve the targets deriving from the respect of the Stability Pact.

The positive impression of the partial improvement of the financial situation is confirmed by Table 5.10 and by Figure 5.1 that show a positive trend in the economic situation of the Province of Ancona. The net income is positive, albeit declining, in all the four years.

Table 5.9   Stability Pact: trends (values expressed in €/000)

	2008	2009	2010	2011
Difference between total revenue and total expenditure (Province of Ancona annual financial result)	+ 4.607	– 4.703	– 3.427	– 4.426
Stability Pact Target	3.276	– 7.547	– 3.455	+ 4.529
Regional Plafond	–	–	–	+ 9.029
Target region				– 4.500
Difference	+ 1.331	+ 2.844	+ 28	+ 74

Table 5.10   Annual economic results (values expressed in €/000).

	2008	2009	2010	2011
Operating Gross Margin	2.462	2.592	3.456	5.314
Financial Revenues and Expenses	–3.957	–2.750	–2.718	–3.044
Extraordinary Revenues and Expenses	7.738	1.394	984	–609
Net income of the year	6.243	1.237	1.722	1.660

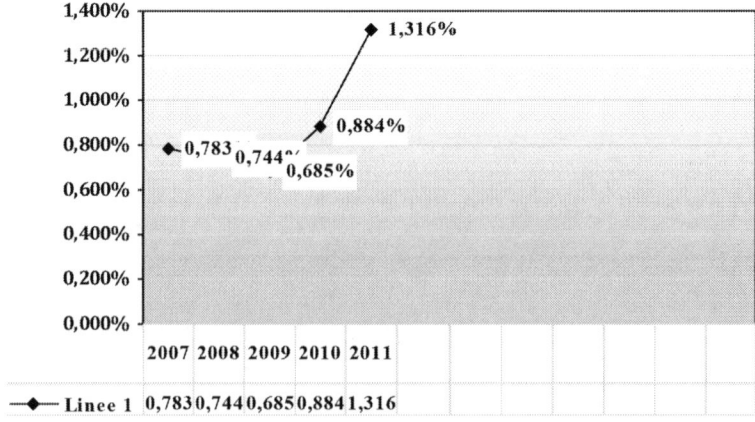

Figure 5.1   Trend of Province of Ancona ROI.

Others indicators were elaborated to measure the financial situations. The indicators were identified by the Head of the management control unit and were used to make useful comparisons (Farneti, Mazzara, Savioli, 1996; Borgonovi, 2004).

Table 5.11 presents the main indicators that show the financial status of the Province of Ancona as it has evolved from 2001 to 2011 (Table 5.12).

Table 5.11   Main financial indicators for the Province of Ancona.

	2011	**2006**	**2001**
1 – Current margin *(current revenues minus current expenditure – percentage on current revenues)*	8,15%	5,02%	18,50%
2 – Degree of financial autonomy *(Tax and non-tax revenues on the total amount of current revenues)*	49,20%	54,30%	66,12%
3 – Fiscal pressure per capita *(tax revenues/inhabitants)*	€ 96,37	€ 108,10	€ 86,11
4 – Degree of structural rigidity – 1 – *(Personnel expenditure, and mortgages and loans payment on the total amount of current revenues)*	30,00%	28,30%	27,30%
5 – Degree of structural rigidity – 2 – *(Personnel expenditure, and mortgages and loans payment on the total amount of current revenues minus revenues with designated destination)*	59,30%	57,80%	45,40%
6 – Per-capita investments *(investments/inhabitants)*	€ 42,55	€ 52,65	€ 40,78
7 – Level of debt *(residual debt of mortgages and loans on the total amount of current revenues)*	83,56%	80,44%	78,72%
8 – Per-capita debt index *(residual debt of mortgages and loans/inhabitants)*	€ 176,23	€ 171,72	€ 109,23
9 – Percentage of fixed rate debt Percentage of variable rate debt	58% 42%	66% 34%	70% 30%
10 – Speed of own revenues collection	93,51%	89,53%	95,21%
11 – Speed of current expenditures payment	69,40%	67,60%	56,46%
12 – Per-capita non-disposable assets *(non-disposable assets/inhabitants)*	€ 195,73	€ 197,53	€ 159,99
13 – Per-capita State properties *(State properties/inhabitants)*	€ 178,29	€ 127,77	€ 61,51
14 – Civil servants per inhabitant *(inhabitants/civil servants)*	909	928	1,181
15 – External rating *assigned by Standard & Poor's*	A + Stable	A	A –

Table 5.12 Benchmarking financial indicators (Ancona/Italy)

	Ancona	Italy
Structural rigidity	28,3%	35,0%
Rigidity per expenditures for personnel	19,2%	23,0%
Rigidity per debt charges	9,1%	11,7%
Ratio debt – current revenues	81,7%	113,6%
Level of incidence of administrative expenditures	19,2%	29,1%
Debt per-capita	€ 183	€ 200

The following trends can be identified:

1. starting from 1999, imposed taxes have steadily expanded, up to 2004; from 2004 onward the tax revenues have declined, in particular in the last financial years: an example of this is the decline of current margin (current revenues minus current expenditures in percentage on current revenues – indicator No. 1). Increase in current margin between 2000 and 2004 means that, in those years, the authority has allocated revenue surplus to financing of investment expenditures: this allowed to absorb better the strong decline of revenues from main taxes. A budget policy envisaging an expansion (a structural expansion) in current expenditure, in line with the expansion in current revenues, would have caused an imbalance in the budget, especially during an economic crisis;
2. between 2005 and 2011, there was a reduction in the level of financial autonomy (indicator No. 2) and fiscal pressure per-capita (indicator No. 3);
3. there was an increase in the level of budget rigidity, as demonstrated by the trend of indicator No.5 (expenditure for personnel, and mortgages and loans payment, on the total amount of current revenues minus revenues with designated destination), which was more significant than the indicator usually considered (Indicator No.4). In 2009, together with the trend of structural costs, the so-called "development expenditure" represented only 5% of the total current expenditure and loan repayment, amounting to €101.6 million;
4. in relation to the debt level, it can be observed that, when the current margin was at high levels (between 2000 and 2005), the ratio between residual debt of bond mortgages and loans, and current revenues, was constant. It then grew because, in order to keep the same level of investments on the territory, debts were contracted to fund Public works (Residual debt of mortgages and loans on the total amount of current revenues – indicator No.7). The level of debt grew in a contained way, thus allowing to improve the external rating, as assigned by Standard & Poor's (indicator No.15). As regards the percentage composition of debt – namely fixed or variable rate – a balancing oriented towards variable rate (indicator No.10) allowed to save on the interests of the last financial years, following a decrease in interest rates (Euribor);
5. although debt per capita increased during the period (indicator No.8), assets per capita grew even more (indicators No. 13 and 14): therefore, it can be affirmed that there was a general increase in wealth;

6. as regards the speed of collection and payment, it must be underlined that there was an increase in the speed of payment of current expenditures, also due to the irrelevance of the current expenditures in the financial budget of the Internal Stability Pact (indicators No. 11 and 12);
7. the attribution of new competences, and the posting of personnel from the Region to Provinces brought about a decrease in the ratio between inhabitants and civil servants (indicator No.15). Because of the new competences, the percentage incidence of regional current postings on the total amount of current revenues reached 47%.

5.4.3   The cost of services in the Province of Ancona

In the Province of Ancona, the determination of the cost of services and indicators comes from the integration of the above mentioned accounting systems; in particular, the system is put in place through the following steps.

First of all, starting from Financial accounting, registrations are made in Management accounting, by matching a "centre" and a "factor" to cost and revenues elements, on the basis of different aggregation viewpoints. The "centre" is yet another detail of the Cost centre as defined in the Executive management plan and is closely related to budget function-service. The "factor" is yet another detail of Productive factors (Budget interventions): this system allows not to weigh down on the Executive management plan, and to have details of costs and revenues in management accounting.

Another common element is accounting of assets-inventories: when a capital expenditure is liquidated, the asset is charged on the assets-inventories procedures, in order for this to be connected to the drawing up of an Assets account divided into different assets categories; the allocation of goods to certain centres allows to detect the necessary amortisations to define the total cost of services.

Later, 15 services are identified ("final centres") in order to assess their costs, and such costs are ascribed to these 15 final centres. Moreover, costs relating to the so-called indirect centres are estimated, and are then divided among the final centres on the basis of the following criterion:

1. some costs (institutional bodies) are divided according to the fifteen services'percentage incidence on the total;
2. other costs (general secretariat, accounting, personnel and organization, offices – building costs) are divided according to the abovementioned criteria, but also according to the percentage incidence of the number of operators of each of the services on the total.

Depreciations are directly ascribed to final centres, whereas those relating to structural costs are divided according to the criterion of percentage incidence on the total number of operators of each of the services.

Finally, these costs have been compared to a number of parameters identified for each service, and costs per inhabitant have then been defined in a homogenous way.

Table 5.13 sums up and presents costs relating to the 15 services, underlining current sources of funding as well, divided into authority's general resources (in practice, tax and non-tax revenues), fixed regional resources, and other revenues with fixed destination (Table 5.14).

Table 5.13 Expenditure per Cost centre in the Province of Ancona (values expressed in €/000)

SPENDING FOR COST CENTRES				
	2009	**2010**	**2011**	**Average for the three-year period**
1100 – Institutional bodies part. Dec.	2.131	1.961	1.989	2.027
1200 – Personnel and organization	6.004	5.889	5.871	5.921
1210 – General Secretariat	2.940	2.488	2.341	2.590
1300 – Accounting – Supply office	1.636	1.089	1.019	1.248
1400 – Tax revenues and Fiscal services	538	1.266	742	849
1500 – Province's building	2.301	2.301	2.211	2.271
2600 – Other buildings	118	94	70	94
1600 – Technical office	1.923	1.768	1.254	1.648
2300 – 2400 Schools and education	7.220	8.243	8.090	7.851
2500 – Professional training	**20.343**	**21.438**	**19.527**	**20.436**
2510-20-30-40 – Training centres	2.016	1.915	1.412	1.781
3200 3100 – Cultural heritage – museums	2.407	2.395	1.703	2.168
4100 – Tourism	574	659	546	593
4200 – Sport and leisure	335	335	359	343
5100 – Transports	21.483	25.233	25.298	24.005
6100 – Roads	**4.901**	**5.227**	**5.680**	**5.269**
6500 – Town planning	1.186	1.182	1.443	1.270
7100 – Soil protection	2.102	2.480	1.537	2.040
7200 – Ecology	1,133	876	788	932
7300 – Organisation of waste disposal	4.010	3.854	3.223	3.696
7400 – Pollution detection	657	660	466	594
7500 – Hunting and fishing	1.360	1.246	1.231	1.279
7800 – Civil Protection services	1.047	247	570	621
8200 – Child care and social services	3.776	2.668	2.814	3.086
9100 – Artes. Ind. Comm.	1.495	1.415	824	1.245
9300 – Labour market	2.241	2.955	2.208	2.468
TOTAL	**95.877**	**99.884**	**93.216**	**96.326**

Table 5.14   Analysis of the costs of Training and Roads services, with relevant indicators (values expressed in €/000)

TRAINING				
	2009	**2010**	**2011**	**Average**
Direct costs	22.357	23.353	20.939	22.216
Indirect costs	3.950	4.271	3.606	3.942
Amortisation	453	676	590	573
TOTAL	**26.760**	**28.300**	**25.135**	**26.732**
Parameters				
People employed	202.000	202.000	202.000	202.000
Authorities and companies which held courses	123	76	46	82
Average cost per people employed	132.48	140.1	124.43	132.33
Parameters	**2011**			
Workforce	217.000			
Male	116.000			
Female	101.000			
Average cost per workforce	115.83			
Yearly average costs between 2009 and 2011				
Personnel	3.264	12,20%		
Puchase of goods	110	0,40%		
Services	3.437	12,90%		
Use of assets belonging to third parties	39	0,10%		
Postings	14.876	55,60%		
Taxes	491	1,80%		
Indirect costs	3.942	14,70%		
Amortisation	573	2,10%		
TOTAL	**26.732**	**100,00%**		
VIABILITY/ROADS				
	2009	**2010**	**2011**	**Average**
Direct costs	4.901	5.227	5.680	5.269
Indirect costs	3.069	2.465	2.903	2.812

(*Continued*)

Table 5.14 Analysis of the costs of Training and Roads services, with relevant indicators (values expressed in €/000) (*Continued*)

Amortisation	2,277	2,427	2,647	2,450
TOTAL Parameters	**10.247**	**10.119**	**11.230**	**10.532**
km of roards	954	954	954	954
*of which former a.n.a.s.	110	110	110	110
*of which mountain roads	215	215	215	215
Operators	68	68	68	68
km./operators	14,03	14,03	14,03	14,03
Average cost per km	10.741,09	10.606,92	11.771,49	11.039,83
Average cost per km: Direct costs	5.137,32	5.479,04	5.953,88	5.523,41
Indirect costs	3.216,98	2.583,86	3.042,98	2.947,94
Amortisation	2.386,79	2.544,03	2.774,63	2.568,48
TOTAL	**10.741,09**	**10.606,92**	**11.771,49**	**11.039,83**
Average annual costs of the three years 2009/2011				
Personnel	2.213	21,00%		
Purchase of goods	341	3,20%		
Services	1.195	11,30%		
Use of goods belonging to third parties	257	2,40%		
Passive interests	1.082	10,30%		
Taxes	182	1,70%		
Indirect costs	2.812	26,70%		
Amortisation	2.450	23,30%		
TOTAL	**10.533**	**100.00%**		

All of the costs are displayed in the following tables in relation to the institutional tasks of the Province. Table 5.15 only takes into account two main costs (Professional training and Roads).

The indicators above have allowed us to measure the degree of efficiency of the Province of Ancona. However, another goal of the management control system is the measurement of effectiveness (Starling, 2005: 21).

Table 5.15 Analysis of the costs of all sectors services, with relevant indicators (values expressed in €/000)

SUMMARY (all sectors)	2009	2010	2011	Average
Total direct costs	78.286	83.028	77.719	79.678
Total indirect costs	17.591	16.855	15.497	16.648
TOTAL	**95.877**	**99.883**	**93.216**	**96.325**
Incidence %	**2009**	**2010**	**2011**	**Average**
Total direct costs	81,7%	83,1%	83,4%	82,7%
Total indirect costs	18,3%	16,9%	16,6%	17,3%
TOTAL	**100.0%**	**100.0%**	**100.0%**	**100.0%**
Total direct costs	78.286	83.028	77.719	79.678
Total indirect costs	17.591	16.855	15.497	16.648
Depreciation and amortization	8.542	8.538	8.698	8.593
TOTAL	**104.419**	**108.421**	**101.914**	**104,918**
Incidence %	**2009**	**2010**	**2011**	**Average**
Total direct costs	75,0%	76,6%	76,3%	75,9%
Total indirect costs	16,8%	15,5%	15,2%	15,9%
Amortisation	8,2%	7,9%	8,5%	8,2%
TOTAL	**100,0%**	**100,0%**	**100,0%**	**100,0%**
VALUES PER INHABITANT (in Euros):	**2009**	**2010**	**2011**	**Average**
Average total cost per inhabitant	219,36	226,67	211,87	219,29
Average direct cost per inhabitant	164,46	173,58	161,57	166,53
Average indirect cost per inhabitant	36,95	35,24	32,22	34,79
Average amortisation cost per inhabitant	17,94	17,85	18,08	17,96
Average total cost per inhabitant	**2009**	**2010**	**2011**	**Average**
Education	28,55	28,93	27,53	28,33
Training	56,22	59,17	52,25	55,87
Culture	5,93	5,81	4,12	5,29
Tourism	1,91	1,84	1,62	1,79
Sport	0,76	0,77	0,93	0,82
Transports	49,27	58,11	57,07	54,83
Roads	21,53	21,16	23,35	22,01
City planning	4,24	4,32	5,17	4,58
Water protection	6,43	7,54	5,00	6,32
Ecology	15,55	14,41	12,02	13,99
Hunting and fishing	4,69	4,24	4,43	4,45
Civil protection	2,58	0,77	1,56	1,63
Social services	9,02	6,39	6,57	7,32
Economic development	4,08	3,73	2,54	3,45
Labour market	8,60	9,49	7,71	8,60
Total	**219,36**	**226,67**	**211,87**	**219,29**

The effectiveness is expressed as the ratio between results and objectives, as the ability to get close to that goal.

However, it should be noted that in the public sector, organizations that are formally effective from the point of view of the indicators, when subject to a more in-depth analysis, reveal a totally different reality.

This paradox stems from the fact that the determination of the objectives could develop into a purely internal logic (with a high risk of self-determination), which allows to demonstrate their achievements because they are constantly set at a level of easy accessibility (not to mention that very often they are not fixed ex-ante, but in progress). In the absence of an external mechanism, which allows an assessment of the adequacy of the performance levels (set and achieved), measuring the effectiveness can become a theoretical exercise (Table 5.16).

Table 5.16 Executive Management Plan 2011 (values expressed in €/000)

2011					
TRAINING					
Revenue					
Initial appropriation	29.888	Assessments	18.608	Collection	1.064
Current expenditures					
Initial appropriation	29.180	Commitments	18.106	Payment	3.156
Capital expenditures					
Initial appropriation	47.500	Commitments	17.250	Payment	–
VIABILITY/ROADS					
Revenue					
Initial appropriation	856	Assessments	590	Collection	590
Current expenditures					
Initial appropriation	1.653	Commitments	1.642	Payment	1.103
Capital expenditures					
Initial appropriation	4.920	Commitments	2.820	Payment	–
TOTAL					
Revenue					
Initial appropriation	138.045	Assessments	121.565	Collection	87.887
Current expenditures					
Initial appropriation	112.640	Commitments	100.037	Payment	70.932
Capital expenditures					
Initial appropriation	25.406	Commitments	20.469	Payment	941

In particular, it emerges that in 2011, for the training, the difference between forecasts and assessments initials of entry is remarkable, having found only 62,3% of appropriation, while current expenditure shows that it was ascertained of appropriation and 62% for capital expenditures 36,3% (Table 5.17).

In the year 2010 the Table shows that, for training, the difference between forecasts and assessments initials of entry is acceptable, having found the percentage of appropriation 84,7%, while current expenditure shows that the 85,7 was found of Commitment and for capital expenditures 50,7%.

For the road, it shows that the difference between forecasts and assessments initials of entry is mild, having found only 91% of appropriation, while current expenditure shows that it was ascertained of appropriation and 108,7% for capital expenditures 120,1%.

Table 5.17   Executive Management Plan 2010 (values expressed in €/000)

2010					
TRAINING					
		Revenue			
Initial appropriation	25.404	Assessments	21.521	Collection	1.416
		Current expenditures			
Initial appropriation	24.427	Commitments	20.931	Payment	2.858
		Capital expenditures			
Initial appropriation	242	Commitments	123	Payment	–
VIABILITY/ROADS					
		Revenue			
Initial appropriation	696	Assessments	634	Collection	593
		Current expenditures			
Initial appropriation	1.760	Commitments	1.912	Payment	1.028
		Capital expenditures			
Initial appropriation	5.105	Commitments	6.130	Payment	324
TOTAL					
		Revenue			
Initial appropriation	150.308	Assessments	128.958	Collection	29.463
		Current expenditures			
Initial appropriation	109.518	Commitments	106.697	Payment	74.747
		Capital expenditures			
Initial appropriation	40.790	Commitments	18.427	Payment	1.030

Table 5.18 Executive Management Plan 2009 (values expressed in €/000)

		2009			
TRAINING					
		Revenue			
Initial appropriation	24.235	Assessments	21.012	Collection	3.166
		Current expenditures			
Initial appropriation	23.832	Commitments	20.231	Payment	3.197
		Capital expenditures			
Initial appropriation	222	Commitments	256	Payment	97
VIABILITY/ROADS					
		Revenue			
Initial appropriation	636	Assessments	645	Collection	605
		Current expenditures			
Initial appropriation	1.578	Commitments	1.549	Payment	1.044
		Capital expenditures			
Initial appropriation	2.760	Commitments	1.506	Payment	–
TOTAL					
		Revenue			
Initial appropriation	148.085	Assessments	124.830	Collection	92.338
		Current expenditures			
Initial appropriation	106.554	Commitments	101.643	Payment	71.894
		Capital expenditures			
Initial appropriation	41.531	Commitments	24.694	Payment	1.105

Substantially it is confirmed, in time, a greater effectiveness in the field roads, in particular on the current expenditure (Table 5.18).

In 2009, it appears that, for training, the difference between forecasts and assessments initials of entry of entry is acceptable, having found the 867% of appropriation, while current expenditure shows that it was established that the 84,9% of committed and for capital expenditure on 115,2%.

For the road, the table shows that the difference between forecasts and assessments initials of entry is mild, having found only of appropriation 101,4%, while current expenditure shows that it was found 98,2% and of appropriation for capital expenditures 54,6%.

Substantially it is confirmed, in time, a greater effectiveness in the field roads, in particular on the current expenditure.

5.5   Discussion

The case of Province of Ancona shows how a public sector organization reacts to an external change occurred in its environment (Andrews, Boyne, 2008; Anselmi, 2005; Borgonovi, 2004; Boyne, 2003,2003b; Sargiacomo, 2000) As we know, public organizations face environments that change in unpredictable ways. In this case, the fiscal federalist reform (Oates, 2008) and the Pact of Stability changed, mainly, the "economic munificence" (Corte dei Conti, 2012; Andrews, Boyne, 2008) of the environment, by reducing the range of the resources available to them (less loans and less state transfers) and the "political munificence" by reducing the support of key external stakeholders (governments, citizen, service users) and increasing the general public distrust towards the political action (Roberts, 2010; Lonti, Gregory, 2007; Pallot, 2003; Le Grand 2003).

There wouldn't be the need to impose a reform if public sector organizations were moving in the desired direction and the trust mechanisms worked (Andrews, Boyne, 2008; Le Grand, 2003). As we have seen in sub-section 5.2.3 the desired direction now is a strong reduction of the Italian Public Sector Debt (Corte dei Conti, 2012; Certet Bocconi, 2011). To be achieved, this goal required Central Government to give execution to the agreed Stability Pact by stopping public sector organizations to increase their debts and by forcing them to reduce their expenses and to obtain a positive margin (positive difference between revenues and expenses) by using Command and Control mechanisms instead of Trust-based ones (Le Grand, 2003; Boyne, 2003b). The choice to give priority to such "corporate goals" derive from the New Public Management framework (section 5.3) that, among others, states that public sector organizations will achieve better results if they adopt and implement market and corporate performance management logics instead of trust-based ones (Hood,1991,1995,2011; Le Grand, 2003). This highlights the fact that any opinion on the success of a reform, on the choice of what is central to change must be theory-driven (Pollitt, Bouckaert, 2009; Boyne, 2003b). The theoretical perspective adopted, therefore, is that of New Public Management. Through this chapter we explored how a particular public sector organization, the Province of Ancona (section 5.4), has tried to implement the change in that direction and how the adoption of a NPM strongly advised tool (a management control system) has or not contributed to that end.

So a number of questions can derive from these observations that will help us to better discuss the case:

1. Did the NPM driven federalist and Stability Pact reforms occur in the Province of Ancona, not only in theory but in practice?

As a starting point of the discussion we observe that the Italian federalist reform process is ongoing and "fluid", not to say confused (Piperata, 2012; Certet Bocconi, 2011). As a proof Italy is currently debating on whether to abolish Provinces in order to reduce, not the costs of the Public sector but "the cost of politics", because politics and administration in Italy are so intertwined that is difficult to understand what is a public sector organization and what is a political organization (De Ioanna, 2013). Both are publicly funded. To reduce public spending and achieve the desired goals of reducing Italian Public Debt, in theory we should delete political organizations from the list of the publicly funded organizations and improve the remaining ones that form the real public sector (Mulazzani, 2006; Borgonovi,2004). What is actually practiced in Italy is the generalized prohibition to increase debts to provide essential public services, the generalized decrease in state transfers (the so-called linear spending cuts) and the pressure to reduce public organizations current expenses to match the declining revenues (De Ioanna, 2013; Longo, Cristofoli, 2007).

How did public sector organizations react to this pressures?

As we saw in sub-section 5.2.3 Italian Provinces strongly reduced their debts but they resisted in cutting their current expenses (Corte dei Conti, 2012; Del Bene, Marasca,2009). From a more general point of view there has been, by the way, a growing emphasis in producing more financial performance information (Bevan, Hood, 2006; Farneti, 2004; De Bruijn,2002). In the case of Provincia of Ancona we observe the same trend: a reduction in State transfers and an increase in the quality of financial information. During an official presentation of the results achieved by the Province of Ancona in the last years, the Head of the Management Control Unit of the Province focused the attention mainly on the efforts made to improve the current financial situation, to improve the economic situation and to meet the targets established by the Stability Pact. As a perfect CFO, the Head of the Management Control Unit elaborated a graphic showing the increase in the Return on Investment (ROI) to confirm the improvement path undertaken by the Province of Ancona. He elaborated, also, a reporting containing 15 key financial performance indicators to show, in wider terms, the changes occurred in the financial situation of the province of Ancona in the last 10 years. Among these, he included the external rating to point out that the growing financial difficulties that characterized the period 2001-2010 have not impeded the improvement of the Province rating (from A– to A +). This improvement is mainly attributable to the fact that in the last years the province of Ancona made strong efforts to reduce its annual debt (from 12.113 millions of euro in 2009 to 4.220 million of euro in 2011) and to increase and make more stable its annual economic result, by reducing the incidence of extraordinary revenues and expenses. We don't know if the essential public services improved or not (Roberts, 2013; Lonti, Gregory, 2007; Carnegie, West, 2005; Kelly, 2005; Pallot, 2003; Meyer, Rowan, 1977). What matters, as the data included in the reporting clearly show, is, in the end, the external financial assessment, the rating (Bevan, Hood, 2006). The global financial deficit of the province of Ancona (total current and capital revenues minus total current and capital expenses) has risen from 2008 to 2011 (from a surplus of 4.607 million of euro registered in 2008 to a deficit of 4.426 million of euro in 2011) but quite in line with the goals established by the Stability Pact, as the tables of Section 5.4 clearly show. So improving the "financial perspective" of a hypothetical Province Balanced Scorecard has been the central preoccupation of the managers of the Province of Ancona in the last years (Modell, 2001, Robinson, 1998; Schick, 1996). In the same way, it is important to occupy a good position in the ranking of financial virtuosity (Rondo-Brovetto, Saliterer, 2007; Triantafillou, 2007; Sargiacomo, 2000).

The "benchmarking table" shows that in all of the most important indicators of the financial well-being, the Province of Ancona is largely better positioned in comparison of the average value referred to the Italian Provinces. What does it mean? Maybe, it means that in Ancona, the NPM reforms are more practiced than in others provinces (Boyne, 2004) and that they are not 'managerial fashions'(Caccia, Steccolini, 2006). The average Italian value signals that there are still strong performance gaps in Italian Provinces and that the "old regime" is alive and well (Andrews, Moynihan, 2002). The

Province of Ancona is, therefore an exception. Here it seems, *prima facie*, that the "new" output-oriented regime has replaced the "old" social and excessively burocratic-oriented one (Pollitt, Bouckaert, 2009; Longo, Cristofoli, 2007). It seems, also, that the importance NPM gives to economic and financial performance information is confirmed with the consequence that the collection and publication of financial performance indicators goes, partially, in the direction established by NPM theory (Bevan, Hood, 2006; Modell, 2001; Brignall, Modell, 2000). Why partially? Because NPM not only emphasize better efficiency but also better quality and outcomes (Le Grand, 2003; De Bruijn, 2002; Kouzmin et al., 1999; Hood, 1991). In this case the attention is focused only on financial information and not on the quality aspects (Radin, 2006; Bozeman, 2004; Pallot, 2003; Noordegraf, Abma, 2003). When effectiveness consideration comes into play they are not presented by means of non-financial indicators but as a ratio of the ex-post and ex-ante expenses, as we can see in the Executive Management Plan tables referred to the period 2009-2011 to various functions (Bevan, Hood, 2006). Also in this case the financial perspective is dominant. Is the emphasis on good financial performance indicators supported by a solid economic and efficiency-oriented management control system? This question anticipates the following:

2. were the expenses and the costs of the Province of Ancona really reduced after the adoption of new, albeit rudimentary, cost control techniques or the better financial indicators reflected the "obsessive" quest by public officials to represent the province performance in the best possible light for legitimacy-seeking purposes (Meyer, Rowan, 1977)? Are we witnessing a gaming "financial number" behaviors (Bevan, Hood, 2006)? We know that the cost information was literally "manufactured" by integrating financial accounting, management accounting, economic-patrimonial accounting, and income and inventory accounting and we don't how accurate was this cost accounting "manufacturing" process (Farneti, 2004; Modell, 2001; Lapsley, Pallot, 2000; Guthrie, 1998; Brignall, 1997; Czarniawska-Joerges, Jacobsson, 1989;). From a NPM perspective setting up new information structures constitute the easy part of the reform implementation ((Anselmi, 2005; Borgonovi, 2004; Pollitt, Bouckaert, 2000). New information structures must then be used and constantly revised and updated. We all know what is the meaning of *loosely coupled* structures and practices (Caccia, Steccolini, 2006; Noordegraf, Abma 2003; Broadbent e al., 2001; Fernandez-Revuelta Perez, Robson, 1999; Meyer, Rowan, 1977). Reducing the gap between structures and practices is, therefore, the main goal of NPM supporters (Starling, 2005; Le Grand, 2003, Sargiacomo, 2000; Hood, 1991). Information is useful only when it is used in such ways to change behaviors and to achieve results (Mason, Swanson, 1979: 4; Flamholtz, 1981: 83). Reducing costs is not important per se but to promote bottom-line improvements. We know that usually public officials resist, or worst, contrast the implementation of the new reform with the result of neutralize it (Piperata 2011; Broadbent et al., 2001; Scapens, Roberts, 1993). If we take a closer look to the Province of Ancona financial data we observe a positive trend in the current margin. The difference between current revenues and current expenditures, in fact, is positive showing an improvement trend. The reduction of current expenditures (from 97,832 in 2008 to 88,203 in 2011) is the main result of the adoption of a management control system that has allowed the global rationalization of the structure of the Province of

Ancona (Del Bene, Marasca, 2009). As we can see current revenues remained stables. The financial improvement is also evident when we consider the Stability Pact Goals. From 2008 to 2011 the financial results obtained were better than expected. Only in 2011 it was necessary to ask for a financial help to the Marche Region, which gave the Province of Ancona a part of its plafond allowing it to respect the target.

What is, also, important to note is the improvement of the operating gross margin during the period (see the increase of ROI in the Figure 5.1) and the decreasing contribution of extraordinary revenues and expenses to the final result. This is an encouraging signal that 'management matters'(Boyne, 2004) in improving the economic situation.

So if we observe the trend of the expenses, the trend of the current balance and the trend of the economic situation, the adoption of management accounting systems has been quite positive, confirming the positive impact of these tools on outputs (Borgonovi, 2004; De Bruijn, 2002; Sargiacomo, 2000). From a formal point of view, we note, also, that cost information is presented in a clear way and is referred to cost centers related to the various institutional tasks (Farneti et al., 2006). In the three-year period of observation we note a generalized improvement of the efficiency of the various functions. From the data, and especially from the discussion we had with the Head of the Management Control Unit of the Province of Ancona, our impression is that in this case cost information were used in reality and not only formally produced (Meyer, Rowan, 1977). The costs of the institutional functions provided show a declining trend signaling an increase of attentions towards efficiency issues. If by "control" we mean the Deming's cycle (Plan – Do – Check – Act), then we cannot avoid to note that, in this case, such cycle is still in its implementation stage. In particular, responsibility centers and cost centers have been identified, but cost standards have not yet been identified thus limiting the possibility to analyze any deviation from an efficient target (Ballantine et al., 1998: 71-94) and aliment a virtuous control cycle. General signs of efficiency improvement, however, are clearly visible from the tables, as well as an improvement in institutional culture, accompanied by a reduction of bureaucracy and an increase in more results-oriented mentality. But only time will tell if the Province of Ancona is now hitting the short term "financial" target but missing the long term "public service outcome" point (Roberts, 2010; Lonti, Gregory, 2007; Radin, 2006; Bevan, Hood, 2006; Bozeman, 2004; Nooordegraf, Abma, 2003; Pallot, 2003). In fact, when interviewed, both the Head of the Management Control Unit and the General Secretary of the Province of Ancona feared the adverse effects of the adoption of this new financial mentality to social outcomes (Kelly,2005). They said that their main goal is now to meet external financial pressure to reduce debts and current expenditures and to respect "accounting more than accountability" (Roberts, 2010; Lonti, Gregory, 2007; Carnegie, West, 2005).

5.6   Conclusions

What was, in the end, the impact of management control system on the Province of Ancona? The financial indicators and the cost accounting systems described are, mainly, an important answer the Province of Ancona gave to the constantly-growing expectations and pressures of financial community at large to improve financial outputs and less, for the moment, of the citizens to improve service outcomes.

It is not easy, however, to adopt new powerful tools such as a management control system.

The critical aspects associated with the introduction of costs and performance measuring systems can be summed up in three main points:

1. the conflict between a process-oriented logic, and a result-oriented logic;
2. difficulties in measuring outcomes;
3. difference between system rationality and its actual capacity to represent real phenomena through measures.

The first criticality derives from a traditionally bureaucratic culture of Public administration (procedures-oriented), as well as from the system of institutional rules, which can clash with the logics of autonomy and/or subjectivity, that are typical of the new systems (Gitto, 2006: 524). An efficient reaction to this could be represented by administrative and/or institutional reforms consistent with the new challenges of Public administration. Nevertheless, the capacity of public management to fully capitalize any space for autonomy can be promoted with incentives related to both result and budget indicators (Newcomer, 2007: 323).

The second critical aspect, connected to the difficulties in measuring outcomes, affects the possibility for stakeholders (for example citizens and politicians, politicians and public managers) to share a common definition of "result", to build on indicators and performance metrics used as legitimate instruments of accountability (Kelly, 2005). This confirms what was expressed also by Noordegraaf and Abma: "empirical texts show that it is very difficult to measure public sector performances. In addition, when performances can be measured, it is not always possible to show improvement" (Noordegraaf, Abma, 2003: 856).

We observed, however, first positive elements in the introduction of management control systems. In particular, together with the review of public accounting systems, they have brought about the rationalization of organizational structures, of activities, of management accountability, and of resources allocation problems. This effect is a consequence of the need to sum up resources, management, and objectives into one single planning and control document, the Economic management plan.

Moreover, the restoration of the authority's activity has triggered a process of confrontation, has clarified the relationship between organizational units and stakeholders, and has stimulated forms of horizontal coordination between managers (De Bruijn, 2002). Such coordination is oriented towards the formulation of budget proposals consistent with the overall constraints of the authority, thus improving company planning in a more general sense.

Therefore, in spite of these positive effects represented by a shift to a new financial and result-oriented mentality, the Province of Ancona has experienced some planning and technical difficulties, such as:

1. a tendency to formally regulate the control process trough directives, and ordinances, which made the process less flexible and slower;

2. the prevalence of traditional accounting logics, where the budget and the informative systems are the core of the control system, whose functioning logic is, therefore, affected by the typical logics of the authorization system;
3. the effective capacity of the measuring system to represent real phenomena in order to be able to properly evaluate them. The main difficulties derive from the informative system, often managed by people who are evaluated on the basis of information they themselves provided; but difficulties also derive from the operational need to manage measuring, something that needs to be done by adequately trained persons;
4. indicators that are not always detected; when they are, their transcription is often delayed and difficult because there are no systematic procedures for data collection;
5. procedural difficulties in the making of the reporting system, because the importance of communicating data coming from informative control systems is still underestimated;
6. a limited personalization of control instruments in relation to differences in organization and processes, through the introduction of standard methodologies and instruments (that is to say, those provided for by current legislation).

In this sense, two important guidelines for the implementation of efficient control systems in the public sector are:

1. looking for more accurate measuring systems that take into account, in a reasonable and rational way, causalities behind results achievement;
2. including performance indicators representing the outcome dimension and not only the financial output one, because "avoiding learned vulnerabilities can become for a government executive the equivalent of earning a profit for a business executive. Each constitutes the bottom line" (Lonty, Gregory, 2007: 480).

Summary

Compared to other countries, the Italian Public sector reforms of 80's and 90's have not substantially affected the way public services were managed and so they have not improved their performance. To boost the improvement process a fiscal federalist reform was approved in Italy and a Stability Pact was established in the European zone. There wouldn't be the need to impose a new reform if public sector organizations were moving in the desired direction and the trust mechanisms worked. New Public Management theory, as we know, states in general that public sector organizations will achieve better results if they adopt and implement market and corporate performance management logics instead of trust-based ones. Italian local governments never seriously applied performance management logics and techniques to improve their public services performance. In light of these premises, our case study described the efforts of the province of Ancona to comply with these new efficiency-oriented logics. General signs of efficiency improvement were clearly visible from the analysis of the financial and cost data, as well as an improvement in institutional culture, accompanied by a reduction of bureaucracy and an increase in more results-oriented mentality. But only time will tell if the Province of Ancona is now hitting the short term "financial" target but missing the long term "public service outcome" point.

References

ANDREWS M., MOYNIHAN D. (2002), "Why Reforms do not Always Have to Work to Succeed?", *Public performance and management review*, Vol. 25, 3.

ANDREWS R., BOYNE G. A. (2008), "Organizational Environments and Public-Service Failure: an Empirical Analysis", *Environment and Planning C: Government and Policy*, 26: 788-807.

ANSELMI L. (2005) (a cura di), *Principi e metodologie economico aziendali per gli enti locali: l'azienda Comune*, Milano, Giuffré.

ANTHONY R. N., HAWKINS D. F., MACRÌ D.M., MERCHANT K. A. (2008), *Analisi dei costi*, Milano, McGraw-Hill.

AUCOIN P., (1990), "Administrative Reform in Public Management: Paradigms, Principles, Paradoxes and Pendulums", *Governance*, 3: 115-137.

BALLANTINE J. A., BRIGNALL T. J., MODELL S. (1998), "Performance Measurement and Management in Public Health Services: a Comparison of UK and Swedish Practice", *Management Accounting Research*, 9: 71–94.

BEVAN G., HOOD (2006), "What's Measured is What Matters: Targets and Gaming in the English Public Health Care System", *Public Administration*, 84 (3): 517-538.

BORGONOVI E. (2004), *Principi e sistemi aziendali per le amministrazioni pubbliche*, Milano, Egea.

BOYNE, G. A. (2003), "What is Public Service Improvement?", *Public Administration*, 81 (2): 211-227.

BOYNE, G. A. (2003B), "Sources of Public Service Improvement: a Critical Review and a Research Agenda", *Journal of Public Administration Research and Theory*, 13 (3): 367-394.

BOYNE, G. A. (2004), "Explaining Public Service Performance: Does Management Matter?", *Public Policy and Administration*, 19 (4): 100-117.

BOZEMAN B. (2004), *Public values and Public interest. Counterbalancing economic individualism*, Georgetown University Press, Washington D. C..

BRIGNALL S, MODELL S. (2000), "An Institutional Perspective on Performance Measurement and Management in the "New Public Sector", *Management Accounting Research*, 11: 281–306.

BRIGNALL, T. J. (1997), "A Contingent Rationale for Cost System Design in Services", *Management Accounting Research*, 8: 325–346.

BROADBENT J., GUTHRIE J. (1992), "Changes in the Public Sector: a Review of Recent "Alternative" Accounting Research", *Accounting, Auditing and Accountability Journal*, 5 (2): 3–31.

BROADBENT J., JACOBS K., LAUGHLIN R. (2001), "Organisational Resistance Strategies to Unwanted Accounting and Finance Changes: the Case of General Medical Practice in the UK", *Accounting Auditing and Accountability Journal*, 14: 565-586.

BURNS J., SCAPENS R. (2000), "Conceptualising Management Accounting Change: an Institutional Framework, *Management Accounting Research*, 11: 3-25.

BURNS J., VAIVIO J. (2001), "Management Accounting Change", *Management Accounting Research*, 12: 389-402.

CACCIA L., STECCOLINI I. (2006), "Accounting in Italian Local Governments: What's Beyond Managerial Fashion?" *Critical perspectives on accounting*, 17: 154-174.

CAMP R. C. (1989), *Benchmarking: The Search for Industry Best Practices that Lead to Superior Performance*, ASQC Quality Press, Milwaukee, WI.

CAMP R. C. (1994), *Business Process Benchmarking: Finding and Implementing Best Practices*, ASQC Quality Press, Milwaukee.

CARNEGIE G., WEST B. P. (2005), "Making Accounting Accountable in the Public Sector", *Critical Perspectives on Accounting*, Vol. 16, No. 7, October 2005: 905-928.

CERTET BOCCONI (2011), *Una proposta per il riassetto delle Province Unione Province Italiane*, Assemblea Unione Province Italiane del 6 dicembre 2011.

COAD A. F., CULLEN J. (2006), "Inter-organisational Cost Management: Towards an Evolutionary Perspective, *Management Accounting Research*, 17.

CORTE DEI CONTI (2012), Relazione sulla gestione finanziaria degli enti locali. Esercizi 2010 – 2011. Deliberazione n. 13/SEZAUT/2012/FRG.

COVALESKI M. A., DIRSMITH M. W. (1983), "Budgets as a Means of Control and Loose Coupling", *Accounting, Organizations and Society*, 8: 323–340. T

COVALESKI M. A., DIRSMITH M. W. (1986), "The Budgetary Process of Power and Politics", *Accounting, Organizations and Society*, 11: 193–214.

COVALESKI M. A., DIRSMITH M. W., SAMUEL S. (1996), "Managerial Accounting Research: the Contributions of Organizational and Sociological Theories", *Journal of Management Accounting Research*, 8: 1–35.

CZARNIAWSKA-JOERGES B., JACOBSSON B. (1989), "Budget in a Cold Climate", *Accounting, Organizations and Society*, 14: 29–39.

DE BRUIJN H. (2002), *Managing Performance in the Public Sector*, London, Routledge.

DE IOANNA P. (2013), *A nostre spese*, Castelvecchi, Roma.

DE TORO, IRVING J. (1995), *Business Process Benchmarking Workshop*, The Quality Network Inc., Rochester, NY, August.

DEL BENE L., MARASCA S. (2009), "Misurare le performance per migliorare la gestione: il caso della Provincia di Ancona", *Azienda Pubblica*, 2: 285-310.

DELLA PORTA A. (2003), *Gli strumenti della contabilità direzionale*, Giappichelli, Torino.

EISENHARDT K. M. (1989), "Building Theories From Case Study Research", *Academy of Management Review*, 14.

EISENHARDT K. M., GRAEBNER M. E. (2007), "Theory Building From Cases: Opportunities and Challenges", *Academy of Management Journal*, 50.

FARNETI G. (2004), *Ragioneria pubblica. Il «nuovo» sistema informativo delle aziende pubbliche*, Milano, Franco Angeli.

FARNETI G., MAZZARA L., SAVIOLI G. (1996), *Il sistema degli indicatori negli enti locali*, Torino, Giappichelli.

FATTORE G. (2005), *Metodi di ricerca in economia aziendale*, Milano, Egea.

FERNANDEZ-REVUELTA PEREZ L., ROBSON K. (1999), "Ritual Legitimation, De-coupling and the Budgetary Process: Managing Organizational Hypocrisies in a Multinational Company", *Management Accounting Research*, 10,4: 383-407.

FLAMHOLTZ G. H. (1981), "Il sistema di controllo come strumento di direzione, *Problemi di gestione*", vol. XII, 3-4: 73-96.

FROST F. A., PRINGLE A. (1993), "Benchmarking or the Search for Industry Best Practice: a Survey of the Western Australian Public Sector", *Australian Journal of Public Administration*, Vol. 52 No. 1, March: 1-11.

GITTO A. (2006), "Gli enti fieristici italiani: evoluzione istituzionale e gestionale", *Azienda Pubblica*, 4: 523-542.

GORI E., FISSI S. (2010), "Un'analisi empirica dei servizi indispensabili e di quelli a domanda individuale nei Comuni italiani per la determinazione degli standard di costo", *Azienda Pubblica*, 3: 369-387.

GRUENING G., (2001), "Origin and Theoretical Basis of New Public Management", *International Public Management Journal*, 4: 1-25.

GUTHRIE J. (1998), "Application of Accrual Accounting in the Australian Public Sector – Rhetoric or Reality", *Financial Accountability & Management*, Vol. 14: 1-19.

HALACHMI A. (1982), "Purpose and Perspective in Evaluation: A Case Study", *Administrative Science Review*, 12 (2): 1-16.

HALACHMI A. (1992), *Evaluation Research: Purpose and Perspective*, HOLZER M. (a cura di), *Handbook of Public Sector Productivity*, New York, Marcell Dekker.

HELDEN G. J., TILLEMA S. (2005), "In Search of a Benchmarking Theory for the Public Sector", *Financial Accountability & Management*, 21: 337-361.

HENRI J. F. (2006), "Management Control Systems and Strategy: A Resource-based Perspective", *Accounting, Organizations and Society*, 31: 529-558.

HOLZER M., YANG K. (2004), "Performance Measurement and Improvement: An Assessment of the State of the Art", *International Review of Administrative Science*, 70 (3): 15-31.

HOOD C. (2011), *The Blame Game*, Princeton University Press, Princeton and Oxford.

HOOD C., (1991), "A Public Management for all Seasons?", *Public Administration*, 69, Spring: 3-19.

HOOD C., (1995), "The "New Public Management" in the 1980s: Variations on a Theme", *Accounting, Organizations and Society*, 20 (2/3): 93-109.

HUMPHREY C., MILLER P., SCAPENS R. (1993), "Accountability and Accountable Management in the UK Public Sector", *Accounting, Auditing & Accountability Journal*, Vol. 6, No. 3.

JACOBS K. (1995), "Budgets: a Medium of Organizational Transformation", *Management Accounting Research*, 6: 59-75.

JACOBS K. (1998), "Costing Health Care: a Study of the Introduction of Cost and Budget Reports into a GP Association", *Management Accounting Research*, 9: 55-70.

KELLY J. M. (2005), "The Dilemma of the Unsatisfied Customer in a Market Model of Public Administration", *Public Administration Review*, 65: 76-84.

KLOOT L., MARTIN J., (2000), "Strategic Performance Management: a Balanced Approach to Performance Management", *Management Accounting Research*, 11.

KOUZMIN A, LOÈFFLER E, KLAGES H., KORAC-KAKABADSE N. (1999), "Benchmarking and Performance Measurement in Public Sectors. Towards Learning for Agency Effectiveness", *The International Journal of Public Sector Management*, Vol. 12 No. 2: 121-144.

LAPSLEY I., PALLOT J. (2000), "Accounting, Management and Organizational Change: a Comparative Study of Local Government", *Management Accounting Research*, N. 11.

LE GRAND J. (2003), *Motivations, Agency, and Public Policy. Of Knights & Knaves, Pawns & Queens*, Oxford University Press, Oxford.

LEIBFRIED K. H. J., MC NAIR C. J. (1992), *Benchmaking: a Tool for Continuous Improvement*, Harper Business.

LONGO F., CRISTOFOLI D. (eds) (2007), *Strategic change management in the public sector*, John Wiley & Sons, UK.

LONTI Z., GREGORY R. (2007), "Accountability or Countability? Performance Measurement in the New Zealand Public Service, 1992-2002", *The Australian Journal of Public Administration*, 66 (4): 468-484.

LOWE A. (2000), "The Construction of a Network at Health Waikato: the "Towards Clinical Budgeting" Project", *Accounting Auditing and Accountability Journal*, 13, 84-114.

MARGINSON D. E. W. (1999), "Beyond the Budgetary Control System: Towards a Two-Tiered Process of Management Control", *Management Accounting Research*, 10: 203-230.

MARKUS M. L., PFEFFER, J. (1983), "Power and the Design and Implementation of Accounting and Control Systems", *Accounting, Organizations and Society* 8 (2/3): 205-218.

MASON R. O., SWANSON E. B. (1979), "Gli indici di valutazione per le decisioni aziendali", *Problemi di gestione*, anno XI, 10: 71-97.

MEYER J. W., ROWAN B. (1977), "Institutionalized Organizations: Formal Structure as a Myth and Ceremony", *The American Journal of Sociology*, Vol. 83 (2): 340-363.

MINISTERO DELL'ECONOMI A E DELLE FINANZE (2009), Relazione Unificata sull'Economia e la Finanza Pubblica per il 2009.

MODELL S. (2001), "Performance Measurement and Institutional Processes: a Study of Managerial Responses to Public Sector Reform", *Management Accounting Research*, 12: 437–464.

MULAZZANI M. (2006) (a cura di), *Economia delle aziende e delle amministrazioni pubbliche. Gli enti locali e le Regioni*, Padova, Cedam.

NEWCOMER K. E. (2007), "Measuring Government Performance", *International Journal of Public Administration*, 30.

NOORDEGRAAF M., ABMA T. (2003), "Management by Measurement? Public Management Practices Amidst Ambiguity", *Public Administration*, vol. 81, n. 4.

OATES W. E. (2008), "On the Evolution of Fiscal Federalism: Theory and Institutions", *National Tax Journal*, 61, 2: 313-334.

OLSON O., GUTHRIE J., HUMPHREY C., (1998), *Global Warning: Debating International Developments in New Public Financial Management*, Oslo, Cappelen Akademisk Forlag.

ORELLI R. L., VISANI F., (2004), "Strumenti di analisi e gestione dei costi: lo stato dell'arte nei Comuni italiani", *Azienda Pubblica*, 4: 587-606.

ORELLI R. L., VISANI F., (2005), "Activity-based cost management nella pubblica amministrazione: una sfida possibile", *Azienda Pubblica*, 3: 381-400.

OSSERVATORIO PER LA FINANZA E LA CONTABILITÀ DEGLI ENTI LOCALI (2006), "LEP e perequazione finanziaria", Ministero dell'interno.

OTLEY D. (1999), "Performance Management: a Framework for Management Control Systems Research", *Management Accounting Research,* 10: 363-382.

PALLOT J. (2003), "A Wider Accountability? The Audit Office and New Zealand's Bureaucratic Revolution", *Critical Perspectives on Accounting*, Vol. 14 (1-2): 133-155.

PIPERATA G. (2011), "Il cammino lento e incerto dei servizi pubblici locali dalla gestione pubblica al mercato liberalizzato", *Munus*, n.1: 1-35.

POLLITT C., BOUCKAERT G. (2004), *Public Management Reform: A Comparative Analysis*, Oxford: Oxford University Press.

POLLITT C., BOUCKAERT G. (2009), *Continuity and Change in Public Policy and Management*, Edward Elgar, Chelthenam-Uk Northampton-Usa.

PRESTON A. M., COOPER D. J., COOMBS R. W. (1992), "Fabricating Budgets: a Study of the Production of Management Budgeting in the National Health Service", *Accounting Organisations and Society*, 17 (6): 561-593.

RADIN E. (2006), *Challenging the Performance Movement. Accountability, Complexity and Democratic Values*, Georgetown University Press, Washington D. C.

ROBERTS J. (2010), "Why Accounting is not Accountability: and Why We Keep Imagining That it is", *Plenary Session Relation*, Apira 2010.

ROBINSON M. (1998), "Accrual Accounting and the Efficiency of the Core Public Sector", *Financial Accountability & Management*, Vol. 14: 21–37.

ROMZEK B. S., DUBNICK M. J. (1987), "Accountability in the Public Sector: Lessons from the Challenger Tragedy", *Public Administration Review*, 47 (3): 227-238.

RONDO-BROVETTO P., SALITERER I. (2007), "Comparing Regions, Cities, and Communities: Local Government Benchmarking as an Instrument for Improving Performance and Competitiveness", *The Innovation Journal: The Public Sector Innovation Journal*, Volume 12 (3), article 13.

SARGIACOMO M. (2000), *Il Benchmarking nell'Azienda Comune*, Torino, Giappichelli.

SARGIACOMO M. (2008), "Benchmarking in Italy: the First Case Study on Personnel Motivation and Satisfaction in a Health Business", *Total Quality Management*, Vol.13, n. 4: 489-505.

SCAPENS R. W., ROBERTS J. (1993), "Accounting Control: a Case study of Resistance to Accounting Change", *Management Accounting Research*, 4 (1): 1-32.

SCHICK A. (1996), *The Spirit of Reform: Managing the New Zealand State Sector in a Time of Change*, State Sevices Commission, Wellington.

SIMONS R. (1990), "The Role of Management Control System in Creating Competitive Advantage: New Perspectives", *Accounting, Organizations and Society*, 15: 127-143.

SOIN K., SEAL W., CULLEN J. (2002), "ABC and Organizational Change: an Institutional Perspective", *Management Accounting Research*, 13: 249-271.

STARLING G. (2005), *Managing the Public Sector*, Thomson Wadsworth, Belmont.

SUBRAMANIAM N., MIA L. (2003), "A Note on Work-Related, Budget Emphasis and Managers'Organisational Commitment", *Management Accounting Research*, 14: 389-408.

TER-MINASSIAN T. (1997), *Fiscal Federalism in Theory and Practice*, International Monetary Fund, Washington, Fiscal Affair Dept.

THOMPSON J. R. (2006), "The Federal Civil Service: The Demise of an Institution", *Public Administration Review*, 66 (4): 496-503.

TRIANTAFILLOU P. (2007), "Benchmarking in the Public Sector: A Critical Conceptual Framework", *Public Administration*, 85.

UPI (2008), *L'evoluzione demografica delle Province dal 1861 ad oggi*.

UPI (2011), *Atlante Statistico delle Province d'Italia*.

WATSON G. H. (1993), *Strategic Benchmarking. How to Rate Your Company's Performance Against the World's Best*, John Wiley & Sons, Inc., New York.

WEINGAST B. R. (2009), "Second Generation Fiscal Federalism: The Implications of Fiscal", *Journal of Urban Economics*, 65, 3: 279-293.

WHOLEY J. S. (1983), *Evaluation and Effective Management*, Boston, Little Brown and Co.

YIN R. K. (2003), *Applications of Case Study Research*, London, Sage Publications.

YIN R. K. (2008), *Case Study Research: Design and Methods* (4th edition), Beverly Hills, CA, Sage Publications.

6

Reforming Public Transport Management in Italy: the Continuous Search for Spending Better[1]

Public sector has been flooded with waves of reforms to improve and make more efficient the services it provides. The local public transport sector has not escaped this major impetus. An intense legislative activity at both the EU and the individual countries parliament is trying to accommodate these new guidelines in order to encourage the emergence of new service organizational forms more output-oriented and more independent from political control. But, local public transport service, compared to education or health, is more problematic to improve because large sums of money are required and significant improvement take many years to achieve. Other European countries have not been trapped in the "make or buy" dilemma, to use or not to use market mechanisms in this particular sector. In a more realistic and pragmatic way they overcame hesitations and chose, for the most part, a path of reforms based on the "market" principles of New Public Management. Surely mistakes were made (to improve the outputs they sacrificed outcomes), but these were followed by corrective action. Italy, unlike other countries, remained stuck in the middle. The objective of this chapter is to show this extreme resistance to experience seriously, deregulation and efficiency-enhanced mechanisms as starting points of the complex service improvement process. The reminder of the chapter is structured as follows. Section 6.2 shows why local transport service improvement is so troubling. Section 6.3 synthetizes the confused reform path followed by Italian central and local governments. Sections 6.4, 6.5, 6.6 explore the main reforms, showing also which were the problems that made problematic the implementation process. In light of these problems we'll illustrate, in section 6.7, which measures were recently imposed by the central government to force this apparently "never ending" reform process. Some concluding remarks will close the chapter.

---

[1] The chapter is the result of a joint effort by the authors who share the formulation. However, the writing of the specific sections has to be divided as follows. Armando Della Porta (corresponding author) wrote paragraphs 6.1, 6.2, 6.3, 6.7, 6.8; Antonio Gitto wrote paragraphs 6.4, 6.5 and 6.6.

Learning objectives

After reading this chapter you should be able to:

- Understand why improving local public transport is so troubling for authorities;
- Understand why the Italian local public transport reforms in the last 30 years have not achieved their goals;
- Recognize the strong difficulties in implementing NPM reforms in Italy.

6.1 Introduction

Public sector has been flooded with waves of reforms (Pollitt and Bouckaert, 2000; Hood, 2000) to improve and make more efficient the services it provides. These reforms come principally from economics and management that are now replacing political and law disciplines as the mainstream public sector organizing framework (Hood, 1991; Hughes, 1994;). Their main goal is to make it more similar to the private one (Boyne, 2002). As a consequence new mechanisms, such as market competition and performance management (de Bruiin, 2007), have been replacing the traditional ones, based on hierarchy and trust on public servants. The literature has problematically described this shift (Gray and Jenkins, 1995; Borgonovi, 2006) as a transition from *Public Administration* to *New Public Management*, which expresses in broad terms the need to focus more on outputs than on inputs, to pay more attention on users satisfaction than on formal compliance with legal rules, to rely more on up-to-date management and strategic tools to achieve the political goals (Ashworth, Boyne, Entwistle 2010; Borgonovi, Fattore, Longo, 2009; Anessi Pessina, 2002). And last but not least, to trust less public managers, traditionally seen as Knights, and to consider them as individuals pursuing their own interests, as Knaves (Le Grand, 2003).

The local public transport sector has not escaped this major impetus. An intense legislative activity at both the EU and the individual countries parliament is trying to accommodate these new guidelines (van de Velde, 2008), not without hesitation and resistance, in order to encourage the emergence of new service organizational forms (van de Velde, 1999) more results-oriented and more independent from political control. The goal is to dismantle excessive political control by placing greater trust on market mechanisms, such as privatization and competition, as levers to solve service efficiency and quality problems (Beesley, 1997; Hensher, 2005). It was not an easy task because local public transport service in some ways has proved difficult to explore (Sargiacomo, Gomes, 2011) and to improve compared to others public services. In more general terms Ubels et al. (2004: 23) observes that "the crux of the problem is that the benefits of car use are very evident to individuals, whereas the problems are more diffuse, hit others rather than car users, with some impinging on future rather than current generation". So, the theme of local public transport improvement "is not […] favoured by politicians, certainly compared to, for example, education and health. For things, to improve significantly, large sums of money are required, and significant improvements take many years to achieve. Transport projects can also be controversial and, even where they are generally accepted, schemes under construction tend to generate hostility at a local level due to the disruption involved. This unequal conflict between choosing immediate and tangible personal benefit over a delayed and far less visible cost to society is behind many of the difficulties faced when addressing the transport crisis".

So, improving local public transport service is a troubling matter for politicians. Things are not so different when market mechanisms are introduced. Even the most fervent advocate of free competition (Hibbs, 2009) cannot fail to recognize, in fact, that market mechanisms can do little to improve the whole performance of transport service. Competition and privatization, if implemented, could reduce the cost of the service, but is unlikely to solve the problems of congestion and pollution (Mees, 2000).

As is evident from these brief and sketchy considerations, it is not easy to find a way out. Other European countries have not been trapped in the "make or buy" dilemma, to use or not to use market mechanisms in this particular sector. In a more realistic and pragmatic way they overcame hesitations and chose, for the most part, a path of reforms based on the "market" principles of New Public Management. They recognized the changing nature of the local public transport service and the public failures and, accordingly, acted to improve the service efficiency through the levers of privatization and competition (free, regulated or both) (van de Velde, Beck, 2010). Surely mistakes were made, to improve the outputs they sacrificed outcomes (Lonti and Gregory, 2007), but these were followed by corrective action (Hefetz, Warner, 2004) such as using free competition or contracting out in a less dogmatic way by introducing more coordination mechanisms (Sorensen and Longva, 2011; Hefetz, Warner, 2012). In more general terms, in the past, the emphasis was on outputs and on the best ways to deregulate the "too much" regulated local public transport sector. Now we are witnessing the reverse process. The emphasis is now on how to better balance output and outcomes. So the question is: which are the best ways to regulate the deregulated local public transport sector? (van de Velde, Wallis, 2013). Italy, unlike other countries, has not embarked on this trial and error learning cycle. It has failed in finding a satisfactory synthesis to the conflicting social and economic pressures and remained *stuck in the middle*, despite being characterized by a desperate financial distress (Boitani, Cambini, 2004; Piperata, 2011).

The objective of this chapter is to show, in some respects, this extreme resistance to experience and test seriously the deregulation as starting point of the difficult and complex local public transport service improvement process. The chapter is structured as follows. In the next section we, briefly, try to show why the local public transport service improvement process is so troubling. Then we describe, principally, the last 30 years stages of the Italian local public transport service reform process that we have defined "confused", showing also, which were the problems that have slowed, if not stopped it. In light of these problems and the resistance showed by Italian Regions we illustrate which measures were recently imposed by the central government to force this apparently "never ending" reform process. Some concluding remarks will close the chapter.

6.2 Improving Local Public Transport Service: a controversial issue

What is Public Service improvement? It is not easy to answer. From the literature (Boyne, 2003) we know that it is a controversial issue, inherently political and contestable. And that "will not go away" (Talbot, 2010). The solution, in the end, is the ability to find an agreement between potentially conflicting perspectives (Christensen and Laegreid, 2007, Borgonovi and Mussari, 2010). This means that public service improvement is the continuous search for a new or a better balance between conflicting stakeholders interests. Boyne (2003) reminds us that service improvement has tangible dimensions (cost, quantity, speed of delivery, etc) and therefore, is the result of a compromise between objective and subjective dimensions in the light of certain circumstances (social, economic, cultural). In the local public transport case, we have to balance on the one hand, the objective reasons of individual companies financial outputs improvement and, on the other hand, the subjective reasons that give substance to the general interest service concept, that has, in the socio-environmental outcomes improvement, the rationale for its existence and for the public service obligations imposition (Ponti, 2006).

Improving local public transport service means, therefore, finding a solution, i. e. a regulatory regime, that is able to reconcile outputs and outcomes (Mele, 2003; Popoli, 1998; Pavan, 1992). It is, obviously, a problematic task. NPM supporters, as we know, give priority to efficiency and financial outputs as starting point, as necessary conditions and constraints to achieve whatever social goal the government subjectively judge as valuable. They prefer deregulation and market initiative organizational forms (van de Velde, 1999). New Public Management (Hood, 1991) has many flaws (deregulation is not at all the new one best way to improve public service performance), but has the merit of focusing attention to the managerial problems of individual firms operating in the public sector. State-owned enterprises, even before being mere "means" pursuing public interest "ends", are firms who have to take care of themselves, of their economic and financial conditions (Cavalieri, 2010).

Over the years the market share of public transport has greatly reduced in favor of the private car (Kenworthy J., Laube F., 1999). Among the causes we have:

- the increase in car ownership and in road infrastructure supply that has both failed to reduce congestion and undermined the local public transport service (Banister, 2005);
- the increase in capital and operative subsidies to local public transport that have not improved its attractiveness, as thought, but only increased its production costs (Lave, 1991).

As a consequence, numerous public transport organizations all over the world became public resources addicted, suffering low productivity, high costs and low tariff revenues. Also due to the severe crisis we are experiencing, which has reduced the public resources availability, the efficiency and productivity issues can no longer be marginalized. It is fundamental, therefore, to reverse this situation and give priority to solutions that minimize the (pathological) dependence on public subsidies (Pucher, Buheler, 2010).

Given the undisputed superiority of the private car, one should take note of this and recognize the public failure (Winston, 2000) in satisfying the changing mobility needs of the people and give the market a new chance. But how and where? In the past, public interest in local transport was principally linked with social inclusion and territorial cohesion, giving priority to *coverage* strategies implemented by public-owned enterprises. Now the paradigm has changed (Marletto, 2004) and public interest is more linked with the financial problem and the satisfaction of new mobility needs as a way to solve congestion and pollution problems.

The fundamental NPM solution to this "new" local public transport problem, therefore, is to use soft regulation instead of integrated planning (Hibbs, 2000) and to give free competition and road price mechanisms a chance to pursue local public transport efficiency, quality and environmental goals (*patronage*) in high density and demand areas and to use, similarly, market mechanisms (in particular competitive tendering) to spending better public money in pursuing planned social *coverage* goals in low demand areas. Public transport can contribute to achieve both environmental and financial goals only if many people ride it instead of cars. This can be interpreted as obvious but, in reality and even in high demand areas, public transport services are often designed for social reasons other than high patronage. The solution, therefore, is, to acknowledge and make finally clear the difference between *patronage* and *coverage* goals (Walker, 2008) and use public resources, principally, to achieve social *coverage goals*, letting market mechanisms the task to achieve *patronage goals*. The confusion between *coverage* and *patronage* goals is one of the principal cause of public failures in the local transport service. Too much public money was spent in (not) pursuing *patronage* goals in high density areas, through bad regulated state-owned enterprises, instead of private ones by means of market mechanisms and, at the same time, too much public money was spent in pursuing *coverage* goals through inefficient state-owned enterprises in low-density areas instead[2] of selected efficient private firms. So, summing up, the advices offered by New Public Management supporters are to:

a. use, fundamentally, soft regulation, congestion charges ("steering not rowing", Barlow and Rober, 1996), privatization and free competition to achieve clear *patronage goals*, to innovate, to satisfy real mobility needs and to make the service more financially and environmentally sustainable by eliminating the internal political and public managerial inefficiencies (poor cost control, unjustified service and personnel expansion and slow tariff adjustment) that are the causes of high public subsidies and users dissatisfaction;
b. use public money, principally, to achieve *coverage goals*, using more efficient selective mechanisms, such as competitive tendering or performance contracts, instead of inefficient ones, such as direct award or automatic concession renewal.

---

[2] "From a theoretical point of view public production of goods and services is somewhat of an embarassment to most economists. It exists, and will in all likelihood increase in importance, but is difficult to explain" (Pashigian, 1976: 1239). Shleifer (1998: 135) states that: "When the opportunities for governmental contracting are exploited, the benefits of outright state ownership become elusive, even when social goals are taken into account. Moreover, it becomes clear that private ownership is the crucial source of incentives to innovate and become efficient".

In giving priority to *outcomes* problems instead of *outputs* ones, the critics of the improvement program proposed by New Public Management supporters argue that:

a. the difference between *patronage* and *coverage goals* is not so sharp (for example even in high density areas we have low-demand problems, like in the evenings and in the week-end) (Mees, 2010);

b. the efficiency problem is not so good as starting point and that, in any case, the question cannot be set at the level of individual companies (organizational effectiveness) but at a higher level (network service whole performance) because it is necessary to take into account the costs of integration of the service network (Pucher, 1996);

c. that the huge subsidies (or the high ticket prices in the deregulated bus sector, like in UK – except London) are not so much due to internal public (or private) management inefficiency and/or opportunistic behavior, but to unfavorable external environmental factors (congestion) that impose higher costs of service planning and management through the increase of the dimension of the area to be served (suburbanization and sprawling), and the reduction of the commercial speed of public transport buses, of their attractiveness and, ultimately, of their load and traffic revenues (Taylor et al., 2009);

d. that the transformation of the local transport service from an *input* to a *result-oriented* one is much more complex and cannot be solved just by looking down at the companies, putting them in competition with each other, with the obsessive goal to reduce costs to solve balance-sheet problems, but, rather, looking up (Stanley, Smith, 2013), to the institutions that have the responsibility to make the service more attractive with less road construction and better network planning and governance mechanisms (eg. dedicated bus lanes, less city car parking, more compact cities) designed to solve congestion (Goodwin, 1997). Therefore, the real challenge is in managing demand with "predict and prevent" policies instead of increasing offer with "predict and provide" or free-market-based policies (Owens, 1995). How can be attractive and performing a public transport service if it is not integrated regarding times, frequencies, tariffs as it is, in fact, the one produced by the invisible hand of the market and if it is not supported by coordinated pro-public transport and environment policies?;

e. that public transport should be considered primarily as a resource, such as an investment to reduce the negative externalities produced by private cars and to increase the efficiency, the competitiveness and the social equity of the territories and not just as a cost to be reduced with privatization policies (Sclar, 2000);

f. that the free competition invoked could be counterproductive both to reduce the internal service production costs and the external ones (pollution and congestion) (Gomez-Lobo, 2007).

To this end, the solution suggested is not in a better functioning of the market mechanisms (especially free competition) but in producing organizational innovations (eg. integrated network planning, Hull, 2005) and policies (eg. Compact cities) that are able to increase the service value and its attractiveness to the users. The external costs (pollution and congestion) are not only the result of a malfunctioning of the market, that does not charge the environmental damages to those who produce them (through congestion charges or road price mechanisms), but the negative effect of policies that have not been able to exploit scale and scope economies in a traffic area (Di Giacomo, Ottoz, 2007) and to offer an high quality integrated service. The high quality of local public transport service is, ultimately, the solution to reduce the public resources addiction. The value innovation, the increase in revenues and in public profits resulting from an integrated service with high frequencies and connections enforced by coordinated environmental policies, rather than cost reduction or retrenchment strategies (Boyne, 2004) is the way that will save both the public transport companies balance-sheets and the congestion problem. It follows that *output* and *outcome* goals can be achieved not by increasing the degree of competition of the local public transport sector but by reducing its organizational and political innovation deficit (Marletto, 2006), by improving performance management systems and public-private partnerships (Entwistle and Martin, 2005; Borgonovi and Mussari, 2010). The advocates of the primacy of the organizational and political innovation through an integrated network planning set by public authorities, offer, as a proof, the public transport successes achieved in diverse metropolitan areas such as London, Zurich or Bogotá (Transmilenio) (Pucher, 1996; Mees, 2000, 2010) that can be defined as real and working public solutions, as opposed to market failures registered in the deregulated areas of UK, New Zealand, Chile, to the local public transport problems.

From the above considerations it appears that is not so easy to sever the link with politics and leave it all to the market. Without a strong political will to fight congestion, hardly the resources invested, high or low as they are, in the public transport service will give results, increasing the service market share, for example, through the increase of the commercial speed of buses or trams, making them more attractive. So is not so easy solve the "make *or* buy" dilemma. Some authors call for an ambitious solution, a proactive public network planning with business delivery (a "make *and* buy" solution), as the key to the efficient repositioning of the service (Barter, 2008). The European Institutions, through Regulation 1370/2007 are very prudent and cautious. While suggesting to use the market in the soft form of regulated competition (competitive tendering and not free competition) as the main rule to award local public transport service by selecting the more efficient provider, they left the decision to use it or not to the individual countries without forcing them and not refuting the "in house" solution, albeit as a second best and only in special cases. This position is a balanced one that try to join public planning and market tools, standing between the defense of the value of competitive pressure, the need to find a mechanism to quantify a fair compensation for the local public transport service obligations and the need to guarantee a quality service network that meets the mobility needs of the people. Leaving aside, for the moment, the quality problems, it is not possible to pay subsidies which do not reflect efficiency criteria in providing the service, as is the case of the direct award to state-owned enterprise. Public subsidies, are not wrong per se, but if they are too high they could be considered a state aid and not a fair price for a service obligation. So we need a benchmark to know what the fair price is. If market mechanisms, or others (efficiency-enhanced regulation with performance contracts), can help to quantify a fair fee for a service obligation is a decision that has to be left to the local governments, or better to the local transport bodies, that should be responsible of the service performance of a whole traffic area. At the end what matters is not if the service provider is a public or private one, but not to pay more than the due (see the Altmark case commented in Zanelli, 2004) and to stay on the budget while respecting certain quality standards. Since it is very difficult, with a shrinking public budget, to achieve at the same time ambitious social, efficiency and quality goals, more pragmatically, improving local public transport services means choosing, in a responsible way, how much social goals sacrifice in order to improve efficiency and quality goals and vice versa. At the end, the problem of improving local public transport service can be solved by finding an agreement regarding how to redefine the meaning of public interest in local public transport by recognizing the changing nature of the service and, accordingly, by choosing which tasks are best performed privately or publicly. One notably balanced solution is that expressed by Gwilliam (2008):

Expectation must be realistic. Aspirations to high quality public transport must be backed either by the fare box or the public budget. Someone has to pay […] The continuing issue is how to align expectations with resource availability.

Incentives matter. Suppliers and regulators have their own objectives and interests […] It should never be presumed that either is necessarily acting in the sole interests of passengers […] The continuing issue is how to mold those private incentives in support of a publicly desirable outcome.

Competitive pressure works. Recent experience has shown not only that costs can be reduced through competitive pressure […] but also that is possible to design competitive structures which are directed at qualitative as well as pure cost reduction objectives […] The continuing issue is how to maintain the competitive impulse as suppliers adjust to eliminate it.

Public sector involvement is inevitable. Because of the prevalence of externality and spill-over effects, unregulated private behavior is very unlikely to coincide with any acceptable concept of the public good. The continuing issue is not whether the public sector has a role, but where and how the public sector involvement is best placed.

Supply structure is important. Fragmentation of supply is not unacceptable per se, but makes many things (service coordination, monitoring) more difficult. Where contracts with incumbent suppliers are negotiated or re-negotiated to overcome these problems the continuing issue is how to keep the market contestable, without losing scale and scope economies.

Governments institutions must be adequate and effective. Poor design of franchises, or inability to control collusion will inevitably get franchising a bad name. Some governments are already cool to the concept of competitive tendering as they perceive difficulties in implementing quality objectives in a market based regime. The continuing issue is whether the contract design and behavioral control skills of the public sector institutions can be developed to the degree necessary to prevent breakdown of managed competitive arrangements."

This six-point list is not a recipe but an invitation to make experiments with those ingredients. Through the continuing experimentation, other countries have learned how to use markets, incentives, public institutions not only to reduce costs but also to innovate and to improve the service quality (Entwistle, Martin, 2005).

They learned that:

a. at the end is the right mix (Borgonovi, Mussari, 2010) of governance modes (hierarchy, markets and networks) that matters (Rhodes, 1997) and not just the magic one (free competition or ambitious but costly public network planning);

b. the mix is specific to each situation;
c. can only be found through experimentation based on realistic expectations.

If it is true that basic governance modes (Powell, 1997) are well known (competition, hierarchy and network-cooperation) it is also true that the right mix can only be discovered through a serious trial and error process. The main point is that markets and private firms have the potential to improve the efficiency and the quality of the local public transport service, but a lot depends on the local authority and its willingness to change.

In the next section we'll describe *the Italian way* in treating local public transport improvement problems.

6.3   The "confused" path to improve the financial sustainability of Local Public Transport in Italy in the last 30 years

The actual impasse of the local public transport service process improvement in Italy is largely dependent on how the Italian central and local governments have (not) been able to effectively implement the various reforms that have been deliberated.

In a broader sense, we can identify three stages of development of local public transport in Italy.

The first phase is mainly focused on the urban dimension and on the social function of the public transport service and lasts about eighty years (1903-1981). It is better known as the municipal capitalism age.

The second phase goes from 1981 to 2012 and marks the Regionalism age. The main goal is to make the local public transport service more efficient and less dependent on public resources. There are two main reforms that have tried to achieve it.

The first, most ambitious, dates back to 1981 (Law 151/1981). It is characterized by an explicit attempt to try and maintain the full social function of the service, reducing, however, the internal production costs. To achieve this goal a concerted and collaborative effort between the Central Government and the Regions (hierarchy + network mechanisms) is required. The Government is committed, through the establishment of the National Transport Fund, to subsidize the local public transport service no longer according to historical expenditure criterion but according to the most efficiency-enhanced one of standard costing. The tasks of the regions are to plan the service in a more rational and integrated way and to calculate standard costs according to their territorial and social specificities.

The second reform, less ambitious and more realistic, is of 1997 (Law 422/1997). It is the consequence of the problems that have occurred with the first one. It draw up a new strategy to reduce costs: the downgrade of the social function of the service and the use of compulsory competitive tendering to select the most efficient provider. Public transport service is not anymore a "full" social service but a "minimum" one. It introduces, in fact, for the first time, the concept of "minimum services".

Given the implementation difficulties of the Law 151/1981, the Law 422/97 fully empowers the Italian regions (devolution) also from a financial point of view, and not just for service planning, so as to make them more financially responsible. In addition, by using compulsory competitive tendering and service contracts, the reform makes use of a new governance mode (from trust and cooperation to distrust and market) to overcome the automatic renewal of the concessions to inefficient local government-owned companies.

In general, the more the legislation opened to efficiency logics (standard costs and competitive tendering), the more the social function of the service was reduced with the introduction of the concept of minimum services and the more local governments and local public transport companies resisted to protect the public monopoly and the full social function of the service, preventing the change and worsening their financial situation. To this kind of behavior has contributed also a confused legislative process that has delayed, if not deleted, once again, the implementation of the planned changes (Cangiano, 2005).

Unlike other countries, Italy, has failed to overcome the resistance to change shown by the main actors of the service (Regions and public transport companies). The central government did not have the strength to impose the change and to reduce the service performance gaps both internal, between different regions, and external, with other countries. Faced, however, with the risk of the financial failure of the service, the government decided to force the change. Hence the need for a third, recent, intervention, more authoritative and more oriented to implement the change by defeating the inertia of the regions. In 2012 the central government decided, in fact, through a normative discontinuity (Law 228/2012) at the limit of the law, to take on the governance of local public transport service. With more powers, central government developed a road map to achieve the main goal of reducing the excess of service supply by making it more "adequate" to the mobility needs and less dependent on public resources. The mechanisms used are the same as in 1981, namely the National Fund of Transport and standard costs, but in a new framework that reverses the responsibility of implementation. Now it is the central government that dictates the executional deadlines, not the regions, that have been downgraded to the role of mere executors, to reward or punish if they do not comply with the new rules. This confused regulatory cycle, swinging between central and local government, is shown schematically in Table 6.1.

6.4 Municipalism Age: 1903-1981: Protecting the social function of the urban transport service

At the beginning of the century the central theme was the destructiveness and usefulness of competition in pursuing the social interest and Italy promptly recognized (with Giolitti's Law of 1903) this social interest and chose, like other countries,[3] to

---

[3] With regard to Ireland, Jakee and Allen (1999: 13), report the statements of the Minister of Transport Lemass in 1944, reflecting the then prevailing conception regarding the use of free competition in the transport sector: "Whatever theoretical case can be made for competition in encouraging efficiency or stimulating enterprise in other commercial spheres, it can, in relation to transport, undermine the stability of services which are necessary to the national commercial life and can in its effect do irreparable damage to the public interest".

Table 6.1   The "Confused" Path to Improve the Financial Sustainability of Local Public Transport in Italy in the Last 30 years

Municipalism Age	Regionalism Age		Statalism Age
(Giolitti's Law 1903)	(Law 151/81)	(Law 422/97)	(Law 228/2012)
A simple solution that lasted almost 80 years: 1) Urban transport: Municipalized firm; 2) Extraurban transport: Regulated Private concession.	Almost full publicization of LPT (urban and extraurban). From Municipal to Special Companies direct award. 16 years of increasing deficit and regional financial irresponsibility. No serious implementation of cost control and reduction strategies. **Command and Control PARTIAL DEVOLUTION Vertical dimension:** State financial control with **NTF** and **Standard Costing**. **Horizontal dimension:** Strategic, Tactical and Operative functions designed and implemented by Regions and Public-owned enterprises (direct award) to provide a **full social** integrated local transport network.	From Special Companies to Public Owned joint stock companies. From direct award to competitive tendering with service contracts. 15 years of resistance and confused market reforms implementation **Choice-Market Oriented FULL DEVOLUTION Vertical dimension:** Strategic (Financial) and Tactical functions under the Regional Government responsibility **Horizontal dimension:** Operative functions with market mechanisms (competition in and for the market) to provide a **minimal** and efficient local transport network.	Normative discontinuity: Top down goals: 1) Resizing transport service. 2) Improve financial autonomy with NTF and Standard Costing 3) Tight executional central control with penalties **Strong Command and Control RE-CENTRALIZA-TION** Strong State financial control with the 1981 solutions: **NTF** and **Standard Costing** More Powers in vertical and horizontal dimensions. Strong State control on service cost information to provide an efficient and **adequate** local transport service.

govern it with the "in house" provision, utilizing the municipalized firms. Giolitti's reform of 1903 opened the municipal capitalism age in Italy (Dell'Alpi, 1928; Laghi, 1919). Before, urban public transport was a private activity carried out in a free market regime. Since then, a lot of problems has become evident (iniquity and uneven covering of the land) calling for direct public intervention to protect the public interest. Free competition was considered wasteful because of the high infrastructure costs (tramways). It was considered better to have only one public municipal operator (natural monopoly). This has led to the rise of large urban public transport firms owned by municipalities with the goal to satisfy social and basic mobility needs (social inclusion and territorial cohesion).

Apart from the usual reasons aimed at preventing private firms to take advantage of the monopolistic nature of the sector and to avoid destructive competition, there are more pronounced reasons of structural weakness and fragility of the private Italian companies which justified the direct intervention of the state (Anselmi, 1995). Rodotà (1995) notes that the Italian intervention in the economy was justified mainly for the historical weaknesses of the Italian economy. Giannini (1985: 8) goes even further when he writes that "the modern Italian economic history is a simple story of requests to the State to assume the burden of providing public services that private firms were not able to deliver for reasons of company size".

If it is true that private firms were not able to provide such services, it is also true that the nascent market of local public services gave sufficient guarantees for the financial autonomy of municipal-owned enterprises.

During the 40s and the 50s the development of car ownership gradually reduced the public transport market share. Between 1950 and 1970 some major reforms began to be discussed. After the 1970, the municipalities, owners of public transport utilities, were finding it increasingly difficult to bear the growing deficit of urban public transport. The financial resources allocated to public transport were reducing the action in other social areas. The state was expected to contribute substantially to fund the deficit. The extraurban transport operated by social regulated private concession during the Seventies showed accounts in surplus. But, the increase in road offer and in car ownership and the strong social regulation did not allow the private transport operators to maintain an economic balance.

6.5 Regionalism Age (part 1): 1981-1997: On trying to introduce efficiency-enhanced mechanisms to control local public transport costs.

The Seventies see the birth of the Italian Regions and the controversial Regionalism Age. The first act that they performed within the functions delegated to them was to solve the extra-urban transportation problem by making it a public one. Regions spent a lot of public money to buy the extra-urban lines by private concessionaries. This decision was motivated by their financial distress caused, for the most part, by a stringent social service obligations impositions. In fact, local public transport market shares deeply declined while the costs necessary to maintain the social function of the service increased. Some data is sufficient to describe the state in which the industry was in the early 80s: if in the early 60s companies were able to cover their operating costs with market revenues for about 80%, in 1982 this same percentage amounted to just above 20% (Baldassarri, 1998).[4]

---

[4] Baldassarri G. (1998), *La riforma del trasporto pubblico locale*, "Riv. Proteo", n. 3.

For urban routes, numerous and patchy laws were enacted to settle the deficit also accompanied by increasingly strict rules limiting the indebtedness of municipalities. To address these problems Italy began to recognize the importance of looking at the LTP service in a more balanced way, as a social and efficient service, by introducing more efficiency-enhanced logics. It was no longer possible to continue to guarantee social mobility rights without taking into account the available resources (rights without resources).

As a consequence a first organic, and ambitious, reform concerning Local Public Transport was launched in 1981, with the Law 151/1981 (Golinelli, 1984). The main points of this reform were:

a. the definition of Local Public Transport as a wider territoral service (from urban to functional traffic zones – basins – inside the Regional.borders) to be planned in an integrated way. With this Law the service remained fundamentally social (local transport is for work, study and tourism purposes);
b. the introduction of the National Fund of Transport to finance the service, the amount of which was set each year by the Finance Act;
c. the introduction of standard costs as a criterion to quantify the right fee to compensate the public service obligations impositions and to improve the service efficiency;
d. the changing of legal form from municipal to special companies, but always publicly owned, to make them more formally independent from political control.

The central government, through the National Fund of Transport and standard costs information would have to control the service efficiency. Local governments, in particular the regions, would have cooperate with the government by:

a. giving right cost data (standard costs);
b. securing the social function of LPT service in a more rational way, through an integrated network planning on a wider territorial dimension (from urban areas to traffic areas within the region) in order to eliminate waste and service duplication.

What results were achieved? Before answering, we think it is necessary to briefly explore the nature of the LTP crisis, as it is conventionally explained by mainstream economic theory. The crisis, in fact, is not only due to the monopoly of the private car with the subsequent decline of the LPT market share. It cannot, in fact, be attributed only to the decline in traffic revenues, although this has been a major component, but also to the political unrealistic ambitions to maintain a universal service without the support of sufficient resources. The economic literature (Lave1991; Viton 1998; Obeng, 2011) is unanimous in stressing the point that if the transport service, especially suburban or rural, had remained in the private sector, firms would have reacted to the market share decline with a reduction in supply through retrenchment and repositioning strategies of the LPT service only in the most profitable segments.

To secure the social function of the service, the State, after careful consideration of costs and benefits, should have provided the service only and exclusively in the segments left uncovered by the retreat of the private firms. It did not happen this way. The state decided, instead, to expand the service by acquiring extra-urban failing private firms. Thanks to subsidies guaranteed by the National Fund of Transport, the suburban transport (which together with the urban one was unified with the Law 151/1981 in the new concept of "local public transport" even though they were of different nature) has continued to grow and expand territorially, causing supply excesses and service duplication without any coordination and, most importantly, without any consideration to the changing mobility needs of the users.

With the National Fund of Transport, Law 151/81 institutionalized the idea that the local public transport sector, as a whole (urban and extraurban) is not self-sufficient and that, therefore, must be funded with public resources albeit with new criteria, standard costs (Golinelli, 1986) and not with those of historical expenditure. If the intention was to find a fair compromise between the social function of service and efficiency, practices have been very different. The regions and LPT companies continued to focus on social outcomes, and not to contain the service costs within the standards that the legislator had established. It was not so effective, also, to change the legal form of the former municipal companies into "special" ones to lessening the political control. So, in order to answer the question posed earlier, as to whether the new regulatory framework has or has not achieved the goal to make LPT more efficient, the answer is an emphatic no. On the contrary, such a solution has exacerbated the financial crisis in the sector.

This solution has been the primary cause of the rise of the public transport deficits. Designed to stimulate with an efficiency-enhanced mechanism (standard costing) the reduction of the service costs, it has become a great incentive to their increase. The Fund was an incentive to increase suburban and extraurban lines and personnel. It was an unexpected consequence. The injection of public money, especially for operating expenses through the National Fund of Transport, has reduced the productivity of services, increased the number of workers, strengthened the role of unions and increased costs when it should only cover its rationalization and restructuration and not a costly expansion.

The L. 151/1981 did not work because it did not change the social and universalistic conception of the transport service, no longer in line with the times, and poorly implemented. This intervention did not recognize the change in individual mobility needs, nor the diversity of needs of different areas (high and low demand areas) and has resulted, in general, only in a greater coverage of the regions rather than in a real service improvement.

It, also, did not work because the National Transport Fund sent wrong signals in relation to efficiency issues. The Fund was composed by two parts: capital and operating subsidies. The literature, for the most part, states that the productivity and efficiency decline observed can be attributed more to the effects caused by the portion relating to operating subsidies than to that caused by the capital subsidies for the fleet bus renewal.

The operating subsidies were, in fact, paid without taking into account the agreed results (gradual improvement – 10% – of the efficiency and productivity). If the capital subsidies were limited to the sole purpose of providing a one-shot injection of capital for the modernization of the bus fleet but not to fully cover the costs, with the operating subsidies paid by continuing to apply the historical cost approach and not the standard costs, the end result was to discourage once for all the control of the efficiency. The coverage of all costs necessary to provide the service in larger basins, identified by using not functional criteria but administrative ones, characterized, for the most part, by very low density areas, provoked what the NPM supporters feared: the confusion between patronage and coverage goals that merged into the single concept of Local Public Transport, conceived as a universal service, which mixes in a financially untenable way distinct objectives.

The Law 151/81, in the absence of a credible sanctions policy, sent a wrong signal to LPT managers and workers. Managers and executives interpreted the guaranteed financial coverage of the historic expenditures, without penalties, as proof that cost control and efficiency were less important than maintaining the social function of the service. Employees and trade unions that represented them, interpreted the signal in the sense that subsidies could be used for the recruitment of personnel not strictly necessary, to improve wages, to reduce working-hours, and, more in general, to improve the employees working conditions, without regard to efficiency, productivity and user satisfaction. The Law 151/81, in its implementation, failed to find a compromise between the social function of the service and its efficiency: on the one hand, it continued to perpetuate a social conception of the service, no longer in line with the actual mobility needs, on the other hand, it provided a tool, standard costs, which was not applied for fear of strikes and service interruptions threatened by the unions. So nothing changed. One of the fundamental errors was, in fact, not to have provided a unique methodology for the calculation of standard costs, leavingthe regions the freedom to define them. The result has been a general alignment of standards to historical costs and to more inefficient firms, in order to protect them, thus negating in practice the efficiency-enhanced nature of the instrument (Buzzo, Margari, Piacenza, 2005).

The end result has been a deterioration of the economic and financial situation of the service in comparison with the previous phase, where the extra-urban transport, operated under license to private firms, was slowly resizing. Under this reform the service growed to serve low density areas. The regions and public transport companies reacted with unnecessary growth strategies rather than cooperate with central government to reduce costs.

The Court of Auditors (2003: 4) underlined very clearly the failure of this reform:[5] "the system based on the Law n.151/1981 [...] in securing the ex-post deficit fixing, produced the uncontrolled growth of public spending relating to local transport, resulting in the need for continuing extraordinary measures to cover the local government-owned deficits".

6.6   Regionalism Age (part 2): 1997-2012: On trying to use competitive tendering to reduce local public transport costs

The deficits of the operators, as seen, not only were "cleaned" through the National Transport Fund but they increased over time. Standard costing methods never worked due to the strong resistance and the difficulties of their calculation. In the face of such

---

[5] Corte dei Conti (2003), *La gestione del trasporto pubblico locale e lo stato di attuazione della riforma a livello regionale – Relazione comparativa e di sintesi sull'andamento dei trasporti locali*, Roma, p. 4.

behavior on the part of public companies and local governments, central government decided to abandon the network-cooperative mode of governance typical of the 80s, by replacing it with new solutions, such as privatization, competition and the downgrading of the universalistic ambitions of the transport service.

This type of solution was initiated by the government delegations in 1996 and 1997, but took the general characteristics with the two legislative decrees, called Burlando after the Minister of Transport, the n. 422/97 and the n.400/99. The main points of this reform were:

a. full devolution of responsibilities (financial and planning) to local authorities;
b. separation between regulation and management by relying on a service contract;
c. exclusive award mechanism: competitive tendering;
d. changing of legal form: from special companies to joint stock companies;
e. minimum obligation to cover costs through tickets revenues (35%);
f. elimination of the National Transport Fund and the budget constraints to centrally transferred resources;
g. less ambitious conception of the local public transport service (minimum service).

With the reform of 1997, the central government eliminated the National Transport Fund and the problematic standard costs system, empowered the Regions on the financial aspects and forced them to plan a less ambitious local transport planning, more compatible with the resources available and closer to the real user mobility needs.

This new approach had its strengths, primarily, in the prohibition of direct and in-house providing, and in the obligation to choose the provider through a competitive tendering system. Given the difficulty in applying the standard costs, the central government decided to rely, above all, on market mechanisms to bring out the hidden inefficiencies of public providers.

Other mechanisms used for this purpose were the further change of the legal form, from special companies to joint-stock companies (once again publicly owned), the requirement (never respected and never sanctioned) to have a minimum coverage of 35% of operating costs with revenues traffic, the use of service contracts (in reality without rewards and penalties).

The compulsory competitive tendering, as it was easy to foresee, did not please local governments and public providers (D'Amico, Palumbo, 2008). Moreover, even the EU Regulation 1370/2007 which rules the awarding procedures for passenger transport services provided by rail and by road, did not provide for compulsory competitive tendering, but allowed freedom of choice between direct award, in house providing and competitive tendering. If the European law allowed freedom of choice why the Italian one was so limiting? Consequently, the implementation of this reform had, in some ways, a schizophrenic path. The direction taken by Italian law, to separate public regulation from day-to day management operations by a mechanism (competition for the market) aimed to select the more efficient providers, was the right one.

What did not work this time? The strong resistance to compulsory competitive tendering through a confused legislative path marked by the following steps:

- a good start, represented by the legislative choice of the compulsory competitive tendering rule (Legislative Decree no. 400/1999);

- a mild and partial application of the rule (not all regions have organized the bidding process in time and the few competitive procedures realized have been won by the incumbents with tiny price reduction);
- to cope with numerous technical difficulties, new deadlines have been allowed by law (from the first deadline of 31.12.2003 set by the Legislative Decree 400/1999, we passed to a new deadline at the end of 31.3.2011 allowed by dl 29/12/2010 No. 225, to the final deadline at the end of 2019 laid down in EU Regulation 1370/2007);
- other rules of awarding the service have been allowed by Law 326/2003; competitive tendering is just one, there are others mentioned by the general legislation on local public services that prevails on the special legislation of public transport;
- after a year, Law 308/2004, restored the compulsory competitive tendering rule in local public transport and then, after various vicissitudes, finally this rule was confirmed by art. 23-bis of Decree Law 112/2008;
- to prevent the use of market mechanisms in local public services (especially in the provision of water service), contained in art. 23-bis of Decree Law 112/2008, a referendum to cancel art. 23bis was organized;
- the referendum was won in the June 12 and 13, 2011 and the market logics of art 23-bis of Decree Law 112/2008 were defeated;
- the central government reacted in a desperate way: ignored the referendum and introduce with art. 4 of Decree Law 13/8/2011 n. 138 the complete liberalization of those local public services not yet liberalized, including LTP and excluding the water service (winner of the referendum);
- some regions appealed to the Constitutional Court against the art. 4 of D.L. 13/8/2011 n. 138, which required the liberalization of local public services;
- the appeal was considered well founded by the Constitutional Court by judgment n.199 of July 2012, with the effect to stopping, for the moment, the deregulation of public services in Italy, including the local public transport one.

The Burlando reform was not only defeated by a schizophrenic legislative production that under the pressure of some regions, has tried in every way to put the brakes to the introduction of market logic in the LPT sector, but also by the concrete practices of the public transport companies and regions in designing the procedures of the competitive tendering mechanism. Compared to what happened abroad, where the literature, in addition to the problems associated with the use of this mechanism, showed also the benefits, with cost reductions from 10 to 40% (Gwilliams, 2008) in Italy the efficiency savings have been minimal, below 10% (Boitani, Cambini, 2004). This is due to various reasons:

- the collusive practices and defensive coalitions strategies (Danovi, Karletsos, 2012) set up by the incumbents;
- the limited number of bidder due to the presence of social clauses that discouraged their participation, because, in case of victory, imposed to keep all the staff with not negotiable salaries.

The attempts to reorganize the public transport sector in Italy with more efficient criteria, as seen, have not been successful (Liberatore, 2001; Mangia, 2005). The attempt to increase productivity and reduce costs through the National Fund of Transport and standard costs had no luck. The same happened to the attempt to restore order using the competitive tendering and the free competition levers, trying to break the taboo that the field of local public transport could not gain a greater financial autonomy. In the face of these failures, due mostly to the strong desire of local governments to prevent the change and do not resolve the conflict of interests that still binds the regions with the local public transport companies (the first are the owners of the second), the central government has reacted, first and foremost, practicing the easiest way, that of the linear cuts. Before embarking upon what we have called the third phase of the reform process of the local public transport service with the return of the National Fund of Transport and standard costs, the central government, in fact, in the 2010-2012 period has reduced the transfers to the transport sector for an average of 12% (ASSTRA 2013). Not all regions have suffered, however, the same reduction in transfers. The most affected were, in order: Campania (-27%), Lazio (– 23.5%), Molise (– 23%), Sicily (– 20%), Sardinia (-14%), Tuscany (– 13%), Abruzzo (– 10%), Veneto (– 10%), Liguria (– 8%), Lombardy (– 8%), and gradually all other regions with smaller percentages (from 5% to 0%). In the latter period, the reaction of the Regions and local public transport companies has been to increase the ticket price, reduce internal costs, ask help to the municipalities, encourage employees exodus, block the turnover, not reconfirm staff figures on fixed-term contracts, reduce expenses for maintenance and modernization of the fleet (average age of the fleet in Italy is 12 years against the 7 average in Europe). But the policy of the linear cuts cannot continue indefinitely. More stronger mechanisms to implement the change in the local public transport sector are needed to start it on more virtuous routes.

6.7   New Statalism Age: 2013 – On trying to force local public transport efficiency improvement with more centralized powers

Starting in 2013, the local public transport sector will be subject to new and more stringent rules to reduce the territorial and dimensional performance gap both internal, between different regions, and external, with the other European countries, resulting from the inertia and the stubborn resistance to change on the part of the regions and public transport companies owned by them. To reduce the performance gaps the Law 228/2012 establishes that the regions must reprogram transport services, replace inefficient modes of transport, revise the service contracts in place. In case of inactivity, the Central Government shall appoint "ad acta" commissioners and relieve the executives of the public transport companies in cases of financial distress, according to certain criteria set out in a separate decree.

The key points of the new path of reform of local public transport service provided for by Law 228/2012 are the following:

1. reprogramming of services by individual regions according to the different goals (i. e patronage/coverage) to be pursued in different geographical areas (optimal traffic zones) from companies with appropriate size, in order to reduce the excesses and the fragmentation of supply. Particular attention will be dedicated to the goal of increas-

ing by 2,5% per year the number of passengers carried on a regional basis and to ensure "adequate levels of employment" through rationalization and turnover block;

2. renegotiation and reassessment of public subsidies through the provision of standard costs to better target the distribution of resources (National Transport Fund) to companies according results-oriented criteria. A progressive increase in the relationship between traffic revenues and operating costs, will have to be secured on an annual basis;

3. effective monitoring of costs and analytical performance information of the public transport companies by the National Observatory of Local Public Transport accompanied by greater powers to sanction the failure to produce the information and the failure to achieve the goals set by central government (appointment of ad acta commissioners and removal of the executives of the public transport companies who do not achieve the objectives assigned).

In this new phase, the efficiency of the TPL sector re-starts from the enhancement of the performance information system about efficiency, productivity, user satisfaction, increasing patronage and the enhancement of the sanctioning system rather than by the use of market mechanisms (performance management/command and control instead of market-choice mechanisms) (Le Grand, 2003).

The fragility of the information base (see the poor quality of information of the National Accounts of Infrastructure and Transport) and often, the reduced ability to provide useful information to decision-makers cannot be the reason to cancel any attempt to establish improvement policies and leave everything to the market (such as the confused legislation of recent years has shown). In a recent parliamentary hearing (23 May 2013) the Minister of Transport and Infrastructure, Maurizio Lupi, reiterated the need for: "strengthening transport information systems, without which real progress in the efficiency of local transport services cannot be achieved" Local public transport is a complex sector where there are enough spaces for public intervention, especially for directing the activities of the various actors (public and private) towards established goals.

But doing so requires reliable cost information that enable the construction of real cross-regional cluster, which go beyond the legal and administrative boundaries of the regions. The publicly available information on the efficiency and productivity of the LPT sector as a whole, and not only on financial deficits, for the most part, came from recent surveys conducted by well-known international consultants (i. e, Bain & Co. or Earchimede).

The OECD report 2009 (*Italy Better regulation to strenghten market dynamics*), in particular, uses data compiled by Earchimede (2005) on behalf of Anav-Asstra to draw a more accurate picture of the conditions prevailing in the TPL in Italy.

After more than thirty years of inactivity and missed reforms, the challenges that the central government will have to face in a more determined way are the following (Earchimede, 2005; Bain & CO., 2012):

- *Reduce the excess supply.* The load factor in Italy (ratio between passengers and offered seats) is just 22% against a European average of 34% (with peaks of 45% in Spain and 42% in France). Some Italian regions have excess, other deficits. Compared to the Italian average of 2.5 thousand seats/km per inhabitant, four regions

(Lazio, Molise, Liguria and Trentino Alto-Adige) are oversized, others undersized (Campania, Calabria, Marche and Sicily). Particularly in extra-urban transport are oversized Abruzzo and Molise;

- *Reduce the excessive concentration of the service in public hands.* Of the more than 1,100 companies operating in the sector about 87% are private. But it is the remaining 13% owned by Local Governments that delivers 68% of the national production mileage. In Uk 5% of the kilometric production is provided by public sector companies, while the 95% is private. In Germany, the public/private ratio is 52/48, France 36/64, Sweden 24/76, Holland 95/5, Belgium 72/28. Media panel 47/53;
- *Reduce the excessive fragmentation of the sector.* In Italy there are more than 1,100 small and medium sized companies poorly integrated. The aggregate production of the top 5 players in Italy is 30% compared to a European average of 49%. Recent studies, however, suggest that there are informal local transport groups that form cartels with anti-competitive aims that make the sector more concentrated than previously thought (Ottoz, 2010);
- *Increase the productivity, efficiency and cost-effectiveness of the service.* The LPT sector in Italy is in a structural loss. Traffic revenues cover on average 30% of operating costs (85% UK, 60% in Germany, 40% in France, 55% in Sweden, 40% Netherlands 33% Belgium, panel average 52,1%). This gap stems from both the lack of ability to generate revenues from traffic, about 1 euro/km in Italy against 1,50 in the UK and in Germany 2,40 – 1,34 average – (usually the fees are lower by 20-50% compared to the European ones), and by higher operating costs (3,6 €/km – 1,8 in Uk – against a European average of 2,7). A negative contribution came also by low productivity per employee mileage (17.060 km/employee in Italy, compared with a European average of 19.763 km/employee). The end result is that LTP in Italy, actually is a loss sector with a negative EBIT of 2,3% which is about 6 percentage points less than in the main European countries (Bain & Co, 2012). In these condition it is not attractive. Usually deregulation occurs where a monopolist has an extra-profit. In Italy we observe, on the contrary, an extra-loss due to inefficient local-government-owned enterprises and inefficient market labour rules.

The biggest challenge, however, will be to overcome the bureaucratic mentality that continues to prevail in Italy and turn it into a more results-oriented one. If positive is the evaluation about the introduction of performance management logics in the field of local public transport by L. 228/2012, many are, however, the doubts about the capacity of central government to exercise successfully substitutive powers with "ad acta" commissioners and managers able to replace those who have not able to achieve the expected results. Forcing companies to be efficient with such strict measures may be appropriate to overcome the resistance and the defensive strategies. In the future, however, the improvement of the service will depend on the capacity of transport companies and local governments to transform their strategic orientations (Coda, 1988, 2010) from reactors to prospectors (Miles and Snow, 1978) to undertake paths of growth and expansion similar to those undertaken by British (Tas report, 2010) and French bus groups.

6.8   Conclusions

The basic idea we conveyed through this chapter is that local public transport in Italy is a sector in crisis because of the resistance in recognizing his changing nature (local public transport is not only a service for social inclusion and territorial cohesion purposes) and by not managing it accordingly by local governments, notwithstanding central government imposed the change with numerous laws.

In Italy public subsidies cover, now, about 70% of operating costs (the average European ratio is 50%). If we think that in Uk the then Prime Minister Margareth Thatcher, in the 80s, completely liberalized local public transport (except in London) because public subsidies were reaching the "dangerous" threshold of 30% (Savage, 1993: 144) we understand the different Italian sensibility, compared to other European countries, in determining what should be the threshold not to exceed to qualify a given situation as "financially unsustainable".

However, others countries, with different socio-economics traditions, but with less hesitation, started to implement the change. As in the classic Deming Plan-Do-Check-Act cycle, they tried, made mistakes, but they, also, learned something.

Italy remained trapped in the plan stage. It planned to adopt mechanisms such as competition, privatization or efficiency-enhanced regulation to make public transport more efficient and attractive, but like Hamlet in the Shakespearean tragedy, it was not able to solve the dilemma: to bid or not to bid having planned to do it? to implement or not to implement regulatory measures to increase efficiency and effectiveness having planned to do it? (Boitani, 2004).

When other countries plan a reform, usually they go to the execution stage, making effective the learning by doing cycle. When Italian Government plan a reform soon starts a long discussion about the opportunity of this reform, with the effects of stopping its implementation and the learning cycle.

This situation resembles the Gramscian notion of Interregnum: "he crisis consists precisely in the fact that the old is dying and the new cannot be born; in this interregnum a great variety of morbid symptoms appear" (quoted in Bauman, 2012: 49).

The "old" organizational forms (Van de Velde, 1999) based on the public authority initiative and on the "in-house" providing or direct award rules, are "dying" because inefficient and unproductive, while the "new" organizational forms prescribed by the reforms, which provide greater openness to market initiative and competition, but also to collaboration, are still at the designing stage, have not been fully assembled yet or are not strong enough to replace the logics that since 1903, with the Giolitti's law, have been imposing in Italy the public monopoly in local services.

Much still remains, therefore, to be done before bringing back the field of local public transport within a perimeter of economic sustainability. Too wide are still the regional disparities that need to be reduced. Regionalism in local public transport, as seen, did not work. The devolution to the regions did not reduce the internal efficiency gap and the external one, between Italy and other countries. The regions themselves were the main responsible in blocking the implementation of standard costs (Law 151/1981) and of compulsory competitive tendering mechanisms (Law 422/97), preferring the status quo. It is now time to give central government a new chance.

With the L. 228/2012 it is the central government which has taken on the burden of carrying forward the process of improving the service through the three actions of:

- resizing the offer;
- reducing the efficiency gaps through the standard costs;
- monitoring more closely the implementation through the National Observatory of Local Public Transport with the provision of greater powers of intervention (replacement of executives of public companies and appointment of "ad acta" commissioners).

The objectives are clear: first reduce the performance gaps to align Italian public transport firms with the European ones and then open up to international competition.

In our opinion this seems to be the lesson learned after about thirty years of inertia on the part of the regions. The future will tell whether the central government will have enough strength to apply it in practice.

In conclusion, it is worth remarking that our new Prime Minister Enrico Letta, that succeeded Mario Monti, has chosen the word "doing" as opposed to "planning", to give meaning to his actions. His program is, in fact, labeled "Decreto del fare" (Decree of Doing) signaling, without any doubts, that is now time to do, to execute what has been planned, and, finally, to learn how to improve public services.

Summary

Improving public services is not an easy task. From the literature we know that it is a controversial issue, inherently political and contestable. The solution, in the end, is the ability to find an agreement between potentially conflicting perspectives. This means that public service improvement is the continuous search for a new or a better balance between conflicting stakeholders interests. Others countries, with different socio-economics traditions, but with less hesitation, tried to find such compromise to improve local public transport service performance. They tried, made mistakes, but they, also, learned something. Italy remained stuck in the middle. The basic idea we conveyed through this chapter is that local public transport in Italy is a sector in crisis because of the resistance in recognizing his changing nature (local public transport is not only a service for social inclusion and territorial cohesion purposes) and by not managing it accordingly by local governments, notwithstanding central government imposed the change with numerous laws. Much still remains, therefore, to be done before bring back the Italian local public transport sector within a perimeter of economic sustainability. Too wide are still the regional disparities that need to be reduced. Regionalism in local public transport, as seen, did not work. The devolution process did not reduce the internal regional efficiency gaps and the external one, between Italy and other countries. The regions themselves were the main responsible in blocking the implementation of standard costs (Law 151/1981) and of compulsory competitive tendering mechanisms (Law 422/97), preferring the status quo. It is now time to give central government a new chance. The future will tell whether the central government will have enough strength to improve this complex public service.

References

ANESSI PESSINA E. (2002), *Principles of Public Management*, Egea, Milano.

ANSELMI L. (1995), *Il processo di trasformazione della P. A. Il 'percorso aziendale'*, Giappichelli, Torino.

ASHWORTH R. E., BOYNE, G. A., ENTWISTLE T. (2010), *Public Service Improvement. Theories and Evidence*, Oxford University Press, Oxford.

ASSTRA (2013), La riscossa, *10° Convegno nazionale*, Bologna 13-14-15 maggio 2013.

BAIN & CO (2012), *Il settore del trasporto pubblico in Italia – Contesto di riferimento e priorità di sviluppo del settore*, Roma.

BALDASSARRI G. (1998), *La riforma del trasporto pubblico locale*, "Proteo", n. 3.

BANISTER D. (2005), *Unsustainable Transport: City Transport in the New Century*, Routledge, London.

BARLOW J., ROBER M. (1996), *Steering not rowing. Co-ordination and control in the management of public services in Britain and Germany*, "International Journal of Public Sector Management", Vol. 9 (5/6): 73-89.

BAUMAN Z. (2012), *Times of Interregnum*, "Ethics & Global Politics", Vol.5 (1), 49-56.

BEESLEY M. A. (1997), *Privatisation, Regulation and Deregulation*, 2nd ed., Routledge, London.

BOITANI A., CAMBINI C. (2004), *Le gare per il trasporto pubblico in Europa e in Italia: molto rumore per nulla?*, "Economia e Politica Industriale", n.122: 65-99.

BOITANI A., CAMBINI C. (2006), *To Bid or not to Bid? The Italian Experience in Competitive Tendering for Local Public Services*, "European Transport", Vol.33: 41-53.

BORGONOVI E. (2006), *La crisi del management nasce dalla debolezza delle teorie*, "Azienda Pubblica", n.3: 389-392.

BORGONOVI E., FATTORE G., LONGO F. (2009), *Management delle istituzioni pubbliche*, Egea, Milano.

BORGONOVI E., MUSSARI R. (2011), *Pubblico e privato: armonizzare gli opposti*, "Azienda Pubblica", n.2: 103-121.

BOYNE, G. A. (2002), *Public and Private Management: What's the Difference?*, "Journal of Management Studies", 39 (1): 97-122.

BOYNE, G. A. (2003), *What is Public service improvement?*, "Public Administration", 81 (2): 211-227.

BOYNE, G. A. (2004), *A 3Rs Strategy for Public Service Turnaround: Retrenchment, Repositioning and Reorganization*, "Public Money and Management", 24 (2): 97-103.

BUHELER R., PUCHER J. (2011), *Making Public Transport Financially Sustainable*, "Transport Policy", Vol. 18 (1): 128-136.

CANGIANO R. (2005), *La liberalizzazione del trasporto locale: dall'affidamento diretto alle procedure a evidenza pubblica …e ritorno*, "Economia Pubblica", 35 (6): 49-98.

CAVALIERI E. (2010), *Le nuove dimensioni dell'equilibrio aziendale*, Giappichelli, Torino.

CHRISTENSEN T., LAEGREID P. (2007), *The Whole-of-Government Approach to Public Sector Reform*, "Public Administration Review", 67: 6, 1059-1066.

CODA V. (1988), *L'orientamento strategico dell'impresa*, Utet, Torino.

CODA V. (2010), *Entrepreneurial values and strategic management*, Bocconi University Press, Milano.

CORTE DEI CONTI (2003), *La gestione del trasporto pubblico locale e lo stato di attuazione della riforma a livello regionale – Relazione comparativa e di sintesi sull'andamento dei trasporti locali*, Roma.

D'AMICO L., PALUMBO R. (2008), *Il trasporto pubblico locale dal protezionismo al mercato,* Franco Angeli, Milano.

DALL'ALPI D. (1928), *Le imprese municipalizzate, provincializzate e statilizzate,* Utet, Torino.

DANOVI A., KARLETSOS D. (2011), *Alleanze e Aggregazioni nel Settore del Trasporto Pubblico Locale. Una prima analisi delle motivazioni strategiche* "Management delle Utilities",, n. 1: 10-24.

DE BRUIJN H. (2007), *Managing Performance in the Public Sector, 2nd ed.,* Routledge, London.

DEMSETZ H. (1968), *Why regulate utilities?,* "Journal of Law and Economics", Vol. 11: 55-66.

DI GIACOMO M., OTTOZ E. (2007), *Local public transportation firms: the relevance of scale and scope economies in the provision of urban and intercity bus transit,* "Hermes Ricerche", Working Paper n. 5.

EARCHIMEDE (2005), *La resa dei conti. Rapporto sul trasporto pubblico locale: situazione attuale e prospettive evolutive,* Asstra-Anav, Roma, 23 marzo 2005.

ENTWISTLE T. MARTIN S. (2005), *From competition to collaboration in public service delivery: a new agenda for research,* "Public Administration", Vol. 83 (1): 233-242.

GIANNINI M. S. (1985), *Il servizio pubblico sotto il profilo giuridico,* PEREZ R. (ED), *Statistica e pubblica amministrazione II. I servizi pubblici,* Giuffré, Milano.

GOLINELLI G. M. (1984), "Le imprese di trasporto pubblico: la legge del 1981 per il controllo della gestione ed i bilanci aziendali tipo", *Atti del seminario di studi sui problemi dei trasporti pubblici di competenza regionale e locale,* Regione Lazio.

GOLINELLI G. M. (1986), "Il recupero di efficienza nelle aziende di servizi pubblici di trasporto", *Atti del seminario di studi su Applicazioni del costo standard nelle politiche del trasporto pubblico locale,* Centro Studi sui sistemi di trasporto, Napoli.

GOMEZ LOBO A. (2007), *Why Competition Does not Work in Urban Bus Networks,* "Journal of Transport Economics and Policy", 41: 2, 283-308.

GOODWIN P. B. (1997), *Solving Congestion,* "Inaugural Lecture for the Professorship of Transport Policy, University College London", 23rd October 1997.

GRAY A., JENKINS B. (1995), *From Public Administration to Public Management: Reassessing a Revolution?,* "Public Administration", 73: 75-99.

GWILLIAM K. (2008), *Bus Transport: is There a Regulatory Cycle?,* "Transportation Research Part A", 42: 1183-1194.

HEFETZ A., WARNER M. (2004), *Privatization and Its Reverse: Explaining the Dynamics of the Government Contracting Process,* "Journal of Public Administration Research and Theory", Vol. 14 (2): 171-190.

HEFETZ A., WARNER M. (2012), *Contracting or Public Delivery? The Importance of Service, Market, and Management Characteristics,* "Journal of Public Administration Research and Theory", Vol. 22 (2): 289-317.

HENSHER D. (ED.) (2005), *Competition and Ownership in Land Passenger Transport,* Elsevier.

HIBBS J. (2000), *Transport Policy: the Myth of Integrated Planning,* Institute of economic affairs, London.

HIBBS J. (2009), *How Can we Call Transport a Utility?,* "Economic Affairs", 29 (4): 55-59.

HOOD C. (1991), *A public management for all seasons?,* "Public Administration", 69 (1), 3-19.

HOOD C. (2000), *The Art of the State. Culture, Rethoric, and Public Management,* Oxford University Press, Oxford.

HUGHES O. (1994), *Public Management and Administration,* London, Macmillan.

HULL A. (2005), *Integrated Transport Planning in the UK: from Concept to Reality,* "Journal of Transport Geography", 13: 318-328.

JAKEE K., ALLEN L. (1998), *Destructive Competition or Competition Destroyed? Regulatory Theory and the History of Irish Road Transportation Legislation*, "European Journal of Law and Economics", 5: 13-50.

KENWORTHY J., LAUBE F. (1999), *An International Sourcebook of Automobile Dependence in Cities 1960-1990*, University Press of Colorado, Boulder, CO.

LAGHI A. (1919), *Aziende Municipalizzate*, Vallardi, Milano.

LAVE C. (1991), *Measuring the Decline in Transit Productivity in U. S.*, "Transportation Planning and Technology", Vol. 15: 115-124

LE GRAND J. (2003), *Motivations, Agency, and Public Policy. Of Knights & Knaves, Pawns & Queens*, Oxford University Press, Oxford.

LIBERATORE G. (2001), *Pianificazione e controllo delle aziende di trasporto pubblico locale*, Franco Angeli, Milano.

LONTI Z., GREGORY R. (2007), *Accountability or Countability? Performance Measurement in the New Zealand Public Service, 1992-2002*, "The Australian Journal of Public Administration", 66 (4): 468-484.

MANGIA G. (2005), *Le alleanze organizzative tra gli operatori del trasporto pubblico locale*, Franco Angeli, Milano.

MARLETTO G. (2004), *Paradigmi dell'intervento pubblico e politica italiana dei trasporti: una rilettura critica*, "Economia Pubblica", Vol. 34 (6): 69-96.

MEES P. (2000), *A Very Public Solution. Transport in the Dispersed City*, Melbourne University Press, Melbourne.

MEES P. (2010), *Transport for Suburbia*, Earthscan, London.

MELE R. (2003), *Economia e gestione delle imprese di pubblici servizi*, Cedam, Padova.

MILES R., SNOW C., (1978), *Organizational Strategy, Structure and Process*, McGraw-Hill, New York.

MINISTERO DELLE INFRASTRUTTURE E DEI TRASPORTI (2012), *Conto Nazionale delle Infrastrutture e dei Trasporti*, Istituto Poligrafico Zecca dello Stato, Roma.

MINISTERO DELLE INFRASTRUTTURE E DEI TRASPORTI (2013), *Audizione del Ministro dell'infrastrutture e dei Trasporti On. Maurizio Lupi alla Commissione Trasporti, Poste e Telecomunicazioni della Camera dei Deputati*, 29 Maggio 2013, Roma.

MUSSARI R. (2011), *Economia delle amministrazioni pubbliche*, McGraw-Hill, Milano.

OBENG K. (2011), *Indirect Product Function and the Output Effect of Public Transit Subsidies*, "Transportation", Vol. 38: 191-214.

OECD (2009), *Italy. Better Regulation to Strengthen Market Dynamics*, OECD Reviews of Regulatory reforms, OECD.

OTTOZ E. (2010), *The Relevance of Groups in Local Public Transport: the Case of Italy*, Hermes Ricerche, Working paper n. 8.

OWENS S. (1995), *From 'Predict and Provide' to 'Predict and Prevent'?: Pricing and Planning in Transport Policy*, "Transport Policy", Vol. 2 (1): 43-49.

PASHIGIAN P. B. (1976), *Consequences and Causes of Public Ownership of Urban Transit Facilities*, "The Journal of Political Economy", Vol. 84 (6): 1239-1259.

PAVAN A. (1992), *Le imprese di trasporto degli enti locali*, Cedam, Padova.

PIPERATA G. (2011), *Il cammino lento e incerto dei servizi pubblici locali dalla gestione pubblica al mercato liberalizzato*, "Munus", n.1: 1-35.

POLLITT C., BOUCKAERT C. (2000), *Public Management Reform*, Oxford University Press, Oxford.

PONTI M. (2006), *La regolazione pubblica dei trasporti: un quadro problematico*, POLIDORI G., MUSSO E., MARCUCCI E. (a cura di), *I trasporti e l'Europa. Politiche, infrastrutture, concorrenza*, Franco Angeli, Milano.

POPOLI P. (1998), *L'azienda di trasporto pubblico locale*, Cedam, Padova.

POWELL W. W. (1997), *Neither Market nor Hierarchy*, "Research in Organizational Behavior", Vol. 12: 295-336.

PUCHER J. (1996), *Verkhehrsverbund: the Success of Regional Public in Germany, Austria, and Switzerland*, "Transport Policy", Vol. 2 (4): 279-291.

RHODES R. A. W. (1997), *From Marketization to Diplomacy: it's the Mix that Matters*, "Public Policy and Administration", Vol. 12 (2): 345-363.

RODOTA' S. (1995), *Le libertà e i diritti*, ROMANELLI R. (a cura di), *Storia dello Stato italiano*, Donzelli, Roma.

SARGIACOMO M., GOMES D. (2011), *Accounting and Accountability in Local Government: Contributions From Accounting History Research*, "Accounting History", Vol. 16 (3): 253-290.

SAVAGE I. (1993), *Deregulation and Privatization of Britain's Local Bus Industry*, "Journal of Regulatory Economics", Vol. 5 (2): 143-158.

SCLAR E. (2000), *You don't Always Get What you Pay for. The Economics of Privatization*, Cornell University Press, Ithaca, NY.

SHLEIFER A. (1998), *State Versus Private Ownership*, "Journal of Economic Perspectives", Vol. 12 (4): 133-150.

SORENSEN C. H., LONGVA F. (2011), *Increased Coordination in Public Transport – Which Mechanisms are Available?*, "Transport Policy", 18 (1): 117-125.

STANLEY J., SMITH A. (2013), *Governance, Contracting, Ownership and Competition Issues in Public Transport: Looking Up not Down*, "Research in Transportation Economics", Vol. 39 (1): 167-174.

TALBOT C. (2010), *Theories of performance. Organizational and Service Improvement in the Public Domain*, Oxford University Press, Oxford.

TAS (2010), *Competition in the UK Bus Industry. A Submission of Evidence to the Competition Commission Local Bus Service Market Investigation*, The Tas Partnership Limited Publishing.

TAYLOR B. D. ET. AL. (2009), *Nature and/or Nurture? Analyzing the Determinants of Transit Ridership across US Urban Areas*, "Transportation Research Part A", Vol. 43: 60-77.

UBELS B., ENOCH M., POTTER S., NIJKAMP P. (2004), *Unfare solutions. Local earmarked charges to fund public transport*, Spon Press, Taylor & Francis, London-New York.

VAN DE VELDE D. (1999), *Organisational Forms and Entrepreneurship in Public Transport. Part. 1: Classifying Organisational Forms*, "Transport Policies", Vol. 6: 147-157.

VAN DE VELDE D. (2008), *A New Regulation for the European Public Transport*, "Research in Transportation Economics", Vol. 22 (1): 78-84.

VAN DE VELDE, D. WALLIS I. (2013), *'Regulated Deregulation'of Local Bus Service – An Appraisal of International Developments*, "Research in Transportation Economics", Vol. 29: 145-159.

VAN DE VELDE D., BECK A. (2010), *Beyond Competitive Tendering*, "Research in Transportation Economics", Vol. 22 (1): 78-84.

VITON P. A. (1998), *Changes in Multimode Bus Transit Efficiency, 1988-1992*, "Transportation", Vol. 25: 1-21.

WALKER J. (2008), *Purpose Driven Public Transport: Creating a Clear Conversation About Public Transit Goals*, "Journal of Transport Geography", Vol. 21 (4): 403-425.

WINSTON C. (2000), *Government Failure in Urban Transportation*, "Fiscal Studies", Vol. 21 (4): 403-425.

ZANELLI E. (2004), *Servizio pubblico e sentenza Altmark: l'anello mancante?*, "Politica del Diritto", Vol. 35 (1): 175-200.

7

Lean thinking practices to enhance performance improvement in Italian healthcare organizations[1]

This chapter explores earlier evidences in the implementation of Lean in the Italian healthcare sector. Findings from the Italian academic literature and three case studies show how the Italian National Health System stands back from the adoption of such a strategy. Furthermore, earlier attempts show a focus on Lean as a set of tool rather than a more holistic approach endeavor. Some conclusions are drawn upon the findings and suggestions for further research are highlighted.

Learning objectives

After reading this chapter you should be able to:

- The main challenges of the Italian National Healthcare System (INHS);
- The principals benefits of lean healthcare practices;
- The most important features of a full lean implementation approach;
- Some evidences from the implementation of Lean in the INHS.

7.1 The need for Performance improvement of Italian healthcare organizations

The Italian National Health Service (INHS) is a tax-funded system aimed to guarantee a universal and uniform provision of comprehensive care throughout the Country (France et al., 2005; Lo Scalzo et al., 2009; Sargiacomo, 2002). The responsibility for

---

[1] The chapter is the result of a joint effort by the authors who share the formulation. The writing of the specific sections however has to be divided as follows: D'Andreamatteo (corresponding author) paragraphs 7.3 (introduction), 7.3.2, 7.3.3 and 7.4; Ianni paragraphs 7.2 and 7.3.1; Sargiacomo paragraph 7.1.

the achievement of *Livelli Essenziali di Assistenza* (essential levels of care) is shared between the central government and the 20 regions. The *Aziende sanitarie locali* (ASLs), public enterprises funded by the regions, are responsible for healthcare delivery, health promotion and prevention activities at the local level. Hospitals are mainly managed directly by the ASL, except for the *Aziende Ospedaliere* (public semi-independent hospitals), the *Aziende Ospedaliere Universitarie* (public semi-independent teaching hospitals), and the private hospitals. Public and private hospitals may act only with an accredited status.

The INHS is known as one of the best healthcare system with reference to life expectancy at birth, that has reached in 2011 a level of 82,7 years compared with an OECD average of 80,1 (OECD Health Data, 2013). Besides, in 2011 Total health spending accounted for 9,2% of GDP and the Health expenditure per capita was of 3012 $ PPPs, against an OECD average, respectively, of 9,3% and 3,339 $ PPPs. Health spending slowed down both in 2010 (-1,8%) and 2011 (-1,6%). In 2011 the number of hospital beds was of 3,4 per 1000 population (OECD average: 4,8 beds).

Nevertheless, the Italian National Health System is dealing with different challenges (Schema di Piano Sanitario Nazionale – National Health Plan, 2011-2013): the growing of the health demand, the increase of chronic sufferers, the ageing of the population, a degree of inappropriateness of hospitalizations, the inhomogeneity of healthcare delivery among regions (structural and qualitative gap), the low integration between hospital care and primary care, the scarcity of resources, the low perceived quality of health services, the inefficiency in purchasing goods and services (technologies) and in human resource management.

In addition the INHS is affected by an inefficient and ineffective cost consumption in several Regions (Lega et al., 2010), which have been asked to countersigning a Government Budgetary Balance Plan in order to reach the break-even as of 2007. What is more, recently single excellent Italian hospitals or ASLs came to the fore for serious financial and economic difficulties, even in more virtuous healthcare regional systems (Carbone et al., 2012). Besides, Italy is facing a major financial crisis since 2009, as many other developed countries. The crisis impacted on the Italian National Health Service (de Belvis et al., 2012) in a multifaceted way and caused a rise in cost-cutting actions (e.g. reduction in the number of hospital beds, co-payments for services added to existing tariffs, mandatory measures to reduce pharmaceutical expenditure). In this context, important national measures aimed to rationalize the Italian public administration and the healthcare sector have been promulgated (among others: the Legislative Decree 150/2009 – on improvement and enhancement of performance management, quality of services and transparency and integrity to prevent corruption, the Law 135/2012 – so-called "Spending Review" and focused on spending containment measures, the Law 189/2012 – containing urgent dispositions to promote the Country development through an higher protection of health).

Together with these pressures Italian hospitals are facing, as modern ones worldwide, other institutional, social, clinical and professional issues (Lega and De Pietro, 2005). As a consequence more and more, Italian healthcare organizations are expected to innovate and improve their performance by means of adequate asset, knowledge and disease management systems (Lega, 2012). In particular there is a growing demand for the application of operations management in healthcare, although the Italian system is behind in introducing related techniques and methods (Bensa et al., 2010). One of the approaches promising to overcome the above mentioned challenges is the strategy of "Lean". Although the relevance of this topic, the way according to which Italian healthcare organizations are implementing Lean is still underexplored. Our work aims to provide first evidences on how and why the INHS is implementing lean. Next paragraph will show the main principles of this strategy and its promises. Subsequently literature on Italian cases and three case studies will be analyzed. Finally some conclusions will be drawn from the previous analysis.

7.2 Benefits and approaches of lean thinking practices in healthcare

In this section, we describe some critical facets in implementing lean in healthcare as emerged from an extensive literature review based on the following keywords: lean production, lean thinking, lean management, lean implementation, healthcare, hospitals. It is not the aim of this chapter to review all the issues of the phenomenon, but to focus on what Lean is, which are its benefits and what approaches are likely to ensure its successful implementation within healthcare organizations.[2]

The literature in the domain of lean healthcare has grown constantly as well as the number of experimentations within the healthcare sector (Spear, 2005; Radnor et al., 2006; Weber, 2006; Kollberg et al., 2007; Papadopoulos et al., 2010). Some organizations also began the lean journey proposing itself, explicitly or not, as the "new Toyota" of the sector, e.g. the Mayo clinic model of care (Berry, 2008), the Virginia Mason Medical Center's Pursuit of the Perfect Patient (Kenney, 2011), The Pittsburgh way (Grunden and Pittsburgh Regional Health Initiative, 2008), or the Bolton Improving Care System (Fillingham, 2007).

The main questions related to the lean journey in public services are linked to its implementation and sustainability (Radnor, 2011): how lean should be introduced and managed in public (and service) organizations, how to make a commitment of the whole system change and how to motivate human resources to adopt such a practice.

Although several definitions have been formulated about Lean, many of which strictly linked to the Japanese concepts of "muda" (identification and elimination of wastes), "mura" (cutting unevenness – reducing process variation) and "muri" (overburden – improving poor work conditions), in our opinion the most powerful in capturing the essence of lean is the one proposed by Moding and Åhlström (2012: p. 117): "lean is an operations strategy that prioritizes flow efficiency over resource efficiency". This definition highlights as Lean is an approach aiming to achieve the former without sacrificing the latter too much and is coherent with the suggestions that Lean must be conceived as a journey rather than an end (Wellman, Jeffries, Hagan, 2010;

---

[2] For more detailed reviews see: Arlbjørn and Freytag (2013); Moyano-Fuente and Sacristán-Diaz (2012); Stone (2012); Bhasin and Burcher (2006); Hines et al. (2004). For lean in healthcare see: Holden (2011); Mazzocato et al. (2010); Poksinska (2010), Radnor (2010), de Souza (2009); Vest and Gamm (2009); Radnor et al. (2006).

Toussaint, Berry, 2013). Accordingly, an organization can be labeled as "lean" if it has improved its state towards flow efficiency when observed at two different points in time, because lean is a dynamic state characterized by constant improvement (Moding and Åhlström, 2012).

Assigning a strategic value to Lean and conceptualizing it as managerial philosophy means to fix its truly essence with a series of fundamental principles (Womack et al., 1990; Womack and Jones, 1996; Soriano-Meier and Forrester, 2002; Emiliani, 2007; Shah and Ward, 2007; Moyano-Fuente and Sacristán-Diaz, 2012): to specify value; to identify the value stream;[3] to avoid interruptions in value flow; to let customer pull value; to pursue perfection continuously; committed management; to respect people; to enhance supply chain management. The underlying assumption behind these principles is that organizations are made of processes (Radnor et al., 2006). Processes should be designed around customer's needs in order to deliver the value they expect, to reach a "flow" state of work centered on these needs and increase the percentage of value added activities, while avoiding wastes and errors and so reducing the resource consumption. The value must be specified from the customer's stand point. Furthermore customers should be allowed to pull product or services just when they need them. As the amelioration is a never-ending process, the organization will be constantly seeking continuous improvement towards perfection. What is more, respect for people is at the very core of any lean initiative: as Sugimori et al. state (1977: p. 553), the second basic concept of Toyota production system is: "to make full use of the workers'capabilities. In short, treat the workers as human beings and with consideration". Soriano-Meier and Forrester (2002) added committed management: managers have to be convinced of the project and support the staff. Lastly, an organization implementing lean production builds a strong supply chain management orientation (Shah and Ward, 2007). It provides suppliers regular feedbacks about their performance, improves supplier involvement in its production processes, offers just in time delivery of supplies and focuses on customer's needs.

As stated, the lean approach allows to recognize several type of waste in daily organizational activities. Graban (2011) identifies as possible wastes in the healthcare sector: defects; waiting; transportation; over processing; inventory; motion; overproduction and human potential. As a consequence specific purposes are to eliminate reworks or repeating things, time spent by the patient waiting for staff, unnecessary equipment, information or movement of material, work not required by the patient, excess of inventory, unnecessary movement of people, work made earlier than needed or in a quantity not required, or waste caused by incorrect human resource management. Wastes can be reduced through a variety of tools. Radnor (2012) explains these tools as means of assessing the processes at the organization level (Customer Analysis, Process Mapping, Six Thinking Hats, Value definition, Value stream mapping), monitoring results of improvement actions (A3s, Benchmarking, Competency framework,

---

[3] In healthcare a value stream results by all the activities composing the patient journey. The value stream mapping is the activity of identifying both value-added and non-value added steps of the journey, from the beginning to the delivery of services (Miller, 2005). Value arise from "any activity which improves the patient's health, well-being and experience" (Westwood et al., 2007: p. 6).

Problem Solving, Standard Work, Visual Management, Workplace Audit) and acting for improving processes (5S, Control Charts, Cross Functional Teams, Daily Meetings, Rapid Improvement Events, Visual Management).

Furthermore, Lean is often pointed out as an excellent way to improve organizational performance, although criticalities remain about the methodology according to which benefits are reported, valorized and discussed (Bhasin and Burcher, 2004). A lot of advantages are normally associated to these initiatives, such as a reduction of process times, wastes, and time to market, an increase in the variety of the production, an improvement in the quality and satisfaction of both staff and customers (Bhasin and Burcher, 2004; Radnor, Holweg and Waring, 2011).

Results of lean are achieved in relation to many dimensions: safety, quality, time, costs and morale of the staff. In next table (see Table 7.1) we list some of the most cited lean benefits, regrouping the items with reference to the subject or object positively affected by lean: the patient, the staff or the organization. In some cases the benefit is listed in more than one level.

Describing the process through which a health organization may become lean is as difficult as defining "lean". Firstly, both the academic and practitioner literature provide a variety of frameworks explaining the supposed correct patterns of implementation. Furthermore, lean is applied around the world in a wide range of ways and not all the lean journeys are successful. Poksinska (2010) affirms that usual implementation patterns build around the work of interdisciplinary teams responsible for change, after having conducted initial lean training and pilot projects. This is consistent with the experience of the international successful cases mentioned above and with what found in a recent research project within a French Teaching Hospital by

Table 7.1 Benefits of lean. Source: Authors based on Fillingham (2007), Westwood et al. (2007), Poksinska (2010), Ballé and Régnier (2011) \

Patient	Staff	Organization
Patient flow improved	Increased productivity	Best use of capacity
Patients treated faster	Improved staff morale	Cost savings
Shorter waiting times	Improved safety	Waste reduced
Reduced length of stay	Respect for front line	Reduced length of stay
Safer, more reliable services	workers	Increased productivity
Improved delivery	Stable working	More patient treated
Reduction in travel	environment	Standardized procedures
time/walking distance	Pride in work	and equipment
	Reduction in travel	Continuous improvement
	time/walking distance	Stable working
		environment
		Flow efficiency
		Organizational learning
		Employee involvement
		Reduced number of errors
		and incidents

one of the authors (Angelé-Halgand and D'Andreamatteo, 2012). Furthermore a lean journey can be started through an external consultant, by developing an internal capability of staff about lean or with both consultants and internal staff; each solution has its own advantages and disadvantages according to quickness of implementation, costs and awareness of staff about the process (Radnor, 2012). Holden (2011), points out that over time staff have to improve own expertise about lean management in order to ensure sustainability after the consultant depart. However, beginning a lean journey may be difficult. The NHS Lean Thinking Network (2006) suggests to start with anything and follow the "4P" model as formulated by Liker (2004): to invest efforts in developing a long term thinking (*Philosophy*), to eliminate waste (*Process*), to respect, challenge and grow staff and partners (*People and Partners*) or to develop a continuous improvement and learning habits (*Problem solving*).

A specific concern refers to the implementation of lean within public services. Radnor and Boaden (2008) stated that, in according to evidences, Lean has been adapted in the sector, rather than adopted. The literature shows that lean can be adapted to reach a wider range of objectives and avoid the simple replication of manufacturing approaches, in some aspects not suitable for public services (Radnor et al., 2006). Nevertheless, the adaption against the punctual manufacturing way of implementing lean is not an obstacle for achieving similar results (Swank, 2003). Most important, a fuller implementation rather than a Rapid Improvement Event (or Kaizen blitz) is the most appropriate approach to build a sustainable lean capability (Radnor and Walley, 2008). A Rapid Improvement Event (RIE), or Kaizen, is a formal event, lasting a few days, in which the staff looks for new ways of working and quickly implements the solutions. A RIE is usually used to start a lean journey.

A full implementation approach is characterized by a wider model of intervention in time and space, aimed to involve the entire organization. It requires a change in culture (Wellman et al., 2010), the redefinition of the strategic vision and the related policy deployment (Radnor et al., 2006), a long-term programme (Radnor, 2011) and an infrastructure for Lean, i. e. a vision for the future healthcare organization, an organizational structure, a strategic plan, a management system, a lean knowledge base of lean leaders, educated staff and consultants (Black and Miller, 2008). A full implementation approach has its own points of strength and weakness. The former are consequence of the specific characteristics of the approach: the link with the strategy, the involvement of more staff, the cultural shift. The latter are strictly linked to the significance of the required efforts that affect timescale, existing management styles and routines (Radnor 2006).

Burgess and Radnor (2013) further developed the framework by extending the typology for evaluating the attempts in implementing Lean. Approaches to lean implementation may be included within the following scheme: 1) Tentative; 2) Productive Ward Only (PW); 3) Few projects; 4) Programme; 5) Systemic. The discriminant between attempts from 1) to 3) and from 4) to 5) is the major impact of lean projects within the hospital due to staff or management involved in the implementation (projects are managed by staff or middle and top manager), the part of the organization affected by improvement initiatives (lean is applied in the hospital as a whole), and the time horizon in which results are expected (the length of programs). An implementation approach like number 4 or 5 is better as it underlines a system view and considers the organization as a whole. There is a consistent literature, indeed, stressing the relevance of a more holistic approach (Womack and Jones, 1996; Pettersen, 2009; Stone, 2012).

As much important, some factors determine a successful implementation of Lean. Based on a critical review about lean thinking in Emergency Departments, Holden (2011) suggests the following successful factors: to be ready for change, to take a human centered approach (to consider the effects of lean on employees), to secure expertise (training and development of internal stakeholders), to obtain top management support and resource allocation (budgetary needs in terms of additional staffing, additional time and funding), to secure leadership, to aim for cultural change (particularly the diffusion of the scientific method into organizational problem solving), to adapt lean to the local context, to improve continuously (to evaluate previous plans and to plan further projects) and to learn from previous experiences. Radnor (2010) highlights other factors such as direct and effective communication with staff and customers; measures and measurement systems aimed to develop a performance culture; the existence of an active and supportive middle management for the engagement of the staff; reward and recognition for all employees; identification of a noteworthy project that can act as catalyst and model for others attempts in the organization (that is, according to the author, a specific success factor for Lean). Further factors influencing lean outcomes could be chosen between the Liker's 13 tips of transitioning a company to a Lean Enterprise (Liker, 2004). Among them Liker includes using the value stream mapping (as a tool that allows to depict the specific activities of a value stream), organising kaizen workshops to teach and to prompt rapid change (i. e. RIE), making the lean transformation project mandatory, being opportunistic in identifying chances for important financial impacts (to choose the right service family in order to obtain – and demonstrate – huge outcomes), developing metrics based on a value stream perspective.

In literature there is evidence of the above-mentioned successful factors for the implementation of Lean. Burgess (2012), for example, in evaluating the experience of the Virginia Mason Medical Center, the Flinders Medical Center and the Royal Bolton Hospital NHS Foundation Trust, highlighted the common points in the process of implementation: the use of process mapping as a central starting point of RIEs; the emphasis upon problem solving; the rigorous application of lean tools; the existence of an internal structure to embed Lean across the organization and the relevance of training of staff.

Finally, the assessment of the lean endeavor is significant in order to evaluate outcomes, to prevent failure and correct action. Toussaint and Berry (2013) propose a frame for health care leaders by focusing on the lean promises, through which they can assess how much the hospital is distant from a flow efficiency state level. An organization that has obtained a deeper implementation of Lean has developed an attitude of continuous improvement, created value, reached unity of purpose through clarification of the priorities, respected front-line workers, tracked improvements thanks to visual tools in dedicated tracking centers and standardized non-standard work processes through continuous adjustment, so as to recognize patients who deviate from the standard and free up resources (time and professionals) for their treatment.

7.3   Evidences from some Italian experiences

In the previous section, we have described the principal benefits and approaches in implementing Lean as emerging from a focused literature review. In regard to the implementation of lean practices in Italian healthcare organizations the peer-reviewed literature is not so rich. A search in the principal academic databases showed only a few works investigating lean in healthcare: all are quite recent publications and according to the scheme proposed by de Souza (2009) all except one are case studies at the operational (micro) level, because they focus on improvements of the physical flow of materials (Portioli-Staudacher, 2008) or the managerial and support area (Agnetis et al,. 2012; Chiocca et al., 2012; Guizzi et al., 2012). The paper of Mignardi (2009) is a case study at an organizational level, as it refers to a local healthcare authority as a whole. The book of Raimondo (2013), instead, assesses some managerial innovations in the Italian healthcare sector, focusing specifically on lean. Two publications does not refer to lean "stricto sensu" but to Lean Six Sigma,[4] a business process improvement approach building on both Lean and Six Sigma (Chiarini and Bracci, 2013; Chiarini, 2012). In contrast to the international literature, only a few articles written by clinicians were found: they are all opinion papers, underling the risks of an uncritical implementation of Lean (Bolognese, 2011; Bovenzi, 2011) or, on the contrary, suggesting the adoption of this strategy (Montesarchio et al., 2012; Plebani and Lippi, 2011). An exception is the work of Zanin et al. (2012), that shows results in implementing Lean within a healthcare department in addition to another technique (case management). The Italian practitioner literature, consisting in books written mainly by consultants is less recent. It describes earlier lean implementation attempts within Italian hospital as well as in the whole public sector (Chiarini et al., 2010; Nicosia, 2010; Patrini and Confortini, 2010; Nicosia, 2008; Nicosia and Nicosia, 2008; Perrella and Leggeri, 2007; Galgano and Galgano, 2006).

In order to broaden the knowledge of benefits that Italian healthcare organizations are achieving in implementing lean, three case studies are analyzed through data gathered both from academic and practitioner literature as well as from internal documents of hospitals (document analysis approach): the Ente Ospedaliero Galliera in Genoa, the Azienda Sanitaria Locale in Florence and the Istituto Cilinico Humanitas in Rozzano (Milan). In the last case, data were gathered through an onsite semi-structured interview to the Director of Operational Directorate, a member of the Lean and Continuous improvement office and four coordinators (from the Operating unit, the Emergency Department, the Oncological Day Hospital and the Preadminission Cen-

---

[4] Six sigma is another well-known quality improvement tool (DelliFraine et al., 2010); it is customer-driven and is characterized by emphasis on decision making and cost reduction (Bisgaard and Freiesleben, 2004). Lean Six Sigma or Lean Sigma is an approach aimed to integrate Lean and Six Sigma, to strength both the improvement philosophies. The following elements characterize the Lean Six sigma framework (De Koning et al., 2006): a structured approach, a project-based deployment; an organizational competency development; an organizational anchoring of solutions; the linking of strategy with project selection.

tralized Unit). These organizations were chosen because they are all examples, at different degree, of Italian full lean implementation cases.

7.3.1   The Ente Ospedaliero Ospedali Galliera

The Ente Ospedaliero Ospedali Galliera in Genoa (Ospedali Galliera), that in 2008 celebrated the first 120 years of activity, is a Hospital Institution that has retained a specific position among Italian public hospitals, maintaining its legal autonomy despite various health system national reforms. It is recognized as Hospital of national importance and of high specialization (Prime Minister's Decree 14/07/1995). The Ospedali Galliera has an availability of nearly 500 beds, a staff of about 1.700 people and works through 9 health departments, 4 administrative departments and 4 inter departments (shared with other hospitals). It owns the RSA Galliera[5], which works with 50 beds.

Due to the INHS's inner difficulties and in order to improve its performance the Ospedali Galliera launched a lean journey in 2007 (Nicosia, 2009) assisted by an external consultant (Nicosia, 2010).

The lean project is aimed to reach the classical benefits of identifying the value streams, improving the patient experience and journey, reducing wastes, redesigning processes, learning to see and solving problems. The attempt is labeled and communicated as "Lean G.E.N.O.V.A." the acronym for Galliera Empowerment by New Organization and Value Analysis (Progetto Lean G.E.N.O.V.A. – Ospedali Galliera).

In particular the lean thinking approach has been chosen as a powerful managerial technique to sustain a major organizational change: the new hospital organization according to three level of intensity of care in which patients are treated in specific areas (intensive or sub-intensive, post-intensive, and rehabilitation) against the traditional organization in specialized operative units. The objective is to complete the reorganization of the hospital by the end of 2013. In addition to this restructuring a major project is the building of the new facility that will allow overcoming the existing structural constraints and better evolving towards the new model of intensity of care. In the meantime the old hospital will function as a laboratory for the change to experiment the new way of work.

To sustain the change and the lean journey the hospital constituted a team ("Lean G.E.N.O.V.A.") coordinated by the Medical Director of the hospital, with the responsibility of selecting consultants, sharing experience with other hospitals, monitoring results and constantly inform the top management about the implementation.

The lean strategy is based on several points:

- to set medium/long-term goals against short-term ones;
- to strengthen the use of PDTA (clinical o critical pathways) to ameliorate clinical decisions and to spread the knowledge of value stream mapping as tools to solve related organizational problems (with the aim of increasing the standardization of activities carried out by physicians);

---

[5] In the INHS a RSA is a skilled nursing residential or semi-residential facility for elderly and disabled people that need of intensive use of health resources (Lo Scalzo et al., 2009).

- to help the healthcare redesign towards the intensity of care model and the cells design;[6]
- to steer the behavior of staff through visual management;
- to train staff continuously.

To realize this strategy some tools have been particularly used by staff to improve processes and reduce wastes, in particular 6S, kanban, value stream mapping and Rapid Improvement Events, along with the Spaghetti Diagram, the Ishikawa Diagram, and 5 Whys.

Personnel gained knowledge about lean principles and tools by means of a specific internal three level training began in 2009 and differentiated in basic, advanced and specialization (Annual Report Ospedali Galliera, 2011). The training scheme "Lean Healthcare at Ospedali Galliera" has been elaborated by the hospital jointly with the external consultant and has been inspired by the Royal Bolton Hospital in UK. Up to November 2012 more than 800 people gained the basic level (each course is attended by groups of 20-25 people). Indeed top management intended to spread the application of Lean and the healthcare redesign thanks to a large scale programme of information-training. The basic level only is obligatory for all the staff. Trainers are selected among the most enthusiast learners of the past basic level course. The objective is to train 40-45 Lean and Intensity of care Model facilitators by 2014 (about 25% of staff). Besides, more than 160 people at the end of 2012 have been trained with special workshops to learn and apply value stream mapping to the processes they personally can control and innovate (for example in order to reduce waiting times). Staff involved in the training is encouraged to communicate and share results, as well (Annual report Ospedali Galliera, 2011).

Another element characterizing the lean attempt is the constant exchange and comparison with other hospitals in Italy or abroad (e.g. the Royal Bolton Hospital – UK). The launch of a not for profit organization, the S.A.L.T.H. – Scientific Association for Lean Training in Healthcare, by the General Manager (Raimondo, 2013) is coherent with the will to share experiences.

In the Ospedali Galliera, several major projects have been carried out in different areas of the hospital, e.g. within the operating theaters (Nicosia and Nicosia, 2008), the ICU (Nicosia, 2011) and the Cyto-Histopathology Laboratory and the Genetic Laboratory (Zanin et al., 2012). The first application of lean resulted in the introduction and development of the Centralized Day Surgery (Nicosia, 2010) along with the redesign of processes, cost saving and set-up of a dedicated Surgical Pre-admission. Results after 5 years of activity were the 50% of surgical activity transferred in day-surgery or one-day-surgery with a concurring improvement of the surgical unit productivity (90% reduction of extra work in a year – measured in hours – in circumstance of the same volume of surgical activity).

All the projects, generally, resulted in promising ameliorations, contradicting the deep-rooted beliefs of professionals that only with more resources it is likely to obtain important improvements, such as waiting times reduction for patients to get tests re-

---

[6] The hospital used the cells design approach to rationalize the use of time, space and other resources to deliver better services.

sponse, reduction of the case cancellation rate, reduction of space floor utilized, reduction of the average of hospital stay and increase in the number of patient treated.

All the efforts in implementing Lean and change the hospital towards the new model are combined with a focus on cost accounting. The Ospedali Galliera is also the co-promoter of a national network, of about 20 Italian Healthcare Organizations, engaged in the elaborations of standard costs of member's healthcare and administrative activities (N.I. San.). According to data gathered by the network, the amount of costs of production of the hospital is about 10% less than the standard (in 2011).

7.3.2   The Azienda Sanitaria Locale in Florence

The Azienda Sanitaria Locale in Florence is one of the healthcare organizations through which the Regional Government of Tuscany deliveries health services to its population.[7] It manages directly 6 public hospitals and 150 health districts, employs about 7.000 people and serves about 800.000 citizens. Two teaching public hospitals (Careggi and Meyer) and 13 private hospitals delivery health care in the same area.

The Azienda Sanitaria Locale (ASL) in Florence faced all the principal issues that other healthcare organizations had to deal with, like, for example, excessive waiting times in the Emergency Department, inefficiency in the operating room management, increasing in expectation about performance and customer satisfaction, need for more complex treatments and technologies. In 2004 the ASL introduced lean thinking with the help of external consultants during two Kaizen weeks (Raimondo, 2013). Lean was adopted as business process improvement methodology because of its points of strength, in particular the focus on the user and the involvement of the worker in the continuous improvement. Two years later the top management decided for a more wider approach and launched a program called "Organizzazione Lean dell'assistenza – OLA (Lean organization of health services), in which Lean was applied as a strategy to survive and, mainly, to prosper (Bilancio Sociale Azienda Sanitaria Firenze, 2007); simplifying the organization, centring processes around the patient and developing staff competencies were the principles inspiring the project. The transition was not painless. Firstly the number of departments was cut down and the new organization resulted in only 9 departments at a company level crossing the six hospitals. Furthermore, in 2006, after a six month period of analysis of all the recovery and outpatient clinical activities, processes were redesigned according to six value streams (lines): Elective Surgery, Emergency Surgery, High Care Medicine (Elective and Emergency), Pregnancy and Birth, Outpatients and Low Care.[8] Each line is now owned by a line

---

[7] The case study has also been developed with data gathered from the presentation that Luigi Marrone, General Manager of the Local Health Authority between 2004 and 2012, made during the Lean Summit 2010 organized by the Lean Enterprise Academy in United Kingdom.

[8] In 2005, the Region Tuscany established (Law n. 40/2005) a new organizational model for the hospitals of its Regional Health System. The model is focused on the principles of homogenous area of hospitalizations according to levels of intensity of care and treatment. This organization overcomes the traditional division of areas into specialist wards. Even though the principal driver of change has been an external factor, the ASL has taken advantage from it through a more comprehensive project of healthcare redesign.

manager (skilled as engineer). According to the new model, patients requiring a homogenous level of care and nursing are now regrouped (and treated) in specific distinct areas.

The methodology for the health care redesign was characterized by a two level intervention: kaizen exemplar events and kaizen local events (Gemmi et al., 2008). The first ones were carried out by multiprofessional teams, named "prototype" groups, with the task to redesign the process at a very high level of abstraction (the company level). The groups identified the "milestones" for the redesign of each line of production (value streams). The latters were run in each hospital involving staff of different qualification. In the earliest phases over 300 people participated in the implementation of the project, whilst over 1,400 people participated until 2011 (clinicians, nurses, executive, project teams, technicians, health technicians, Department Directors). At a very micro-level the work was reorganized according to the model of "cell of production", characterized by a multidisciplinary way of work, a focus on flow and not on tasks (each nurse takes care of a group of patients), a redistribution of responsibilities among clinicians and nurses and a rational use of resources.

Even though the process improvement was generally labeled as "lean", it was supported both with Business Process Reengineering and lean thinking. The principal tools used for the latter were kaizen, visual management, value stream mapping, Kanban, 5S and Standard work.

The approach of implementation was mixed. The process was top down in the earlier phases and bottom up in the following ones. The new strategy formulated by the top management was not negotiable (Mignardi, 2009: p. 161), but, at the same time, the support of the Board to the change agents was strong during the whole lean journey. Indeed, once defined the "milestones", the practical translation of the basic model (the OLA structure) and principles was responsibility of the healthcare professionals. The major tool for the "translation" was the kaizen event, as stated earlier. Each event, lasting 8 weeks in average, has been structured in three phases: an informative phase, a second operative one and a final of control one (Menchi, 2009). The aim of each stage has been different. In the first one the heads of the involved structures explained the event. The second phase was twofold. In the first step, lasting one week, the ASL's staff analyzed the situation pre-improvement, set out the pathway of change, identified possible criticalities, verified data and proposed solutions. In the second step the staff implemented solutions. In the last stage the healthcare professionals gathered data and communicated results. All the staff share the same approach. Firstly they try to specify the value for the patients and to identify the value stream for each group. Subsequently they detect the elements of waste affecting the care pathways. Eventually they try to develop further the internal capability of the unit to predict the demand of healthcare services.

In order to sustain the OLA Project various actions were launched. A specific focus was established on communication towards staff and a wider programme of competencies development was started. Moreover, exchanges were promoted with other national and international healthcare organizations, by means of conferences such as "Assistere nel presente" (To care today) held by the ASL since 2008, which is the occasion to verify the engagement on the OLA Project and share results. Along with the conferences the ASL organized a program of certified training on Lean, based on 4 levels aimed to learn core knowledge and practical skills on how to utilize lean tools. Every person working in the hospital has to pass the first level.

As much important, the ASL launched a programme ("lean administration") to extend the implementation of Lean to the administrative processes in order to improve its support to the health staff (Bilancio Sociale Azienda Sanitaria Firenze, 2009-2010). At the same time a system of performance measures was implemented both to monitor clinical outcomes and the state of implementation of the OLA project. Another relevant project was the "Just one patient", aimed to overcome the fragmentation of care among hospitals and Basic Health Districts[9] through a lean, unique and easier pathway of care. In brief, Lean resulted a strategy of the whole local health authority (hospital, primary care, administrative and managerial processes and architectural design of new buildings).

Some of the results in eight years (2004-2012) of lean implementation (Marroni, 2012; Raimondo, 2013) have been an increment of the production of about 30%, even though staff is decreased (-15% of full time equivalent), an augmentation of the number of patients per bed in a year (over 60) while the number of beds is decreased at 856 (from 1.180 beds), the reduction of over 10% in the length of stay and up to 18% reduction of length of stay before surgery, an increase in time spent by nurses with the patient (+ 50%) and in customer satisfaction, a reduction in the number of warehouses (– 50%), of paper forms (-50%), of duplicated information (-40%) and an increase of standard procedures (+ 30%).

An important criticality was the engagement of physicians (De Pietro et al., 2011), which saw in the transition a loss of power (some of them lost the position of head unit in favour of another pattern of career), and generally the motivation of the staff (lower in the public sector than in the private). Furthermore, in the earlier phases the local community and the ASL were engaged in a strong debate about the opportunity of the healthcare redesign. These specific challenges were faced with a more effective human resource management, a strong commitment of the top management, a huge investment in the credibility of the project (the personal success of the project leader – the General Manager at the top level – was linked to the success of the project) and continuous maintenance (follow up of the project to achieve sustainability).

7.3.3   Istituto Clinico Humanitas

Istituto Clinico Humanitas (ICH), a Harvard case study (Bohmer, 2006; Bohmer 2004, Bohmer et al., 2001), is the 2nd largest private hospital in the Milan Area. It receives about 50,000 admissions per year and has a high focus on Surgery. It can be defined as a tertiary care hospital, as it provides complex medical and surgical interventions. Since its opening, in 1996, the organizational design has been based on two well dis-

---

[9] In the INHS a Basic Health District is a geographical unit "responsible for coordinating and providing primary care, non-hospital-based specialist medicine and residential and semi-residential care to their assigned populations" (Lo Scalzo et al., 2009: p. 75).

tinguished service lines: inpatient and outpatient. Even though the ownership is private, most of Humanitas'patients are public (about 90%); indeed the hospital has obtained is accredited status in 1997. It is also credited by Joint Commission International (since 2002), a global leader in releasing quality and safety certifications for healthcare organizations. Among others, a clear sign of excellence is the strong commitment on research: the hospital hosts the University of Milan's International Medical School and has its own research center. The quality of research allowed the hospital to obtain the status of IRCCS (National Institutes for Scientific Research) in 2005. Most of clinical specialties services are offered, except obstetrics, pediatrics and mental health. The success of the initiative is due to a series of factors. Historically there is a strong focus on asset management, which resulted in some principles: shared assets, need-based allocation, flexible physical space and separated patient flows. The first assumption is that no one is the owner of beds or operating rooms (that is a revolutionary idea for the traditional Italian culture). As a consequence, patients are treated in multi-specialty wards, with an advantage in flexibility for the hospital to deal with peaks. Equipment and clinicians rotate according to where they are needed. The second principle means that the allocation of assets is centered on needs: there is a frequent tuning of assets, according to the results of monitoring activities waiting lists, OR utilization, length of stay and other indicators. Furthermore, spaces are continuously re-built thanks to the use of plasterboard in construction. The last principle means that, in order to reduce variability and complexity, inpatient and outpatient paths never cross. Pathways are designed to minimize patient walking distances, as well. The success of such an approach builds on a clear organizational setting: an Operational Directorate is responsible for the achievement of the asset management objectives.

As new challenges affected the functioning of the hospital (the complexity of the system, physical constraints and the increasing of patient needs), managers began to evolve the historical model focused on asset efficiency. Since 2010, the challenge has been to maintain the high efficiency while developing a higher focus on care pathways, through the constitution of "centers". Each center is a collection of multidisciplinary teams assembled around care pathways aimed to generate positive internal tension between quality and efficiency. The first one was the Cancer Center, launched in 2010. The last challenge of the hospital is to evolve further towards a "disease management" model, with a focus on coherence and appropriateness of contents according to pathology and improvement of outcomes.

Another important innovation is the inception of a lean transformation programme in 2012. The initiative for the implementation of Lean was undertaken by a unit expressly set up in the Operational Directorate, the "Lean and continuous improvement" office that is responsible for organizational innovation, clinical process redesign and change management. The unit works as a team offering services to professionals within the hospital. Up to now the hospital hasn't been helped by external consultants in implementing Lean. The office drives improvement projects (project management), provides support for clinical and organizational issues and offers training and coaching about continuous improvement tools and concepts, contributing to the development of a lean culture in the hospital. Two elements distinguish the efforts of the team. Firstly a clear methodological approach built on process mapping and analysis, tools for issue identification and solution design, project management and monitoring of results.

Moreover, the attempts at building a lean culture are realized through a 3-level training programme, from basic to team training. The basic programme is intended to spread key concepts and tools for daily continuous improvement. Typical contents of the session are the core concepts of "muda", "mura" and "muri" and the principal instrument of problem solving (5S, value stream mapping, Root Cause Analysis, 5 Whys analysis, Pareto Diagram, Spaghetti Diagrams, Visual management, Poka-Yoke Systems, kanban, check list, procedures, clinical algorithms and pathway maps for standard work). Over 300 workers earned this level, to date. In the advanced level, staff learn how to master project management techniques and lean and change management tools. While the first level is opened to all staff, the second one is directed only to selected lean champions. The final one (team training) has the objective to train the staff towards a more effective team working in highly complex and multidisciplinary environment.

Importantly, staff trained for the basic level has been encouraged to carry out improvement projects, particularly in occasion of a "Lean contest" organized in 2012 by the "Lean and continuous improvement" office. 65 people participated in such competition, for a total of 20 projects submitted. Expected results were the diffusion of the best practices around the hospital, an increase of the staff motivation and benefits for patients, e.g. reduced and predictable waiting times in DHO (Oncological Day Hospital). The winner was a project carried out within the Emergency Department (ED) with the aim to improve the percentage of patients discharged by 4 hours (the target was internally set at 80%). A value stream map allowed to highlight the huge amount of time spent on average by the patient in non-adding value activities: people had to wait during the diagnostic process mainly because the difficulty for clinicians in retrieving patient status info within the available software. A new software screen enabled clinicians to visual tracking the patient path and status. The percentage of in-time discharged patients increased of about 10% in a six month period and, most important, changes were sustained over time. Besides, many other positive results were achieved thanks to all the projects carried out in different areas of the hospital: most projects improved quality, safety and patient and staff satisfaction; a significant amount of waiting times was decreased; unnecessary exams and visiting were eliminated; supply chain was optimized; waiting list had even been halved; more patients were treated per day; patients improved their experience. No particular criticisms or important difficulty were reported about the lean journey, except the need for a careful management of the transformation process and of the motivation of people involved in the change.

7.4   Discussion and conclusion

Building upon the main topics synthetized in the previous literature review and the three Italian cases (see Table 7.2 for principal actions), in this paragraph we highlight the principal features of lean implementation in Italy.

Data gathered from the three Italian case studies confirm that Lean, if applied with a full implementation approach, allow obtaining the typical advantages at individual (patients and workers) and organizational level. Specifically they concerned the waiting times, the case cancellations in the operating theatre, the average of hos-

Table 7.2 Main actions of implementation

	Ospedali Galliera	LHA of Florence	ICH
Ownership	Public (with special legal autonomy)	Public	Private
Approach	Full implementation, with the help of external consultants	Full implementation, with the help of external consultants only in the earlier phases	Full implementation, without the help of external consultants
Principal Actions of implementation	• Redesign of the traditional health care model • Constitution of the Lean G.E.N.O.V.A. team • Basic, advanced and specialized training of staff on lean • Constitution of the S.A.L.T.H. – Scientific Association for Lean Training in Healthcare • Organization of conferences • Launch of several projects in different areas of the hospital • Strong focus on cost accounting	• Redesign of the traditional healthcare model • Establishment of "prototype" groups • Four level training of staff on lean • Start off of several projects, in different areas of the hospitals and of the Basic Health Districts • Improvement of the performance measurement system • Launch of a wider programme of staff competencies development • Increase in communication towards staff • Organization of conferences • Combination of Lean thinking and Business Process Reengineering	• Constitution of a "Lean and continuous improvement" office • Basic and advanced training of staff on lean • Launch of the "lean Contest" • Launch of several projects concerning all the areas

pital stay, the space floor utilized, the time spent with the patient, the productivity of the staff, the patient experience, the safety for both patient and staff, the supply chain optimization, the reduction of wastes of administrative activities.

Consistently with the suggestions of the literature, Lean has been conceived and applied as more than a set of tools, and decisions have been taken at a company level, in order to spread and sustain the implementation. Fundamentally, basic and advanced training on Lean, and specific preparation of change facilitators have been conducted, jointly with the constitution of stable working teams supporting both top management and staff and operating synergically with other improvement teams.

Among the factors that enabled the lean implementation, the strong commitment of top management, long-term objectives, celebration and diffusion of best practices, as well as sharing information about the implementation with other organizations were the most important elements. In particular the long tenure of the General Manager as head of the organization was a factor of success both in the Ospedali Galliera and in the ASL in Florence.

The main difficulty in implementing lean was the cultural resistance of the staff, particularly of the physicians, used to work alone (not in multidisciplinary teams) and in a self-referential way.

Interestingly, lean appears to keep its promises both in private and public organizations, in absence or presence of external help by consultants, though in the private sector the improvement seems to be faster.

Although the findings cannot be statistically generalizable (Silverman, 2001) to the INHS, some considerations may be made about the implementation of lean healthcare practices in Italy from the literature and the three cases.

First of all the practices of lean management (Nicosia, 2010; Raimondo, 2013) and more generally of operations management (Bensa et al., 2010) appear to be not so diffused in Italy as they are in other healthcare systems (e.g. in the UK NHS; Radnor and Osborne, 2013). With reference to Lean the reason may be that neither national nor local politicians able to decide strategies for Italian public organizations have promoted such a strategy. In other words Lean has not been chosen as a reform strategy for the Italian public sector to improve public services. Nevertheless Lean may be considered, along with other service improvement methodologies, to solve organizational performance issues of Italian healthcare organizations. Due to the prevalent public nature of the healthcare delivery provision, Lean should be applied within "a public service dominant business logic" (Radnor and Osborne, 2013) to enhance its potential and overcome possible failures such as those of the UK National Health Service, where implementation has been tool-based rather than system-wide and characterized by a "product dominant logic". Accordingly, it is necessary to avoid that Lean become the last managerial fad (or, worse, used as a policy to enhance a spending review) in a context, the Italian one, that over the last decade has already been characterized by a huge amount of reforms and resistance of healthcare professionals towards managerial innovation.

Second, two of the three cases of full implementation show that lean has been implemented jointly with a major project of healthcare redesign towards "the hospital for intensity of cure and care model". Even though the underlying assumption of the new model is to meet patient needs effectively, which is at the same time a core characteristic of Lean, actually there is a misunderstanding of the community of Italian physicians about the two phenomena (e.g. Bolognese, 2011; Bovenzi, 2011): Lean should not be confused with the model of "the hospital for intensity of care" but, as stated, is a strategy for the operational excellence (Modig and Åhlström, 2012). As a consequence not every hospital starting a lean journey has to transform itself according the intensity of care model and vice versa. Accordingly, the lesson is that Italian health care organizations must not apply Lean uncritically and without a deep knowledge about what the approach really is.

Third, basic stability is a condition to enhance lean practices (Ballé and Régnier, 2007). In the ICH case, where Lean was introduced about a years ago, there was a starting condition in which processes were already efficient and patients'needs were taken into account in order to evolve the organizational model, so the new strategy allowed further and quick gains in efficiency and effectiveness. Consequently Lean is not a "magic" set of tools to solve problems of inefficiency but, again, a strategic choice to reach flow efficiency.

Fourth, Lean is compatible with other business process improvement methods. In the health care sector, as also shown by the cases and the Italian literature, clinical care algorithms (e.g. clinical pathways, protocols, guidelines, and so on) used for the management of health care problems, Six Sigma (Chiarini, 2012), Business Process Reengineering, or other methodologies (Radnor, 2010), have all different features but identic purpose, the improvement of processes. What is more, they can coexist in order to achieve the expected results and support each other. Certainly, attention may be paid for the careful harmonization of the various methods when applied simultaneously. A promising combination is among Lean and Six Sigma, with interesting examples from Italy (Chiarini and Bracci, 2013).

Fifth, as the case of the ASL in Florence highlights, in Italy (but probably wherever the health care sector is mainly public), stakeholders (local politicians, trade unions, local community) may play a role in spreading (or slowing down) the adoption and diffusion of business process methodologies.

Sixth, Lean has proven to facilitate, in the ASL in Florence, the integration among different facilities and overcome the fragmentation of healthcare delivery among levels of care (hospital care, health district and primary and community health care), a strategic issue for Italian ASLs.

More generally, even though in the Italian healthcare literature interesting cases of lean healthcare practices have been described, most of the endeavors can be labeled as "tentative" or "few projects" (Burgess and Radnor, 2013). Furthermore it seems that earlier lean attempts in healthcare focus more on improving risk management activities (Chiarini, 2012; Patrini and Confortini, 2010) and on exploring modalities to reach simultaneously the potentiality of different business process improvement methodologies (Chiarini and Bracci, 2013), even though without trying a more holistic approach ("systematic approach"). Chiarini and Bracci (2013) highlighted some interesting implications from two Italian publicly-owned healthcare organizations: savings are not the mandatory or the most important purpose to launch Lean Six Sigma projects in the public sector; in Italy there is a lack of statistical culture among doctors and nurses that limits the use of Six Sigma; as a consequence there is more use of basic Total Quality Management and Lean tools than statistical ones.

Ultimately, we can extend to the INHS the claim of Jones (2006: p.16) that "the existing model in which the hospital doctor acting as a skilled craftsperson effectively manages their own waiting list of patients, clinics and operations inside someone else's mass production general hospital is reaching the end of the road". Accordingly, as Lean is a promising strategy to improve the performance of Italian hospitals, it is useful to spread the diffusion of lean in the INHS, that stands back from other national healthcare system, such as, for instance, the UK NHS.

To gain more knowledge about Lean healthcare in Italy further qualitative and quantitative research is needed about the diffusion of the strategy and the modalities of implementation. A more rigorous analysis about the benefit-cost ratio is important in order to assess the advantage of implementing Lean, as well. Furthermore the relationship between lean practices and the overall organizational performances is not well understood. What is more, another issue of interest is how to overcome resistance of healthcare professionals to change. Lastly, attention may be paid to develop key indicators both to monitor the lean journey and assess the outcomes of lean.

Summary

The Italian National Healthcare System is facing challenges concerning the growing of the health demand and the increase in the expectation of patients on quality and safety of care in a context of continuous reduction of funding for the healthcare expenditure. Moreover, structural and qualitative gaps among regions, low integration between hospitals, primary and social care, the presence of regions under Recovery plans or single local health authorities and hospital struggling for turnaround because of important deficits, and traditional lack of healthcare operations management culture, call for innovation and implementation of managerial practices already experimented in the manufacturing sector.

Lean healthcare has proven to be extremely efficient in several healthcare organizations of different healthcare systems in order to improve productivity, reduce costs, increase quality, safety and timely delivery of services. Reported benefits are likely to be reached in organizations trying a "programme" or a "systematic" approach (Burgess and Radnor, 2013). Failure in the implementation of lean initiatives may be linked also to a mistaken conception of lean, not understood and applied in its truly essence: a strategic choice that prioritizes flow efficiency (Modig and Åhlström, 2012). Attention has to be paid to overcome the typical barriers in the introduction of lean and to follow successful pattern of implementation.

Several critical factors of success in implementing Lean emerged from the three Italian cases: the commitment of top management and the long permanence of the General Manager; the existence of a structure mediating between top management and staff asked to change the way to perform work; the collaboration between the team responsible for lean management at an organizational level and other improvement teams; the long-term orientation of the project; the training of staff and change facilitators; a bottom-up process of implementation; the celebration and diffusion of best practices; an effective human resource management and the continuous "maintenance" of the implementation.

The findings from earlier Italian experiences in healthcare are consistent with the international literature about benefits and approaches of lean thinking practices, even though Italy stands back from other healthcare systems in the implementation of lean practices, nor the Country has chosen Lean explicitly as means of public reform. Few applications are described in the academic literature and most of them are examples of "few project" implementations (Burgess and Radnor, 2013). Nevertheless some lessons can be drawn upon the case studies and the academic literature. In case of adoption of Lean as approach for Public reforms, policies have to be embedded within a "public service-dominant logic" (Radnor and Osborne, 2013). Efforts are necessary to overcome possible misunderstandings of the nature of Lean, especially when confused with the hospital for intensity of care model. Furthermore the reaction of stakeholders to the implementation or their support may not be undervalued.

Finally, further quantitative and qualitative research is needed to extend the knowledge about the diffusion of Lean in the INHS and its modalities of implementation.

References

Agnetis A., Coppi A., Corsini M., Dellino G., Meloni C., Pranzo, M. (2012), *Long Term Evaluation of Operating Theater Planning Policies*, "Operations Research for Health Care", 1 (4): 95-104.

Angelé-Halgand N., D'Andreamatteo A. (2012), *Lean Implementation in a Health Care Setting: the Case of a French University Hospital*, 7th International Conference on Accounting, Auditing and Management in Public Sector Reforms.

Annual report Ospedali Galliera (2011), accessible on line: http://www.galliera.it/20/56/1344/file-ar/Annual%202011%20Galliera.pdf [accessed 20/07/2013].

Arlbjørn J. S., Freytag P. V. (2013), *Evidence of Lean: a Review of International Peer-reviewed Journal Articles*, "European Business Review", 25 (2): 174-205.

Ballé M. – Régnier A. (2007), *Lean as a Learning System in a Hospital Ward*, "Leadership in Health Services", 20 (1): 33-41.

Bensa G., Giusepi I., Villa S. (2010), *La gestione delle operations in ospedale*, Lega F., Mauri M. – Prenestini A. (a cura di), *L'ospedale tra presente e futuro. Analisi, diagnosi e linee di cambiamento per il sistema ospedaliero italiano*, EGEA, Milano, 243-288.

Berry L. L. (2008), *Management Lessons from Mayo Clinic : Inside One of the World's Most Admired Service Organizations*, McGraw-Hill, New York.

Bilancio Sociale Azienda Santiaria Firenze (2007), accessible on line: http://www.asf.toscana.it/images/stories/bilanci/bilancio_sociale2007.pdf [accessed 01/07/2013].

Bilancio Sociale Azienda Santiaria Firenze (2009-2010), accessible on line: http://www.asf.toscana.it/images/stories/bilanci/bilancio_sociale2009-2010.pdf [accessed 01/07/2013].

Bisgaard S., Freiesleben J. (2004), *Six Sigma and the Bottom Line*, "Quality Progress", 37 (9): 57-62.

Black J. R., Miller D. (2008), *The Toyota Way to Healthcare Excellence Increase Efficiency and Improve Quality with Lean*, Health Administration Press, Chicago.

Bohmer R. (2004), *Istituto Clinico Humanitas (B)*, Harvard Business School, Boston, Massachusetts.

Bohmer R. (2006), *Istituto Clinico Humanitas (C)*, Harvard Business School, Boston, Massachusetts.

Bohmer R., Pisano G., Tang N. (2001), *Istituto Clinico Humanitas (A)*, Harvard Business School, Boston, Massachusetts.

Bolognese L. (2011), *Sviluppare e verificare nuovi modelli assistenziali in sanità: la prospettiva di un cardiologo*, "Giornale italiano di cardiologia", 12 (1): 5-9.

Bovenzi F. M. (2011), *Lean Hospitals: Lean Thinking is Difficult to Implement in Practice*, "Giornale italiano di cardiologia", 12 (1): 21-22.

Burgess N., Radnor Z. (2013), *Evaluating Lean in Healthcare*, "International Journal of Health Care Quality Assurance", 26 (3): 220-235.

Carbone C., Del Vecchio M., Lega F., Longhi F., Prenestini A. (2012), *Se l'azienda è a rischio default*, "Il Sole24Ore sanità", 21-27 febbraio, 8.

Chiarini A. (2012), *Risk Management and Cost Reduction of Cancer Drugs Using Lean Six Sigma Tools*, "Leadership in Health Services", 25 (4): 318-330.

Chiarini A., Bracci E. (2013), *Implementing Lean Six Sigma in Healthcare: Issues from Italy*, "Public Money and Management", 33 (5): 361-368.

CHIARINI A. (2010), *Lean Organisation for Excellence: Hoshin Kanri, Supply Chain Accounting, Lean Metrics. Toyota Production System nel mondo manifatturiero, dei servizi*, FrancoAngeli, Milano.

CHIOCCA D., GUIZZI, G., MURINO T., REVETRIA R., ROMANO E. (2012), *A Methodology for Supporting Lean Healthcare*, W. DING, H. JIANG, M. ALI, M. LI (Eds.), *Modern Advances in Intelligent Systems and Tools*, Springer Berlin Heidelberg, 93-99.

DE BELVIS A. G., FERRÈ F., SPECCHIA M. L., VALERIO, L., FATTORE G., RICCIARDI W. (2012), *The Financial Crisis in Italy: Implications for the Healthcare Sector*, "Health Policy", 106 (1): 10-16.

DE KONING H., VERVER J. P. S., VAN DEN HEUVEL J., BISGAARD S., DOES R. J. (2006), *Lean Six Sigma in Healthcare*, "Journal for Healthcare Quality", 28 (2): 4-11.

DE PIETRO C., BENEVENUTI C., SARTIRANA M. (2011), *Gli ospedali per intensità di cura in Toscana: un'esperienza in corso*, CANTÙ, E. (a cura di), *Rapporto OASI 2011. L'aziendalizzazione della sanità in Italia*, Egea, Milano.

DE SOUZA L. B. (2009), *Trends and Approaches in Lean Healthcare*, "Leadership in Health Services", 22 (2): 121-139.

DELLIFRAINE J. L., LANGABEER J. R., NEMBHARD I.M. (2010), *Assessing the Evidence of Six Sigma and Lean in the Health Care Industry*, "Quality Management in Healthcare", 19 (3): 211-225.

EMILIANI B. (2007), *Real Lean: Understanding the Lean Management System*, Center for Lean Business Management, LLC.

FILLINGHAM D. (2007), *Can Lean Save Lives?*, "Leadership in Health Services", 20 (4): 231-241.

FRANCE G., TARONI F., DONATINI A. (2005), *The Italian Health-care System*, "Health Economics", 14 (S1): S187-S202.

GALGANO A., GALGANO C. (2006), *Il sistema Toyota per la sanità. Più qualità meno sprechi*, Guerini e Associati, Milano.

GEMMI F., MECHI M. T., GEDDES DA FILICAIA M., TURCO L., APPICCIAFUOCO A. (2008), *Il Progetto Ola-Organizzazione Lean dell'Assistenza. Una reingegnerizzazione dei servizi ospedalieri basata sul lean thinking, per una disposizione più efficiente delle risorse*, "L'Ospedale", n. 3: 76-81.

GRABAN M. (2011), *Lean Hospitals: Improving Quality, Patient Safety, and Employee Engagement, Second Edition (2° ed.)*, Productivity Press.

GRUNDEN N. – PITTSBURGH REGIONAL HEALTH INITIATIVE (2008), *The Pittsburgh Way to Efficient Healthcare: Improving Patient Care Using Toyota-based Methods*, Healthcare Performance Press, New York.

GUIZZI G., CHIOCCA D., ROMANO E. (2012), *Healthcare Lean Thinking: Simulation of an Intensive Care Unit (ICU)*, Advances in Computer Science, Proceedings of the 6th WSEAS European Computing Conference (ECC'12), Prague, Czech Republic, 394-400.

HINES P., HOLWEG M., RICH, N. (2004), *Learning to Evolve: a Review of Contemporary Lean Thinking*, "International Journal of Operations and Production Management", 24 (10): 994-1011.

HOLDEN R. J. (2011), *Lean Thinking in Emergency Departments: a Critical Review*, "Annals of emergency medicine", 57 (3): 265-278.

JONES DT. (2006), *Leaning Healthcare*, "Management Services", 50 (2): 16-17.

KENNEY C. (2011), *Transforming Health Care: Virginia Mason Medical Center's Pursuit of the Perfect Patient Experience*, CRC Press, Boca Raton.

KOLLBERG B., DAHLGAARD, J. J., BREHMER P. O. (2006), *Measuring Lean Initiatives in Health Care Services: Issues and Findings*, "International Journal of Productivity and Performance Management", 56 (1): 7-24.

LEGA F. (2012), *Oltre i pregiudizi e le mode: natura e sostanza dell'innovazione organizzativa dell'ospedale*, in CANTÙ, E. (a cura di), *Rapporto OASI 2011. L'aziendalizzazione della sanità in Italia*, Egea, Milano.

LEGA F., DE PIETRO C. (2005), *Converging patterns in hospital organization: beyond the professional bureaucracy*, Health Policy, 74 (3), 261–281.

LEGA, F., SARGIACOMO, M., IANNI, L. (2010), *The Rise of Governmentality in the Italian National Health System: Physiology or Pathology of a Decentralized and (Ongoing) Federalist System?*, "Health Services Management Research", 23 (4): 172-180.

LIKER J. K. (2004), *The Toyota Way: 14 Management Principles from the World's Greatest Manufacturer*, McGraw-Hill, New York.

LO SCALZO A., DONATINI A., ORZELLA L., CICCHETTI A., PROFILI S., MARESSO A. (2009), *Italy: Health System Review*, "Health Systems in Transition",11 (6): 1-216.

MARRONI L. (2012), *Nuova organizzazione nell'Azienda Sanitaria Firenze: intensità di cure, processi, lean, report for the national conference "Modelli di assistenza ospedaliera per intensità di cura"*, Bologna 29-30 march, accessible online: http://www.saluter.it/documentazione/convegni-e-seminari/convegno-ospedale-intensita-di-cura-2012 [accessed 01/07/2013].

MAZZOCATO P., SAVAGE C., BROMMELS, M., ARONSSON H., THOR, J. (2010), *Lean Thinking in Healthcare: a Realist Review of the Literature*, "Quality and Safety in Health Care", 19 (5): 376-382.

MECHI M. T. (2009), *L'esperienza dell'ASL 10 di Firenze: il progetto OLA, report for the international seminar "Redesigning care"*, Genova, the 23rd of October, accessible online: http://www.galliera.it/1372/redesigning-care/redesigning-care/?searchterm=mechi [accessed 21/07/2013].

MIGNARDI L. (2009), *L'accesso ospedaliero: un'esperienza di riorganizzazione secondo l'approccio Lean Thinking*, "Salute e Società", Suppl. 1: 155-165.

MILLER D. (2005), *Going Lean in Health Care*, Institute for Healthcare Improvement, Cambridge, MA.

MODIG N., ÅHLSTRÖM, P. (2012), *This is Lean: Resolving the Efficiency Paradox*, Rheologica, Stockholm.

MONTESARCHIO V., GRIMALDI, A. M., FOX, B. A., REA, A., MARINCOLA, F. M., ASCIERTO, P. A. (2012), *Lean Oncology: a New Model for Oncologists*, "Journal of translational medicine", 10 (1): 74.

MOYANO-FUENTE J., SACRISTÁN-DIAZ M. (2012), *Learning on Lean: a Review of Thinking and Research*, "International journal of Operations and Production Management", 32 (5): 551-582.

NHS LEAN IMPLEMENTATION HANDBOOK (DRAFT) NHS LEAN THINKING NETWORK (2006), http://www.networks.nhs.uk/uploads/06/01/lean_implementation_handbook.doc [accessed 20/06/2013].

NICOSIA F. (2008), *L'ospedale snello. Per una sanità a flusso controllato e intensità di cure*, Franco Angeli, Milano.

NICOSIA F. (2009), *Galliera, caccia agli sprechi con "Lean"*, "il Sole24Ore Sanità", 3-9 novembre, 20.

NICOSIA F. (2010), *Il nuovo ospedale è snello. Far funzionare gli ospedali con il Lean Healthcare: consigli pratici e sostenibilità*, Franco Angeli, Milano.

NICOSIA F. (2011), *Così "Lean" taglia gli sprechi*, "il Sole24Ore Sanità", 26 aprile – 2 maggio, 20.

NICOSIA P. G., NICOSIA F. (2008), *Tecniche lean in sanità. Più valore, meno spreco, meno errori col sistema Toyota*, Franco Angeli, Milano.

PAPADOPOULOS T., RADNOR, Z., MERALI, Y. (2011), *The Role of Actor Associations in Understanding the Implementation of Lean Thinking in Healthcare*, "International Journal of Operations and Production Management", 31 (1-2): 167-191.

PATRINI E., CONFORTINI M. C. (2010), *Lean management e qualità in sanità. La metodologia applicata in corsia,* Il Sole 24 Ore, Milano.

PERRELLA G., LEGGERI R. (2007), *La caccia e la lotta agli sprechi in sanità. Metodi e strumenti operativi per le strutture sanitarie pubbliche e private,* Franco Angeli, Milano.

PETTERSEN J. (2009), *Defining Lean Production: Some Conceptual and Practical Issues,* "The TQM Journal", 21 (2): 127-142.

PIANO SANITARIO NAZIONALE – Schema di (National Health Plan), 2011-2013.

PLEBANI M., LIPPI G. (2011), *Closing the Brain-to-Brain Loop in Laboratory Testing,* "Clinical Chemistry and Laboratory Medicine", 49 (7), 1131-1133.

POKSINSKA B. (2010), *The Current State of Lean Implementation in Health Care. Literature Review,* "Quality Management in Healthcare", 19 (4), 319-329.

PORTIOLI-STAUDACHER A. (2008), *Lean Healthcare. An Experience in Italy,* Lean Business Systems and Beyond, Springer US, 485-492.

PROGETTO LEAN G.E.N.O.V.A. – OSPEDALI GALLIERA, accessible online: http://galliera. it/files/documenti/Lean_GENOVA/progetto_Galliera. pdf [accessed 20/07/2013].

RADNOR Z. J. (2011), *Debate: How Mean is Lean Really?,* "Public Money and Management", 31 (2): 89-90.

RADNOR Z. J. (2012), *Why Lean Matters Understanding and Implementing Lean in Public Services,* Advanced Institute of Management Research, London.

RADNOR Z. J. (2010), *Review of Business Process Improvement Methodologies in Public Services,* AIM Research.

RADNOR Z. J., BOADEN R. (2008), *Editorial: Lean in Public Services—Panacea or Paradox?,* "Public Money and Management", 28 (1): 3-7.

RADNOR Z. J., OSBORNE, S. P. (2013), *Lean: A Failed Theory for Public Services?,* "Public Management Review", 15 (2): 265-287.

RADNOR Z. J., WALLEY P., STEPHENS A., BUCCI G. (2006), *Evaluation of the Lean Approach to Business Management and its Use in the Public Sector,* Scottish Executive Edinburgh.

RAIMONDO C. (2013), *Innovazioni gestionali nelle imprese sanitarie. Modelli ed esperienze di lean management,* Youcanprint.

SARGIACOMO M. (2002), *Benchmarking in Italy: the first case study on personnel motivation and satisfaction in a Health Business,* in Total Quality Management, 13 (4): 489-505.

SHAH R., WARD P. T. (2007), *Defining and Developing Measures of Lean Production,* "Journal of operations management", 25 (4): 785-805.

SILVERMAN D. (2001), *Interpreting Qualitative Data: Methods for Analyzing Talk, Text and Interaction,* 2nd edition, Sage, London.

SORIANO-MEIER H., FORRESTER P. L. (2002), *A Model for Evaluating the Degree of Leanness of Manufacturing Firms,* "Integrated Manufacturing Systems", 13 (2): 104-109.

SPEAR S. J. (2005), *Fixing Health Care from the Inside, Today,* "Harvard Business Review", 83 (9): 78.

STONE K. B. (2012), *Four Decades of Lean: A Systematic Literature Review,* "International Journal of Lean Six Sigma", 3 (2): 112-132.

SUGIMORI Y., KUSUNOKI K., CHO F., UCHIKAWA S. (1977), *Toyota Production System and Kanban System Materialization of Just-in-Time and Respect-for-Human System,* "International Journal of Production Research", 15 (6): 553-564.

SWANK C. K. (2003), *The Lean Service Machine,* "Harvard Business Review", 81 (10): 123-130.

TOUSSAINT J. S., BERRY L. L. (2013), *The Promise of Lean in Health Care*, "Mayo Clinic Proceedings. Mayo Clinic", 88 (1): 74-82.

VEST J. R., GAMM L. D. (2009), *A Critical Review of the Research Literature on Six Sigma, Lean and Studer Group's Hardwiring Excellence in the United States: the Need to Demonstrate and Communicate the Effectiveness of Transformation Strategies in Healthcare*, "Implementation Science", 4: 35.

WEBER D. (2006), *Toyota-style Management Drives Virginia Mason*, "Physician executive", 32 (1): 12.

WELLMAN J., JEFFRIES H., HAGAN P. (2010), *Leading the Lean Healthcare Journey. Driving Culture Change to Increase Value,* Taylor & Francis.

WESTWOOD N., JAMES-MOORE M., COOKE M. (2007), *Going Lean in the NHS,* NHS Institute for Innovation and Improvement, London.

WOMACK J. P., JONES D. T. (1996), *Lean Thinking: Banish Waste and Create Wealth in your Corporation,* Simon and Schuster, New York, NY.

WOMACK J. P., JONES D. T., ROOS D. (1990), *The Machine that Changed the World: How Japan's Secret Weapon in the Global Auto Wars Will Revolutionize Western Industry,* Rawson Associates, New York.

ZANIN T., ANELLI E., MURA I., SIMONDO, P. (2012), *Lean Healthcare: Application of the Lean Techniques and "Case Management" to Network Services in a Reorganization of the Cyto-Histopathology Laboratory and Genetic Laboratory within the Diagnostic Service Department with Equal Resources,* "GSTF International Journal on Bioinformatics and Biotechnology", 2 (1): 73-77.

8

The impact of future introduction of standard costing on healthcare management[1]

This chapter aims at investigating and describing the multi-faceted effects triggered by the future introduction of standard costing on healthcare management in the light of the latest federalist reform in Italy (Legislative Decree 68/2011). Indeed, in order to better address the financial funds and healthcare delivery and guarantee more efficiency and effectiveness within the Italian National Health System (INHS), it is necessary to shift to an alternative model to replace the per capita and retrospective expenditure criteria. The analysis is conducted by illuminating some strengths and weakness deriving from the potential reform deployment and the respective impact on management and delivery of the healthcare services.

Learning objectives

After reading this chapter you should be able to:

- Italian National Healthcare System (INHS);
- Funding and management of the healthcare in Italy;
- The future introduction of the standard cost in the INHS;
- Its impacts and effects on healthcare management and providing services.

8.1 Introduction

In the last years there has been much debate about the regional healthcare expenditure and the reason why some regions, other things being equal, spend less than others and even with the same share of per-capita funding. Some scholars have attributed

---

[1] The chapter is the result of a joint effort and formulation. However, Luca Ianni (corresponding author) wrote paragraphs 8.1, 8.4, and 8.5; Antonio D'Andreamatteo wrote paragraphs 8.2 and 8.3; Massimo Sargiacomo wrote paragraph 8.6.

this to the multi-tier situation featuring the Italian National Healthcare System (INHS) where "historically northern regions were faster in developing administrative and technical capacity than southern regions" (Tediosi, Gabriele, Longo, 2009). Anyway, there are still many differences among Italian regions in terms of incurred expenses, funding models in comparison also with regional GDP (Gross Domestic Product) as a "fiscal capacity" index. Therefore, among other causes that generally may affect efficiency and effectiveness in the different National Healthcare Systems (e.g. trend economy, changing of the GDP, cutbacks policies and so on), funding for healthcare sector in Italy is the crucial variable to address the related expenditure level, thereby reaching the governmental public health goals, since total funds destined to INHS mostly stem from taxes (national/regional-based) collected from taxpayer. Consider, for example, that in 2010 they represented 78,4% of the overall available resources while the remainder was constituted by private source in terms of reduced charge (co-payments) and out-of-pocket payments (de Belvis et al., 2012). In this respect, funding "mechanisms" would make the improvement of the public health performances possible by putting pressure on each regions towards the achievement of positive financial and healthcare outcome, as long as these "pressure tools" are linked to achieved regional results (Del Vecchio, 2001) rewarding the best regions and punishing the bad ones in terms of funds to be transferred.

Unfortunately, the actual financing model (briefly described later), is mainly based, on one hand, on the regional incurred expenses (drawn from previous financial statement) as estimated financial requirements; on the other hand, per capita criterion for allocation funds rather than on the regional performances obtained thanks to effective strategic actions taken by politicians, good managerial skills and, in other words, "good management practices" in order to make their own systems financially sustainable.

Regarding the first point, this means that regions which in past times had spent more, also providing low quality services, could claim higher sums as past expenditure is the measure used to appraise the needed regional funds. Moreover, as to pro-capita parameter for distributing them, albeit it seemingly ensures fairness, ease of calculations, and equality of conditions (Del Vecchio, 2004), such criterion could lead to the assignment of excessive or not enough money compared to regional health needs to be satisfied, incomplete and insufficient of the healthcare expenditure coverage, even if it is necessary, as well as to increasing the differences among regions in terms of inefficiency (also for the incurred expenses), inappropriateness (for delivering services) and overspending (Ceruzzi-Sorano, 2013).

Here-hence, the need of revising of the previous model by introducing the standard costing criterion instead of per capita one, in order to better assign the available funds and in doing so to make them more consistent with the effective regional financial requirements and so as to avoid, among other things, that some regions have additional and unneeded money to burn.

All that in the attempt of accomplishing a regional federalist system, not well-defined yet, aiming at improving management public health and at the same time enhancing regional accountability and pushing politicians to do good work.

Therefore, the aim of this chapter is to describe and investigate the multi-faceted effects triggered by the future introduction of standard costing on healthcare management in the light of the latest federalist reform (Legislative Decree 68/2011) in

Italy. Admittedly, standard costing is part of the broad management accounting system and, accordingly, its implementation can be seen as the result of the impetus triggered by New Public Management related ideas and practices (Hood, 1991, 1995).

8.2   Brief notes about Italian National Health System (INHS)

The Italian National Health System (INHS) was established in 1978 by Law 833/1978 as a result of the extant fragmentation and disorganization occurred in that period and where different institutions and organizations (located at both national and local level) were involved. Bear in mind the overall healthcare was entrusted to the Interior Minister who acted at a peripheral level through the prefects and related provincial healthcare offices, while dedicated authorities (a sort of hospitals) were concerned with providing cares and other services to the admitted patients. In this respect, the INHS was defined as "the ensemble of functions, structures, services and activities intended to promote, maintain, restore the physical and psychical conditions of all population regardless of distinctions about individual and social states, and according to procedures assuring non-discrimination towards the citizens using the services" (art. 1 – L. 833/78). Furthermore, referring to institutions in charge "the delivering and providing health care services are the responsibility of the State, Regions, and Municipalities, guaranteeing the involvement of the citizens" (art. 1 – L. 833/78).

To do this, healthcare was, basically, provided by means of "municipal subdivisions" referred to as Local Health Units (LHU) with the task of delivering, among others, outpatient and hospitalization services by hospital units.

Unfortunately, a significant inefficiency and ineffectiveness (along with an irresponsible public funding model) was ascertained, while the overall expenditure was increasingly growing over time, partly because of the LHU governance structure featured by political delegates who very often deviate from the protection of the public health in favor of their own self-interests or to gain power, control and dominance.

Therefore, the first very "innovative" reform was launched in 1992 by Decree 502/92 (and later integrated and modified) in order to better handle the healthcare in Italy by introducing some tools and principles drawn from the New Public Management (NPM) framework.

Particularly, such changes have mainly resulted in (Ianni, 2008):

- "regionalization" of the healthcare and regional accountability for delivering services within central monitoring system and without involvement of the municipalities (except for advisory functions). Indeed, the Central government has exclusive power to set system-wide rules and health services that must be guaranteed throughout the country as healthcare entitlements (Tediosi, Gabriele, Longo, 2009);
- establishment of a new entity for healthcare, referred to as Local Health Authorities (LHA), with the task of providing outpatients services and hospitalization (both for acute care and long stay and rehabilitation), by means of directly managed hospital units to residential patients;
- "independent" public hospital (also as converted former hospital units) and private healthcare provider acting upon regional rules;

- introduction of a "competitive" system or "quasi-market" cash-based both among public providers (in or out region) and public-private ones in delivering healthcare services in order to push them to improve their financial and healthcare performances.

First attempts to introduce regional federalist system in healthcare was established by Legislative Decree 56/2000 with the purpose of enhancing regional accountability to citizens in the managing public health and at the same time, consequently, to turning the previous funding criterion ("incremental" fund transfers by State founded on annual reporting of the regional incurred expenses) into regional assignment based on revenue. In fact, the central government allocated some additional funds only in case of insufficient regional revenue destined to cover healthcare expenditure and to achieve equalization goals in order to balance the economic and social differences featuring the Italian regions, thereby acting as a "regulator" State.

Yet, essential levels of the care (EHL) were determined by Decree of the President of the Council of Ministers (DPCM) November 29, 2001 (later modified) so as to identify the health services (by listing them) to be provided within the INHS and thus the respective expenses covered by internal revenue. It goes without saying, all the other "extra-EHL" services will be delivered to the citizens "out-of-pocket", on their demand.

Finally, on March 23rd in 2005, a State-Regions Agreement set rules and procedures to be followed by regions so that Central Government could carry out monitoring and control activities with the intent of making INHS efficient, effective and sustainable as a whole. Bear in mind, for example, the introducing of the Budget Recovery Plan to be presented and transmitted by deficit regions to the Economic and Finance Ministry (MEF) as a condition to get a part of the funds due, once monitored and verified that the planned actions have been taken and the related objectives reached.

This gave the impression of a presumed and pathological nearly re-centralization, as reported by some scholars (Tediosi, Gabriele, Longo, 2009). But, since regional (decentralized) policies could not be completely free – because of multi-tier situations of the Italian regions and the mixed and variables results obtained from the decentralization process – there was the need for a governmentality structure equipped with external supervision, strong stewardship, aiming to coordinate systems that supported dialogue between the Central Government and regions in the light of the public health objectives. Therefore, "looking back at the INHS experience in recent years, it is clear that decentralization has to coexist with centralization in highly decentralized (almost federalist, and aiming at becoming fully federalist in a short time span) [...] thus reintroducing a governmentality approach in the relation between centre and periphery" (Lega, Sargiacomo, Ianni, 2010).

In 2006 and in 2009 two very important agreements between State and regions were signed. They were referred to as "Pact for Public Health" intended to accomplish and strengthen what had been previously established (in 2005) in the building of the regional federalist system.

Respectively, we can summarize these as follows:

- increasing of healthcare financial resources for the 2007-2009 years;
- revision of essential levels of care;

- setting of criteria to properly identify the regions to be considered in distress (e.g., the reaching or exceeding a given percentage of the losses in respect to the assigned health funds and the regional revenue);
- fulfilments to be followed by regions (e.g. cap pharmaceutical expenditure, standard for public and private "accredited" hospital beds, standard for appropriateness healthcare services, etc.);
- "automatic" increasing of some regionally based taxes, i.e. tax on productive activities (IRAP) and the surcharges on personal income tax for defaulting regions.

Finally, at a later stage, to the purpose of enforcing the signed agreements, further rules were established, i.e. Law 42/2009 for authorizing government to issue legislative decrees about federalism, within two years, such as the one for regulating the source of revenue to be directly collected by regions and of which they are accountable for their usage towards regional population and, at the same time, implementing the "standard cost model" as new mechanism of funding healthcare.

8.3   Funding and healthcare delivery

As already outlined above, from 2001 on, the funding of the National Healthcare in Italy (INHS), is based, at large, on regional revenue (i.e., regional tax on productive activities (IRAP), the surcharges on personal income tax (IRPEF), shares of the value-added tax (VAT), excise tax on petrol and car tax). Indeed, central State intervenes only to give additional funds devoted to the healthcare expenditure and not covered by regional receipts (because probably not adequate) or to balance and limit the existing economic and social "gaps" among regions ("equal distribution").

Particularly, this can be split into the following groups:

- weighted "per capita" funding;
- DRGs – Prospective Payment System (PPS);
- fee-for-service (FFS);
- additional funds;
- co-payments, out-of-pocket payments, other receipts (e.g. for rent).

The first one consists in dividing the funds to be assigned at the regional level in respect their financial requirement, by regional resident population ("per capita"), then weighted in depending on some parameters (e.g. mortality rates, age class, differently used over time). Once such funds has been transferred, each region provides its own Local Health Authorities (LHA) with financial resources to be used for delivering health care services, weighted, in turn, on the basis of the different features of the regional population and in some cases by levels of care (see Table 8.1).

DRGs – Prospective payment system (PPS) is mainly used in Italy for the reimbursement of the costs incurred by public or private hospitals for providing health care services to the inpatients during their hospital stay. It is substantially based on classifying, codification and grouping of the diseases listed in the International Classification of Diseases, Clinical Modification, 9th Edition (ICD9CM) into 25 Major Diagnostic Categories (MDC) and divided into 579 Diagnosis Related Groups (DRGs),

Table 8.1 Some regional weights used to assign "per capita" funds to LHA

Region	Weighting	Levels of care	Criteria
LOMBARDY	Yes	Yes	Age class Gender (15-44 years old) Mortality rates (at a given level of cares)
VENETO	Yes	Yes	Age class Altitude/Isles Equipment Other criteria
TUSCANY	Yes	No	Regional Morphology (7%) N. inhabitants within residential area (3%) Age class (90%)
MARCHE	Yes	Yes	Age class Gender Index of population dispersion
SICILY	Yes	Yes	Age class Gender Population density Regional Orography Isles

Source: adapted from JOMMY (2004).

identified by a specific code, so that every hospital episode may be included in one of those groups (e.g. carpal tunnel syndrome: DRG 6, MDC 1 "Nervous System").

In order to attribute a correct DRG to the different "cases", it is necessary to get a discharge summary written by physicians and summarizing all clinic-diagnostic information about patients released from the hospital or clinic (i.e. treatment course, the status at release, post-discharge expectation, instructions for physical therapy, etc.). Through a particular software named "GROUPER" the reimbursement is arranged multiplying the detected DRG by established "price" (higher for those entailing surgical interventions) equivalent to the "prospective" standard costs, on average, incurred to care the concerned inpatients (Preston, Chua and Neu, 1997). Indeed, the main assumption is that within the given DRG the related cost of the different hospital cases are assumed the same. In addition, before definitively computing the overall sum to be reimbursed, the complexity level of care has to be considered to further increase or decrease the earlier attributed DRG along with hospital stay days-threshold above which the final amount due will be correspondingly diminished. An example (Box 8.1) about eye socket operations (DRG 37, MDC 2 "Eye") is useful to understand what we have just described.

To be more precise, in the most of regional funding models, each region is concerned with funds to be assigned to LHA for providing healthcare services (specially, hospitalization, by hospital units directly managed, and outpatients services) and to coordinate the activities among public providers and public and private ones, in the

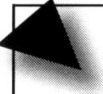

Box 8.1

Calculate reimbursement for DRG 37: Eye socket operations

Patient "A" has been admitted to hospital "X" in order to subject himself to eye socket operations. At the time of his release, the summary discharge, among other information about the patient, reported overall 20 days of hospital stay. Therefore, given that the "correction factor" set for such DRG in depending on complexity level of the care amounted to 1.47 (thereby increasing the total sum to be paid), € 4,930.00 is the "price" (per inpatient) drawn from latest "list of hospitalization price" DRG-based (Gen. 2013) as maximum value to be assigned within each region (regional lower price are certainly permitted) with 17 days-threshold. Therefore, the Region will have to pay € 7,247.10 (4,930*1.47) plus a lower amount for each extra-day (€ 254.00) at the discharge time (3 days), for a total of € 8,009.10.

light of reaching of the regional public health objectives. But then, the LHA have also the task of paying and reimbursing (with funds at their disposal) "independent" public and private hospitals for delivering healthcare services "purchased" by them for satisfying the needs of care of their patients/users.

The next Figure (Figure 8.1) sums up the overall funding model adopted by most regions referred to as "funding LHA-based".

Fee-for-service (FFS) is generally used for outpatient services purchased and provided by other regional LHA or belonging to other regions. It is mainly grounded on the payment of separate treatments depending on quantity (or volume) of cares at a given "price" listed for each service, respectively, in a regional or national ("one-price") rate (price) payment table. It is in some way similar to Outpatient Prospective Payment System in the US Medicare.

DGRs-PPS could be also included within the FFS model, since there is a "rate" established for hospitalization as well, but the underlying mechanism is different, firstly, because the related services are linked to Diagnosis related Groups and based on

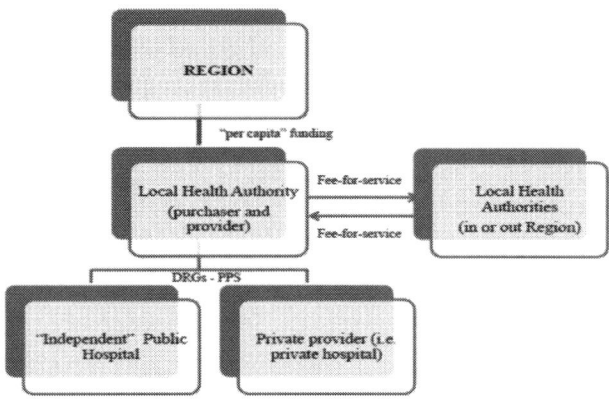

Figure 8.1   General funding model adopted by Regions (LHA-based).

"standard" average costs, as a measure of those prospectively incurred to care the in-patient whose diseases fall among one of them. Even though this model focuses on the quantity rather than the quality of the delivered services, it makes possible to better align funding to healthcare activities so as to drive physicians to achieve efficiency, make the relation price-cost of providing care more congruent and adequate, and bring about more attention to patients by introducing competitive mechanism among organizations (Jommi, 2004).

What is more, regions can assign additional and residual funds in order to further provide financial support to the regional LHA in the pursuing of the financial and health results, enabling to gradually move to new funding criteria, correct and balance the effects arose from the "per capita" funding.

Regional healthcare system is also funded by co-payments for pharmaceutical and outpatient care paid by users to partially cover the related incurred expenses but, actually, to the purpose of making citizens more responsible in the requiring healthcare services, thereby avoiding to trigger an expenditure which is useless or out of control for not needed requests.

Finally, out-of-pocket payments normally made for services extra-EHL (because not covered by taxes and accordingly by INHS) and other revenue such as rent, income from patent, gain from disposal or selling fixed asset.

8.4 The future introduction of standard costing in the INHS

Firstly, broadly speaking, the standard cost can be defined as an estimated value of what it should cost to make one unit of production at a fixed level of efficiency as target to be achieved. In short, it is a cost determined in relation to well-defined objectives to reach (Brusa, 2009). With respect to healthcare organizations it "would be the expected cost to treat a specific type of patient" (Finkler et al., 2007) or related to healthcare services, clinically-defined episodes of care, cost or revenue (responsibility) centers (e.g. ward, department, etc.), being regarded as *object cost*, that is to say the item of which we want to know the respective cost through the attribution process of direct costs (clearly ascribable) and allocating a fair share of indirect ones, such as overheads and the like.

Standard costs may be normally used by managers in order to control costs and efficiency, make the budget (budgeting) (e.g. Pettersen, 1995; Macinati, 2010), motivate and push personnel to meet the set goals by means, normally, of a reward-punishment system, support a management by objective (MBO), analyze cost-effectiveness for making some decisions, analyze the variances between the budgeted amounts (standard) and the costs (or revenues) actually incurred so as to lead the organization to the defined performances. The introduction of standard costing in the Italian National Healthcare Service (INHS) witnesses again "the invasive influence of financial measures and imperatives" (Lapsley, 1998) in the focal activities of healthcare organizations (Jacobs, Marcon, Witt, 2004; Kurunmäki, 2004; Kurunmäki, Melia, Lapsley, 2004; Pizzini, 2006).

Needless to say, in order to correctly determine standard costs, it generally needs to draw on historical past data because they are easily available, even though they can include inefficiency such as wastage of direct materials or not to incorporate any changes expected, for example, for the budget period (Horngren at al., 2011), processes mapping, observation and studying times and motions, theoretical calculations as well.

Secondly, in regards to its implementation in the INHS as an alternative and a new funding model, the legislative decree n. 68/2011 seems to refer to regional standard cost for providing healthcare as a whole. Particularly, the reform, as a first step, has specified that regional "standard" financial requirement is equivalent to a given percentage of the national one, obtained on the basis of the mean value (per capita weighted by age class) of the costs recorded and ascertained for the benchmark regions. In other words, this value should represent what the regions need in terms of funds to guarantee the essential level of cares as well as the regional "standard" costs, then attributed to each of the different type of them. These are constituted by three regions out of the five best having reported good performances and quality in the delivering healthcare services by way of the financial resources at disposal. The overall procedure and specific criteria have been consequently established by Council of Ministers deliberation (11th of December 2012) with the intent to identify the best five regions from which select the benchmark ones.

To sum up, it starts off with identifying the regions to be included in the ranked list, i.e., those who have proved:

- to ensure the essential level of cares in the latest year receiving a score greater than or equal to median value calculated by a particular supervision committee of the Health Ministry;
- to achieve positive results for two earlier consecutive years, as reported from regional healthcare financial statement in the providing the related services by the available assigned funds and other regional own revenue;
- not to have been subject to "Budget Recovery Plan Procedure";
- to have fulfilled what the central State has ruled for governing public health, as verified by a specific supervision committee of the Economics and Finance Ministry.

This ranking, in turn, is grounded on the following criteria:

- ascertained score for providing essential level of cares (determined by aforementioned ministerial committee);
- surplus or deficit as a percentage of the assigned total funding;
- quality, appropriateness and efficiency indicators for healthcare services delivered, e.g. variance between the estimated standard and actual reported value of the hospital expenditure as a percentage of the total amount, pre-operative hospital average length of stay, percentage of the patients discharged from wards that have not DRG entailing surgical interventions ("medical type" DRG), hospitalization of "surgery type" DRG as a percentage of the total admitted to hospital, average cost per hospitalization for acute patient, average cost per admission to hospital post-acute, expenditure on clinical laboratory, expenditure on the general practitioners, pharmaceutical expenditure per capita.

To elaborate the ranked list, the calculated value for each region will be reported in terms of quality and efficiency index (IQE), ranging from 1 to 10, and derived from a formula (see Box 8.2) based on summing of the regional normalized value for each indicator and a "grade point average" (GPA) per region whereby rank the best five.

Box 8.2

Calculation of Quality and Efficiency Index (IQE)

Normalization

Each indicator (19 in all) of a given region (R) is normalized by the following formula:

$$\text{Normalised Value}^t_R = \frac{\text{Value of the indicator}^t_R - \text{Mean value of the regional distribution}}{\text{Standard Deviation of the regional distribution}}$$

Then, by summing every regional normalized value we get the total score per region.

$$\text{Total Score}_R = \Sigma^{10}_i \text{ Normalized Value}^t_R$$

Finally, for each region, the quality and efficiency index is calculated (see formula below) on the base of its total score and in relation to the minimum and maximum value recorded on the whole.

$$IQE_R = \frac{\text{Total Score}_R - \text{Minimum Value of the Total Score}}{\text{Maximum Value of the Total Score} - \text{Minimum Value of the Total Score}} \times 10$$

Obviously, in the selection of the regions will have to be followed a representative criterion so as to include northern, central, southern Italian regions and those having small size.

Practically, once the five best regions have been identified, and the benchmarks among them chosen, the average of their recorded cost of providing healthcare (as "standard" cost) will be multiplied by resident population, weighted by class age, getting the regional standard financial requirement. The related percentages of the total will be then applied to the financial resources destined to healthcare sector to the purpose of estimating the funds to be assigned per region.

The next table (Table 8.2) shows the financial effects likely to arise from standard costing according to the latest reform, supposing that Lombardy (north of Italy), Tuscany (center), Basilicata (South and small size region) have been selected as benchmark regions (highlighted in bold) and 102 billion Euros is the available money.

As we can see at first glance from the exhibited table, the reported "standard" would be nothing but a constant that multiplies the weighted population (Mapelli, 2010) rather than being the average regional "standard" cost for delivering healthcare services. As a matter of fact, it could be readily proven that a different value would have not changed the percentage of allocation because of the underlying calculation mechanism. What is more, the funds at their disposal (e.g. € 102 Billions) could not be able to cover the total healthcare expenditure which should be incurred (e.g. € 104.478 Billions) in case of standard costs greater than national average unless funding is adjusted to what the regions need, as well as having a surplus (as "savings") to redirect towards other public sectors, in case of standard cost lower than national average. Indeed, financing will be able to be aligned to regional financial requirement

Table 8.2 Prospective financial effect deriving from using standard cost in the INHS

Region	Resident Population weighted by class age (WP)	Cost per capita (supposed) (C)	Regional "standard" financial requirement (FR) (CST = 1.740)		Regional funds to be assigned (P * 102 Billions) (€/000.000)
			CST * WP (€/000.000)	% (P) (FR/Tot)	
PIEDMONT	4.592.748	1.768	7.991	7,65	7.802
V. AOSTA	127.526	1.736	222	0,21	217
LOMBARDY	**9.663.413**	**1.727**	**16.814**	**16,09**	**16.415**
PA BOLZANO	472.468	1.683	822	0,79	803
PA TRENTO	506.093	1.713	881	0,84	860
VENETO	4.813.916	1.722	8.376	8,02	8.178
FRIULI V.G.	1.279.475	1.773	2.226	2,13	2.173
E. ROMAGNA	4.441.054	1.761	7.727	7,40	7.544
LIGURIA	1.783.987	1.866	3.104	2,97	3.031
TUSCANY	**3.862.159**	**1.773**	**6.720**	**6,43**	**6.561**
UMBRIA	925.661	1.768	1.611	1,54	1.572
MARCHE	1.615.387	1.759	2.811	2,69	2.744
LAZIO	5.383.659	1.721	9.368	8,97	9.145
ABRUZZI	1.358.737	1.743	2.364	2,26	2.308
MOLISE	336.719	1.773	586	0,56	572
CAMPANIA	5.579.109	1.673	9.708	9,29	9.477
PUGLIA	4.030.182	1.645	7.013	6,71	6.846
BASILICATA	**607.792**	**1.731**	**1.058**	**1,01**	**1.032**
CALABRIA	2.008.954	1.710	3.496	3,35	3.413
SICILY	5.001.227	1.695	8.702	8,33	8.496
SARDINIA	1.654.799	1.717	2.879	2,76	2.811
TOTAL	**60.045.065**	**1.730**	**104.478**	**100,00**	**102.000**

Source: adapted from CERUZZI-SORANO (2013).

on condition that it complies with government spending objectives which often require cutbacks policies, thereby entailing financial restrictions.

Yet, the "virtuous" regions that have spent less for governing public health could receive less money as a consequence of a presumed lower financial requirement and not necessarily those incurring higher healthcare expenses should be considered as "bad" regions because such costs have probably been intended to efficaciously provide higher quality of care.

Hence, the need for setting standard costs directly by regions (*bottom-up* approach), attributing them to the various healthcare services so as to better identify the benchmark among them (Pammolli, Salerno, 2010), instead of using a *top-down* approach at a macro-level (central government).

In summary, the standard costing reform in the INHS seems to propose again a per-capita financing even if enhanced in considerations of a standard mean value of what regions should spend to provide healthcare.

8.5   Managerial implications and impact on healthcare delivery

Admittedly, NPM-inspired reform – such as the one investigated in this book chapter – may have relevant managerial implications both at macro and at micro level. Standard costing in INHS could be very useful if it were linked to planning and control activities in the light of the set governmental purposes.

At a macro-level (State), this would enable to better arrange the financial resources to destine to public health sector by abolishing the mechanisms of allocation centred on per capita criterion (even though weighted by specific parameters), which could result in overspending, inappropriateness, increasing regional differences, so as to push the regions to achieve a given efficiency level reflected in the standard cost and, as a consequence, improving the healthcare management. At the same time, it would allow to avoid to incur in healthcare costs which are higher than those incurred in regions having the similar features, for example, in terms of population density, regional morphology, mix of treated patients, etc.

At a micro-level (Region), standard costing could enhance regional budgeting in consideration of what is effectively needed to guarantee the essential levels of care and be able to lead its own Local Heath Authorities and public hospitals to achieve, in turn, regional targets, thereby ensuring well-being of the resident citizens.

Particularly, standard cost must be firstly estimated by regions (and not by State) according to a bottom-up approach and, secondly, based on some technique and tools drawn from the literature on management and cost accounting for healthcare organizations (e.g. Finkler et al., 2007; Horngren et al., 2011; Dennis, 1989; Fass and June, 1997; Zimmerman and March, 1996) in order to predict the expenses that will have to be incurred in the future rather than relying only on historical data. In this respect, we can mention the using of groups for calculating costs (e.g. Delphi and nominal group technique), indexing for inflation, linear regression, forecasting for prediction patient volume and so on.

Unfortunately, on the one hand, most Italian regions have a costing accounting system not entirely working yet, making these calculations more difficult to realize. On the other hand, the expenses recorded in the Italian National Healthcare Information System (INHIS), cannot represent, in replace of them, the standard cost because these information could embrace more or less high levels of inefficiency, very changeable among regions, and do not reckon with type or mix of patients, hospitalization level, volume of patients treated and progressively aging population.

In the standard costing reform (Legislative Decree 68/2011) some of these issues have been taken into account only to the purpose of identifying the best five regions within which to select the benchmarks. For instance, indicators such as pre-operative hospital average length of stay, percentage of the patients discharged from wards that have not DRG entailing surgical interventions, average cost per hospitalization for acute patient, expenditure on clinical laboratory, expenditure on the general practitioners, etc. Notwithstanding, the funding will mainly relate to mean value of the expenses incurred by the three regions benchmark, irrespective of whether these may not reflect the amount of money needed to provide healthcare and, in the bargain, according to the available financial means.

Therefore, the fundamental introduction of a simple average expenditure recorded by "virtuous" regions, as standard, would mean propose again "old" mechanisms based on "historical" costs (Cisalghi, 2010), albeit partly improved.

This could probably result in more attention for the financial variable at the expenses of quality of care and public health on the whole. Indeed, regions would be able to spend only what it has been assigned in relation to the regional standard financial requirement, thereby becoming de facto a regional healthcare system almost completely finance-driven regardless of the actual health needs.

Moreover, there are too many differences among regions that portray the INHS insomuch as it would be very difficult to adopt a "standard" average cost to which regions should tend, as healthcare spending is heavily affected by the following causes (Falcinelli et al., 2010):

- age of population and aging rate;
- regional morphology;
- Gross Domestic Product (GDP) per capita, unemployment rate, enrolment rate at upper secondary school and passage rate from upper secondary school;
- condition of family environment, level of diffusion of the public services;
- propensity to require healthcare and social services;
- capacity of the LHA of dealing with the demand of healthcare without requiring necessarily the increasing of hospitalization, but enhancing primary care units and general practitioner activities.

Accordingly, government would consider as "good" regions those not having overspending with respect to funding, neglecting such variables and in doing so attributing less funds to regions that, for example, have a higher level of aging rate and, for this reason, a greater demand of healthcare services to satisfy.

Besides, it would be ignored the inverse distribution that could occur among regions, between hospitalization rate and their cost given that these could not be easily reduced over time, if that were the case, because of difficulty to decrease the personnel costs. So, the region, for public budgeting purposes, would find itself forced to set new hospitalization upper limits (Falcinelli et al., 2010).

It goes without saying that to accomplish a regional federalist system, the financial resources appertaining by virtue of new funding model, will be contingent on regional fiscal capacity (tax revenue). It would entail, as usual, a disadvantage for center and southern regions, that have, normally, fewer firms than those northern.

To solve this problem, the reform has established interventions of equalization by government through the part of tax revenue collected to a greater extent than the national average per capita, to allocate in favor of regions with lesser fiscal capacity, thereby diminishing the differences among regions. However, this would not enable the "bad" regions to ameliorate, knowing that the state will intervene in their aid, included also those that, having a quite high tax evasion rate, would record revenues lower than national average.

Finally, on the one hand, standard costs should be estimated directly by the regions, so as to consider the various regional features and reflect what these spend to provide healthcare. In this respect, it is necessary to make the cost accounting system operating within each region, so that these are be able to implement the needed calculations. On the other hand, the allocations of funds should effectively be regionally-based, i.e. differentiated by region according to social, economic, and epidemiological indicators, and in doing so reflecting the demand of healthcare services.

8.6   Discussion and Conclusion

Admittedly, after decades of centralization, the attempt of accomplishing the federalist system in Italy is not an easy task because of the multi-tier situation that characterizes it for historical, cultural, political reasons. After the first laws in the nineties, aiming at granting powers from central government to regions, provinces and municipalities (*devolution*) a process of decentralization of some public sectors (e.g. public health sector) was later started in order to gradually bring to completion a regional federalist system where regions have to be accountable for activities and the decisions made towards its own citizens.

Moreover, there have been re-centralizations interventions by some countries that had recently experienced the decentralization in healthcare (Tediosi et. al, 2009) probably deriving from the changes of the European policy and the objectives to be achieved and in the relations among the different levels (Europe, State, Region) or from the incapacity of the healthcare regional systems of pursuing targets in step with the national public health ones.

Particularly, the decentralization process within INHS has engendered varied results over time, as "some regions have taken advantage of it to strengthen their system, whereas others have not been able to develop an effective steering role" (Lega et al., 2010). Anyway, such presumed re-centralization would be "an effective way for the State to maintain control over the equity and efficiency of its healthcare system while decentralizing at a regional level" (Lega et al., 2010) without jeopardizing regional autonomy in the managing of the healthcare.

The real fundamental "step" in the implementation of the federalist system is represented by the fiscal decentralization, whereby each region can collect what has been earned by resident and firms, in terms of tax revenue, by abolishing, as a consequence, central government transfer funds except for equalization interventions. As already said, this decentralization was "weakly" introduced by decree 56/2000 and, later, by Law and related decrees about federalism.

Nevertheless, the funding of the healthcare sector is still managed by the central government since it has the task of assigning the funds owed to regions, albeit as a function of their revenue. Moreover, this mechanism of allocation is grounded on a weighted per-capita criterion which is not able to push regions to improve the healthcare management and to achieve a higher level of efficiency and of quality of care.

Hence, the revision of the previous funding model, realized by launching the standard costing, which can be seen as the introduction of another NPM-inspired reform, involving the deployment of private sector techniques and practices (i.e., Otley, 1978) whose implementation deserves investigation in non-Anglophone (Llewellyn-Northcott, 2005) public sector organizations and societies (Kurunmäki-Lapsley-Miller, 2011).

As we have noticed, by analyzing its functioning, it acquires as standard the mean value of the expenses incurred by the best regions and linked to the population "weighted" by class age. Thus, it would not be representative of what the regions need for providing healthcare services, but rather an attempt of making the regional expenditure uniform, at the level of the regions in financial balance, considered, to a greater extent for this reason, as "virtuous".

Indeed, not necessarily a region in financial balance and that has provided good quality of care, will present a lower spending, but, on the contrary, will produce a greater standard cost, and if chosen as benchmark, will contribute to increase the regional standard financial requirement.

Yet, the weighting has been attributed to the resident population (and not to financing as a whole) taking as a parameter only the age class at the expense of other economic and social indicators more useful to portray the actual healthcare needs.

We do not have to forget, furthermore, that once determined the regional standard financial requirement, central government could allocate an amount greater or lesser according to the available funds, forcing the regions to, respectively, increase or decrease their expenses independently from the demand of healthcare.

Such reform doesn't seem to be concerned about the marked differences that feature the regions in the INHS in Italy, since it does not contemplate remedial so as to create a funding model, multi-level, differentiated regionally-based.

In summary, this proposes again a "bad copy" of "old" mechanisms of funding incapable of supporting the health needs and achieving the public health objectives, paying more attention to the financial aims rather than to the patients. So, the regions would run the risk of not being able to guarantee essential level of cares because of the incapability in managing their money in an efficient and proper manner.

It is also worth noting that the global and financial crisis, at the present moment, is resulting in a heavy impact on the Italian healthcare system (de Belvis et al., 2012) mainly in terms of public health funding. Therefore, the future introduction of standard costing, according to the decree, would contribute to reduce over time, in financial restriction conditions, the expenditure to be incurred by the regions and money to spend for healthcare services, worsening the access to care, quality of healthcare and well-being of residents, as well as increasing of the regional deficits for those unable to cut costs.

Finally, considering the above remarks, we might argue that standard costing reform as established by decree 68/2011 might compromise the completion of a regional federalist system which should be characterized by clear mechanisms of funding linked to the social and economic indicators, accountability to citizens for using the funds for public health, giving importance to patients, users and well-being of the residents, and, especially, autonomy in the collecting and managing revenue so that the services can promptly be provided.

Thus, albeit the reform has attributed specific sources of revenue to the regions in the federalist perspective, the expected "model" is resulted unbalanced and hard to carry out, above all in managing in terms of fiscal pressure, fiscal autonomy factually obtained by the regions, arrangement of the taxes and their impact on the coordination of the fiscal policy among the different level of government such as state, regions, municipalities, etc. (Court of Auditors, 2013).

To conclude, the financing model is very important within the Italian healthcare sector, because most of funds available are drawn from fiscal system. Accordingly, the financial mechanisms deeply affect the conduct of the regions in public health management, as well as in putting governmental objectives into practice. Here-hence, the importance for making the central State aware of what are the health needs to be satisfied and the respective costs, estimated with proper techniques, and not only based on historical expenditure, for delivering healthcare services within the different regions.

At the same time, it is necessary to deeply analyze the single "variables" that constitute the "equations" of demand and supply of care (e.g. type or volume patients, aging rate, cases of patients treated), thereby improving the allocation process of the funds, more adjusted to the health needs, and making INHS much more sustainable in view of the challenges which will must be faced in the forthcoming future. We're sure that the "actual" introduction of standard costing to support healthcare management in near future will deserve further investigations by the academic community eager to unveil both the managerial performance results, and the interactions of accounting and the context in which it operates (Hopwood, 1983; Broadbent and Guthrie, 2008).

Summary

In this chapter we tried to understand the effects triggered by the latest federalist reform in the introduction of standard costing as alternative financing model within the Italian National Healthcare System (INHS) and its impact on management and delivering healthcare, and, at the same time, whether it brings to completion the regional federalist system. We have also discussed about the opportunity of implementing a funding model multi-level and more regionally-based to take into account the marked differences among the Italian regions in terms of providing health services thanks to which ensure the essential levels of care and the sustainability of system as a whole.

References

BROADBENT J., GUTHRIE J. (2008), *Public Sector to Public Services: 20 Years of "Contextual" Accounting Research*, "Accounting, Auditing and Accountability Journal", Vol. 21, n. 2.

BRUSA L. (2009), *Analisi e contabilità dei costi*, Giuffrè, Milano.

CERUZZI P., SORANO E. (2013), *Il controllo di gestione nelle aziende sanitarie ai tempi dell'armonizzazione contabile*, Ipsoa, Milano.

CISALGHI C. (2010), *Riflessione sui criteri da utilizzare per il riparto del fabbisogno sanitario*, Age. na. s, Roma.

COURT OF AUDITORS (2013), *Rapporto 2013 sul coordinamento della finanza pubblica [Report year 2013 on coordination of public finance]*, Roma.

DE BELVIS A. G., FERRÈ F., SPECCHIA L., VALERIO L., FATTORE G., RICCIARDI W. (2012), *The Financial Crisis in Italy: Implications for the Healthcare Sector*, "Health Policy", Vol. 106, n.1.

DEL VECCHIO M. (2001), *Dirigere e governare le amministrazioni pubbliche*, Egea, Milano.

DEL VECCHIO M. (2004), *Il sistema di finanziamento delle aziende sanitarie pubbliche: un'interpretazione*, JOMMI C. (a cura di), *I sistemi di finanziamento delle aziende sanitarie pubbliche*, Egea, Milano.

DENNIS D. K. (1989), *Estimating Cost Behavior Organizations*, CLEVERLEY W. O. (ed.), *Estimating Handbook of Health Care Accounting and Finance*, Aspen Publisher, Maryland.

FALCINELLI N., GENSINI G. F., TRABUCCHI M., VANARA F. (2010), *Rapporto Sanità 2010. Federalismo e Servizio Sanitario Nazionale*, Il Mulino, Bologna.

FASS S. (1997), *Forecasting Technique Improve Hospital Budgeting*, "Hospital Cost Management and Accounting", Vol. 9, n. 3.

FINKLER S. A., WARD D.M., BAKER J. J. (2007), *Essential of Cost Accounting for Health Care Organizations*, 3rd Edition, Jones & Barlett Learning, Burlington, Massachusetts.

HOOD C. (1991), *A Public Management for All Seasons?*, "Public Administration", Vol. 69, n. 1.

HOOD C. (1995), *The "New Public Management" in the 1980s: Variations on a Theme*, "Accounting, Organizations and Society", Vol. 8, n. 2-3.

HOPWOOD A. G. (1983), *On Trying to Study accounting in the Context in which it Operates*, "Accounting, Organizations and Society", Vol. 8, n. 2-3.

HORNGREN C. T. – DATAR S. M. – RAJAN M. V. (2011), *Cost Accounting: a Managerial Emphasis*, 14th Edition, Prentice Hall, New Jersey.

IANNI L. (2008), *Profili economico-aziendali e contabili nel nuovo sistema informativo sanitario (NSIS)*, Franco Angeli, Milano.

JACOBS K. G., MARCON G., WITT D. (2004), *Cost and Performance Information for Doctors: an International Comparison*, "Management Accounting Research", Vol. 15, n. 3.

JOMMI C. (2004), *I sistemi regionali di finanziamento delle aziende sanitarie: cinque realtà regionali a confronto*, JOMMI C. (a cura di), *I sistemi di finanziamento delle aziende sanitarie pubbliche*, Egea, Milano.

KURUNMÄKI L. (2004), *A Hybrid Profession: the Acquisition of Management Accounting Expertise by Medical Professionals*, "Accounting, Organizations and Society", Vol. 29, n. 3-4.

KURUNMÄKI L., LAPSLEY I., MILLER P. (2011), *Accounting Within and Beyond the State*, "Management Accounting Research", Vol. 22, n. 1.

KURUNMÄKI L., MELIA K., LAPSLEY I. (2003), *Accounting vs. Legitimization: a Comparative Study of the Use of Accounting Information in Intensive Care*, "Management Accounting Research", Vol. 14, n. 2.

LAPSLEY I. (1998), *Research in Public Sector Accounting: an Appraisal*, "Accounting, Auditing and Accountability Journal", Vol. 21, n. 1.

LEGA F. – SARGIACOMO M. – IANNI L. (2010), *The Rise of Governmentality in the Italian National Health System: Physiology or Pathology of a Decentralized and (Ongoing) Federalist System*, "Health Service Management Research", Vol. 23, n. 4.

LLEWELLYN S. – NORTHCOTT D. (2005), *The Average Hospital*, "Accounting, Organizations and Society", Vol. 30, n. 6.

MACINATI M. S. (2010), *NPM Reforms and the Perceptions of Budget by Hospital Clinicians: Lesson from Two Case-studies*, "Financial Accountability and Management", Vol. 26, n. 4.

MAPELLI V. (2010), *Se il costo standard diventa inutile*, Lavoce. info, articolo 8 ottobre 2010.

OTLEY D. T. (1978), *Budget Use and Managerial Performance*, "Journal of Accounting Research", Vol. 16, n. 1.

PAMMOLLI F. – SALERNO N. C. (2010), *Benchmarking tra sistemi sanitari regionali: evidenze per decidere*, "Short Note", n.8, CERM.

PETTERSEN I. J. (1995), *Budgetary Control of Hospitals: Ritual, Rhetorics and Rationalized Myths*, "Financial Accountability and Management", Vol. 11, n. 3.

PIZZINI M. J. (2006), *The Relation Between Cost-system Design, Managers'Evaluations of the Relevance and Usefulness of Cost Data, and Financial Performance: an Empirical Study of US Hospital*, "Accounting, Organizations and Society", Vol. 31, n. 2.

PRESTON A. M. – CHUA W. F. – NEU D. (1997), *The Diagnosis-related Group Prospective Payment System and the Problem of Government of Rationing Health Care to the Elderly?*, "Accounting, Organizations and Society", Vol. 22, n. 2.

TEDIOSI F. – GABRIELE S. – LONGO F. (2009), *Governing Decentralization in Health Care Under Tough Budget Constraint: What Can We Learn from the Italian Experience?*, "Health Policy", Vol. 90, n. 2.

ZIMMERMAN S. (1996), *Forecasting and its Importance to Health Managers in the Ever-changing Health Care Industry*, "Hospital Cost Management and Accounting", Vol. 7, n. 12.

Using performance measurement to make italian universities more financially sustainable[1]

The changes that are affecting state universities are rather clear. The institutional and managerial profiles which characterized these secular institutions have been deeply questioned. The "old" model that considered higher education as a public good and conceived university as a social institution easily accessible to all, is declining. It has been replaced by a new one which considers universities rather as companies able to pursue efficiency, effectiveness and financial sustainability. This new "managerial" model has never been popular in Italy, where the traditional "social" one continued to prevail. The main idea we want to expose in this chapter is that Italian state university system, which is also characterized, for the most part, as being closed to competition and to international comparison, only recently has begun to change, taking the first steps in this new direction. Only with the Gelmini reform of 2010, performance management logics and tools, typical of the managerial model, has begun to scratch a closed and self-referential system like the Italian one. Considering the above mentioned aspects, the aim of this chapter is to show how Italian state university system was forced to change, to rethink itself. The chapter is structured as follows. After the introduction, section 9.2 describes the process of reform of Italian state university system. Sections 9.3, 9.4, and 9.5 discuss in depth the three main waves of reform that occurred over the last thirty years. The conclusion provides some reflections upon the characteristics of the reform process and its implications for Italian universities.

Learning objectives

After reading this chapter you should be able to:

- Understand which changes are affecting the Italian University System;

---

[1] The chapter is the result of a joint effort by the authors who share the formulation. However, the writing of the specific sections has to be divided as follows: Armando Della Porta (corresponding author) paragraphs 9.1, 9.2; Massimo Sargiacomo paragraphs 9.5, 9.6; Michela Venditti paragraphs 9.3, 9.4.

- Understand why the Italian university reforms in the last 30 years have not achieved their goals;
- Recognize the strong difficulties and resistances in improving Italian University System

9.1 Introduction

The changes and issues that are affecting state universities in recent years are rather evident (e.g., Ansell, 2008; Mazza, Quattrone, Riccaboni, 2008). The Institutional and managerial aspects that have characterized these secular institutions have been indeed deeply challenged. If, on one hand, it is reaffirmed the centrality of universities as engines of new knowledge creation, which is an essential factor for growth and development, on the other hand the methods used to produce it are harshly criticized. The "humboldtian" methods that give academic staff total power and autonomy in determining what kind of knowledge should be produced and the State the role of mere moneylender, have not worked (Tessitore 1970). The trust and the freedom to manage given to professors produced, mostly, self-referent behaviours and financial irresponsibility. They acted as Knaves, not as Knights (Le Grand, 2003). In general, we can say that the need to rethink the autonomy of state universities can be interpreted as a reflection of the waves of reforms experienced in the last two decades by the public sector (Osborne & Gaebler 1992; Meneguzzo1999; Pollit & Bouckaert, 2002; Borgonovi, Fattore, Longo 2009). This has led single states to intervene with a series of reforms in order to make universities more accountable to stakeholders (State, households, businesses, students), more competitive and, above all, more financially sustainable. These changes contributed, indirectly, to redefine the system qualitatively and quantitatively, but also making more problematic, the contents of the activities of academic staff. In addition of teaching and research activities, academic staff is now charged with several other organizational and managerial activities (Sargiacomo 2001, 2002) certainly not easy to integrate with the traditional ones. In general, we can say that the "old" model that consider higher education as a public good and that conceives, therefore, state university as a social institution easily accessible to all, is declining (Hansmann, 1999; Webster et al., 2000).

Its place is being taken by a new model which conceives state university as a "firm" able to:

- depend less on state funding by expanding and diversifying its own revenues, by increasing the ability to obtain revenues, in addition to students'fees, also from the development of new educational and research products;
- control the efficiency and effectiveness of its activities and processes adopting up-to-date management techniques;
- recruit a qualified staff with managerial and administrative skills with the dual purpose of separating governance activities from managerial ones, and of limiting, above all, academic power and scope of action;
- continually generate new knowledge that is not only abstract but also useful in solving problems;
- take on new and more flexible forms, make alliances with other parties, both national and international, (businesses, public institutions and non-profit organizations, other research institutions) according to the Triple-Helix model (Etzkowitz

& Leydesdorff, 1996, 1997, 2000), maintaining, at the same time, an identity consistent with its own mission;
- develop a third mission to contribute to the economic and social development (Klein, 2000; Laredo, 2007; Molas-Gallart et al., 2002; Rothaermel et al., 2007; Sanchez & Elena, 2006).

The idea of a state university as a market oriented firm (Slaughter, Leslie, 1997; Slaughter, Rhodes, 2004; Agasisti, Catalano, 2005; Munch, 2009), adopting value management and entrepreneurial principles:

- that pursues excellence in the research activity;
- that manages strategically intellectual property;
- that creates local and international networks;
- that develops spin-off and participates in the commercialization of the results;
- that is responsive to the student needs;
- that recognizes the labour market logics and incorporates them in its own courses of study;
- that recognizes the value of practical experiences;
- that stimulates and promotes personal initiatives;
- that set clear strategic objectives;
- that identifies alternative funding sources;
- that accurately plans its economic, financial and patrimonial growth;
- that competes successfully in the markets in which it has chosen to operate;
- that controls and manages its cost drivers;
- that secures the quality of its teaching offer;
- that, finally, develops an effective performance management system, never settled down in Italy (except in some excellent isolated cases).

On the contrary, Italy represented and, in some cases, still is, in the international scene, one of the last strenuous and stubborn defenders of the traditional model. There are currently more than 90 universities among state and private ones. We might not agree with the idea of a university capitalism (Slaughter, Rhodes, 2004), with this new market-oriented model of university, which is subject of animated criticisms (Ansell, 2008), but we cannot avoid to recognize the continued reduction of state funds (Garlatti, 1996, Genua, Sylos Labini, 2013) and the strong pressure from external stakeholders, on the quality and on the impact of university activity. These pressures pose concrete challenges that need to be addressed and cannot be ignored. Other countries accepted this challenge (e.g. Australia) (Mazza, Quattrone, Riccaboni, 2008) and changed through a trial-and-error process. The main idea we want to convey through this chapter is that Italian state university system, which is characterized, above all, as being closed to competition and to international comparison, began only recently a deep process of renewal and change, taking the first steps towards the new emerging model of university capitalism briefly described above. This happened also following the stimuli provided by New Public Management ideas (Hood, 1991, 1995), whose deriving practices have been embedded in the so called Gelmini reform of 2010. By doing so, the performance management logics, typical of this model, have begun to scratch a closed and self-referential system as the Italian one (Sargiacomo, 2002). In light of this premises, the aim of this chapter is to show how Italian state university system was forced, in the end, to begin this difficult process of reform. Indeed in the last thirty years, the path of change has been, uncertain and uneven, fluctuating between centralization and decentralization, without facing seriously the real problems that affected state universities (Geuna, Sylos Labini, 2013). It was not easy to win the strong resistance to change. Only in 2010, after a severe conflict between the social actors, the Gelmini reform, became a law. As mentioned, this reform was a first step in the direction of change. A first step that marks the transition from a model based on autonomy and trust towards a new one based on strict central Government command and control (Le Grand, 2003). The main goal of this reform is to try to remedy the errors accumulated in the previous decades that led part of the system itself on the edge of a financial collapse and to scientific and academic national and international blame.

The chapter is structured as follows. The next section describes the process of change that occurred in Italian state university system during the last thirty years (1980-2010). The whole period can be divided into three phases which together constitute a cycle. These phases will be discussed and analyzed in the next three sections. The last section of the work will present some concluding remarks upon the characteristics of the reform process and its implications for Italian universities.

9.2   The waves of reform of Italian universities

The current crisis of Italian state universities is, mainly, the consequence of how central government chose to govern their autonomy in relation to a changing environment, which, as mentioned, placed greater emphasis on outputs (efficiency and quality of university results) and less on inputs (accessibility to masses). In particular, the "big bang", the origin of the problems Italian universities are currently facing, was a lack of control over results that had disastrous effects, primarily upon their financial situation. Italy, unlike other countries, continued to defend strenuously the idea of a mass university (Catturi, Mussari, 2003), funded almost entirely by public funds and managed, in full autonomy and freedom, by academic staff, without any effective internal and external control mechanism. What did the central Government to change this view? The process of change was substantially soft, at least until 2010. And it is precisely because of this softness, that the government was forced, mainly to avoid the risk of financial distress, to intervene in 2010 with the so-called (by the name of the Ministry that enforced the law) Gelmini reform.

The financial distress of the university system did not depend so much by the small amount of resources invested in the Italian university system, but, as previously said, by the absence of strict controls on how these resources were used and managed. To understand what has caused this situation, we identified, in the last thirty years, three waves of reforms which together constitute a regulatory cycle that starts and returns to the centre after a period of decentralization and autonomy (lasted 17 years). The periodization is the following (see Figure 9.1):

- the first wave, which goes from 1980 to 1993, is mainly characterized by a centralized control of financial resources, more rigid and inflexible rather than strict and rigorous;

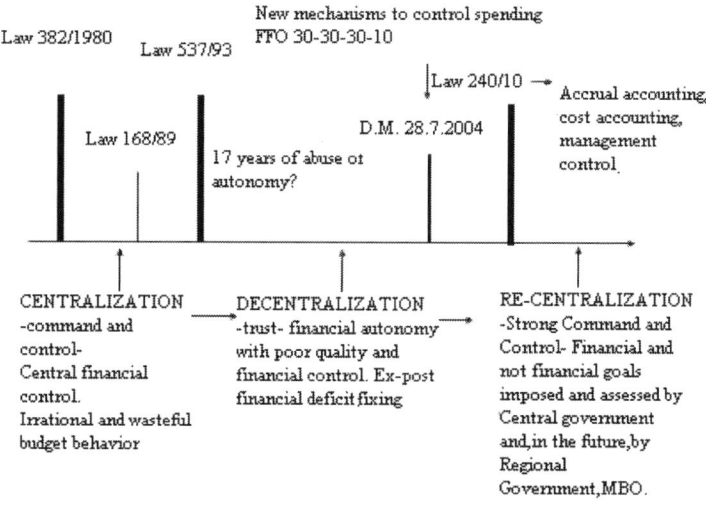

Figure 9.1 The reform process of Italian public universities from 1980.

- the second goes from 1993 to 2010 and is characterized by decentralization (financial autonomy and "accountability" without an effective control system);
- the third, that began in 2010, is characterized by the restoration of central financial control supported by a rigorous system of internal and external checks and assessments of economic, educational and research results linked with the provision of rewards and sanctions.

We chose to start from 1980 because in previous years, from a financial and accounting perspective, universities were regulated, since their nationalization, by archaic and patchy laws (Garlatti, 1996) present even in a consolidated law on higher education (Law 1592/1933) and in the Bottai's circular in 1939. From 1980 to 2010, however, a number of regulatory measures occurred with the intent of "modernizing" Italian universities in order to make them more output and results-oriented. However, these measures were not decisive. Hence Italian universities (and the Ministry) found themselves, up to 2010, as being spectators and protagonists, both positively and negatively, of a formal, loosely coupled, process of change, not by chance labeled as "new public management by law" (Borgonovi 1993), that produced a situation of financial distress for many universities. The first period we identified, 1980-1993, is characterized mainly by a top-down approach and limited financial autonomy of universities. The second period, 1993-2010, can be considered as a reaction to the problems created by the prevailing logics of the previous phase. In this phase, we witness a greater university financial autonomy that will be the cause of many problems. The third period started in 2010 with the Gelmini reform and represents the restoration of a centralized power and control system to contrast the abuse of autonomy registered previously.

The preceding analysis *prima facie* suggests that the path of change is not linear and progressive but fluctuating and, somewhat, regressive. Regrettably, the errors of the first wave of reforms are not corrected but amplified by the second wave. Hence the need to restore more effective and tight coupled control and performance measurement logics, to steer the state university system in the direction described in the opening. Let's now examine in more detail the different phases.

9.3 The centralization wave: 1980-1993: Limited financial autonomy of universities

The most important element of this phase is the limited and formal financial autonomy of universities. It is the Ministry who decides how much resources to assign to universities and how should be allocated within universities among the various functions. In 1980 university departments come up as autonomous centres of responsibility (Presidential Decree, Presidential Decree 382/80). Subsequently (Presidential Decree, DPR 371/82) it is adopted a basic financial type scheme for the budget. In that budget public funding are recorded in different chapters (about 20) tightly tied to specific spending aims.

The ministry decides the *"quantum"* (how much) and the allocation of resources to various spending areas through direct assignment to faculties and departments.

In particular:

- the 40% of costs for teaching staff, non-teaching staff, and a part of research funds, are directly assigned by the Ministry to faculties and departments;
- the 60% of financial resources are assigned, instead, to universities to cover costs for researchers, for operating expenses, for the building maintenance costs and the research funding still to be covered.

From the 80s to the early 90s, the whole system is characterized by a strong centralised system where the Ministry has almost the total control over funding allocation (Catturi, Mussari, 2003).

What problems did derive from this strong and deep centralised financial control? How did universities react? Universities were not interested in pursuing better efficiency and cost reduction because of the lack of freedom in using the saved resources (Venditti, 2012). This allocation mechanism did not encourage virtuous behaviours. As a consequence, the most important task for universities was the "negotiation" with the Ministry to obtain more funding (self-interested network behaviours in the shadow of hierarchy). What happened was that the tightness of the centralised financial control caused an opportunistic behaviour that forced universities to spend all the resources that they would otherwise lose.

It is probably for these reasons that, in the late 80s, the Ministry took a first step towards universities financial autonomy with a measure (Law 68/89), which allowed them to adopt their own regulations for administration, financing and accounting systems. At the conclusion of this first wave, uniform criteria were established for the preparation of homogeneous accounting rules in order to allow the Ministry to control the final expenditure and the fiscal consolidation of public university sector spending.

This reform is, essentially, characterized by a top-down approach of command and control (Le Grand, 2003) and by a rigid financial control. It is, however, more

tied to the form than to the substance of the problems and is absolutely discon-
nected from any form of output or outcome control. The choice of a strong input
control, adopted to cope with the rising costs of the mass university model, failed
both to reduce costs and to reduce the opportunistic behaviour of spending all that
was available in the specific budget chapter, although not necessary. The final result
was to further increase the financial dependence of universities from the central
government.

The following table shows the increase of dependence of universities on public resources over time. In 1990, public funds accounted for the 88,8% compared to 62,2%
in 1957 (Table 9.1). On the expenditure side, in 1990, 68,49% of the total amount was
intended to cover personnel costs (Catturi, Mussari, 2003).

9.4 The decentralization wave: 1993-2010: Financial Autonomy and Formal Accountability

The second wave of reform (1993-2010) can be interpreted as a reaction to the rigid
central formal control which, as seen, limited universities freedom to use financial
resources. In this phase the most important thing is that Law 537/93 allows a budgetary system formulated independently by each university. The idea is to provide
greater organizational and financial autonomy to universities in order to make them
more financial responsible and accountable; to let them the necessary freedom to develop their own distinctive strategy to cope with the external changing environment.
While the previous reform used command and control style as a central spending
control mechanism, the latter reform relies, perhaps too much, on trust mechanisms.
It is thought that a responsible and competent academic staff will use financial autonomy to improve the quality of economic, teaching, and research performances.
Therefore, at the beginning of the 90s, Italian universities become, by law, autonomous
institutions, quasi-firms. With the Law 537/1993 the Ministry introduce a more balanced system than the previous one, completely focused on a rigid input-oriented
central control. This reform, in fact, balance the autonomy of the universities in the
use of resources transferred from the Ministry with a system of internal control and
external reporting to the Government (Geuna, Sylos Labini, 2013) with the goal to
make Italian universities more efficient and more results-oriented. Public funding is,

Table 9.1 Composition of state universities resources (1957/1990)

Resources	1957 (L/000.000)	%	1990 (L/000.000)	%
Public resources	2.4522,8	62,22	8.853,303	88,8
Private resources	1.4887,7	37,78	1.116,547	11,2
Total resources	3.9410,5	100	9.969,850	100
% self-financing	38,91%		14,29%	

Source: our elaboration from Catturi, Mussari, 2003.

therefore, transferred without any constraint about allocation in order to empower the universities about their results.

The resources allocated to universities are divided only into three main macro classes that each university can use with full autonomy within each macro-class:

a. fund for the ordinary financing of universities (FFO). The FFO finances universities operating costs and institutional activities. In this fund are included expenses for teaching staff, researchers and non-teaching staff, costs for facilities routine maintenance. In the fund there are also included expenses for scientific research excluding amounts earmarked for research projects of national interest. The strongly innovative aspect, that goes in the direction of making universities more efficient and results-oriented, is that the FFO is formed by two parts: a basic part and a rebalancing one. The first is allocated to universities using historical spending criteria. The second part of the fund is distributed using more meritocratic criteria defined by the Ministry (standards costs of production per student, and quality goals achieved taking into account contextual and structural conditions of each university). The purpose is clear: to eliminate gradually the historical spending criterion and to replace it with a more results-oriented criterion, i.e. on standard costs. The goal is to introduce a new funding regime that should reward more virtuous behaviours (Geuna, Sylos Labini, 2013);

b. fund for university building and scientific equipment investments. This fund is allocated according to equity criteria (rebalancing the national housing availability) and meritocratic ones (financing those research projects of relevant national interest);

c. fund for specific initiatives, activities and projects, such as the financing of new educational initiatives.

Subsequently, the entire FFO is fully allocated using only results-oriented criteria. With the Ministry Decree 28/7/2004 the allocation of the FFO is based on the following criteria:

- 30% of FFO is related to the ability of attracting students, measured by the number of recruited students;
- 30% of FFO is related to the results of training processes, measured through credits earned each year;
- 30% of FFO is related to the quality of scientific research;
- 10% of FFO is related to specific purposes (teaching staff mobility, support to disability).

These new output-oriented resource allocation criteria were further reinforced by Law 1/2009. The central idea was to replace historical spending criteria without any link to results with a virtuous circle based on autonomy, results and results-based financing. From an accounting point of view universities were free to structure their budgets in a format like the budget type scheme of 1982 or even draw up integrated systems of financial and economic capital accounting. The majority of Italian universities continued to prepare annual financial budget statements structured on the base of the type schema of 1982. Accrual accounting has been adopted primarily by private universities. In some cases they have not even been respected the requirement of homogeneous preparation of final accounts.

Which were the consequences of this reform?

Unfortunately, the majority of Italian universities, have not used the autonomy to design and implement repositioning strategies to strengthen their reputation and competitiveness, or to reorganize themselves by eliminating inefficiency and waste (Boyne, 2004). On the contrary, they worsened both these aspects. An example in this sense can be seen in the way in which control was circumvented.

Control over the use of resources was assigned mainly to Internal Evaluation Units (i.e., Nuclei di Valutazione), composed for the most part, not by independent experts, but by academic staff internal to universities themselves. Their task was to secure the proper use of public resources, to monitor the productivity of teaching and research activities and to verify the impartiality and efficiency of administrative action. To achieve these goals, these evaluation units had to carry out comparative analysis of the costs and returns and forward them to the Ministry for further inspection and corrective actions. Nevertheless monitoring and reporting activities carried out by evaluation units were mostly formal. Relatedly, due to the internal academic pressures, often they did not reveal the real problems, weakening the effectiveness of the control system itself and thwarting the necessary corrective actions. And it is precisely because of this lack of control, caused by an obvious conflict of interest (the absence of impartiality and independence of the members of the evaluation units) that this phase has been illustrated by many commentators as the most disastrous for the entire Italian university system. Indeed, the evaluation units were the weakest link of the control chain designed by Law 537/93.

This lack of control is evident when we consider (Figure 9.2), the increase of public resource transferred by central government. In absolute terms public transfers increased from around 7,1 billion euro in 2001 to around 8,3 billion euro in 2009. The revenue from students'by law, cannot exceed 20% of the FFO and so they cannot contribute to rebalance the increased deficit. This is a rule that reflects the social value of public higher education in Italy and that perpetuates the idea of a mass university.

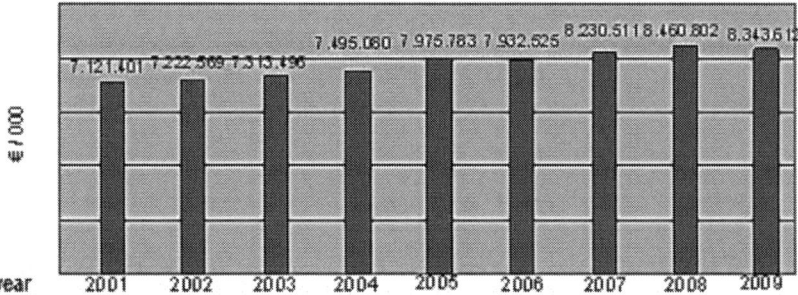

Figure 9.2 FFO and MIUR resources from 2001 to 2009. Source: our elaboration from MIUR data.

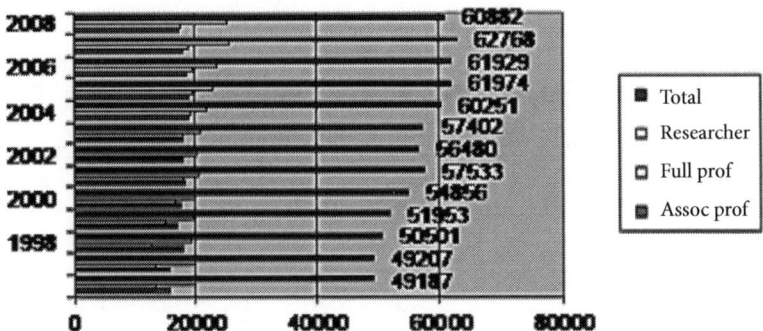

Figure 9.3 Academic staff of Italian universities 1997-2009. Source: our elaboration from MIUR data.

How did universities use these resources? They used the resources, for the most part, to promote the exponential growth of the academic population (Figure 9.3). As already underlined in the 18th century by A. Smith (1776) "if the authority to which a teacher is subject resides in the body corporate, the college, or university, of which he himself is a member, and which the greater part of the other members are, like himself, persons who either are or ought to be teachers, they are likely to make a common cause, to be all very indulgent to one another, and every man to consent that his neighbour may neglect his duty, provided he himself is allowed to neglect his own". In this sense, also if at the beginning of the 21st century, Italian universities seemed to not have learnt the lesson considering that most of the available resources were spent primarily for the recruitment of academic staff and not for the improvement of technical facilities. In summary, there has been, for the most part, an over-investment in human capital and a consequent weakening of the technical capital needed to improve teaching and research activities. The academic population grew by about 26% in the period 1997-2009, while in the same period, the student population grew by about 9% (our elaboration of MIUR data).

In particular, some commentators highlighted that there has been an abuse by universities and their academic leaders in the use of public resources for personal or "school" aims, as well as in choosing professors and researchers irrespective of the quality of their CVs (e.g., Pierotti, 2008; Rizzo, Stella, 2008; Stella, 2008). The result of this behaviour was an unbalanced composition of academic staff which was inadequate to cope with external challenges. Too many professors (full and associate) compared to the number of researchers pointed outside that an easy and fast career progression was one of the main goals of the moment and that teaching activities were more important than the research ones. As further proof of such behaviour, it is in this period that the number of undergraduate courses increased exponentially. This growth represented a mere cosmetic and marketing strategy to recruit students and to foster career progression. Italian universities looked like inverted pyramids, with a number of professors (full and associates) higher than that of the researchers. This occurred because public resources, as just said, were used more for the academic staff career progression rather than for recruiting new researchers. In addition, the real career progression costs were not signalled by internal evaluation units with the consequence to make even more inefficient and less competitive the whole Italian state university system (MEF 2007).

The predictable growth of the academic population did not, however, escape the attention of the Ministry, which, since 1998, began to pose constraints. In particular, it imposed that the relationship between fixed costs for the staff, and the total FFO could not exceed the maximum threshold of 90%. This limit did not work sufficiently. Many universities irresponsibly exceeded it, being in serious difficulties and at risk of financial distress. Also in this case we detect a lack of rigorous controls in the application of what was previously defined. The severity of the consequences of this lack of control is evident in the following (Figure 9.4) which shows how the 90% rule has been circumvented and overcame. As we can see, the entire Italian university system, in this period, walks dangerously on a clear path of financial unsustainability. It is impossible, indeed, that staff expenses arrive in 2009 to represent even 115% of the total amount of FFO. Our calculations include all staff (including fellows and others who carry out teaching and research activities) and not only researchers, associate and full professors. In our opinion, this is the overall picture of the financial condition of Italian universities. Official statistics take into account only the restricted composition of the academic staff, instead we look at a broader composition on the basis of data provided by the Ministry. It is not by chance that in the following year, the 2010, the Government would launch a new reform, the so-called Gelmini reform.

It should be said that there are different situations within the Italian university system, which clearly shows a multi-tier situation. In a broad sense we can identify at least two clusters (Venditti, 20012). In particular, at the end of 2007, compared to universities that are in serious danger of financial distress, we have a cluster of about a third of universities that are part of an association (AQUIS) for the quality of Italian state universities. To take part of it at least two indicators, among the following, must be achieved:

- fixed costs for staff/FFO <90%;
- international reputation witnessed by the presence in at least one international ranking list;
- size of at least 15.000 students (http://www.aquis-universitas.it/).

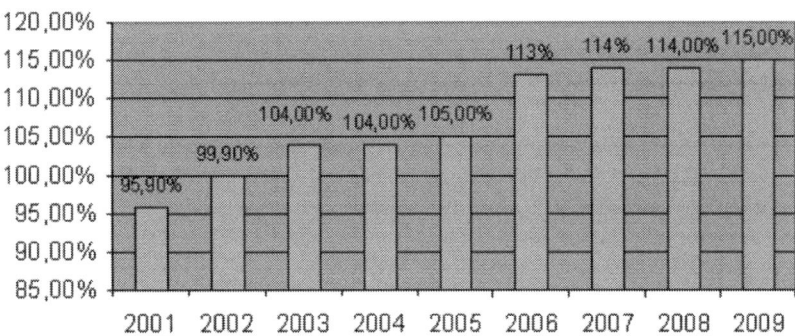

Figure 9.4   On the road to financial distress: Ratio between 'whole' staff costs and FFO in percentage from 2001 to 2009. Source: our elaboration from MIUR data.

How did the Ministry react to such abuses? At least until 2004, the Ministry has been "the great absent" in the sense that it financed the system without exercising any serious form of control. The idea that the cure of Italian universities evils was in the combination of autonomy and responsibility was not wrong. The error was, as usual, in the reform implementation and consisted, as previously mentioned, in a control deficit. We cannot grant autonomy without designing, at the same time, a serious control system over the quality of spending, recruitment, research, etc. Furthermore, in light of what has happened, it was not sufficiently taken into account the fact that Italian university system is not homogenous, but that has very different dimensional and territorial performance gaps which would require different courses of action. A general intervention as the one provided by Law 537/93 could not fit all universities. The worst ones, as expected, abused the given autonomy in the described ways (overstaffing) while the responsible ones used it to enhance their reputation and their competitiveness.

9.5   The recentralization wave: 2010 today: The "Loss" of Italian University financial autonomy and the Restoration of the Government Central Control

The third phase has begun in 2010 with Law 240/2010 – the Gelmini reform –and can be defined as a true restoration of central control and power (strong command and control system) through a MBO type, performance management system. Gelmini Reform represents a normative discontinuity, a break with the past, that has the main objective of restoring a financially sustainable university system as an essential condition for it to continue to exist. The new philosophy is evident in the following statements:

"We must, first of all, well spend the available resources and we must work together to promote a virtuous collaboration between the Ministry and the universities, based on a clear distinction of tasks: the first must credit, evaluate, promote, and above all ensure compliance with quality standards, the seconds must ensure to the national and international community, high quality education, high-level research, according to agreed economic and quality parameters" (Government's Guidelines for universities, 2010)

It is a real change of course. Tasks are clarified for the first time. The Ministry impose and check overall goals, universities must execute by adapting their activities to the qualitative and economic parameters imposed "de facto" by the Ministry. These parameters are not negotiable.

In light of this new framework has emerged that 36 of 66 state universities are at risk of financial default. Relatedly, 12 have a ratio between costs for permanent staff and FFO exceeding the maximum past limit of 90% i.e. the threshold established by law (Pacelli, 2011).

Responsibility, reduction of public funding, financial sustainability, greater accountability and merit, are the pillars of this new reform. The goals of the Gelmini reform, in reality, are not so challenging because the Italian university system, in the light of the disasters of the previous two decades, is not able to bear too ambitious aims and must begin his new course facing "basic" financial issues (back to basics). The Italian university system governance, as seen, fluctuated between centralization and decentralization without finding a satisfactory balance, but rather worsening its already fragile financial condition. In order to achieve this objective it needs to be structurally reformed. The 2010 reform recognizes this state and provides guidelines for the reconstruction. The focus of the reform is represented, indeed, by the prevision of a strict and rigorous, economic and financial control system. The new reform law, indeed, removes autonomy and powers from single universities, caging them in a "not easy to stay in" system of rules in order to promote greater attention to financial issues.

Gelmini reform, certainly imperfect, but necessary, in its vertical dimension, defines a system of accounting and financial statements of the universities, where together with the financial accounting, it introduces the accrual accounting, the cost accounting, the standard cost per student unit of training, and the consolidated financial statements. Universities that do not perform the essential functions or are not able to cope with the debts towards third parties risk the financial default. Financial default is, however, not immediate. Before the definitive closure of the university, the reform gives a last chance with the introduction of a system of "controlled administration of the universities" that have difficulty or are not able to manage according the new rules.

In its horizontal dimension, the reform foresees, on the contrary, for universities, the possibility to merger or to federate themselves, also with the aim to improve management quality, efficiency and effectiveness.

Gelmini reform actually implements what was the spirit of the 1993 reform i.e. to drive resources to those universities that do better in teaching and research, but with a new governance style, no longer based on autonomy and trust. This new style relies fully on the Command and Control model (Le Grand, 2003), with little tolerance for deviations from targets. This model brings together several tools. Firstly, it enhances the internal control through an evaluation unit composed, this time, by independent members that report to a new Board of Directors that identifies scope for improvement. Secondly, the reform pays particular attention to the external reporting, forcing the diffusion of information through internet. Public reporting of information will cause students and other stakeholders to switch from university with poor results to those with better performance. Thirdly a reputation-oriented information system that ranks universities in a way that the public can understand (see the recent Anvur VQR evaluation exercise http://www.anvur.org/index.php?lang=it). This new system, a sort of blame game (Hood, 2012), seems a powerful one and generates, apart from anxiety and stress, incentives for poorly performing universities to remedy the damage to their reputation. More penetrating internal controls, the use of external reporting and ranking constitute a powerful mix, at least in theory, to facilitate the transformation of the Italian universities system from an input to a result-oriented one.

Gelmini reform, as mentioned, is a complex mosaic of actions that are still in the implementation phase: Pres. Decree 76/2010, Legislative Decree 199/2011, Decree 1819/2012; Decree Law 2012/49; ANVUR Doc. Jan. 2013; Min. Decree 47/2013.

The implementing regulations concerned, so far:

- the arranging and functioning of the National Agency for the Evaluation of University and Research – ANVUR (Presidential Decree 76/2010);
- the definition of the rules for the controlled administration of universities that have distressed budgets when the economic situation and financial position of the university reaches a level of severity that it cannot ensure the sustainability and the performance of its essential functions and when a university cannot cope with debts towards third parties (Legislative Decree 199/2011, Article 2);
- the introduction of a reward system in the distribution of public resources on the basis of criteria defined *ex ante* through an initial and recurrent system of accreditation of university courses and offices. It is introduced a system of evaluation and assurance of quality efficiency and effectiveness of both teaching and research. It enhances the self-assessment system of both the quality and the effectiveness of teaching and research activities of the universities (Legislative Decree 2012/19);
- the introduction of a balance-sheet and profit and loss analytic accounts to ensure transparency and homogeneity of accounting systems and procedures in order to allow the recognition of the budgetary situation and the evaluation of the overall management. It obliges universities to prepare a single financial statement and consolidated financial statements. The planning and budget system is thus formed by: 1) single annual budget of the university for spending authorization, consisting, for each university, of an integrated economic and investment budget; 2) single three-year planning budget, consisting of an economic budget and an investment budget, in order to ensure the sustainability of all activities in the medium term; 3) single operating budget for each university, drawn up with reference to the calendar year, consisting of balance sheet, income statement, cash flow financial notes and accompanied by a report on the management activities; 4) the consolidated financial statements with their own businesses, companies or other controlled entities, with or without equity securities, regardless of their legal form, consisting of the balance sheet, income statement and notes. To allow, then, the consolidation and monitoring of public administrations accounts, universities prepare the comprehensive financial accounting budget and statement. (Legislative Decree 2012/18). Notably, the above mentioned accounting and reporting tools and practices have already been implemented in Anglophone countries (e.g. Edwards, Ezzamel, Robson, 2005; Ezzamel, Robson, Stapleton, 2012), and are part of the previously mentioned comprehensive accounting and accountability transformation, which is challenging the broad Italian Higher Education System (Bracci, 2009);
- the introduction of new limits to the expenses for debts (Dl 49/2012).

One of the first concrete actions of the Ministry was a reduction of public resources to universities, in particular through the reduction of FFO (see Figure 9.5) and the strengthening of external actors powers (Ministry of Education joined by CUN; CRUI; ANVUR, Internal Evaluation Units). These actors are charged with the primary responsibility to overseeing and evaluating the complex process of reorganization and repositioning of Italian university system. More precisely, the FFO has registered a decrease of 4.9% in 2013 compared to 2012 and a decrease of 20% compared to 2009. This means that in 2013 some universities will not be able to autonomously cover

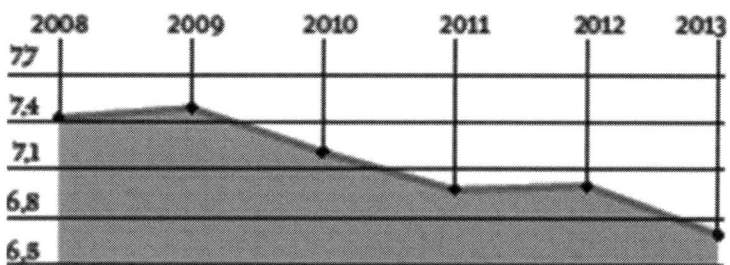

Figure 9.5   FFO amount from 2008 to 2013 (in billions euro). Surce: revised by the authors from "Il Sole 24ore", 2012.

staff expenses. It has already started the "final count-down" in that universities that are next to default and that could be forced to close in the subsequent years. The Conference of Italian University Rectors (CRUI) in the assembly of the 23rd of May 2013 (CRUI 2013) has noted that the heavy generalized cuts planned on FFO take half of Italian universities in a default situation according to the new limit of 82% (staff plus debts) foreseen by the Law Decree 49/2012 with the consequence of blocking the academic recruitment turnover and weakening the competitive position of virtuous universities. These statements, in our opinion, underline the full meaning of this reform that, as fully described, has its "centre of gravity" in fiscal consolidation and in top-down imposed improvement strategy.

9.6   Conclusions

It is not easy to reform a system as complex as that of university. Even more difficult is to reform a state university system like the Italian one which by tradition, or convenience, decided to defend the social function of higher education, avoiding confrontation with the market or, more generally, refusing to adopt more output and results-oriented logics. From a general point of view change is inevitable and does not necessarily represents a threat rather than an opportunity. Contextual changes, stakeholders'pressures towards a higher quality of university products, the reduced availability of public financial resources naturally push the central Government to change the regulatory regimes searching for new ones more attuned with user needs. History teaches us, in general, that any resistance to change that tries to keep intact the "*status quo*" is doomed to fail. The Italian case confirms this. The stubbornness to defend the mass university model has led to swing the pendulum of reforms between centralization and decentralization without, however, being able to achieve the objectives which had been set in the various reforms, bringing, indeed, the entire state universities system on the edge of a financial collapse. For about thirty years the change was resisted at least until 2010 when more rigorous central control logics were restored.

These centralist approaches (command and control), however, are not the same of 1980 ones. It has not been a mere back to the past. The 1980 reform foresaw a central control of resources to be allocated to universities but, in reality, it was only a rigid spending control system, not a rigorous results-oriented one. The 2010 reform starts again with a central government control but with more stringent logics and also with penalties. The new sanction is the failure of those universities that do not rigorously comply with targets, standards and indicators imposed by the central government. It has been thus closed a circle, but the arrival point has not been the same as the starting point. In both cases, however, it has been recognized the fundamental role played by central government but with the awareness, now, that without a "virtuous collaboration between universities and Ministry" there will be no any way out, as in the past. Central Government, indeed, will no longer be willing to cover inefficiencies and errors of single universities and the latter, in order to continue to exist, will have to undertake truly virtuous paths attentive to economic and financial issues. What does it mean, in conclusion, for Italian state universities to undertake such a virtuous paths? In our opinion this basically means:

a. formulate more realistic goals to pursue. The idea of continuing to propose a model of mass higher education must be carefully considered in light of the financial sustainability of the same. Without careful planning and continuous searching for alternative sources of funding, accompanied by focused cost reduction activities, it will be difficult to continue to survive. Indeed it will not be, anymore, possible to increase unnecessary and "useless" degree courses having a little impact on the labour market which have ended up only in a multiplication of the number of academic staff;

b. pursue these objectives with professional managers with proven competence. The model based on trust in the academic staff as people with good governance and management skills produced only disasters;

c. overcome localism and provincialism that mostly characterize Italian state universities system by activating networks and aggregations both nationally and internationally;

d. implement seriously, not just formally, a disciplinary control system that includes rewards and sanctions. As we have seen, it was the lack of control and the absence of sanctions that brought Italian state universities system on the edge of financial collapse. The Internal Evaluation Units did not work as they were supposed to. The problem is how to carefully dose control activities avoiding the opposite risk, i.e. that evaluation units are working "too well". An excess of tight controls might weaken a system already debilitated. It may be a good solution, in first phase, to restore financial autonomy, but in the long run it can cause even more dangerous side effects. After a "chemotherapy" style, the control system should reorient itself towards expansion and growth issues;

e. discuss and recognize the nature of its own mission. Not all universities can excel in research. There should be a clear differentiation in the assessment and incentive for research-oriented or teaching-oriented universities. Accordingly, the national professors salary should become only a base to which an incentive scale should be attached, and linked with clear research-teaching performance criteria;

f. do not discredit the system of actors responsible for monitoring and evaluating state universities system. Any attempt to devalue their work by always questioning their results, will be harmful in the long run. It is necessary to build an atmosphere of trust around assessment and evaluation tools, whilst the past Italian experience has rather demonstrated the opposite.

In closing, we can say that Italian university system in recent years enjoyed a path of conquest and subsequent loss of financial autonomy caused by the prior irresponsible freedom shown by some public universities, and their respective academic staff. In such scenario the dramatic public funding reduction triggered by the economic crisis – as well as by the concurrent effort to meet the euro thresholds at December 31, 2013 – has also accelerated the change stage towards more sophisticated government performance measurement systems in order to obtain a more financially sustainable university system. We think it will take many years, and especially huge efforts to proceed further towards a truly virtuous path, and it is not sure that all Italian universities will survive to near future challenges and issues.

Summary

The changes that are affecting state universities are rather clear. The "old" model that considered the higher education as a public good is declining, being replaced by a new one which is more focused on the efficiency, effectiveness and financial sustainability issues. Italy represented and, in some cases, still is, one of the last strenuous defender of the traditional model.

The main idea we wanted to convey through this chapter was that Italian state university system started only recently a deep process of change in this new direction. We identified three waves of reforms, in the last thirty years, which together constitute a regulatory cycle that starts and returns to the centre after a period of decentralization and autonomy (lasted 17 years) that created many problems.

Our analysis brought us to the conclusion that it is not easy to reform a system as complex as that of universities. Even more difficult is to reform a state universities system like the Italian one which by tradition, or convenience, decided to defend the social function of higher education refusing to adopt more results-oriented logics. We described as, in the last thirty years, the path of change has been, uncertain and uneven, fluctuating between centralization and decentralization, without facing seriously the real problems that affected Italian state universities. Only in 2010, with Gelmini reform, Italian university system has begun to experiment more rigorously a change in the direction of a more output and outcome oriented system. The new sanction will be the failure of those universities that will not be able to comply with the new rules imposed by central government.

Within these thirty years of reforms it has been thus closed a circle, but the arrival point has not been the same as the starting point. Central Government, indeed, will no longer be willing to cover inefficiencies and errors of single universities and the latter, in order to continue to exist, will have to undertake truly virtuous paths attentive to economic and financial balances.

References

AGASISTI T., CATALANO G. (2005) *I quasi-mercati nell'istruzione universitaria Un modello interpretativo per un confronto europeo*, Hermes ricerche http://www.hermesricerche.it/ita/semconv/Agasisti-Catalano.pdf.

ANSELL B. W. (2008), "University Challenges: Explaining Institutional Change in Higher Education", *World Politics*, 60 (2): 189-230.

BOYNE, G. A. (2004), "A 3Rs Strategy for Public Service Turnaround: Retrenchment, Repositioning and Reorganization", *Public Money and Management*, 24 (2): 97-103.

BORGONOVI E., FATTORE G., LONGO F. (2009) *Management delle istituzioni pubbliche*, Egea Milano.

BORGONOVI E. (1993) "Non cercare nelle leggi ciò che in esse non si trova", *Mecosan*, 6: 2-6.

BRACCI E, (2009), "Autonomy, Responsibility and Accountability in the Italian School System", *Critical Perspectives on Accounting*, 20 (3): 293-312.

CATTURI G., MUSSARI R. (2003) "Il finanziamento del sistema pubblico universitario dal dopoguerra all'autonomia", *Annali di storia delle università italiane*, VII.

CRUI (2013), Documento CRUI per il novo Governo – Assemblea del 23 maggio 2013 http://www.crui.it/(accessed 19/08/2013).

EDWARDS P, EZZAMEL, M, ROBSON, K (2005), "Budgetary Reforms: Survival Strategies and the Structuration of Organizational Fields in Education", *Accounting, Auditing and Accountability Journal*, 18 (6): 733-755.

EZZAMEL M, EDWARDS P, STAPLETON, P. (2012), "The Logics of Budgeting: Theorization and Practice Variation in the Education Field", *Accounting, Organizations and Society*, 37 (5): 281-303.

ETZKOWITZ H., LEYDESDORFF L., (2000) "The Dynamics of Innovation: From National Systems and "Mode 2" to a Triple Helix of University-Industry-Government Relations", *Research Policy*, 29 (2): 109-123.

ETZKOWITZ H., LEYDESDORFF L., (1997) *Universities and the Global Knowledge Economy: A Triple Helix of University-Industry-Government Relations*, Cassell, London.

ETZKOWITZ H., LEYDESDORFF L., (1996) "Emergence of a Triple Helix of University-Industry-Government Relations", *Science and Public Policy*, 23: 279-86.

GARLATTI A. (1996), *Bilancio e controllo economico nelle università degli studi*, Milano, Egea.

GEUNA A., SYLOS LABINI M. (2013) "Il finanziamento pubblico delle università italiane: venti anni di riforme incompiute" *Working Paper Series Department of Economics and Statistics "Cognetti de Martiis"*, 19/13.

GIARDA P. (2004) *Il finanziamento dell'università italiana*, relazione presentata al 2° convegno CODAU:. Quindici anni di riforme nell'Università italiana. Quali prospettive?, Università Cattolica di Milano, 30.09.2004.

HANSMANN H., (1999) "Proprietà e Concorrenza nell'Istruzione Universitaria" (A Ownership and Competition in Higher Education), *Mercato Concorrenza Regole*, (1 – 1999): 475-96.

HOOD C. (1991) "A Public Management for All Seasons", *Public Administration*, 6: 3-19.

HOOD C. (1995) "The New Public Management in the 1980s: Variations on a Theme", *Accounting, Organization and Society*,20: 93-109.

HOOD C. (2011), *The Blame Game*, Princeton University Press, Princeton.

KLEIN, J. (2002) 'More to Third Mission Than Counting Pounds', *Times Higher Education*, 9, August <http://www.timeshighereducation.co.uk/accessed 28 June 2013.

LAREDO, P. (2007) 'Revisiting the Third Mission of Universities: Toward a Renewed Categorization of University Activities?'*Higher Education Policy*, 20: 441–56.

LE GRAND J. (2003), *Motivations, Agency, and Public Policy. Of Knights & Knaves, Pawns & Queens*, Oxford University Press, Oxford.

MAZZA C., QUATTRONE P., RICCABONI A (2008) (Eds). *European Universities in Transition: Issues, Models and Cases*, Edward Elgar, Cheltenham, UK.

MEF – MINISTERO DELL'ECONOMIA E DELLE FINANZE (2007) Commissione Tecnica per la Finanza Pubblica Misure per il risanamento finanziario e l'incentivazione dell'efficacia e dell'efficienza del sistema universitario, Doc. 2007/3 BIS Roma, 31

MENEGUZZO M. (1999) "Dal New Public Management alla Public Governance: il pendolo della ricerca sulla amministrazione pubblica", Meneguzzo M. (edited by), *Managerialità Innovazione e Governance la PA verso il 2000*, Aracne, Roma.

MOLAS-GALLART, J., SALTER, A., PATEL, P., SCOTT, A. AND DURAN, X. (2002), "Measuring Third Stream Activities". Final Report to the Russell Group of Universities. Brighton, UK: SPRU, University of Sussex.

MÜNCH, R. (2009), *Globale Eliten, lokale Autoritäten. Bildung und Wissenschaft unter dem Regime von PISA*, McKinsey & Co., Frankfurt a. M.

OSBORNE P., GAEBLER T. (1992) Reinventing Government. How the Entrepreneurial Spirit is Transforming the Public Sector, Reading, Mass: Addison-Wesley.

PACELLI B. (2011), "Sul lastrico 36 università", *Italia Oggi*, 16.02.2011.

POLLIT C., BOUCKAERT G. (2002), *La riforma del management pubblico*, Università Bocconi Editore, Milano.

RIZZO, S., STELLA, G. A. (2008), *La Deriva. Perché l'Italia rischia il naufragio*, Milano, Rizzoli.

ROTHAERMEL, F. T., AGUNG, S. D., JIANG, L. (2007), "University Entrepreneurship: A Taxonomy of the Literature", *Industrial and Corporate Change*, 16: 691–791.

SANCHEZ, M. P., ELENA, S. (2006), "Intellectual Capital in Universities: Improving Transparency and Internal Management", *Journal of Intellectual Capital*, 7: 529–48.

SARGIACOMO M. (2001), *Comportamento manageriale dei presidi delle Facoltà di economia e scienze statistiche*, Libreria Campus, Pescara.

SARGIACOMO M. (2002), "Budgeting Behaviours negli Atenei pubblici italiani", *Azienda Pubblica*, 15 (4-5): 371-397.

SLAUGHTER, S., LESLIE, L. L. (1997) *Academic Capitalism*, London, The John Hopkins University Press.

SLAUGTHER, S., RHOADES, G. (2004), *Academic Capitalism and the New Economy*, London, The John Hopkins University Press.

SMITH, A. (1776), *An Inquiry into the Nature and Causes of the Wealth of Nations*, Book V Part III Art.2.

STELLA, G. A. (2008), "La prof che non pubblicò una riga", *Corriere della Sera*, 30 Settembre.

TESSITORE F. (1970) "Il modello Humboltiano di università", Tessitore F. (edited by) Università e umanità/W. von Humboldt, Guida Napoli.

VENDITTI M., (2012) "La crisi dell'Università italiana e l'evoluzione delle funzioni degli atenei: il contributo della Tripla Elica", Sargiacomo M. (edited by) *Banche, imprese università: out of the crisis*, Giappichelli, Milano.

WEBSTER A., GEBHARDT C., TERRA, B.R.C. (2000), "The future of the university and the university of the future: Evolution of ivory tower to entrepreneurial paradigm", *Research Policy*, 29: 313–30.

http://www.aquis-universitas.it/

http://hubmiur.pubblica.istruzione.it/Linee_Guida_del_Governo_per_Universita.pdf

http://www.anvur.org/index.php?lang=it

10

Human Resource Performance Management in Italian Universities[1]

This chapter explores the dual role of Human Resource Performance Management, namely diagnostic and interactive, and its relationships with the individual well being via the mediation role of social capital. To this end we present PLS regression analysis of survey data collected from a sample of 424 academics and administrative employees in 77 Italian Universities. Empirical results show how different uses of HRPM are differently related with social capital, sense of community and individual well-being. Also, the mediation role of social capital described in our theoretical model is fully supported in the sample.

Learning objectives

After reading this chapter you should be able to:

- why Human Resource Management has become a central feature of much Contemporary Performance Management Research in universities worldwide.
- how Human Resource Management Performance in Italian Universities is providing new insights about practices and policy-making in Italian Higher Education.
- the dual role of Human Resource Performance Management, namely Diagnostic and Interactive in Italian Universities.
- the relationships between Human Resource Performance Management and the Individual Well Being via the mediation role of Social Capital in Italian Universities.

10.1   Introduction

With the advent of the New Public Management (Hood 1991), many Universities have attempted, either voluntary or under pressure, to adopt new management sys-

---

[1] Although this article is the result of joint research, Sections 1, 2, 3 and 5 can be attributed to Lorenzo Lucianetti (corresponding author) while the remaining Sections to Monica Franco.

tems originally designed to meet the needs of business or private sector organizations (Smeenk et al. 2009). Themes like budget transparency, output measurement, increased competition, and use of private sector management techniques have become common in many Universities around the world (Aucoin, 1990; Pollitt, 1993).

These organizations, characterized by wide collegiality, academic freedom and autonomy, are now facing severe tasks in line with the concept of *managerialism* and the new societal demands for public accountability and competitiveness (Salter and Tapper, 2002; Townley, 1997). As a result of this process, new tensions are emerging, some of which are generating unintended consequences in staff's behavior and outcomes (e.g., Bryson, 2004; Deem, 1998; Prichard and Willmott, 1997).

Economic and political pressures have led many Universities to adopt managerial tools for identifying, measuring and enhancing individual and team performance (Brennan and Shah, 2000; Middlehurst, 2004; Ferlie et al., 2008; Decramer, Smolders, Vanderstraeten and Christiaens 2012); and to align it to the strategic goals of the organization (Aguinis and Pierce 2008, p. 139). Most of these tools are included in what many researchers refer to as Human Resource Management Performance (den Hartog, Boselie and Paauwe 2004, Delery and Doty 1996; Ichniowski, Kochan, Levine, Olson and Strauss, 1996) that have led to the introduction of new management practices and new performance measurement systems (Townley, 1997; Lapsley and Miller, 2004).

The financial crises has clearly had a substantial influence on recent developments in the universities pushing them towards a "managerialistic model" that emphasises accountability, efficiency, cost-effectiveness, marketization and quality assessment in academic work (ter Bogt & Scapens, 2012). Also, the rise of managerialism has increased the role of professional managers while the traditional managerial role of academics has decreased (Salter and Tapper, 2002; Deem, 1998, 2004).

The recent economic and political crises in Italy have generated a turbulent climate in the Higher Education sector. Italian Universities are now facing dramatic financial pressures from Central Government due to overall budget restrictions. In 2009 the cumulative expenditure per student was around $ 43,218 about 37 percent less than the OECD average and 50 percent less compare to the rest of European Countries (see the OECD report Education at a Glance 2010). Furthermore, in a sample of OECD Countries, Italy occupies one of the last positions regarding the expenditure on educational institutions for core services, R&D and ancillary services as a percentage of GDP, at the tertiary level of education (source: OECD report Education at a Glance 2013, p.182). Even more indicative is the data which highlights the impact of the economic crisis on public expenditure on education: Italy is one of the Countries that have cut more investments in Education system (source: OECD report Education at a Glance 2013, p.187).

In Italy, the government funding of universities has become increasingly contingent on their performance in research and teaching. These performance seem to play an increasingly important role in the management of most universities, although their meaning and usefulness is often debated.

The last Italian reforms on education system have given a central role to the National Agency for the Evaluation of Universities and Research Institutes which has introduced extensively performance targets and league tables to classify Universities, Departments and Academic Journals with the aim to allocate a part of public resources.

In this complex contest Human Resource Management in all its various forms has become a central feature of much contemporary performance management research. However, it seems to be very little research in the management literature on Human Resource Performance Management (HRPM) in universities and into the nature of its consequences. Instead, a considerable amount of research on performance management has been conducted in the public sector (Carter, 1991; Propper and Wilson, 2003; Johnsen, 2005; de Bruijn, 2007).

In theory, HRPM is thought to facilitate the development of a skilled workforce that engages in functional behavior for the organization (Wright, Dunford and Snell, 2001). Functional behavior (i.e., behavior that is in line with what the organization expects and wants to achieve) is thought to result in increased operating employee performance, which in turn engenders higher organizational performance (Boselie, Paauwe and Jansen 2001; Boxall, Purcell and Wright 2007).

Empirically, HRPM has been positively associated with a greater sense of community (relatedness) and employee well-being in private sector organizations (see for example Veld, Boselie and Paauwe 2010; Van de Voorde, Paauwe and Van Veldhoven, 2011) as well as in public sector organizations (Gould-Williams 2004). Specifically, research has shown that HRPM ultimately results in lower employee absence, higher satisfaction, greater willingness to stay with the organization and higher effort (Paauwe and Richardson 1997).

The paucity of research aimed at understanding how HRPM influences individuals'well being in the context of Higher Education Institutions allow us to widen the concept of HRPM trying to link some of HRPM practices with other important factors like social capital and sense of community.

For this reason, this chapter describes a set of HRPM practices related to the vision, mission, key success factors, key performance measures, target setting, performance evaluation and reward systems of an organization. These practices seem necessary to realize the shift from professional to managerial values among employees.

Building upon the literature related to HRM (Guest, Conway and Dewe 2004), social capital (Nahapiet & Goshal 1998, Leana & Van Buren 1999), and individual well being (Fletcher 2001; Armstrong and Baron 2004; den Hartog et al. 2004; DeNisi and Pritchard 2006) this chapter describes the dual role of Human Resource Management Performance in Italian Universities providing new insights about procedures and policy-making in Italian Higher Education.

Specifically, the aim of the chapter is to explore the relationships between two main different but complementary uses of HRPM, namely interactive use and diagnostic use, and their relationships with social capital, sense of community and academics and employee Well-being.

Understanding antecedents and consequences of HRPM in the particular context of Higher Education is important for two reasons mainly:

1. to understand how Italian Universities manage their institutional performance.
2. to analyze the impact of different human resource management approaches at the individual level.

The chapter is organized as follows. The next section introduces the concept of HRPM. The third section explains the theoretical framework followed by a review of empirical studies that have examined and defined the same constructs of our hypothesized model. We then describe the method used for our study. The empirical analyses and results are then presented and discussed. The chapter closes with conclusions, limitations of the study and implications for future research.

10.2   Human Resource Performance Management

The consequences of the financial crisis are becoming increasingly visible and the Italian Government has reduced substantially the amount of public funds spent on Italian universities. Funding pressures has increased the emphasis on performance measurement at the university level and, in turn, the focus on individual performance evaluations and the related anxiety and stress.

HRPM is associated with creating a shared vision of the purpose and aims of the organization, helping each individual employee to understand and recognize their part in contributing to them, and, in so doing, to manage and enhance the employee performance of both individuals and the organization (Fletcher and Williams 1996, p. 169). Hence, any organization needs of a variety of HRPM practices through which seek to assess employees, develop competences, enhance employee performance and distribute rewards (Fletcher 2001, Aguinis and Pierce 2008).

Over the past two decades, these systems have been converted into strategic and integrated processes (Aguinis and Pierce 2008). Proponents of HRPM assume that this strategic and integrated approach is necessary to achieve organizational success and to develop individual capabilities (Bach 2000; Fletcher 2001; Armstrong and Baron 2004; Aguinis and Pierce 2008).

The alignment between HRPM and the organization's strategy represents an important strategic fit. For this reason, it becomes important to link individual employee performance appraisal to corporate objectives, ensuring that there is a clear line of sight between organizational and individual goals (Boswell 2006).

However, other important factors, like social interactions, are also positively related to individual well being (e.g. Wallace, 1995a). Specifically, academics'commitment may be influenced by structural factors such as social involvement with colleagues (Igbaria and Wormley; 1992). With the advent of more demanding HRPM, we propose that this is an area where social capital is likely to have a deeply influence on individual working behavior.

For example studies are now investigating how academics are shifting their time in response to multiple pressures coming from different tasks in research, in teaching and in administrative roles (Decramer et al., 2013). So, HRPM may provide relevant information about what performance drivers must be managed in order to achieve deliverable performance. If academics are aware of the institution strategy, then, the measures contained in HRPM will provide the manager with useful job relevant information. Providing managers with feedback information on progress relative to objectives creates opportunities for learning and for keeping the energy people's work-related activities focused on personal and institutional goals. Hence, the content of HRPM will provide the manager with job relevant information useful for making decisions.

HRPM has shifted from an operational focus to a more strategically oriented concept, i.e. where they may play an integral role in the formulation and implementation of the strategy (Armstrong and Baron 2004) seeking to align employee goals and institutional objectives (Fletcher 2001). The alignment of academics and institutional interests, is critical if organizations hope to manage their human capital effectively and ultimately attain strategic success (Becker, Huselid and Ulrich 2001). Employees with greater understanding of their organization's strategic objectives, and how to contribute to them, report higher satisfaction with their job, feel greater affective commitment towards the organization and ultimately desire to stay with the organization (strategic aligned behavior) (Boswell and Boudreau 2001; Boswell 2006; van Riel et al. 2009). That should increase HRM satisfaction and individual well being (Boswell 2006) in a period where the pressure on academics to perform appropriately has increased considerably.

Townley (1997) distinguished between "developmental" and "judgmental" types of performance evaluation. The first type seeks to identify the individual's strengths and weaknesses and to develop his/her skills as a way of securing the commitment and trust of individuals within the organisation. At the opposite, the judgmental type seeks to evaluate the individual via other individuals in the organization.

Nowadays, Academic's performance is measured quantitatively and can be the basis for promotion and remuneration as such it focuses on past performance (Anderson, 1994; Townley, 1997; Redman, 2001). After the introduction of the last Education system Reform in 2010, Italian universities are experiencing a strong judgmental form of performance evaluation.

For this reason this chapter describes 14 HRPM practices currently adopted by Italian university presenting a theoretical research model where such practices are distinguished based upon their different usage: diagnostic and interactive, respectively. The diagnostic use of HRPM (see paragraph 3.2) tends to have a more judgemental role for the organizations (for example the University uses specific performance indicators or "critical success factors" to monitor its performance, or sets specific performance targets to differentiate good and bad performance, or has an useful performance reporting system). Instead the interactive use of HRPM (see paragraph 3.3) tends to have a more developmental role (for example the organizations provide employee with the necessary resources to do their work well, and equally promote and recognize excellence in research, teaching and management/administration or provide constant opportunities for learning and development).

In our theoretical model, both of these HRPM uses are related to the concepts of social capital, sense of community and individual well being. Next paragraph introduces and defines these constructs and presents the theoretical research model providing the related hypotheses.

10.3 Definition of Constructs and Research Theoretical framework

10.3.1 The role of Social capital

In this study we define social capital following the works of Leana & Pil (2006), Nahapiet & Goshal (1998), Leana & Van Buren (1999), Collins & Smith (2006). We adapt the social capital concept to describe three important features: information sharing, trust and shared vision.

Nahapiet and Ghoshal (1998) sustain how the structural aspect of social capital refers to the connections among actors with whom and with what frequency they share information. Also, they argue that such information flows create competitive advantage by enhancing the organization's ability to absorb and assimilate knowledge.

Information sharing may play an important role in enhancing competitive advantage by facilitating individual learning. Such learning is thought to enhance performance, particularly in knowledge-intensive organizations as Universities.

Information sharing increases the likelihood that individuals will have the requisite knowledge to make good decisions feeling confident to perform their work (Spreitzer 1996). The sharing of information may also increase individuals'competence fostering their abilities to quickly uncover problems as they arise, and to integrate and coordinate actions. Hence, academic can respond to suboptimal solutions and increase their understanding of how the system works (Weick and Sutcliffe 2001).

Individuals can focus on larger institutional contributions instead of focusing only on narrow tasks (Weick and Roberts 1993). Consequently, they can relate more heedfully with one another.

The following items have been used to operationalize the construct of Information Sharing (IS): In this institution people engage in open and honest communication with one another; In this institution people share and accept constructive criticisms without making it personal; In this institution people are willing to share information with one another; In this institution people keep each other informed about institutional matters at all times.

Nahapiet and Ghoshal (1998) suggest that the relational aspect of social capital "describes the kind of personal relationships people have developed with each other through a history of interactions". Hence, among its attributes the level of trust among actors is preponderant (Leana and Van Buren 1999).

Coleman (1990) and Onyx and Bullen (2000) point out that trusting relations facilitate collaborative behaviors and collective action in the absence of explicit mechanisms to foster and reinforce those behaviors. So trusting relations allow the transmission of richer and potentially more valuable information. Also members who trust one another are more likely to exchange sensitive information and less likely to fear opportunistic behavior.

The following items have been used to operationalize the construct of Trust (T): In this institution people can rely on each other when doing their work; In this institution people feel comfortable being creative because superiors understand that sometimes creative solutions don't work; In this institution people have confidence in one another; In this institution people show a great deal of ethics and integrity; In this institution overall, people are trustworthy.

Another aspect of social capital refers to the fact that if individuals may interact with one another as part of a collective, they should be better able to develop a common set of goals, and a shared vision for the institution. Coleman (1990) suggests that the shared vision and goals, and the collectively held values that under lie them, help to promote integration and to create a sense of shared responsibility and collective action. Leana and Van Buren (1999) define this phenomenon in terms of *associability* ("the willingness and ability to define collective goals that are then enacted collectively", 1999, p. 542).

If an institution collectively holds a set of goals, the likelihood of free-rider problems is diminished. As correctly point out by Leana & Pil (2006, p. 354): "In these ways, social capital may be a substitute for the formal contracts, incentives, and monitoring systems that organizations devise to control individual self-serving behavior that may hamper the attainment of collective goals". Also, for Mohammed and Dumville (2001), people who share the same mental models about their work are also more likely to have high-quality relations with one another and to interact with one another and share information regularly.

The following items have been used to operationalize the construct of Shared Vision (SV): In this institution people share the same ambitions and vision for the institution; In this institution people enthusiastically pursue collective institutional goals; In this institution there is a commonality of purpose among people; In this institution people view themselves as partners in charting the institution's direction.

10.3.2 The Diagnostic Use of Human Resource Performance Management

HRPM in its diagnostic use can be defined as a set of formalized procedures that use information to maintain or alter patterns in an organizational activity (Henri 2006). These procedures may include strategic plans, reporting systems, and monitoring procedures and similar that are based on information use like strategic plans and performance results communicated to all staff, conceptual model for understanding the drivers of organizational success or how excellence is achieved like (success map or strategy map), specific performance indicators or critical success factors to monitor organizational performance, specific performance targets to differentiate good and bad performance, combination of quantitative and qualitative information to assess organizational performance, performance reporting system (i.e., organizational data are accurate, reliable, easily accessible and comes in an appropriate format).

One of the most known reporting system is the performance measurement system (PMS) that represents a set of metrics used to quantify actions (Neely, Gregory, & Platts, 1995). These metrics can be financial or non-financial, internal or external, short or long term as well as ex post or ex ante (Franco et al, 2012).

Six items have been used to operationalize the construct of Diagnostic Use of Human Resource Performance Management (see the Appendix 10. B), specifically: my institution uses specific performance indicators or critical success factors to monitor its performance, my institution sets specific performance targets to differentiate good and bad performance, my institution relies on a combination of quantitative and qualitative information to assess its performance, my institution uses a conceptual model for understanding the drivers of its success or how excellence is achieved, my institution has an useful performance reporting system, my institution's mission, strategic plans and performance results are communicated to all staff.

The diagnostic use of HRPM reflects two important features associated with mechanistic controls: (i) tight control of operations and strategies, and (ii) highly structured channels of communication and restricted flows of information (Burns & Stalker, 1961).

The diagnostic use of HRPM is associated with tight control of task and strategies through sophisticated management practices. These practices include action plans derived from strategies, detailed financial targets, comparison of actual outcomes with targets, and explanation of variances. This formal use of HRPM provides a mechanistic approach to decision making to signal when productivity and efficiency have fallen (Henri 2006).

However, as a mechanistic control, diagnostic use has been associated with several dysfunctional behaviors in terms of smoothing, biasing, focusing, filtering, and illegal acts (Birnberg, Turopolec, & Young, 1983; Hofstede, 1978; Simons, 1995). These distortions constitute defensive routines that aim to reduce potential embarrassment or threat, or to improve personal interest. They consequently impede the potential for important aspects related to the social capital. Also, the diagnostic use of HRPM may be associated with highly structured channels of communication and a restricted flow of information reinforcing the existing lines of authority and responsibility (Henri 2006). These arguments lead to the following first hypothesis:

Hypothesis 1. A diagnostic use of HRPM will be negatively related to social capital.

10.3.3   The Interactive Use of Human Resource Performance Management

The interactive use of HRPM may represent a positive force used to expand opportunity seeking and learning throughout the institution. The interactive use focuses attention and forces dialogue throughout the institution by reflecting signals sent by academic leaders. This should stimulate the development of new ideas and initiatives (Henri 2006).

When HRPM is used interactively, the information generated is a recurrent and important agenda for academic leaders; frequent and regular attention is fostered throughout the institution; data are discussed and interpreted among academics and non-academics of different hierarchical levels; and continual challenge and debate occur concerning data, assumptions and action plans (Henri, 2006).

These practices include less formalized procedures compared to diagnostic use in order to looking for new ways for the institution to improve. The following eight items have been used to operationalize the construct of Interactive Use of Human Resource Performance Management (see Appendix 10. B), specifically: my institution provides constant opportunities for learning and development, my institution is effective at retaining its best talent, my institution is able to attract the best talent, my institution equally promotes and recognizes excellence in whatever shape or form it comes in terms of teaching, research, management/administration, my institution has an effective probation system, my institution provides us with the necessary resources to do our work well, my institution is effective at dealing with systematic or continuous under-performance, my institution is always looking for ways to improve.

So, an interactive use of HRPM may focus organizational attention on specific targets for which knowledge must be generated and cause–effect relationships understood. HRPM may reinforce important mechanisms used to collect information to develop new and existing capabilities (Henri 2006).

Furthermore, by fostering institutional dialogue and debate, and encouraging information exchange, interactive use contributes to knowledge dissemination, sharing information and communication. Hence, an interactive use of HRPM contributes to expanding the organization's information processing capacity and fostering interaction among institutional actors. These arguments lead to the following hypothesis:

Hypothesis 2. An interactive use of HRPM will be positively related to social capital.

10.3.4   Sense of Community

The sense of community represents the need for *relatedness* (Van den Broeck et al, 2010). Baumeister & Leary (1995) define *relatedness* as individuals'inherent propensity to feel connected to others, that is, to be a member of a group, to love and care and be loved and cared for. To measure the academics'perception of social interactions, we adapted Sheldon's instrument (1971).

The following four items have been used to represent this construct: at work, I feel part of a group; at work, I can talk with people about things that really matter to me; some people I work with are close friends of mine; I feel fairly treated and rewarded at work.

As suggested by Deci & Ryan (2000) the need for relatedness is satisfied when people experience a sense of communion and develop close and intimate relationships with others. The assumption that individuals have the natural tendency to integrate themselves in the social matrix and benefit from being cared for is equally emphasized in developmental approaches such as Attachment Theory (Bowlby, 1969). It may be consistent with concepts in organizational psychology such as social support (Viswesvaran, Sanchez, & Fisher, 1999) and loneliness at work (Wright, Burt, & Strongman, 2006).

These arguments lead to the following hypothesis:

Hypothesis 3. The sense of community will be positively related to social capital.

10.3.5   Individual Well Being

Individual Well-being focuses on happiness, pleasure attainment, pain avoidance and self-realization. Individual Well-being is defines in terms of the degree to which a person is fully functioning and it lies in the actualization of human potentials.

Individual Well-being is subjective and resides within the experience of the individual including the absence of negative factors and the presence of positive measures.

Veenhoven and Jonkers (1984) define Individual Well-being as the degree to which an individual judges the overall quality of her or his life as a whole in a favorable way or how well the person likes the life he or she leads (p. 22). Andrews and Withey

(1976) define Individual Well-being as "both a cognitive evaluation and some degree of positive or negative feelings, i.e., affect" (p. 18).

As suggest by Spreitzer and Sonenshein (2003), Spreitzer & Porath (2012) subjective individual well being refers to how people evaluate their lives affectively and cognitively.

The following four items have been used to represent this construct: I feel alive and vital at work; I have energy and spirit at work; I feel alert and awake at work; I am looking forward to each new day at work.

We posit the following hypothesis:

Hypothesis 4. Individual well being will be positively related by individual's perceptions of a sense of community.

10.3.6   Research Theoretical Model

Figure 10.1 presents the research theoretical model that reflects the relationships among the two uses of HRPM (diagnostic and interactive), social capital, sense of community and individual well being. As previously mentioned, the aim of this model is to understand the specific contributions of these different uses of HRPM on sense of community and on individual well being and to understand the role of social capital (mediation effect).

Research theoretical model considers the effect of diagnostic and interactive uses of HRPM, separately. When examined specifically, a diagnostic use is expected to have a negative influence on the social capital, while interactive use is expected to be positive. Lastly, the usage of HRPM is expected to have an indirect effect on individual well being via sense of community.

Relationships and hypotheses are depicted graphically in figure 10.1.

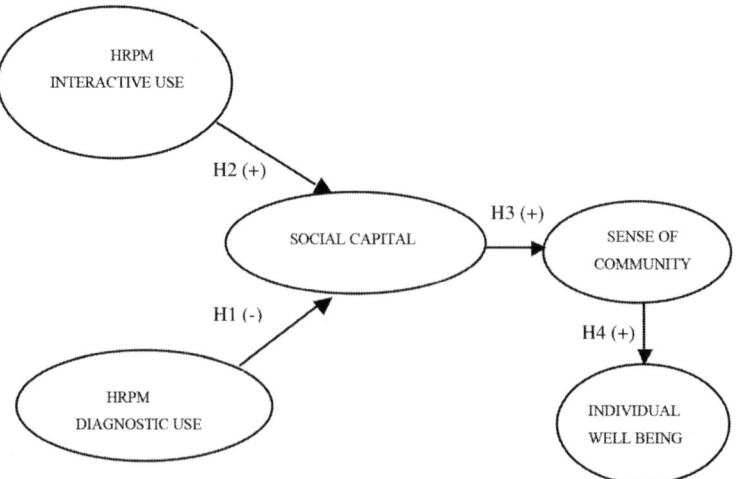

Figure 10.1   Research Theoretical Model.

10.4   Research method

Data were gathered using a structured questionnaire addressed to academics involved in teaching and research and address to technical and administrative employees involved in administrative management. Questionnaires were distributed using Qualtrics online survey platform.

Survey instrument resulted from multiple discussions and brainstorming sessions and was subjected to pre and pilot testing. The aims of these procedure were to improve the quality of the survey by increasing clarity and avoiding misunderstanding of survey questions. A preliminary draft of the questionnaire was discussed with academic scholars to assess the content validity prior to pilot testing. Inputs were used to improve the clarity, comprehensiveness and relevance of the survey instrument. The pre-test was useful in discarding and modifying some questions, and to focus more on specific constructs. Also, to achieve high levels of content validity, most of the measures used in the survey were already tested in earlier research. All items were measured using a seven-point Likert response scale ranging from 1 (strongly disagree) to 7 (strongly agree).

After a period of intensive follow-up via internet mails and telephone calls, the survey resulted in 668 respondents from a population of around 2.500 individuals, representing a response rate of approximately of 26.72%. This is consistent with the mean response rate found in previous studies (Cook, Heath and Thompson 2000). However, due to missing data and incomplete responses, only 424 questionnaires were considered to be usable to test our research theoretical model. Furthermore, given that the survey had a relatively low response rate, we assessed potential non response bias. This procedure is important because there is a possibility that the target respondents have self selected some survey variables, thus posing a threat to the theoretical generalizability of the survey results (Van der Stede et al. 2007, p. 467).

As suggested by Oppenheim (1966), two separate procedures were conducted to find evidence for possible bias from respondents. A first test based on time response was undertaken as suggested by Armstrong and Overton (1977), however, the independent samples t-test failed to detect any significant difference between early and late respondents. Afterwards, a comparison was made based on two characteristics of surveyed respondents (respondent age and role, see table 10.1). Also in this case, no significant differences were found ($p < 0.05$) between these two groups. Hence, it appears that non-response bias is not a greater concern in this sample.

Totally, people from 77 Italian Universities have participated to this research (see Appendix 10.A1) belonging to 17 different academic research fields (see Appendix 10.A2).

Various demographic characteristics were assessed to describe the study's sample population. Table 10.1 shows respondents demographic characteristics in terms of age, employment, gender, roles and job place.

10.5   Results

To test empirically our research theoretical model we used the Partial Least Squares (PLS) approach for structural equation modeling (Wold, 1985). PLS is more appropriate than LISREL when models are complex, there is low theoretical information,

Table 10.1 Respondent demographic characteristics

Demographic variables	Frequency	Percent
Respondent age		
26 – 35	9	2,12%
36 – 45	67	15,80%
46 – 55	172	40,57%
56 – 65	146	34,43%
66 and over	30	7,08%
Total	**424**	**100,00%**
Respondent employment		
Full time	414	97,64%
Part time	9	2,12%
Other	1	0,24%
Total	**424**	**100,00%**
Respondent gender		
Female	154	36,32%
Male	270	63,68%
Total	**424**	**100,00%**
Respondent role		
Academic leader (e.g., Vice Chancellor, Pro–Vice Chancellor, Head of Faculty/School/Department)	156	36,79%
Academic (e.g., Professor, Reader, Senior Lec turer, Senior Researcher, Lecturer, Researcher, Post-Doc)	119	28,07%
Professional services leader (e.g., Registrar, Director of Finance, Director of Human Resources)	30	7,08%
Professional services manager (e.g., Head of Train & Devel, Head of Stud Affairs, Head of Planning)	36	8,49%
Support (e.g., Assistants)	3	0,71%
Technical (e.g., Technician, Officer)	44	10,38%
Others	36	8,49%
Total	**424**	**100,00%**
Respondent job place		
Central Services	115	27,12%
A Faculty or School	297	70,05%
Others	12	2,83%
Total	**424**	**100,00%**

and the measures are not well established in literature (Fornell & Bookstein, 1982). PLS generates estimates of standardized regression coefficients (beta values) for the model's paths, which are then used to measure relationships among latent variables. PLS also generates factor loadings for measurement items, which are interpretable similarly to loadings generated by principal component factor analysis.

Moreover, PLS does not make assumptions about data distributions to estimate model parameters, observation independence, or variable metrics (Bass et al., 2003). Therefore, we used PLS to effectively manage the high number of variables in the model and the low theoretical support in the identification of the causal relations among the constructs.

Appendix 10. B describes measures and labels related to the constructs of the model. Reliability and validity of the scales are examined in the PLS measurement model. This process led to the exclusion of some items that loaded on more than one factor.

In the following sections we describe both the measurement model and the structural model. The measurement model specifies relations between observed items and latent variables. The structural model specifies relations between latent constructs.

Although in PLS the measurement and structural models are estimated simultaneously (Barclay, Thompson, & Higgins, 1995), the model is typically interpreted in two stages. First, the reliability and validity of the measurement model is assessed. Second, the structural model is assessed (Barclay et al., 1995). This ensures that the constructs'measures are reliable and valid before assessing the nature of the relations between the constructs (Barclay et al., 1995; Hair et al., 1998; Hulland, 1999). As such, the results from the measurement model are presented first followed by the hypothesized relations between the constructs.

10.5.1   Measurement model validation

Statistics from the PLS measurement model are used to examine the psychometric properties of the variables. First we examine the factor loadings for each variable. All items load on their respective constructs. Low item loadings add very little to the explanatory power of the model while potentially biasing the estimates of the parameters linking the constructs (Chin, 1998a; Hulland, 1999).

Our hypothesized model contained 37 directly observed measures (or indicators), 2 first-order unobserved (or latent) variables and 3 higher-order latent variables. The items were validated via Confirmatory Factor Analysis (CFA) using SmartPLS 2.0 (Ringle et al., 2005). CFA provides a more stringent test of construct validity and unidimensionality using latent and manifest variables. The factor loadings from the final PLS measurement model are reported in Table 10.2

We assess the reliability of each variable using Fornell and Larcker's (1981) measure of composite reliability and Cronbach's (1951) alpha. As shown in table 10.3 the composite reliability and alpha scores for each variable are above 0.80, which demonstrates good reliability (Nunnally, 1978).

Convergent validity of the variables is assessed by examining the average variance extracted (AVE) statistics. Table 10.3 shows, also, that the AVE for each variable is above 0.50, which demonstrates adequate convergent validity (Chin, 1998a; Hair et al., 1998). The AVE statistic is also used to assess discriminant validity by comparing

Table 10.2 Factor loadings from final PLS Measurement Model

	HRPM INTERACTIVE USE	HRPM DIAGNOSTIC USE	SENSE OF COMMUNITY	SOCIAL CAPITAL	INDIV. WELL BEING
HRPM1	**0,824**	0,759	0,323	0,632	0,205
HRPM2	**0,778**	0,550	0,218	0,535	0,174
HRPM3	**0,859**	0,664	0,317	0,653	0,228
HRPM4	**0,828**	0,595	0,245	0,556	0,147
HRPM5	**0,773**	0,537	0,273	0,543	0,224
HRPM6	**0,838**	0,577	0,281	0,584	0,182
HRPM7	**0,876**	0,591	0,289	0,653	0,206
HRPM8	**0,788**	0,582	0,184	0,574	0,103
HRPM9	0,587	**0,762**	0,275	0,490	0,186
HRPM10	0,611	**0,830**	0,261	0,456	0,081
HRPM11	0,582	**0,865**	0,253	0,391	0,063
HRPM12	0,590	**0,861**	0,244	0,416	0,057
HRPM13	0,630	**0,845**	0,277	0,441	0,128
HRPM14	0,663	**0,797**	0,290	0,495	0,151
SOC2	0,290	0,313	**0,817**	0,378	0,373
SOC3	0,239	0,242	**0,869**	0,343	0,426
SOC4	0,061	0,097	**0,627**	0,253	0,227
SOC5	0,353	0,302	**0,764**	0,420	0,449
SOCAP1	0,596	0,425	0,426	**0,850**	0,278
SOCAP10	0,615	0,489	0,368	**0,831**	0,231
SOCAP11	0,649	0,511	0,395	**0,858**	0,221
SOCAP12	0,635	0,501	0,384	**0,861**	0,223
SOCAP13	0,664	0,535	0,369	**0,829**	0,211
SOCAP2	0,581	0,440	0,332	**0,821**	0,207
SOCAP3	0,548	0,385	0,365	**0,816**	0,249
SOCAP4	0,572	0,430	0,413	**0,821**	0,270
SOCAP5	0,585	0,422	0,401	**0,873**	0,245
SOCAP6	0,548	0,439	0,308	**0,713**	0,190
SOCAP7	0,576	0,420	0,405	**0,875**	0,238
SOCAP8	0,611	0,461	0,408	**0,830**	0,249
SOCAP9	0,630	0,451	0,396	**0,837**	0,219
IWB1	0,229	0,124	0,466	0,294	**0,891**
IWB2	0,184	0,113	0,422	0,253	**0,918**
IWB4	0,198	0,130	0,462	0,213	**0,895**
IWB5	0,112	0,087	0,204	0,139	**0,519**

HRPM INTERACTIVE USE (HRPM1-HRPM8); **HRPM DIAGNOSTIC USE** (HRPM9-HRPM14); **SENSE OF COMMUNITY** (SOC2-SOC5); **SOCIAL CAPITAL** (SOCAP1-SOCAP13); **INDIVIDUAL WELL BEING** (IWB1-IWB5)

Table 10.3 Descriptive statistics, reliability and average variance extracted (AVE) statistics, and correlations from PLS model

	Mean	Dev std.	Range	Min	Max
HRPM DIAGNOSTIC USE	4,11	1,46	1-7	1	7
HRPM INTERACTIVE USE	4,05	1,33	1-7	1	7
SOCIAL CAPITAL	4,88	1,22	1-7	1	7
SENSE OF COMMUNITY	4,10	1,21	1-7	1	7
INDIVIDUAL WELL BEING	4,97	1,09	1-7	1	7
	AVE	Composite Reliability	R Square	Cron. Alpha	Commun.
HRPM DIAGNOSTIC USE	0,685	0,929	0,000	0,908	0,685
HRPM INTERACTIVE USE	0,675	0,943	0,000	0,931	0,675
SOCIAL CAPITAL	0,694	0,967	0,523	0,963	0,694
SENSE OF COMMUNITY	0,600	0,855	0,225	0,776	0,600
INDIVIDUAL WELL BEING	0,677	0,889	0,242	0,830	0,677
SQ AVE Diagonal	HRPM diagno-stic use	HRPM interactive use	Social capital	Sense commu-nity	Indiv. well being
HRPM DIAGNOSTIC USE	**0,827**				
HRPM INTERACTIVE USE	0,742	**0,821**			
SOCIAL CAPITAL	0,547	0,723	**0,833**		
SENSE OF COMMUNITY	0,325	0,328	0,460	**0,774**	
INDIVIDUAL WELL BEING	0,139	0,226	0,280	0,492	**0,823**

n = 424; Diagonal elements are the square roots of the AVE statistics. Off-diagonal elements are the correlations between the latent variables calculated in PLS. The number on the diagonal should be larger than the numbers on the corresponding column and row to demonstrate discriminant validity. All correlations above 0.20 are statistically significant (p < 0.01, two-tailed).

the square root of the AVE statistics to the correlations among the latent variables (Chin, 1998b). This tests whether a construct shares more variance with its measures than it shares with other constructs (Fornell & Larcker, 1981).

Table 10.4 shows that the square roots of the AVEs (diagonal) are all greater than the respective correlations between constructs. In addition, table 10.4 shows that each item loads higher on the construct it intends to measure than on any other construct

Table 10.4 Results from final PLS Structure Equation Model

Path coefficient and expected sign	Original Sample	Stand. Deviat.	T Stat	P Value
HRPM DIAGNOSTIC USE -> SOCIAL CAPITAL (–)	0,024	0,110	0,214	0,830
HRPM DIAGNOSTIC USE -> SOCOMMUNITY (–)	0,171	0,145	1,185	0,237
HRPM INTERACTIVE USE -> SOCIAL CAPITAL (+)	**0,705**	**0,094**	**7,498**	**0,000**
HRPM INTERACTIVE USE -> SOCOMMUNITY (+)	-0,135	0,169	0,798	0,426
SOCIAL CAPITAL -> SOCOMMUNITY (+)	**0,464**	**0,135**	**3,437**	**0,001**
SOCOMMUNITY -> INDIVIDUAL WELL BEING (+)	**0,492**	**0,082**	**6,027**	**0,000**
Total effects	**Original Sample**	**Stand. Deviat.**	**T Stat**	**P Value**
HRPM DIAGNOSTIC USE -> SOCIAL CAPITAL (–)	0,024	0,110	0,214	0,830
HRPM DIAGNOSTIC USE -> SOCOMMUNITY (–)	0,182	0,151	1,210	0,227
HRPM DIAGNOSTIC USE -> INDIVID. WELL BEING (–)	0,090	0,076	1,177	0,240
HRPM INTERACTIVE USE -> SOCIAL CAPITAL (+)	**0,705**	**0,094**	**7,498**	**0,000**
HRPM INTERACTIVE USE -> SOCOMMUNITY (+)	0,192	0,146	1,319	0,188
HRPM INTERACTIVE USE -> INDIVID. WELL BEING (+)	0,095	0,079	1,201	0,230
SOCIAL CAPITAL -> SOCOMMUNITY (+)	**0,464**	**0,135**	**3,437**	**0,001**
SOCIAL CAPITAL -> INDIVIDUAL WELL BEING (+)	**0,228**	**0,083**	**2,760**	**0,006**
SOCOMMUNITY -> INDIVIDUAL WELL BEING (+)	**0,492**	**0,082**	**6,027**	**0,000**

(Barclay et al., 1995; Chin, 1998b). The results of these two tests demonstrate adequate discriminant validity. Overall, the results from the PLS measurement model indicate that each construct exhibits satisfactory reliability and validity. We can now proceed to test the structural model.

10.5.2 Empirical testing of hypothesized structural model

The objective of PLS is to maximise variance explained rather than fit, therefore prediction orientated measures, such as R^2, are used to evaluate PLS models (Chin, 1998b). The R^2 for each endogenous variable is shown in Table 10.5

PLS produces standardised βs for each path coefficient, which are interpreted in the same way as in OLS regression. As PLS makes no distributional assumptions, bootstrapping (500 samples with replacement) is used to evaluate the statistical significance of each path coefficient (Chin, 1998a). Statistical significance is determined using the reported original PLS estimates and bootstrapped standard (table 10.4).

Next table shows the standardized PLS path coefficients. To assess the statistical significance of the path coefficients, which are standardized betas (β), a bootstrap analysis was performed. The use of this as opposed to traditional t-tests allowed the testing of the significance of parameter estimates from data that were not assumed to be multivariate normal.

Results (table 10.5) show how different uses of HRPM lead to different influences on social capital and in turn on sense of community and individual well being.

The diagnostic use of HRPM is not related neither to social capital nor to sense of community. So H1 of this model is not supported in this dataset.

Instead, as expected, the interactive use of HRPM is positive related to social capital ($\beta = 0.705$, $p < 0.001$) that in turn is positively related with sense of community

Table 10.5   PLS structural model: path coefficients, t-statistics and R^2

Dependent variables	Independent variables				
	HRPM interactive use	HRPM diagnostic use	social capital	sense of community	R square
SOCIAL CAPITAL	0,705 (7,498)***	0,024 (0,214)	–	–	0,523
SENSE OF COMMUNITY	–0,135 (0,798)	0,171 (1,185)	0,464 (3,437)***	–	0,225
INDIVIDUAL WELL BEING	0,095 (1,201)	0,090 (1,177)	0,228 (2,760)**	0,492 (0,6027)***	0,242

n = 424. Each cell reports the path coefficient (t-value).
* p < 0.05 (one-tailed); ** p < 0.01; *** p < 0.001

(β = 0.464, p < 0.001). However, there is no significant relation between HRPM interactive use and sense of community. Hence, social capital fully mediate the relationship between HRPM interactive use and sense of community. So H2 and H3 are fully supported in this model.

Finally, sense of community is strongly and positively related to individual well being (β = 0.492, p < 0.001). So H4 is fully supported. However, given that social capital is also positively related to individual well being (β = 0.228, p < 0.01), the sense of community partially mediate the relationship between social capital and individual well being.

Final empirical model is represented in figure 10.2.

Next table 10.6 shows the summary of the empirical results.

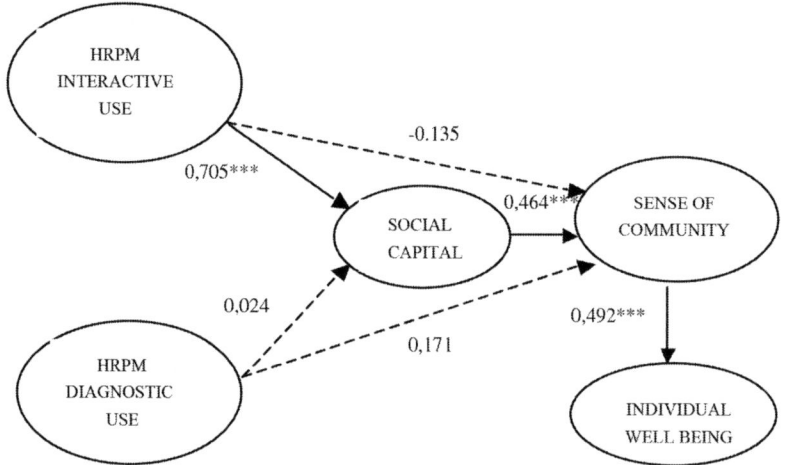

Figure 10.2 Final empirical model. Pls Structural model *** significant at p < 0.001; ** significant at p < 0.01; * significant at p < 0.05; ns = not significant.

Table 10.6 Summary of main results

Hypothesis		Results
Hypothesis 1	*A diagnostic use of HRPM will be negatively related to social capital*	Not Supported
Hypothesis 2	*An interactive use of HRPM will be positively related to social capital*	Supported
Hypothesis 3	*The sense of community will be positively related to social capital*	Supported
Hypothesis 4	*Individual well being will be positively related by individual's perceptions of a sense of community*	Supported

10.6   Discussion

In these last ten years, in many Countries have taken place institutional level reforms concerning the higher education sector. In Italy, Universities have been influenced by social, economic and political developments that have pushed the Italian Government to introduce new type of management doctrines such as management-by-results to steer Italian universities. Specifically, in search for efficiency and modernization new decentralization and severe budget constraints have been introduced.

The wave of reforms, known as "New Public Management" (NPM) or "managerialism" (Hood, 1991; Pollitt and Bouckaert, 2004) involves greater managerial power, structural reorganization, and more emphasis towards performance-related targets. These developments have reinforced the trend in academic institutions to adopt organizational forms and managerial practices commonly found in the private business sector (Deem, 1998).

Following the increasing transparency of government funding mentioned earlier, Italian Government is now introducing a resource allocation model based upon judgmental forms of performance evaluation. The National Agency for the Evaluation of Universities and Research Institutes (ANVUR) has introduced extensively performance targets and league tables to classify Universities, Departments and Academic Journals. As a result, Italian universities are now facing considerable uncertainty. This new performance evaluation system clearly based on the judgmental dimensions may lead to more pressure to perform well and, consequently, the level of stress is perceived to have increased considerably.

Recent studies about the consequences of these new performance evaluation system indicate that scholars working in academia are increasingly experiencing a sense of losing their academic freedom and autonomy (ter Bogt & Scapens, 2012).

For this reason this chapter has empirically examined the effects of some management practices on individual well being. Specifically, we have concentrated on the HRPM role (Aguinis and Pierce 2008), and widened the concept of employee performance management by using a set of HRPM practices. In a combination with such practices we pinpoint the strategic importance of social relations in academia (Gersick et al. 2000) to find out whether social capital and sense of community have significant and positive relationships with individual well being.

Overall, our propositions were inspired by the HRPM literature implying that a HRPM system is more than a single HR practice. Specifically, we have distinguished two main different roles of HRPM (diagnostic and interactive) and we have analyzed their consequence at the individual level.

The diagnostic use of HRPM represents the traditional feedback role as Human Resource Management Systems are used on an exception basis to monitor and reward the achievement of pre-established goals. Based upon the traditional mechanistic notion of control, a diagnostic use of HRPM may provide motivation and direction to achieve goals by focusing on and correcting deviations from preset standards of performance. This diagnostic use comprises the review of critical performance variables to monitor and coordinate the implementation of intended strategies focusing on mistakes and negative variances. On the contrary, the interactive use of HRPM may stimulate participation and social interactions which are factors extremely important in university working life.

The interactive use of HRPM focuses on a development role helping individuals to improve their future performance while the diagnostic use of HRPM based on a more judgemental and quantitative role may decrease individual performance.

By presenting significant relationships between several HRPM, social capital, social interactions (relatedness) and individual well being, this study contributes to the theory on the effects of HRPM practices and antecedents on individual well being. Specifically, these findings contribute to our understanding of how different usage of HRPM may influence social capital and in turn individual well being. Also these findings highlight the importance of incorporating employee perspective into the examination of performance management systems. However, the applicability of the concept of HRPM in other settings should be better explored. Although we have no reason to believe that the relations observed are unique to the Italian Universities, generalizations to other Countries should be made with caution since HRPM may differ in Universities of other Countries due to institutional factors or different individual culture.

On the other hand, this research represents an ideal setting for studying the relationship between HRPM features and individual well being due to the large number of Universities involved, the presence of different kinds of academic employees and their different academic backgrounds.

10.7 Limitations and implications for future research

A first limitation of our research theoretical model is that we did not investigate whether the joint use of diagnostic and interactive HRPM creates dynamic tension that reflects competition (positive versus negative feedback) and complementarities (focus on intended and emergent strategies). As suggested in the literature for the case of Performance Measurement Systems (Henri 2006), the diagnostic and the interactive use of HRPM may represent two complementary uses that work simultaneously but for different purposes. Hence, while, diagnostic use of HRPM may represent a mechanistic control used to track, review and support the achievement of predictable goals, interactive use maybe considered as an organic control system supporting the emergence of communication processes and the mutual adjustment of organizational actors. Also, a diagnostic use limits the role of HRPM to a measurement tool, while an interactive use of HRPM expands its role to a strategic management tool (Kaplan & Norton, 2001).

A second limitation is that like all cross-sectional analyses, this study is unable to solve the ambiguity in the direction of causality. Inferences about causal processes are, therefore, tentative and partial, at best. The data were gathered at one point in time, making it difficult to draw inferences of causality and rule out the possibility of reverse causality (i.e., endogeneity). Hence, we should have examined the impact of HRPM developing a pre and post test type of study. In this way we could examine the HRPM impact of the academic employees prior to its implementation. Then, after a sufficient amount of time, we have could reexamine their perceptions regarding the HRPM and the associated individual well being.

Third, the reliance on self-reported questionnaire data causes concern about possible mono method variance.

Fourth, this research have not demonstrated how academic identity may influence the set of HRPM practices and antecedents affecting individual well being. Practitioners in the field of University HRPM should be careful in applying generally approved HRPM. We think it is wise to account for the academic identity while implementing a HRPM strategy.

Lastly, future research should examine whether satisfaction with these HRPM practices has an impact also on organizationally relevant outcomes.

Summary

With the advent of the New Public Management (Hood 1991), many Universities have attempted, either voluntary or under pressure, to adopt new management systems with themes like budget transparency, output measurement, increased competition, and use of private sector management techniques became common in Universities.

In Italy, the government funding of universities has become increasingly contingent on their performance in research and teaching and the National Agency for the Evaluation of Universities and Research Institutes (ANVUR) has introduced extensively performance targets and league tables to classify Universities, Departments and Academic Journals.

In this contest Human Resource Management has become a central feature of much contemporary performance management research. However, while a considerable amount of studies on performance management has been conducted in the public sector, it seems to be very little research in the management literature on HR performance management (HRPM) in universities.

In theory, HRPM is thought to facilitate the development of a skilled workforce that engages in functional behavior for the organization (Wright, Dunford and Snell, 2001). Functional behavior (i.e., behavior that is in line with what the organization expects and wants to achieve) is thought to result in increased operating employee performance, which in turn engenders higher organizational performance.

For this reason, this chapter has described a set of HRPM practices related to the vision, mission, key success factors, key performance measures, target setting, performance evaluation and reward systems of an organization. These practices seem necessary to realize the shift from professional to managerial values among employees.

Building upon the literature related to HRM (Guest, Conway and Dewe 2004), social capital (Nahapiet & Goshal 1998, Leana & Van Buren 1999), and individual well being (Fletcher 2001; Armstrong and Baron 2004; den Hartog et al. 2004; DeNisi and Pritchard 2006) this chapter has focused on Human Resource Management Performance in Italian Universities providing new insights about practices and policy-making in Italian Higher Education.

Specifically, the aim of the chapter was to explore the relationships between two main different but complementary uses of HRPM, namely interactive use and diagnostic use, and their relationships with social capital, sense of community and individual Well-being. The diagnostic use of HRPM tend to have a more "judgemental role" (i.e., the institution uses specific performance indicators or "critical success factors" to monitor its performance, or sets specific performance targets to differentiate good and bad performance, or has an useful performance reporting system) while the interactive use of HRPM tend to have a more "developmental role" for the HR.

To test our model we presented PLS regression analysis of survey data collected from a sample of 424 academics, technical and administrative employees in 77 Italian Universities.

Results have broadly supported the mediation role of social capital described in our research theoretical model. Specifically, results have shown how different usage of HRPM led to different influences on social capital and in turn on sense of community and individual well-being.

References

AGUINIS, H., & PIERCE, C. A. (2008). *Enhancing the relevance of organizational behavior by embracing performance management research.* Journal of Organizational Behavior, 29, 139–145.

ANDREWS, F. M., & WITHEY, S. B. (1976). *Social indicators of well-*being: Americans'perceptions of life quality, pp. 19–35.

ARMSTRONG, J. S. AND OVERTON, T. S. (1977) *Estimating non response bias in mail surveys,* Journal of Marketing Research, 14 (3), pp. 396–402.

ARMSTRONG, M., AND BARON, A. (2004), *Managing Performance: Performance Management in Action (1st ed.),* London: Chartered Institute of Personnel and Development.

ANDERSON, G. (1994) *Performance appraisal,* in: B. Towers (Ed.) The Handbook of Human Resource Management, pp. 186–207 (Oxford and Cambridge: Blackwell).

AUCOIN, P. (1990) *Administrative Reform in Public Management: Paradigms, Principles, Paradoxes and Pendulums,* Governance: An International Journal of Policy and Administration, 2 (2): 115–37.

BACH, S. (2000), *From Performance Appraisal to Performance Management, in Personnel Management: A Comprehensive Guide to Theory and Practice,* eds. S. Bach and K. Sisson, Oxford: Blackwell, pp. 241–286.

BARCLAY, D., THOMPSON, R., & HIGGINS, C. (1995). *The partial least squares (PLS) approach to causal modelling: personal computer adoption and use as an illustration.* Technology Studies, 2 (2), 285-309.

BAUMEISTER, R. F. & LEARY, M. R. (1995). *The need to belong: Desire for interpersonal attachments as a fundamental human motivation.* Psychological Bulletin, 117, 497-529.

BECKER, B., HUSELID, M., AND ULRICH, D. (2001), *The HR Scorecard: Linking People, Strategy, and Performance,* Boston: Harvard Business School Press.

BIRNBERG, J. G., TUROPOLEC, L., & YOUNG, S. M. (1983). *The organizational context of accounting.* Accounting, Organizations and Society, 8 (2–3), 111–129.

BOSELIE, P., PAAUWE, J., AND JANSEN, P. (2001), *Human Resource Management and Performance: Lessons from the Netherlands,* International Journal of Human Resource Management, 12, 1107–1125.

BOSWELL, W. (2006), *Aligning Employees with the Organization's Strategic Objectives: Out of Line of Sight, Out of Mind,* International Journal of Human Resource Management, 17, 1489–1511.

BOSWELL, W., AND BOUDREAU, J. (2001), *How Leading Companies Create, Measure and Achieve Strategic Results Through Line of Sight,* Management Decision, 39, 851–860.

BOURNE M., FRANCO-SANTOS M., PAVLOV A., LUCIANETTI L., MARTINEZ V., MURA M. (2008), *The Impact of the Investors in People Standard on people management practices and firm performance,* Centre for Business Performance, Cranfield School of Management.

BOURNE M., FRANCO-SANTOS M., PAVLOV A., LUCIANETTI L., MURA M. (2013), *Generating Organisational Performance: The Contributing Effects of Performance Measurement and Human Resource Management Practices,* International Journal of Operations and Production Management, IJOPM, Emerald, Vol. 33, Iss. 11.

BOWLBY, J. (1969), *Attachment and loss*, VOL. 1: ATTACHMENT. NEW YORK: BASIC BOOKS.

BOXALL, P., PURCELL, J., AND WRIGHT, P. (2007), *The Oxford Handbook of Human Resource Management*, Oxford: Oxford University Press.

BRENNAN, J., AND SHAH, T. (2000), *Quality Assessment and Institutional Change: Experiences from 14 Countries*, Higher Education, 40, 331–349.

BRYSON, C. (2004) *The Consequences for Women in the Academic Profession of the Widespread Use of Fixed Term Contracts*, Gender, Work and Organization, 11 (2): 187–206.

BURNS, T., & STALKER, G. M. (1961). *The management of innovation*. London: Tavistock Publications.

CARTER, N. (1991) *Learning to measure performance: the use of indicators in organizations*, Public Administration, 69 (1), pp. 85–101.

CHIN, W. W. (1998b). *The partial least squares approach to structural equation modelling*. IN G. A. MARCOULIDES (ED.), *Modern methods for business research* MAHWAH, NJ: Lawrence Erlbaum, 295–336

CHIN, W. W (1998a), *Commentary: Issues and opinion on structural equation modelling*, MIS Quarterly, Vol. 20, No. 1, pp. 7-16.

COLEMAN J (1990). *The foundations of social theory*. Cambridge, MA, Harvard University Press.

COLLINS, C. J., SMITH, K. G. (2006). *Knowledge exchange and combination: The role of human resource practices in the performance of high technology firms*. Academy of Management Journal, 49, 544-560.

COOK, C., HEATH, F., & THOMPSON, R. L. (2000). *A meta-analysis of response rates in web– and internet-based surveys*. Educational and Psychological Measurement, 60, 821-836.

CRONBACH, L. J. (1951). *Coefficient alpha and the internal structure of tests*. Psychometrika, 297–334.

DE BRUIJN, H. (2007), Managing Performance in the Public Sector (London and New York: Routledge).

DECRAMER, A., SMOLDERS, C., VANDERSTRAETEN, A., AND CHRISTIAENS, J. (2012), *The Impact of Institutional Pressures on Employee Performance Management Systems in Higher Education in the Low Countries*, British Journal of Management, 2, S88–S103.

DECRAMER, A., SMOLDERS, C., AND VANDERSTRAETEN, A. (2013), *Employee performance management culture and system features in higher education: relationship with employee performance management satisfaction*, The International Journal of Human Resource Management, 24: 2, 352-371.

DEEM, R. (1998) *"New Managerialism" and Higher Education: The Management of Performances and Cultures in Universities in the United Kingdom*, International Studies in Sociology of Education, 8 (1): 47–70.

DELERY, J., AND DOTY, D. (1996), *Modes of Theorizing in Strategic Human Resource Management: Tests of Universalistic, Contingency, and Configurational Performance Predictions*, The Academy of Management Journal, 39, 802–835.

DEN HARTOG, D. N., BOSELIE, P., AND PAAUWE, J. (2004), *Performance Management: A Model and Research Agenda*, Applied Psychology: an International Review, 53, 556–569.

DENISI, A. (2000), *Performance Appraisal and Performance Management: A Multilevel Analysis*,'in Multilevel Theory, Research and Methods in Organizations, eds. K. Klein and S. Kozkowski, San Fransico, CA: Jossey-Bass, pp. 121–156.

FELTHAM, G. A. AND J. XIE. *Performance Measure Congruity and Diversity in Multi-Task Principal/Agent Relations*. Accounting Review (July 1994): 429-453.

FERLIE, E., MUSSELIN, C., AND ANDRESANI, G. (2008), *The Steering of Higher Education Systems: A Public Management Perspective*, Higher Education, 56, 325–348.

FERREIRA, A., OTLEY, D., 2009. *The Design and Use of Performance Management Systems: An Extended Framework for Analysis*. Management Accounting Research 20, 263–282.

FLETCHER, C. (2001), *Performance Appraisal and Management: The Developing Research Agenda*, Journal of Occupational and Organizational Psychology, 74, 473–487.

FLETCHER, C., AND WILLIAMS, R. (1996), *Performance Management, Job Satisfaction and Organizational Commitment*, British Journal of Management, 7, 169–179.

FORNELL, C., & LARCKER, D. F. (1981). *Evaluating structural equation models with unobservable variables and measurement error*. Journal of Marketing Research, 18, 39–50.

FORNELL, C., BOOKSTEIN, F. L. (1982), *Two structural equation models: LISREL and PLS applied to consumer exit-voice theory*, Journal of Marketing Research, Vol. 19 (November), 440-452.

FRANCO M., LUCIANETTI L., BOURNE M. (2012), *Contemporary performance measurement systems: A review of their consequences and a framework for research*, Management Accounting Research, 23 p. 79-119.

GEFEN, D. STRAUB, D. W. (2005), *A practical guide to factorial validity using PLS-graph: tutorial and annotated example*, Comm. Association of Information Systems, Vol. 16, No. 5, 91-109.

GERSICK, C. J. G., BARTUNEK, J. M. AND DUTTON, J. E. (2000) *Learning from Academia: The Importance of Relationships in Professional Life*, Academy of Management Journal, 43 (6): 1026–44.

GOULD-WILLIAMS, J. S. (2004), *The Effects of High Commitment HRM Practices on Employee Attitude: The Views of Public Sector Workers*, Public Administration, 82, 63–81.

GUEST, D., CONWAY, N., AND DEWE, P. (2004), *Using Sequential Tree Analysis to Search for 'Bundles'of HR Practices*, Human Resource Management Journal, 14, 79–96.

HAIR, J. F., ANDERSON, R. E., TATHAM, R. L., & BLACK, W. C. (1998). *Multivariate data analysis*. Upper Saddle River: Prentice Hall.

HENRI, J. F., 2006a. *Organizational culture and performance measurement systems*. Accounting Organizations and Society 31 (1), 77–103.

HENRI, J. F., 2006 b. *Management control systems and strategy: a resource based perspective*. Accounting Organizations and Society 31 (6), 529–558.

HOFSTEDE, G. (1978). *The poverty of management control philosophy*. Management control philosophy, 3 (3), 450–461.

HOOD, C. (1991). *A Public Management for All Seasons*. Public Administration, 69 (Spring), 3-19

HULLAND, J. (1999). *Use of partial least squares (PLS) in strategic management research: a review of four recent studies*. Strategic Management Journal, 20, 195–204.

HULT G. T., KETCHEN D. J. (2001), *Does market orientation matter?. A test of the relationship between positional advantages and performance*. Strategic Management Journal, 22, pp.899-906.

JOHNSEN, A. (2005), *What does 25 years of experience tell us about the state of performance measurement in public policy and management?*, Public Money and Management, 25 (1), pp. 9–17.

ICHNIOWSKI, C., KOCHAN, T., LEVINE, D., OLSON, C., AND STRAUSS, G. (1996), *What Works at Work: Overview and Assessment*, Industrial Relations: A Journal of Economy and Society, 35, 299–333.

KAPLAN, R. S., NORTON, D. P., 2001. *The Strategy-Focused Organization: How Balanced Scorecard Companies Thrive in the New Business Environment*. Harvard Business School Press, Boston, MA.

KUVAAS, B. (2008), *An Exploration of How the Employee–Organization Relationship Affects the Linkage Between Perception of Developmental Human Resource Practices and Employee Outcomes*, Journal of Management Studies, 45, 1–25.

LAPSLEY, I., MILLER, P. *Foreword: Transforming Universities: The Uncertain, Erratic Path*. Financial Accountability & Management, 2004, 20.2: 103-106.

LEANA, C., PIL, F. K. 2006. *Social capital and organizational performance: Evidence from urban public schools*. ORGANIZATION SCIENCE, 17 (3): 353-366.

LEANA, C., VAN BUREN, H. 1999. *Organizational social capital and employment practices*. Academy of Management Review, 24 (3): 538-555.

LINDELL, M. K., WHITNEY, D. J. (2001), *Accounting for common method variance in cross-sectional research design*, Journal of Applied Psychology, Vol. 86, No. 1, pp. 114-121

LUCIANETTI L. (2010), *The impact of strategy maps on balanced scorecard performance*, International Journal of Business Performance Management, (IJBPM), Inderscience Publishers, Vol. 12, 1, pp. 21-36.

MIDDLEHURST, R. (2002), *The International Context for UK Higher Education*, in *The Effective Academic: A Handbook for Enhanced Academic Practice*, eds. S. Ketteridge, S. Marshall and H. Fry, London: Kogan Page, pp. 13–31.

MOHAMMED, S., & DUMVILLE, B. C. (2001). *Team mental models in a team knowledge framework: expanding theory and measurement across disciplinary boundaries*. Journal of Organizational Behavior, 22, 89-106.

NAHAPIET, J. & GHOSHAL, S. 1998. *Social capital, intellectual capital, and the organizational advantage*. Academy of Management Review, 23: 242-266.

NEELY, A., GREGORY, M., & PLATTS, K. (1995). *Performance measurement system design: a literature review and research agenda*. International Journal of Operations & Production Management, 15 (4), 80–116.

NUNNALLY, J. C. (1978), *Psychometric methods*, New York: McGraw Hill.

ONYX J, BULLEN P (2000). *Measuring social capital in five communities*. The Journal of Applied Behavioral Science 36 (1): 23–42.

OPPENHEIM, A. N. (1966) *Questionnaire design and attitude measurement*, London, Heinemann.

PAAUWE, J., AND RICHARDSON, R. (1997), *Introduction Special Issue on HRM and Performance*, The International Journal of Human Resource Management, 8, 257–262.

POLLITT, C. (1993) *Managerialism and the Public Services: Cuts or Cultural Change in the 1990s?* Oxford: Blackwell.

POLLITT, C., AND BOUCKAERT, G. (2004), *Public Management Reform: A Comparative Analysis*, Oxford: Oxford University Press.

PRICHARD, C. AND WILLMOTT, H. (1997) *Just How Managed is the McUniversity?*, Organization Studies, 18 (2): 287–316.

PROPPER, C. AND WILSON, D. (2003) *The use and usefulness of performance measures in the public sector*, Oxford Review of Economic Policy, 19 (2), pp. 250–267.

REDMAN, T. (2001) Performance appraisal, in: T. Redman and A. Wilkinson (Eds) Contemporary Human Resource Management, pp. 57–97 (Harlow: Financial Times/Prentice Hall).

RINGLE, C. M., WENDE, S., WILL, A. (2005), *SmartPLS 2.0 (M3) Beta*, Hamburg, Germany.

RYAN, R. M., & DECI, E. L. (2000). *Self-determination theory and the facilitation of intrinsic motivation, social development, and well-being*. American Psychologist, 55, 68-78.

SALTER, B. AND TAPPER, T. (2002) *The External Pressures on the Internal Governance of Universities*, Higher Education Quarterly, 56 (3): 245–56.

SARGIACOMO M. (1999), *Antichi valori e nuovi strumenti gestionali per migliorare la qualità nel sistema universitario: una proposta per il CUEIM*, in Sinergie n. 49, pp. 207-230.

SARGIACOMO M. (2002), *Benchmarking in Italy: the first case study on personnel motivation and satisfaction in a Health Business*, in Total Quality Management, Vol.13, n.4, pp. 489-505.

SARGIACOMO M. (2002), *Budgeting Behaviours negli atenei pubblici italiani: risultanze di una ricerca sulle caratteristiche di good budgeting*, Azienda Pubblica n. 4/5, pp. 371-397.

SHELDON, M. E. (1971). *Investments and involvements as mechanisms producing commitment to the organization.* Administrative Science Quarterly, 16, 142-150.

SIMONS, R. (1995). *Levers of control: How managers use innovative control systems to drive strategic renewal.* Boston: Harvard Business School Press.

SMEENK SGA, EISINGA RN, TEELKEN JC AND DOOREWAARD JACM (2006) *The effects of HRM Practices and antecedents on organizational commitment among university employees*, International Journal of Human Resource Management 17 (12): 2035-54

SPREITZER G, PORATH C (2012). *Creating sustainable performance*, Harvard Business Review, The Magazine, January-February 2012.

SPREITZER, G. M., & SONENSHEIN, S. (2003). *Positive deviance and extraordinary organizing.* IN K. CAMERON, J. DUTTON, & R. QUINN (EDS.), Positive organizational scholarship (pp. 207-224). San Francisco: Berrett-Koehler.

SPREITZER, G. M. (1996). *Social structural characteristics of psychological empowerment.* Academy of Management Journal, 39 (2): 483-504.

STRAUB, D., BOUDREAU, M. C., GEFEN, D. (2004), *Validation guidelines for IS positivist research*, Comm. Association of Information Systems, Vol. 14, 380-426

TER BOGT, H., SCAPENS, R. (2012), *Performance management in universities: effects of the transition to more quantitative measurement systems.* European Accounting Review, 21.3: 451-497.

TOWNLEY, B. (1997) *The Institutional Logic of Performance Appraisal*, Organizational Studies, 18 (2): 261–85.

VAN DE VOORDE, K., PAAUWE, J., & VAN VELDHOVEN, M., (2012). *Employee well-being and the HRM-organizational performance relationship: a review of quantitative studies.* International Journal of Management Reviews, Volume 14, Issue 4, pages 391–407.

VAN DEN BROECK, A., VANSTEENKISTE, M., DE WITTE, H., SOENENS, B., & LENS, W. (2010). *Capturing autonomy, competence, and relatedness at work: Construction and initial validation of the Work-related Basic Need Satisfaction scale.* Journal of Occupational and Organizational Psychology, 83, 981-1002.

VAN DER STEDE, W. A., YOUNG, S. M. AND XIAOLING CHEN, C. (2007) *Doing management accounting survey research*, in Chapman, C. S. and Hopwood, A. G. and Shields, M. D., (eds.) Handbook of management accounting research, Elsevier Science, 445-478.

VAN RIEL, C. B. M., BERENS, G., AND DIJKSTRA, M. (2009), *Stimulating Strategically Aligned Behaviour Among Employees*, Journal of Management Studies, 46, 1197–1226.

VEENHOVEN, R., & JONKERS, T. (1984). *Conditions of happiness* (Vol. 2). Dordrecht: Reidel.

VELD, M., BOSELIE, P., AND PAAUWE, J. (2010), *HRM and Strategic Climates in Hospitals: Does the Message Come Across at the Ward Level?* Human Resource Management Journal, 20, 339–356.

VISWESVARAN, C., SANCHEZ, J. I., AND FISHER, J. (1999). *The role of social support in the process of work stress: A meta-analysis.* Journal of Vocational Behavior, 54 (2), 314-334.

WALLACE, J. E. (1995) *Corporatist Control and Organizational Commitment among Professionals: The Case of Lawyers Working in Law Firms*, Social Forces, 73 (3): 811–40.

WEICK, K. & ROBERTS, K. 1993. *Collective mind in organizations: Heedful interrelating on flight decks*. Administrative Science Quarterly, 38: 357-381.

WEICK, K. E., & SUTCLIFFE, K. M. 2001. *Managing the Unexpected: Assuring High Performance in an Age of Complexity*. University of Michigan Pressing Problem Series. San Francisco: Jossey-Bass.

WOLD, H. (1985). *Partial Least Squares*. In S. Kotz and N. L. Johnson (Eds.), Encyclopedia of Statistical Sciences, Vol. 6, pp. 581-591, New York: Wiley.

WRIGHT, P., DUNFORD, B., AND SNELL, S. (2001), *Human Resources and the Resource Based View of the Firm*, Journal of Management, 27, 701–721.

WRIGHT, S. L., BURT, C. D. B. & STRONGMAN, K. T. (2006). *Loneliness in the workplace: Construct definition and scale development*. New Zealand Journal of Psychology, 35 (2), 59-68.

Appendix

Appendix 10.A1 Italian Universities in the sample

University Name	Frequency	Percent
Istituto Universitario Suor Orsola Benincasa	8	1,89%
Libera Università "Maria ss. Assunta" LUMSA	2	0,47%
Libera Università degli Studi San Pio V	1	0,24%
Libera Università di Bolzano	4	0,94%
Libera Università di Lingue e Comunicazione IULM	1	0,24%
Libera Università "Guido Carli" LUISS	1	0,24%
Libera Università Mediterranea – LUM	1	0,24%
Politecnico di Bari	5	1,18%
Politecnico di Milano	1	0,24%
Politecnico di Torino	9	2,12%
Scuola Internazionale Superiore di Studi avanzati SISSA	3	0,71%
Scuola Normale Superiore Pisa	3	0,71%
Scuola Superiore di Studi Universitari – Pisa	1	0,24%
Seconda Università degli Studi di Napoli "SUN"	8	1,89%
Università "Cà Foscari" di Venezia	9	2,12%
Università Campus Bio-Medico di Roma	3	0,71%
Università Carlo Cattaneo LIUC	2	0,47%
Università Cattolica del Sacro Cuore	6	1,42%

(Continued)

Appendix 10.A1 Italian Universities in the sample (*Continued*)

University Name	Frequency	Percent
Università Commerciale Luigi Bocconi	12	2,83%
Università degli Studi del Molise	2	0,47%
Università degli Studi del Piemonte Orientale	3	0,71%
Università degli Studi del Salento	7	1,65%
Università degli Studi della Basilicata	3	0,71%
Università degli Studi della Tuscia	3	0,71%
Università degli Studi dell'Aquila	7	1,65%
Università degli Studi dell'Insubria – Varese e Como	3	0,71%
Università degli Studi di Bari	9	2,12%
Università degli Studi di Bergamo	6	1,42%
Università degli Studi di Bologna	7	1,65%
Università degli Studi di Brescia	5	1,18%
Università degli Studi di Cagliari	15	3,54%
Università degli Studi di Camerino	4	0,94%
Università degli Studi di Cassino	2	0,47%
Università degli Studi di Catania	3	0,71%
Università degli Studi di Chieti e Pescara	12	2,83%
Università degli Studi di Ferrara	3	0,71%
Università degli Studi di Firenze	12	2,83%
Università degli Studi di Foggia	9	2,12%
Università degli Studi di Genova	17	4,01%
Università degli Studi di Macerata	4	0,94%
Università degli Studi di Messina	5	1,18%
Università degli Studi di Milano	4	0,94%
Università degli Studi di Milano Bicocca	1	0,24%
Università degli Studi di Modena e Reggio Emilia	2	0,47%
Università degli Studi di Napoli "Federico II"	11	2,59%
Università degli Studi di Napoli "L'Orientale"	1	0,24%
Università degli Studi di Napoli "Parthenope"	1	0,24%
Università degli Studi di Padova	20	4,72%

(*Continued*)

Appendix 10.A1   Italian Universities in the sample (*Continued*)

University Name	Frequency	Percent
Università degli Studi di Palermo	6	1,42%
Università degli Studi di Parma	9	2,12%
Università degli Studi di Pavia	6	1,42%
Università degli Studi di Perugia	7	1,65%
Università degli Studi di Pisa	4	0,94%
Università degli Studi di Roma "Foro Italico IUSM"	1	0,24%
Università degli Studi di Roma "La Sapienza"	10	2,36%
Università degli Studi di Roma "Roma 3"	9	2,12%
Università degli Studi di Roma "Tor Vergata"	21	4,95%
Università degli Studi di Salerno	7	1,65%
Università degli Studi di Sassari	10	2,36%
Università degli Studi di Scienze Gastronomiche	2	0,47%
Università degli Studi di Siena	6	1,42%
Università degli Studi di Teramo	2	0,47%
Università degli Studi di Torino	9	2,12%
Università degli Studi di Trento	6	1,42%
Università degli Studi di Trieste	9	2,12%
Università degli Studi di Udine	3	0,71%
Università degli Studi di Urbino "Carlo Bo"	3	0,71%
Università degli Studi di Verona	4	0,94%
Università degli Studi Europea di Roma	1	0,24%
Università degli Studi Mediterranea di Reggio Calabria	5	1,18%
Università della Calabria	3	0,71%
Università della Valle D'Aosta	4	0,94%
Università IUAV di Venezia	6	1,42%
Università per Stranieri di Perugia	1	0,24%
Università per Stranieri di Siena	2	0,47%
Università Politecnica delle Marche	6	1,42%
Università Vita-Salute San Raffaele	1	0,24%
Total	424	100,00%

Appendix 10.A2 Academic discipline

Academic discipline	Frequency	Percent
Agriculture	13	3,07%
Architecture	16	3,77%
Biology	14	3,30%
Business and Management	19	4,48%
Informatics	4	0,94%
Design & Arts	1	0,24%
Economics	28	6,60%
Education	15	3,54%
Engineering e Technology	29	6,84%
Literature, Languages, Archaeology	31	7,31%
Law	16	3,77%
Maths & Physics	25	5,90%
Medicine and Health	31	7,31%
Personal services, Transport, Security services	1	0,24%
Social Sciences	21	4,95%
Veterinary	6	1,42%
Other, please specify	27	6,37%
Missing	127	29,95%
Total	**424**	**100,00%**

Appendix 10.B Items and constructs

Human resource performance management – Interactive Use

HRPM1 My institution is always looking for ways to improve

HRPM2 My institution provides us with the necessary resources to do our work well

HRPM3 My institution equally promotes and recognises excellence in whatever shape or form it comes (e.g., teaching, research, management/administration)

HRPM4 My institution is able to attract the best talent

HRPM5 My institution has an effective probation system

HRPM6 My institution is effective at retaining its best talent

HRPM7 My institution provides constant opportunities for learning and development

HRPM8 My institution is effective at dealing with systematic or continuous under-performance

---

Human resource performance management – Diagnostic Use

HRPM9 My institution's mission, strategic plans and performance results are communicated to all staff

HRPM10 My institution uses a conceptual model for understanding the drivers of its success or how excellence is achieved (e.g., success map, strategy map)

HRPM11 My institution uses specific performance indicators or 'critical success factors'to monitor its performance

HRPM12 My institution sets specific performance targets to differentiate good and bad performance

HRPM13 My institution relies on a combination of quantitative and qualitative information to assess its performance

HRPM14 My institution has an useful performance reporting system (i.e., its data is accurate, reliable, easily accessible and comes in an appropriate format)

Sense of community

SOC2 Work environment At work, I feel part of a group

SOC3 Work environment At work, I can talk with people about things that really matter to me

SOC4 Work environment Some people I work with are close friends of mine

SOC5 Work environment I feel fairly treated and rewarded at work

---

Social capital

SOCAP1 In this institution... People engage in open and honest communication with one another (IS)

SOCAP2 In this institution... People share and accept constructive criticisms without making it personal (IS)

SOCAP3 In this institution... People are willing to share information with one another (IS)

SOCAP4 In this institution... People keep each other informed about institutional matters at all times (IS)

SOCAP5 In this institution... People can rely on each other when doing their work (T)

SOCAP6 In this institution... People feel comfortable being creative because superiors understand that sometimes creative solutions don't work (T)

SOCAP7 In this institution... People have confidence in one another (T)

SOCAP8 In this institution... People show a great deal of ethics and integrity (T)

SOCAP9 In this institution... Overall, people are trustworthy (T)

(Continued)

Appendix 10.B Items and constructs (*Continued*)

SOCAP10 In this institution... People share the same ambitions and vision for the institution (SV) SOCAP11 In this institution... People enthusiastically pursue collective institutional goals (SV) SOCAP12 In this institution... There is a commonality of purpose among people (SV) SOCAP13 In this institution... People view themselves as partners in charting the institution's direction (SV)
Individual well being IWB1 I feel alive and vital at work IWB2 I have energy and spirit at work IWB4 I feel alert and awake at work IWB5 I am looking forward to each new day at work

Printed in Great Britain
by Amazon